# Literary Reading, Cognition and Emotion

## An Exploration of the Oceanic Mind

## Michael Burke

Routledge
Taylor & Francis Group
New York   London

First published 2011
by Routledge
711 Third Avenue, New York, NY 10017

Simultaneously published in the UK
by Routledge
2 Park Square, Milton Park, Abingdon, Oxon OX14 4RN

*Routledge is an imprint of the Taylor & Francis Group, an informa business*

First issued in paperback 2011

© 2011 Taylor & Francis

The right of Michael Burke to be identified as author of this work has been asserted by him in accordance with sections 77 and 78 of the Copyright, Designs and Patents Act 1988.

Typeset in Sabon by IBT Global.

*Library of Congress Cataloging in Publication Data*
Burke, Michael, 1964–
   Literary reading, cognition and emotion : an exploration of the oceanic mind / Michael Burke.
      p. cm. — (Routledge studies in rhetoric and stylistics)
   Includes bibliographical references and index.
   1. Reading, Psychology of.   2. Mental representation.   3. Literature—Psychology.
4. Books and reading—Psychological aspects.   I. Title.
   BF456.R2B655 2010
   418'.4019—dc22
   2010017763

ISBN13: TK 978-0-415-87232-4 (hbk)
ISBN13: TK 978-0-415-52068-3 (pbk)
ISBN13: TK 978-0-203-84030-6 (ebk)

*For my mother and father (†) – the caring authors of my days*

# Contents

# Figures

# Tables

# Acknowledgments

This book is based on my dissertation *The Oceanic Mind*, which I wrote at the University of Amsterdam for the ASCA research school. I am indebted to Peter Verdonk and John Neubauer for feedback and guidance during that project and, before that, to the lecturers at Amsterdam who inspired me as a student to become the scholar I am today. Most prominently, these are Paul Werth †, Teun van Dijk, Mieke Bal and, most importantly, Peter Verdonk. I am also grateful to Cathy Emmot, Ray Gibbs, Patrick Colm Hogan, Willie van Peer, Peter Stockwell, Sonia Zyngier, and two anonymous Routledge reviewers for their invaluable feedback on the most recent version of the manuscript. Thanks also to Erica Wetter and the copy editor at Routledge and to Michael Watters at IBT for all their guidance and advice during the final stages of preparing this book. I am furthermore indebted to all my rhetoric, stylistics and creative writing undergraduate students at Roosevelt Academy, Middelburg (the liberal arts and sciences honours college of Utrecht University) for keeping me young of mind and for continually introducing me to new books and new reading experiences. Another source of continual inspiration for me is my fellow members of the International Poetics and Linguistics Association (PALA), whom I meet with every year to exchange ideas, views and theories. Finally, none of this could have been possible without the support of my mother, brother and sister back in the UK, and the intellectual stimulation, companionship and love of my wife, Helle K. Hochscheid.

Michael Burke
Middelburg, April 2010

# 1 The Secret Lives of Reading and Remembering

Have you ever stopped to think what happens when you read a work of fiction? By this, I mean what happens to your mind and body, as well as what makes the literary reading event so special, so intense, so emotive? This is something that, as an avid reader of literature, has intrigued me for a long while. It may seem odd, but if things are just right when I read a book, I appear to go to places and feel things that are beyond my immediate comprehension. But what does "just right" mean, and what "things" am I referring to? Let us put the answers to these questions on hold for a moment. Equally peculiar, perhaps, is that as I go about my everyday business, those feelings appear to be only just below the surface of my everyday cognition; ready to be reactivated by a new literary reading experience. How can I account for this? Well, F. Scott Fitzgerald, the celebrated author of *The Great Gatsby*, once wrote in a letter to his friend and colleague, Ernest Hemmingway that "the purpose of a work of fiction is to appeal to the lingering after-effects in the reader's mind." (Turnbull 1964). He had taken this basic idea from Joseph Conrad and it was to become his artistic credo. Now, it is likely that fiction has more than just one purpose—recall, for example, how Horace said that the purpose of literature is to delight and instruct—but I somehow understand what Fitzgerald means by this. So how does a literary text appeal to the so-called lingering after effects in a reader's mind, and what exactly are they? These are issues that this book seeks to explore.

Let me begin by saying that this work investigates the act of literary reading as a process, not as a product. As will become clear in the subsequent pages of this volume, it views that process as highly flexible, but with a basic underlying structure. In metaphorical terms, one could say that the processes essential to the reading mind are not mechanical or computational, but more oceanic, that is, dynamic, fluvial and fluctuating. This seemingly paradoxical process of "predictable arbitrariness", for want of a better expression, is what I will consider in this work. I will start by unpacking some of the mystery that lies behind both the secret, private act of reading literature and the human memory systems needed to facilitate reading and its associated cognitive processes. I then explore the elements that go into what can be called the optimum rhetorical situation of literary reading. These include (i) textual elements, e.g. the rhetoric, style and themes on the page, (ii) contextual elements, e.g. the place of a reading event, and (iii) cognitive-emotive elements, e.g. the mood of a reader, as well as the literary reading-induced mental imagery that literature conjures up so well and so enigmatically. I then go on to model how the three notions of memory, cognition and emotion interact with these elements to produce that unique and cherished "feeling of reading". I conclude by looking at the cognitive-emotive nature of heightened emotive events, which I term 'disportation', and by considering what philosophical and biological purposes such bodily phenomena might serve in the narrative life of the literary reader. The conclusions I draw touch on the very essence of what it means to be a feeling, thinking human being. All this will be done primarily using theoretical conjecture combined with the qualitative feedback of a group of readers. Far from being an empirical study, these data merely offer an illustration and are thus not meant as unequivocal evidence nor should they be read as such. Let us now turn to the matter at hand and explore the secret lives of reading and remembering.

Unlike speaking, reading is a relatively recent phenomenon, emerging less than 5,000 years ago. Developing written signs in order to convey units of meaning was as much a socio-cultural phenomenon as it was a cognitively-mediated one. The social aspect is highlighted by the fact that reading skills are not acquired naturally; rather they must be explicitly taught, often with varying results. It is believed that the first writers, and hence the first readers, were the Sumerian scribes, who lived in the fourth millennium BC in present-day Iraq. These people did not engage in acts of reading and writing to give or receive aesthetic pleasure, as is common these days in the case of literature, but rather largely for purely pragmatic reasons. They had administrative motives for learning to recognise these essentially iconic, cuneiform-style pictograms that were etched on stone and clay tablets. It is therefore not surprising to learn that most of the tablets that have been unearthed from this period by archaeologists have turned out to record nothing more than everyday financial transactions, produced in order to provide a kind of visual, mnemonic prompt. Hence, reading seems to have evolved from a simple registering device that was probably developed when people began to realise that human memory was not the ideal place to accurately store and recall detailed past events of primarily numerical transactions. The cognitive act of reading therefore has, at its very source, the basic mnemonic function of recovering an incident in our past life that would otherwise have been either lost or irrevocably distorted by human memory.

Today, both reading and remembering are principally known as silent cognitive procedures. This also holds for the reading of literature, which, in itself, is a relatively new form of "entertainment", emerging in Europe in its present form in the eighteenth century in the period when the novel came to the forefront. Since reading, including novel reading, takes place silently in the privacy of our individual minds, the act of reading seems very personal. Nevertheless, although one might think of silent reading as the default mode, it is a socio-cultural rather than a biological development. It may seem strange from a twenty-first century perspective, but texts were almost always written to be read aloud, as indeed they still are in some religions today like Judaism and Islam. In the past, therefore, reading was anything but a silent pastime.

One of the first recorded silent readers in Western history was St. Ambrose, the fourth-century bishop of Milan. His friend and colleague St. Augustine wrote about him in his *Confessions*, with much amazement:

> When he read his eyes scanned the page and his heart sought out the meaning but his voice was silent and his tongue was still. Anyone could approach him freely and guests were not commonly announced, so that often when we came to visit him we found him reading like this in silence, for he never read aloud. (1998, VI, 3)

Clearly, St. Ambrose was considered a bit of an oddity and it would be a long while before silent reading became the norm in the West. So although it is these days taken for granted that we read silently, it is important to remember that this soundless reading, like the earlier development of reading itself, must have come about as a result of socio-cultural necessities. One reason might be that one can read more quickly when reading silently than when reading aloud: this would not have gone unnoticed by scribes and accountants faced with volumes of text and numbers to get through on a daily basis. Examples like the one above serve to remind us that history and culture can, and indeed still do, play a role in the cognitive act of reading.

Any study of reading processes, such as this one, must try to work out the relationship between so-called "bottom-up" or "stimulus-driven" processes on the one hand and "top-down" or "concept-driven" processes on the other. This study, which deals exclusively with literary reading in the English language, will also have to carry out this task. The first of these processes is mainly concerned with how a text might "trigger" or "guide" a reader's meaning-making faculties. This may incorporate such things as the written medium, the rhetorical text structure, the style, the genre, the syntax, the graphology, the vocabulary, etc. The second of these processes primarily focuses on what a reader brings to bear on a text. This may include the act of vision itself and the cognitive and emotive processing that takes place, as well as reading-induced mental imagery, which involves mnemonic input, i.e. prior knowledge, previous experiences, etc. One of the main reasons why text and discourse scholars wish to try and work out this relationship is to discover which of the two, i.e. top-down or bottom-up, plays the greater role in meaning-making in particular contexts and, more importantly, why. Another reason is to explore the shifting boundaries of individual, intersubjective and social aspects of cognition in reading processes. Let us now look more closely at some of those processes.

Stimulus-driven studies on reading and comprehension are largely concerned with which formal features of a text guide a reader's meaning-making faculties. Some of the first linguistically-orientated studies into reading processes were the very formal readability tests of the 1940s. The most famous of these was devised by the linguist Rudolf Flesch. His test measured the average number of syllables per word and per sentence and his general claim was that shorter sentences with shorter words should be easier to read. Although still useful today in very formal composition teaching environments, such readability tests are otherwise limited as they pay little or no attention to the actual context of the reading situation. Take, for instance, a couple of simple words like "April" and "thirteen". According to Flesch's readability test these disyllabic lexical items should be processed relatively swiftly and without much cognitive effort. This is probably the case in a sentence like "his son will turn thirteen in April". But put these two seemingly "easy-to-process" words in the hands of a literary artist and you may get a sentence like "It was a bright, cold day in April and the clocks were striking thirteen", which some of you may recognize as the opening line of George Orwell's classic novel *1984*. Here, it becomes evident that readability and comprehension rely to a large extent on something far more fundamental than merely counting up the number of syllables in a word or the words in a sentence. By their formal nature, such readability tests appear to look at texts in isolation and entail perhaps the most pronounced bottom-up approach that there is.

Early work conducted in the fields of discourse psychology and discourse analysis also tended to rely heavily on "words on the page" in describing how concepts are formed. For example, in their influential 1983 work on text comprehension Teun van Dijk and Walter Kintsch set out three levels of representation in meaning making. The first of these they called the surface level of representation, which included the linguistic surface features of the text. The second category, which included any inter-sentential and intra-sentential aspects of meaning making, they called the text-base level of representation. This is what is more commonly known as the co-text, i.e. the immediate linguistic environment of a stretch of discourse that is being processed. Both these categories can be said to be language-based. The third level of representation, which they called the situation model level, concerns the referential state of affairs in the world that the text describes. This can be either real or imaginary. This third category does indeed leave open the option for reflection on a more extensive amount of cognitive input. Nevertheless, the model was still very much text-based, as linguistic elements here play a far more dominant role in the construction of mental representation. Similar approaches in this period that emphasised the importance of stimulus-driven aspects of the processing continuum tended to focus on such core linguistic issues as referential or clausal cohesion, such as the work of Trabasso, Secco and van den Broek (1984).

Technological advances of the late 1980s helped to move this research forward. New approaches, including methods such as eye-tracking techniques, led to a focus on the actual on-line reading process itself. What happens to readers when they process written discourse became a central concern. Hence, the actual reader, and not just the text, was becoming an important focus. This heralded a move to attempt to include top-down processes more fully in addition to bottom-up ones. During this period many of the models that were developed started to look at the role of cognitive inference in meaning-making strategies. One problem that these scholars had to come to terms with was the imbalance between the large number of inferences that must be made in order to comprehend a text, and the very limited processing capacity of working memory. Two of the more prominent models at this time included Kintsch's developing Construction-Integration (CI) model, first set out in the late 1980s, and Gail McKoon and Roger Ratcliff's far more bottom-up, minimalist model from the early 1990s. Although these continue to produce interesting and relevant data, the focus today appears to be much more on trying to integrate more fully bottom-up comprehension processes on the one hand and top-down recall strategies on the other. One particularly persuasive model of reading that attempts to combine equally both comprehension *and* recall is van den Broek et al.'s "Landscape model of comprehension and memory" (1996; 1999), about which more will be said later in this chapter.

Some of the earlier accounts of reading comprehension in cognitive psychology did try to address both bottom-up and top down matters. One drawback, however, is that reading was still largely viewed as a linear procedure that usually involved the four stages of (i) decoding, (ii) literal comprehension, (iii) inferential comprehension and (iv) comprehension monitoring. John B. Best summarises the first three of these as follows:

> Decoding refers to feature analysis of letters and clusters of letters and pattern recognition. At this stage, the graphemic code is mapped onto another internal representation. In the second stage, the reader accesses his lexicon. As we have seen, this process is apparently done directly from the graphemic code in most cases. In the third stage, the reader accesses larger units of cognitive organisation to integrate separate sentences. (1986: 361)

Of the fourth stage "comprehension monitoring", Best suggests that although it is not involved in the actual translation of the graphologcial symbols on the page to semantic meaning, it is an important aspect of reading (361). He states further that reading involves a two-way procedure:

The stages of reading indicate that both bottom-up and top-down processes are involved. For example, decoding is largely a bottom-up process. Literal comprehension for skilled readers is probably also a bottom-up process, although top-down processes play a definite role in limiting the locations within the lexicon that might be activated. Inferential comprehension is almost completely a top-down process. (1986: 362)

Current cognitive psychology and cognitive linguistics assume that comprehension is dependent on the activation and availability of experience-based prior knowledge that is located in the mind. I will now discuss this process within the context of a schema theory.

Schemata can be defined as a portion of background knowledge relating to a particular type of entity, situation or event. Schema theory can be traced back to the work of the psychologist Sir Frederick C. Bartlett, who produced his seminal book *Remembering* in 1932 (reprinted in 1995) while working in the Gestalt tradition of psychological experimentation in the 1920s and early 1930s. Bartlett's work may seem dated, however, psychologists Keith Oatley and Jennifer M. Jenkins state in their book *Understanding Emotions* that a strong case can be made that Bartlett's *Remembering* is the most important study of memory completed so far (1996: 267). One of the central tenets of modern schema theory is that no definitive meaning is to be found in texts or in words alone; rather, meaning comes into existence at the moment of interaction between the textual base on the one hand and the reader's background knowledge on the other. This is also the case for literary reading. As Elena Semino puts it "we make sense of new situations—and texts in particular—by relating the current input to pre-existing mental representations of similar entities, situations and events" (1997: 123).

In his original qualitative empirical investigations Bartlett showed how knowledge plays an important role with regard to understanding, perception and memory by suggesting that the comprehension of a new situation depends on the activation of relevant areas of existing knowledge. He described such basic schematic units of prior knowledge as "an active organisation of past reactions, or past experiences" (1995: 201). Bartlett's experiments suggested that readers' expectations, based on their knowledge of previous texts and previous experiences, produce powerful interpretations of a text which can override the semantic content of the textual information. In practice, this actually means that culturally unfamiliar events, actions and episodes in texts are overruled, as it were, by reader-based knowledge and by the corresponding familiar mental imagery produced by the intersubjective, individual reader. He showed this in his famous "War of the Ghosts" experiment whereby British middle-class students at Cambridge read a Native American story through the distorting filter of their own cultural subjectivism. Thus words in specific texts are not processed on the basis of their formal, decontextualised semantic content, but rather their contextualised, pragmatic situation. Moreover, Bartlett did not just claim that comprehension requires the activation of appropriate areas of background knowledge, he was also convinced that the organisation and activation of knowledge is crucially affected by factors such as emotions, interests and attitudes (1995: 206–7). Although Bartlett explored the influence of emotions and affective attitudes in minimal detail only, he did have some interesting things to say, the crucial importance of which, as Semino has already noted, has not been fully realised in subsequent developments of schema theory in literary reading environments since the early 1930s (1997: 127). This largely absent emotive dimension in modern literary text processing studies is something that I shall seek to address.

Soon after the publication of Bartlett's work, the Gestalt tradition became swamped by the emergence of behaviourism. As a result, the study of cognitive processes was to remain unpopular for some forty years until its revival in the 1970s due, in part, to the rise of artificial intelligence. Three theories related to schema theory are usually mapped out during this period: the ones developed by (i) David E. Rumelhart, (ii) Roger C. Schank and Robert Abelson, and (iii) Schank, this time working alone. The cognitive scientist Rumelhart conducted work on "story grammars" in the mid-1970s, an analytic approach which assumes that comprehension and recall rely heavily on story structures. Perhaps paradoxically, comprehension was grounded in a predominantly language-based, bottom-up approach. As a result, story grammars, with their formal methods of sentence parsing came under fire because of their inherent inflexibility (see for example, Morgan and Sellner [1980] who argued that this type of linguistic analysis that relies on formal markers like referring pronouns cannot explain or even relate "coherence" and "meaning assimilation" processes in a reader's head). A decade later, in the mid-1980s, Rumelhart et al. (1986) conducted work on his theory of "parallel distributed processing". To some extent this idea counters the claim of schema theory that knowledge is first of all ordered in blocks "top-down", by positing that instead it is distributed across lower level units. Once again, this theory of Rumelhart's was, in effect, primarily focusing on stimulus-driven processes.

Two other researchers interested in schema theory were Schank and Abelson, who worked chiefly in the field of artificial intelligence. In the mid-nineteen seventies they developed the notion of "script", which can be said to be a specific mental structure, like a visit to the dentist or to a restaurant. Schank, reflecting on them much later in his 1999 work, says that they are knowledge structures that are valuable in text processing in that that they direct the inference process and connect pieces of input (1999: 4). Thus "input sentences are connected together by referring to the overall structure of the script to which they make reference" (1999: 4). In this view, as the author himself concludes, scripts are "a kind of high-level knowledge structure that can be called upon to supply background information during the understanding process" (1999: 4). Like Rumelhart's story grammars, this theory was also quite formal and rigid despite its advantages and did not seem to cohere to a satisfactory level with real discourse interactions and memory structures. Schank would claim that in some senses stories can be the opposite of scripts when viewed from the perspective of memory functions since we do not tell a story unless it deviates from the norm in some interesting way (1999: 89).

Schank, this time working alone, came up with a pliant theory of cognition he called "dynamic memory", which he updated in his book *Dynamic Memory Revisited*.[1] In these works Schank moves away from scripts and develops the notion of "scene". Thus, whereas scripts were specific structures, scenes transcend the specifics of a situation (1999: 19). A scene refers to an event in a larger chain. Take, for example, a van rental episode. This is a scene in a larger organising structure which could be moving house or going on a camping vacation or going to buy furniture, etc. Schank also developed two higher-level processing mechanisms, which he termed memory organisation packets (MOPs) and thematic organisation points (TOPs). MOPs basically organise the scenes. They are the larger organising structures mentioned above, like the house moving episode in my example. They are flexible as well, in that they allow new information to be integrated into existing expectations. TOPs are somewhat different. They are "high-level structures under which memories are organised" (1999: 81). Three types of information are stored in TOPs: expectational, static and relational (1999: 81). To employ a literary discourse processing analogy as an illustration, TOPs account for how readers draw on a whole host of similar experiences to flesh out an ongoing reading experience.

Both MOPs and TOPs move away from the text-base towards the processing qualities of the human mind, where Bartlett had begun some fifty years earlier. In his updated 1999 work Schank says that he "now sees language understanding as an integrated process", adding "people don't understand things without making reference to what they already know" (1999: 4). In that same discussion he adds "we don't break down the tasks of understanding language into small components" (1999: 5). In effect he appears to be arguing against linear models of discourse processing. Schank concludes by suggesting that "expectations are the key to understanding" (1999: 79). He goes on to qualify this by stating "in a great many instances these expectations are sitting in a particular spot in memory, awaiting the call to action. Frequently, they are prepackaged like scripts" (1999: 79–80). Although Schank adds that it is not always that simple, the implications of this claim for top-down processing in reading comprehension situations is significant. In this same discussion he further observes:

> More often we do try to figure out what will happen in a situation we encounter . . . In attempting to imagine what will happen next we must construct a model of how things will turn out. (This model can often

be quite wrong of course). Sometimes during the construction of the model, we come across memories that embody exactly the same state of affairs that we are constructing; this is an instance of outcome-driven reminding. (1999: 80)

Perhaps one reason why much of this earlier work did not account fully for the pivotal role that cognitive processes played was that almost all of this psychological work was based on simple, pre-fabricated sentences. In other words, the sentences studied were not real or natural language that had been produced in real discourse situations. They were often very short and isolated pieces of text lacking meaningful co-text as well as context. It is easy to see how under such minimalist and artificial circumstances there was little scope for exploring the processes involved in reading literary texts. It was to remain so for a long time. This is odd since literary texts are essentially stories and storytelling is fundamental to human communication. This is supported by Schank who writes that "whatever the means and whatever the venue, storytelling seems to play a major role in human interaction" (1999: 89). Despite the neglect of literary discourse processing there were some admirable models developed at the end of the twentieth century. These included Rolf Zwaan's model of literary reading (1993), Paul Werth's text world theory (1999) and Catherine Emmott's study on narrative comprehension (1997). There was also work conducted on applying schema theory to the analysis of literary texts. Guy Cook claimed, for example, in his work on the interplay of form and mind in literary discourse processing that literary language, and by default the inherently slippery notion of "literariness", rests on what he terms the "refreshment" and subsequent "reinforcement" of cognitive schemata (1994: 9–11).

The lack of attention to top-down processes in many discourse processing studies in the 1990s is something that van Dijk has highlighted by proposing a view of text processing based on what he terms "context models". Context models are a type of experience model in that they represent "the ongoing, subjective interpretation of everyday episodes in the lives of social actors" (1999: 125). Experience models are characterised by how they are built by "the primacy of personal experiences" (1999: 127). Unlike situation models (often now referred to as "event" models), the focus of context models is on pragmatics rather than on providing a cognitive base for the semantics of the text: involving cohesion, coherence, reference, etc. Van Dijk argues that it is not contexts themselves that influence discourse or language use but rather how they are subjectively interpreted by discourse participants (1999: 124). During communicative events in social situations "participants actively and ongoingly construct a mental representation of only those properties that are currently *relevant* to them" (1999: 124, emphasis as original). Thus such things as opinions and emotions are important in the workings of mental models (1999: 126). Such subjective interpretations of contexts are located in episodic memory and have a crucial role in controlling text and talk. Van Dijk's focus is on reading newspaper discourse. However, because reading literature is a communicative event in a broadly social situation, there seems to be no reason why this general idea could not be extended to literary discourse processing, in which an author or implied author/narrator communicates with a reader, whose mental models of the discourse situation are subjective, relevant to the reader involved and based on emotions.

Current reading research broadly falls either into the category of memory-based research, involving such methods as questionnaires or think-aloud protocols or the more technological domain of on-line processing research, such as the aforementioned eye-tracking and even some basic neural-scanning procedures. These involve either what readers remember about reading or what readers do when they read. As van Dijk has noted, "linguists and discourse analysts have paid a great deal of attention to the role of context but have failed to develop explicit theories of text-context relationships" (1999: 123). Recently, however, there has been a general growing realisation that a combination of both approaches might prove to be most effective. In essence, what one is looking for is an approach that seeks not to subjugate either language or the mind, but rather one that seeks to understand the contextualised complexities of their confluent interaction in any given discourse comprehension situation.

One persuasive current model of text processing that appears to do this is van den Broek et al.'s earlier mentioned "landscape model of reading". This theory goes some way towards emphasising the dynamic, complex and bi-directional process that takes place during the bottom-up activation of concepts and the top-down deployment of conceptual networks. These authors are interested in finding out how readers construct representations from a text based on memories. They are also interested in how the process of comprehending individual sentences translates into mental representations that, to cite the authors, "linger far after the reader has put down the book" (1999: 71). This description may call to mind in you, as it does in me, F. Scott Fitzgerald's views set out on the first page of this chapter that "the purpose of a work of fiction is to appeal to the lingering after effects in the reader's mind".

The authors view each new sentence as a reading "cycle". They claim that there are four sources of activation in such a cycle (1999: 73). The first is from the text that is currently being processed, i.e. the present reading cycle. The second concerns the activation of a concept from the preceding reading cycle. This can occur because this conceptual representation is still fresh in the mind and may override the current input. The third concerns the reactivation of a concept from even earlier reading cycles. This reactivation need not be due to the (re)occurrence of a literal, textual reference; it can be triggered as well by available background knowledge. This purely top-down input is thus the fourth and final source. Van den Broek et al. label these four sources: (i) text, (ii) carryover, (iii) reinstatement (from prior cycles), and (iv) background knowledge. Crucially, the authors stress that the latter three can all influence the first, i.e. the sentence that is currently being read. To take this to its most expanded form, background knowledge can affect the text itself, which is a claim not too dissimilar from that made by Bartlett as we saw earlier. Van den Broek et al. particularly note that "there is ample evidence that readers routinely—and often automatically— activate background knowledge that is associated with what they read" (1999: 74). The authors further claim that "together, the limited attentional capacity and the access to these sources of activation cause text elements constantly to *fluctuate* in activation as the reader proceeds through a text" (1999: 74, my emphasis). By considering the simultaneous activation of what the authors go on to term "peaks" and "valleys" for each concept across a reading cycle, they arrive at their notion of "a landscape of con- ceptual activation in reading processes". This empirically grounded sense of a "fluctuation" of textual elements or, one might say, "an undulation" of both textual elements and cognitive elements, is central to their landscape model of reading. Van den Broek et al. also point out that concepts will be activated to different degrees, so some can be at the centre of attention, while others are "hovering in the background, still active but less so" (1999: 76). On the subject of retrieval, van den Broek et al. say that it is a matter of the activation vector and the memory representation. They suggest that retrieval of representations can occur both during and after reading and that, if after reading, it can be immediate or delayed. If retrieval is initiated immediately after reading has been completed, the activation vector for the last cycle is still active and will enter into the equation of the retrieval process, but if recall is delayed it will play no role (1999: 92).

Three important concepts in contemporary text processing studies that warrant some explanation at this stage are "immediacy", "incrementation" and "inferencing". The immediacy theory proposes that linguistic informa- tion is processed word by word. This means that decoding leads to spon- taneous conceptual processing. This idea was primarily put forward in the cognitive psychological experiments of Marcel Just and Patricia Carpen- ter in the early 1980s. Their "immediacy assumption" in text comprehen- sion is based partially on the idea that working memory is limited and as such cannot hold onto too much uninterpreted information. However, this was thought by other researchers to be too one-sided. Later work, includ- ing eye-tracking experiments conducted by Lyn Frazier and Keith Rayner (1987; 1990) on the complexities of processing purely syntactic structures, and especially on the differences between processing patterns of lexical ambiguities compared to sense ambiguities, led to the adjustment of this model and to the development of what these authors term the "immediate partial interpretation hypothesis".

Two other researchers influential in this field are Anthony J. Sanford and Simon Garrod. In the work they did in the 1990s, which builds on their earlier reading research, particularly *Understanding Written Language*, they distinguish two general modes of discourse processing. The first of these is broadly incremental in fashion and is concerned with the ways that discourse is built up in interpretation strategies. The second concerns both local and global knowledge and focuses on the ways in which patterns in the input may match those types of knowledge. With regard to the second of these two modes, the authors argue that processing is immediate and not incremental, and can operate on a whole scale of language processing, from the syntactic level right up to the discourse level (1999: 4). These authors suggest that the general availability of background knowledge will determine the speed of processing. This means that incoming information that cannot rely on background information but instead has to be "computed" on-line, as it were, will take more time. They have also suggested that this predominantly syntactic distinction between either computing alternative interpretations, as opposed to being able to rely on pre-stored knowledge, is applicable as well to semantic and discourse processing levels (1999: 6). In addition they have developed a theory of "scenario-mapping and focus" where they state that "language input is related to world knowledge at the earliest opportunity" (1999: 23). They propose too that despite being sometimes constrained by processing factors, specific scenario knowledge in immediate interpretation is powerful enough to override local syntactic and semantic interpretations of sentences (1999: 24). A claim such as this ties in with their telling observation that states "human language processing may often be incomplete" (1999: 25). This finding echoes the similar one mentioned earlier by Bartlett.

The amount of background knowledge that is available to a specific reader can be considered too by means of the notion of "inference generation" during discourse comprehension. McKoon and Ratcliff's earlier mentioned minimalist hypothesis claims that the only real inferences that readers make are local bridging ones. The authors suggest that sometimes use is made of background knowledge but only if there are strong pre-existing multiple associations (1992; 1995). In their work, the role of top-down processing is very limited and to a certain extent predictable. This position has been challenged by a number of scholars including Graesser and Kreuz (1993); Graesser, Singer and Trabasso (1994) and Singer, Graesser and Trabasso (1994), who generally argue for a more global position with regard to inferencing in text processing. Two inferences that they seem to agree on as necessary in order to achieve some valid sense of global coherence are thematic inferences and the emotional reactions of characters. This position has its roots in Graesser's earlier 1981 work on literary discourse processing in which he suggests that if readers are asked to make inferences from a story, and if they are then given enough time in which to make them, the number that they can come up with is unlimited.

A further account of the global nature of inferencing has recently been explored by Emmott in her earlier-mentioned work on literary narrative comprehension. She argues that "a global representation of a textual world is necessary to make basic inferences" (1997, 270). Emmott notes that "whenever events are set in a fictional context, the reader has to make priming and focusing inferences and repeatedly update entity representations" (1997, 269). The mental agility required for this constant mental monitoring and updating in inferencing is expressed in her notions of "frame switches" (i.e. flashbacks/forwards) and "frame recall" (i.e. returning to the main story). Emmott accordingly claims that "naturally occurring sentences", such as those found in fiction, "depend for their interpretation on a knowledge of the full text" (1997, 269).

These then are some of the basics of discourse processing that go to make up "the secret life of reading". It will not have gone unnoticed that the concept of memory has come up in many of the above discussions as it is fundamental to any study on reading and text processing. Some aspects from that mnemonic domain that are relevant to this study will now be sketched out below: first from a cognitive perspective and thereafter from a neurobiological one.

Cognitive psychology traditionally makes a clear distinction between what is known as "short-term memory" and "long-term memory". The first, also often referred to as "working memory" or sometimes even "consciousness", is a very limited system that is characterised by its on-line processing capacity. It is believed to last for just a few seconds and is only able to deal with and retain about six or seven items of very concise information. Long-term memory, on the other hand, is often described as a kind of theoretical storage system that is available to cueing and is characterised by the notions of duration, accessibility and size. There are obvious links between long-term memory and the notions of unconscious and subconscious mind processes.

A second traditional classification is made between "semantic" and "episodic" memory. M. W. Eysenck and M. T. Keane, for example, describe the first of these as "our decontextualised memory for facts about the entities and relations between entities in the world" (1990, 250). Semantic memory, therefore, is broadly word-based, as it encompasses the storage of words and meanings, even though some concepts and world knowledge are stored too. But the emphasis in semantic memory is always on knowledge of "facts". Episodic memory, on the other hand, is described by Eysenck and Keane as "our memory about specific situations and events that occurred at a particular time" (1990, 250), which can be said to be more "mind-based". This type of memory also accounts for the names of people and places. Episodic memory, therefore, refers to the sort of memory that concerns information about time-related episodes and events together with the relationship between such events. The emphasis here, then, is on a kind of "experiential" knowledge. In fact, episodic memory is in many ways similar to the notion of autobiographical memory in which emotion plays a pivotal role. This is illustrated by the clinical neurologist Antonio Damasio, who states in *The Feeling of What Happens* that "the autobiographical self depends on systematized memories of situations in which core consciousness was involved in the knowing of the most invariant characteristics of an organism's life—who you were born to, where, when, your likes and dislikes, the way you usually react to a problem or a conflict, your name and so on" (1999, 17).

There is another type of memory that specifically links memory to place. It has its roots in the rhetorical work of Cicero and his well-known story about the Greek poet Simonides and the collapsed building, which involves associating items to be remembered in conjunction with a specific physical location. It also involves revisiting those actual sites during recall. This rigid type of memory is known more commonly as the "method of loci". Other types of memory include (i) *echoic memory*, which involves the memory of sounds and their general availability for further processing, (ii) *eidetic memory*, which is an extremely vivid kind of memory, as if an event is actually perceived, (iii) *flashbulb memory*, which stores events of short duration in vivid detail, and (iv) *iconic memory*, which refers to the fleeting persistence of images and their brief availability for further processing.

Many of these types of memory appear to suggest just how vivid many memories can be. This, however, is becoming an increasingly debatable point. Flashbulb memories, for example, stress clear photographic detail. However, ample new empirical evidence questions this notion of clarity. For example, Kintsch has claimed that "flashbulb memories are not notably accurate; it is just that people have great confidence in them" (1998, 420). Ronald A. Finke makes a similar observation too when discussing how memories are likely to never truly be photographic in nature (1989: 16). Arguably then, several of these "vivid" types of memory might not be as detailed or clear as many psychologists first thought back in the mid-twentieth century.

Schank also stresses the difference between conscious and non-conscious knowledge bases. He does this in part by suggesting we try for a moment not to think in words. If we are successful, what we are left with are images, feelings, attitudes, expectations, etc. (1999: 239). He further states that none of his structures (MOPs, TOPs, scenes, etc.) rely on conscious knowledge. In fact, procedures like understanding sentences and generating expectations are also non-conscious forms of knowledge (1999, 241). He places them in the same category as what he calls "the racing mind", i.e. acts of daydreaming or that moment before you fall asleep or "when you are calm, alone, and deprived of visual and auditory stimuli and find your mind taking off on its own" (1999, 247). Schank explains further how memory is inextricably linked to stories. He holds the view that "the major processes of memory are the creation, storage and retrieval of stories" (1999, 90–91). In short, at its core, the mind is a collection of experience-based stories. This idea is in part supported by neurobiologist James E. Zull who claims that "stories engage all parts of the brain" (2002, 228). Schank stresses further the familiarity and stereotypicality of those stories.

No memories are new since we must have already experienced them during creation and storage. He suggests further that in order to build memory structures we need to be able to recognise that the experience we are currently undergoing is in some way related to a previous experience (1999, 155). Recall, however, is not a random process; it appears that we just use the nearest match and replay it (1999, 91). He argues as well against the idea that every sentence one may ever produce is sitting in the mind, word for word, ready for activation. He adds that stories themselves do not exist as entities in the mind (1999, 100). Instead, because all humans evolve during their adult lives, so too do their views. So even if an utterance, or for that matter a thought, is slightly different from its original, the relationship between them will be robust (1999, 91). These stories, and the events that drive them, will, of course, be unique and personal to each individual. However, some may be intersubjective as well, by which I mean communities of readers may share similar interpretations and effects under certain conditions, a process described in detail by literary theorist Wolfgang Iser in his book *The Act of Reading* (1978).

Let us move now from the mind to the brain. Drawing on earlier studies Zull has argued that from a neurobiological perspective brain imaging experiments have shown that when we recall stories, i.e. the episodic kind of remembering, we use our right frontal cortex. This he points out is unique, as all other things linked to stories, such as the recall of facts or the encoding of stories, etc., employs the left frontal cortex (2002: 229). This is an interesting conundrum, which leads us nicely into an account of the mnemonic biological world of reading and memory.

Using a variety of neural imaging techniques, recent research in cognitive neuroscience has made three very general discoveries with regard to the neurobiology of human memory systems. The first is that memory has different stages. The second is that long-term memory is represented in numerous regions throughout the human brain—this claim undermines a more modular argument for neural memory. The third is that what are known as "explicit" and "implicit" memory—both of which can be subsumed under long-term memory—involve quite different neuronal circuits in activities like processing, storage and retrieval. Very generally speaking, the remembering and receiving parts of the brain are towards the rear, while the more "action" part is towards the front. Zull, for example, places memories of stories and place, flashbacks, long-term memory, emotions related to experiences, etc., at the back of the cortex, also known as the integrative cortex (a region bordering the parietal and temporal lobes) (2002: 155). He locates the integrative cortex between the three main sensory areas: visual, auditory and somatic, thus making it in his own words "a short journey for signals to travel from these sensory regions to the integrative back cortex" (2002: 155). But we are getting ahead of ourselves a little here. Let us start this discussion of neurobiological memory with a look at what are termed explicit and implicit memory.

Explicit and implicit refer to two different aspects of long-term memory. Explicit memory processes refer to the learning of facts, like the names of people and places. This is a highly flexible kind of memory that must be reactivated by conscious effort. It can be recalled verbally and is also sometimes referred to as declarative memory. One could say that semantic memory, pertaining to facts, and episodic memory, pertaining to events and personal experiences, both fit into this explicit category of neurobiological recall.

From a purely physiological perspective, the long-term storage of explicit memory is now widely believed to take place in the medial temporal lobe system. The temporal lobe system is the area of the cerebral cortex located just above the ear. It is chiefly, though not exclusively, concerned with hearing. There are four main lobe areas in the cerebral cortex. The other three are the frontal, parietal and occipital lobes. The frontal lobe is mainly concerned with movement and the planning of future action, while the parietal lobe is responsible for somatic issues and with the forming of a body image and relating that image to extra-personal space. The occipital lobe is predominantly concerned with vision. Attached to the brain stem is the cerebellum which helps in coordinating movement and balance.

It is now widely believed that the kind of knowledge that gets stored as explicit memory is first acquired through processing that takes place in one or more of the temporal, prefrontal or limbic cortices, which is an area of neural structures bordering the brainstem, and the cerebral hemispheres associated with all the emotions and basic drives such as food and sex. In these areas, a confluence of visual, auditory, somatic and emotive information takes place. The so-called entorhinal cortex has specifically been highlighted in the medial temporal lobe system as being crucial for processing explicit memory storage and for sending it to and from other areas in the brain—especially to the hippocampal region of the sub-cortex, which is an important region for memory processing. The hippocampus is also believed to send some signals directly to the amygdala: two almond-shaped neural centres in the limbic system that register emotion, (Zull 2002: 82). It is important at this stage to note that long-term memories of childhood are not stored in the hippocampus; rather they are only processed there. This is known because patients with amnesia, which causes damage to that specific region, are able to remember their childhood memories and other factual knowledge that occurred prior to the damaging of the hippocampus. The hippocampus therefore is only a kind of temporary resting point for long-term memory. In sum therefore, explicit memory storage can be said to be primarily mediated by the hippocampus and the (medial) temporal areas of the cortex.

The hippocampus is also the area that mediates spatial memories in the right hemisphere of the brain, while words, objects and people are mediated in the more dominant left hemisphere (Kandel, Kupfermann and Iversen 2000, 1233). Moreover, as already alluded to, the hippocampus is an important centre of emotion as well as memory. As neural scientist Joseph LeDoux puts it in *The Emotional Brain* "when the elements of the sensory world activate these cells, the tunes they play are the emotions we experience (1998: 95). Additionally, as can be gleaned from the previous discussion, the vast majority of neurobiologists place the storage of factual semantic knowledge in the neo-cortex in a fundamentally *distributed* fashion. However, they often situate the storage of episodic or autobiographical knowledge, which tends to deal with time, people and places, solely in the pre-frontal cortex (Kandel, Kupfermann and Iversen 2000, 1233–37). As a result of experiments conducted on patients with brain lesions, it is widely believed that semantic knowledge is stored across a number of neo-cortical areas. When a person with a normal functioning brain is asked to recall an object, let us say, for example, a hippopotamus, then this seems to occur in one smooth, cognitive activity. Nevertheless, it would be wrong to assume that this has come from one general region of the brain. There is no single location in the brain for the storage of this semantic, mnemonic information pertaining to an object like a hippopotamus or indeed any other object. Different aspects and elements of the concept of this semi-aquatic mammal are stored in quite different anatomical areas across the neo-cortex. When a person is prompted to evoke this concept, then a kind of fluvial parallel process takes place whereby all the relevant elements get activated and come together in what might be called a "confluence of cognition" to produce the concept or mental image. This is known because people with damage to certain areas of the neo-cortex would, for example, be unable to activate certain aspects of a particular object. In the case of my "hippopotamus" example, this could be its bulk, colour, gait, etc. Alternatively, a patient might be able to identify a hippopotamus in its entirety but might be unable to label it linguistically.

This idea of information ebbing back and forth in synaptic tidal flows across the neural basin of the brain may seem somewhat esoteric, but it is one that is becoming increasingly popular among neurobiologists. Zull, for example, in a discussion on the executive capacities of the integrative frontal cortex and its relationship with the integrative back cortex says "many, if not most, pathways of signaling in the brain include a combination of neurons that send signals in the other direction" (2002: 193). He describes a "back and forth" movement between these areas, adding that this traffic is especially active during the recollection of images (2002: 194). This idea of continual patterned movement in the mind is prominent too in the recent interdisciplinary work of neuroscientist György Buzsáki. In *Rhythms of the Brain* (2006) he puts forward a case for neuronal synchronisation and argues that it is this rhythmic regularity that organises meaning that in turn allows the brain to function the way it does. Similarly, in *The Wet Mind* Stephen M. Kosslyn and Olivier Koenig discuss how the whole idea of neural computation might best be based on a hydraulic metaphor. The virtue of this view is that although it dictates a relatively strict anatomical location for most mind functions, it stresses the complex interactive nature of brain activity. They suggest that such a metaphor "encourages us to think about how emotion and motivation can alter information processing" (1995, 447–48).

As mentioned, the storage of episodic knowledge that deals with time, people and places is, unlike its semantic counterpart, primarily situated in one central area, namely in the pre-frontal cortex: "primarily" because other areas of the neo-cortex are also sometimes activated in order to allow the recollection of "when" and "where" a past event occurred (Kandel, Kupfermann and Iversen, 2000: 1237). In his discussion on the neurobiology of memory, Damasio says that the pre-frontal cortex consists of "a vast array of higher-order cortices" (1999: 158), some of which can hold personal or autobiographical memories. These can relate to temporal, spatial or linguistic events but to memories of certain categories of events or somatic states as well (1999: 158). The prefrontal cortex, he adds, also plays a pivotal role in working memory. According to Damasio, not only is the prefrontal cortex crucial for consciousness, and thus working memory, but, since it plays an important role in autobiographical memory, it is "relevant to autobiographical self and extended consciousness" (1999: 158).

Explicit memory in general can be said to have at least four distinct aspects. These are (i) encoding, i.e. how incoming information is dealt with and processed, (ii) consolidation, i.e. how new information is dealt with in order to make it more reliable for long-term retention, (ii) storage, i.e. how limitless amounts of information are retained in long-term memory, and, (iv) retrieval, i.e. the process that allows the recall and activation of stored information. As mentioned, retrieval is centrally about bringing bits of information together from lots of different anatomical sites that have been stored separately. Kandel, Kupfermann and Iversen note that "retrieval of memory is much like perception; it is a constructive process and therefore subject to distortion, much as perception is subject to illusions" (2000: 1238). They go on to suggest that recall is never an exact copy of the information that is originally stored. Rather during recall a whole host of cognitive strategies might be employed. These can include the activation of inferences, comparisons, guesses and suppositions (2000: 1239).

It should be noted that in cognitive psychology there is a distinct relationship between encoding and recall, particularly with regard to what might be called affective mnemonic situations. For example, if a person is feeling happy, then that person is more likely to remember things they learned and stored while in a happy state of mind, than things learned and stored in a negative state of mind. Two of these processes are known as mood-state-dependent retrieval and mood congruity effects (Frijda 1986: 121). Interestingly, it has been shown on many occasions that positive affective states lead to better retrieval of positive material. In light of this there one could argue that there is no reason why episodes of discourse processing, and, in particular, literary discourse processing, should be any different. After all, when a person chooses to read literature, a main factor for such a decision is often for reasons of pleasure, unless of course the reading is compulsory for purposes of edification.

There is an important conclusion to be drawn here too as to the difference between emotion and the nature of human memory that is best summarised by Alice M. Isen, who suggested that if positive affective states are essentially retrieval cues, then the events and experiences that are stored in memory must be tagged according to the feelings that are associated with them (1984: 218). Hence, and in anticipation of my argument to come in the later chapters, the activation of highly emotive memories can plausibly occur during certain literary reading situations far more readily than other kinds of memories. In some ways, this maps onto one of Bartlett's earlier mentioned ideas, namely, that affective attitudes influence recall. Interestingly, Bartlett added that this "may tend, in particular, to produce stereotyped and conventional reproductions which adequately serve all normal needs, though they are very unfaithful to their originals" (1995: 55).

Another type of memory, alluded to previously and of some significance here, is short-term memory. This kind is not subsumed under either semantic or episodic memory, nor for that matter explicit or implicit memory.[2] It can also be said to be less complex than its long-term counterpart. Often referred to as "working memory", short-term memory is cited by specialist scientists like Alan Baddeley as having three distinctive component systems. These are often termed (i) the attentional control system or "central executive", (ii) the articulatory loop, and (iii) the visuo-spatial sketch-pad. The first of these, thought to be located in the pre-frontal cortex, has a very limited storage capacity. Its attention is focused on events in the perceptual environment and it functions to regulate the flow of information to the two other areas, which are believed to hold memory for temporary use. These two areas are known too as "rehearsal systems" a term coined by Baddeley. The first one, the articulatory loop, is a storage system where words and numbers are remembered and can be recalled orally. The articulatory loop, however, is said to have a memory capacity that decays very quickly. The second rehearsal system is the visuo-spatial sketch-pad. This is another ephemeral, mnemonic storage system. It does not merely deal with the visual properties of things to be remembered, as the name suggests, but also with their actual spatial location. It should be noted that no information that enters into either of these two rehearsal systems has to decay. Indeed, it can pass into long-term memory for subsequent consolidation and storage, ready for later retrieval. I will return to Baddeley's model in the final chapter of this work.

Motivation, be it conscious or subconscious, is thought to play an important role in transforming new short-term memories into stable, long-term ones. An important link between long-term memory and short-term memory is to be found in the notion of "retrieval structures", first introduced by Chase and Ericsson in 1982. Kintsch, for example, argues in his book

*Comprehension* that retrieval structures are activated by cues in short-term memory. One such cue can activate an entire event or episode in a relatively wholesale manner. Hence, all of our memories are potentially just one step away, i.e. they can be retrieved in one operation by a single cue (1998, 244–46). Kintsch further points out that such structures do not occur naturally; instead, they have to be learned through repetition and practice (see also Ericsson and Kintsch 1995). Such cues might, for instance, be words. It is, however, questionable as to whether textual inferences are even necessary at all as generators of meaning and subsequent mental image construction. As Kintsch explains further, in a familiar domain the expert reader does not even need inferences from the text for a familiar retrieval structure to be activated immediately. Hence, not only does such information not have to be inferred, it need not even have to be installed in short-term memory or consciousness (1998: 245). With that final thought in mind, we turn to the domain of implicit memory.

Implicit memory processes are markedly different from explicit ones and can be said to refer to more perceptual, motor and especially affective activities. Unlike its explicit counterpart, this type of memory involves little conscious effort, and there is no explicit conscious search to try and recall information. Furthermore, it does not tend to use verbal channels of communication; rather it is more expressed in what might be termed "performance" (Kandel, Kupfermann and Iversen 2000: 1239). It is also known as "non-declarative" memory and is far more inflexible than explicit memory, as it tends to be tied to the original conditions under which a particular stimulus was learned. There are different forms of implicit memory which are learned in different ways and are housed in different parts of the brain. As stated above, emotion plays an important role in this kind of memory. One affective aspect of implicit memory is fear conditioning. This type of memory, dealt with in detail by LeDoux (1998), is thought to involve, in particular, the amygdala which registers and processes emotive, implicit memories. Another affective aspect of implicit memory is something known as operant conditioning, which uses the striatum, in the sub-cortex, and cerebellum for memory. A third type occurs through an exposure to such things as "classical conditioning", "habituation" and "sensitisation" and centrally involves the sensory and motor systems (see LeDoux 1998: 138–224 for more on this). From this it is likely that studying reflex systems may give an insight into this kind of Pavlovian "response-type" memory. It is worthwhile to note that some types of learned behaviour involve both implicit *and* explicit forms of memory. As Kandel, Kupfermann and Iversen explain, although something like classical conditioning involves associating an unconscious reflexive response with a certain stimulus, it may also involve explicit memory when the response is processed cognitively (2000: 1243). For example, avoiding danger or pain is not merely an automatic, unidirectional, skeletal-muscular response, as behaviourism would have us believe; rather it is a cognitive response, because differing flight situations will require different exit strategies that invariably use different limbs and muscles. Moreover, repeated exposure to a fact or an experience can turn it from an explicit learned response into an implicit, automatic one.

Implicit long-term memory thus generally involves the more subcortical areas of the brain in memory storage probably including the cerebellum, the sensory and motor areas and especially the main central emotive area: the amygdala. Clearly, the type of implicit memory needed to perform certain tasks requires numerous brain structures and diverse areas. This ultimately means that a form, or forms, of parallel processing must take place during mnemonic acts within implicit processing. Furthermore, it must be remembered that explicit and implicit memory essentially differ as to the areas that get activated during memory storage and retrieval procedures. Kandel, Kupfermann and Iversen make a clear distinction between the two modes when they say "implicit memory flows automatically in the doing of things, while explicit memory must be retrieved deliberately" (2000: 1245). This fluvial aspect to implicit memory is facilitated by the very nature of memory itself, since cerebral blood flow plays a crucial role in memory-production, as indeed does neurotransmitter activity at the level of the synapse; a process Zull refers to as "a chemical cascade" (2002: 226).

Since some aspects of implicit memory make use of the amygdala, this type of memory might also be termed "emotional". LeDoux makes an interesting distinction between explicit and implicit memory in the framework of emotions. He calls hippocampal (explicit) memory "a memory of an emotion" and amygdaloidal (implicit) memory "an emotional memory" (1998: 182). He adds that both implicit and explicit memory systems are activated when an emotive memory occurs, and uses the following example as an illustration: if you have been hurt in a car accident while driving down the road whereby the horn gets stuck, then the sound of a horn can bring back that negative memory in later life, since this sound has been conditioned as a fear stimulus LeDoux 1998: 200–201). This involves both explicit and implicit memory systems. LeDoux explains that "the sound of the horn goes straight from the auditory system to the amygdala and implicitly elicits bodily responses that typically occur in situations of danger" (1998: 201). This then is the activation of an "emotional memory" that can open the floodgates to emotive arousal and make the past experience feel seamlessly current in conscious experience (1998: 201). LeDoux states that "the sound also travels through the cortex to the temporal lobe system where explicit declarative memories are activated" (1998: 201). It is at this point, in close interactive proximity to the hippocampal region that memory probably becomes conscious, i.e. it becomes a "memory of an emotion". So, here, it would appear that emotive memory processing has a kind of "primacy" over purely cognitive memory processing.

LeDoux suggests further that in order for a person to have a fully embodied emotive experience the amygdala system must be activated (1998: 201). Expanding on the role of that system he explains that "there are in fact abundant connections from the hippocampus and the transition regions, as well as many other areas of the cortex, to the amygdala" (1998: 203). The amygdala, however, does not just receive information; it has projections to many other cortical areas as well. Indeed, there is probably more outgoing information from the amygdala than there is incoming. It projects back to the visual system, long-term memory, the lateral pre-frontal cortex, short-term memory and many other areas. In sum, in addition to information flowing into the amygdala from the cortex, it also flows back to attention, perception and memory areas (1998: 284). Indeed during emotive and cognitive episodes, many parts of the human brain can be active at once "in neuronal networks of incomprehensible complexity" (Zull 2002: 100). This general principle is also supported by Stephen Kosslyn and Olivier Koenig, when, during their discussion of "the confluence of bottom-up and top-down processing that constitutes a specific emotion" they speak of how an emotion can "feed back" once it has been interpreted (1995: 463).

Interestingly, and perhaps somewhat controversially, LeDoux says that "it is also possible that processed stimuli activate the amygdala without activating explicit memories or otherwise being represented in consciousness" (1998: 203). This unconscious processing of stimuli can occur, he claims, "either because the stimulus itself is unnoticed or because its implications are unnoticed" (1998: 203). To return to his road accident example: the memory of the accident may be long forgotten by what one might term the "cognitive" memory system, but it may not be forgotten by the emotive memory system housed in the amygdala region. So, in such a situation, "you may find yourself in the throes of an emotional state that exists for reasons you do not quite understand" (1998: 203). This experience, LeDoux further suggests, "is all too common for most of us" (1998: 203). Emotive implicit memory, therefore, might be said to be more fundamental than explicit memory in the sense that it only contains basic links between cues and responses. There is an implicit suggestion in LeDoux's claims that the memory systems located in the amygdala region may be more "reliable" than those in the hippocampal region. He appears to back this up by explaining that although the explicit memory system is notoriously fragile, the implicit memory system is very robust. Indeed, not only does the implicit system maintain emotive memories, but it can even strengthen them as time passes (1998: 203). Additionally, the emotive memory system is in place and functioning normally long before the cognitive system is. This may account for the phenomenon known as infantile amnesia. It is thought that adults cannot recall childhood traumas before the age of three or four because in children the hippocampus has not yet matured to the point of forming conscious memories. The amygdala, however, is there and is functioning perfectly, recording emotive memories (see the work of Nadel and Jacobs 1996). A purely linguistic, and quite pragmatic, reason may be that young children have too few linguistic labels at their disposal which they can use as retrieval cues.

Despite all of the above-mentioned differences in memory systems, neural imaging techniques have suggested that both implicit and explicit memories are often stored and retrieved more or less in parallel (see also Zull 2002: 86). This fluvial parallelism and seemingly general absence of the explicit notion of "primacy" one way or the other is a point to which I shall return in the next chapter when discussing cognitive appraisal. In order to try and illustrate all this more clearly, below is a basic diagram (Fig. 1.1) that attempts to represent the main points of what has been said about memory in this section. It is basic in the sense that it does not show those less strong yet important links that connect long-term to short-term memory, explicit memory to implicit memory and the varied projections back from the amygdala. The rudimentary diagram below shows some of the basic memory functions discussed thus far and their essential relationship to each other.

Having now concluded this brief discussion on both cognitive and neurobiological memory, I want to recall and summarize some concepts discussed earlier. From a discourse perspective, memory appears to play at least two different roles in any text comprehension situation, irrespective of the nature of the text. First, it has to be able to access previous sentences or discourse units that have just been read while processing a current sentence. This broadly falls into the bottom-up aspect of text comprehension sketched out earlier. Secondly, and of equal importance, since text representations are not based solely on the text itself, a significant contribution to meaning making has to be supplied by the continual activation and ebbing and flowing of relevant, affect-driven schemata from long-term memory. This type of memory

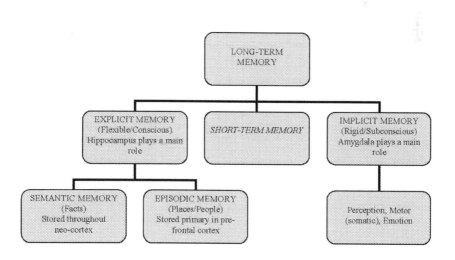

*Figure 1.1* Some basic memory functions.

is of a top-down nature. Both types of memory, what might be termed the co-textual and the contextual, are crucial to everyday comprehension.

As we saw earlier, our memory storage system is both fragile and fragmentary. In the words of cognitive scientist Daniel Schacter it contains mere "snippets of conversation, glimpses of faces, an occasional scent or taste" (1996: 91). The fragmentary nature of memories is clear; their fragility on the other hand lies in the fact that they decay, often bottom-up—i.e. the details tend to go first. As we also learned, memory is an act of construction and composition, it is not a simple act of replay. Moreover, that construction might have as much to do with how we feel in the present, as it has to how we felt in the past. As Schacter notes "even the seemingly simple act of calling to mind a memory of a particular past experience . . . is construed from influences operating in the present as well as from information you have stored about the past" (1996: 8). He goes on to suggest that sometimes the present conditions virtually create the memory (1996: 104–13).

Kintsch's aforementioned Construction-Integration (CI) model of comprehension deals with memory too, as it focuses on three aspects: (i) the integration of knowledge, (ii) the memory of the text, and (iii) other non-textual elements (1998: 409). Indeed, it gives special attention to the environment to be comprehended and the long-term memory that does the comprehending (1998: 409). In a similar fashion to van den Broek et al.'s work on reading processes, the CI model is persuasively described in terms of successive cycles of comprehension processes (1998: 409–13). In this domain of discourse psychology, long-term memory is generally viewed as an extensive network of nodes representing such core cognitive issues as "beliefs", "experiences" and "knowledge", whereby only a small part of the system needs to be triggered from working memory in order to activate a whole schema from a person's background knowledge. In neurobiological terms, one now knows from what has been set out earlier, that the brain region being referred to here by this term will depend on what type of explicit knowledge is being processed, namely, "semantic" or "episodic".

What the previous discussion on the neurobiology of memory suggested was that some aspects of implicit long-term memory do not solely contain so-called purely, cognitive "belief-based" elements in their interaction with working memory. Instead, both emotive and somatic elements appear to play a major role in recall. An increasing number of cognitive scientists and discourse psychologists appear to agree with this. In a chapter entitled "Beyond Text" in *Comprehension*, Kintsch also embraces the idea that emotive and somatic markers are crucial to the dynamic and fluvial meaning-making processes that take place in working memory (1998: 411). He states that the processes that take place in working memory are like "a dynamically changing stream", referring to this further as "shifting patterns of activation" (1998: 411). He also claims that it is highly plausible that such somatic markers can act as cues that activate retrieval structures in long-term memory about one's body:

When I look out the window of my study on the scene below, I see the city nestled in the trees, the flat curve of the horizon, and the sky above speckled with afternoon clouds. I move my head as the eyes scan the horizon, the familiar view makes me feel good, and I stretch my legs and take a deep breath . . . When I recreate the image later, traces of my movements, the way I sat in my chair, and the somatic reactions that occurred in the first place are regenerated with it. I experience a little of that good feeling that went with the original perception. (Kintsch 1998: 410).

The image reconstructed in the brain, through a blend of working memory and the visual cortices, will include bodily reactions that had occurred in the previous experience. Mnemonic images, it seems, are not solely reliant on external retinal information; far from it, they also crucially depend on internal visceral and motor input. As Kintsch puts it "cognition does not occur in a vacuum or in a disembodied mind but in a perceiving, feeling, acting body" (1998: 410). Kintsch further notes that somatic nodes in long-term memory may represent limbs, muscles and the position of the body in space as well as diverse balances and imbalances in the body, whether felt or actual, adding that the sense we have of our body is context-dependent (1998: 411–12). All this seems to suggest that seemingly "less prominent" motor-based senses, such as proprioception and the vestibular balance faculty, can play a significant role in meaning making both in long-term memory and, when activated, in working memory too. Cognitive mnemonic images that are activated and processed during all acts of perception, including reading, appear to be saturated with affective-embodied input. This addition of such fundamental emotive and somatic aspects to working memory offers a procedure recognised in neurocognitive science to account for the role of emotion in the cognitive processing of literary texts.

We may conclude from what has gone before that that the kind of memory that is employed while reading must consist of at least five dynamic, one might even say fluvial, inputs, which include a number of external and internal elements as well as some that fall exclusively into neither category. In the specific context of literary reading, these can be preliminarily listed as:

- the immediate text that is being read
- sections of the previous text, either the last sentence that was read or more salient past sentences or fragments that are still available for recall
- a reader's projected knowledge of how such texts often unfold and conclude
- subconscious background information about previous reading experiences and previous experiences in general

- various affective and somatic inputs either via the body to working memory from the affective and somatic areas of the brain or directly from the affective and somatic areas of the brain to working memory simulating the mediation of the body

Here, not only the importance of internal or top-down aspects of text processing in memory become evident, but also affective, embodied aspects. This is something that is increasingly being acknowledged by specialists in the field of cognitive science (see Damasio 1994, 1999; Kintsch 1998, etc.).

This chapter looked at the secret lives of reading and remembering. These are two processes fundamental to any study on literary discourse processing. The next chapter will expand on this by setting out yet more basic yet essential phenomena. Reading is primarily a visual act that involves the recognition and interpretation of socially-constructed semiotic signs. A study of literary reading processes should therefore devote some discussion to perception. When one speaks of perception one cannot avoid addressing the notion of cognitive appraisal because the former appears to involve the latter. Correspondingly, as this chapter has started to show, no discussion on cognition can circumvent emotion. Hence, three topics—seeing, thinking and feeling—will be the main focus of discussion in the second chapter. Like this one it will seek to highlight the many dynamic cognitive and neural processes that take place during reading.

One final observation before we move on is that the terms "bottom-up" and "top-down" have been used repeatedly in this chapter. However, to my mind, the first of these does not distinguish clearly enough between visual stimuli in the world, such as images and pictures, and the kind of culturally constructed semiotic stimuli we know as writing that one encounters on the page or computer screen. As such, this bottom-up term needs some modification in order to make clear that in this work I am discussing the processing of written language and not visual stimuli in general. For the purposes of clarity, I will henceforth use the term "sign-fed" when referring to visually appraised language-based written input, as this seems far more appropriate to represent this linguistic stimulus-driven category. Correspondingly, the term "mind-fed" appears apt to present the top-down, concept-driven category. It should be noted that these are merely temporary terms of convenience.

# 2   Seeing, Thinking and Feeling

The roots of the Western study of perception in cognitive neuroscience and cognitive psychology lie in the philosophy of ancient Greece. One of the first accounts of vision and the brain comes from the fifth century BC philosopher Empedocles. He believed that the eye had come down to man from the goddess Aphrodite, who had "confined a fire in the membranes and delicate cloths; these held back the deep waters flowing around, but let through the inner flame to the outside" (fragment 84, DK). This might be a somewhat fanciful account of perception, but it is surprisingly modern too in its dynamic and fluvial nature. A century later, the philosopher Epicurus in his "Letter to Herodotus" claimed that perception was a matter of films that were "given off by the object and that convey an impression to the eyes" (O'Connor 1993: 24). This bottom-up view of perception, also known as an atomist account, was later adopted by the first-century BC Roman poet and philosopher, Lucretius in his *On the Nature of Things*. Epicurus added that these emanations occur "at the speed of thought, for their flow from the surface of bodies is constant" (1993: 24). Like Empedocles's claim, that of Epicurus involved a fluvial dimension, as he suggested that his theory of perception was like a kind of "ascending rain, drenching us in all the qualities of the object (cited in Manguel 1996: 28; see also Lindberg 1983). In *On the Soul* Aristotle, with his empirical world-view, also came down on the side of the philosophers who believed in the notion that visual information, including written information, streams upward into the mind of a viewer or reader through the retina.

Another theory of perception was proposed by Epicurus' contemporary, the mathematician and geometrician, Euclid. Euclid's ideas on the nature of perception were arguably less fanciful than the two already mentioned. They were still basically mono-directional, but in contrast to Epicurus's views they were exclusively top-down. This is best seen in Euclid's idea that rays are projected from a person's eyes in order to apprehend an object (cited in Manguel 1996: 29; see also Lindberg 1983). The ancient Greeks therefore were quite divided on whether perception was a stimulus-driven or concept-driven process.

Six hundred years later, the Roman physician Galen took a more unified view of perception than the Greeks had, although his starting point was still essentially a top-down perspective. In his work *On the Natural Faculties* he claimed that a "visual spirit" in the brain "crossed the eye through the optic nerve and flowed out into the air" (cited in Manguel 1996: 29, see also Lindberg 1983). This was the first stage of a three-stage process. The second stage, he claimed, involved the air somehow becoming "imbibed" with the qualities of perception. The third and final stage involved the essence of the perceived object then being transported "back through the eye to the brain and down the spinal cord to the nerves of sense and motion" (cited in Manguel 1996: 29, see also Lindberg 1983). Despite being linear and hierarchical in its structure, Galen's theory did attempt to account for both a top-down and a bottom-up processing of perception.

This interaction between stimulus-driven perception, sometimes known as intro-missionism, and concept-driven visual processing, known as extra-missionism, was meaningfully expanded only in the Middle Ages, when the Basra-born Arab scholar, al-Hasan ibn al-Haytham, known as "Alhazen" in the West, suggested a subtle division in what "seeing" actually means. Inspired by the work of the second century Alexandrian scientist, Ptolemy and while studying optics in the first half of the eleventh century at the celebrated "Dar el-Ilm" ("the House of Science") in Cairo, he set about combining some of Aristotle's bottom-up ideas with some of Euclid's top-down ones, finally coming down on the side of intro-missionism. In doing so, he was able to make a radical distinction between "pure perception" and "pure sensation" (see Smith 1990; 2001). In Alhazen's view, pure perception would refer to something like consciously focusing on words or calculations set out on paper, whereas "pure sensation" might occur if you were to take your eyes away from those black marks on the page by simply turning your head sideways and gazing out of an adjacent window to apprehend an object like a piece of paper being carried playfully by the wind. Alhazen was thus arguing that perception involves a gradation of awareness that fluctuates from the conscious to the unconscious and, in effect, from cognitive processes to subconscious affective processes. This was one of Alhazen's crucial observations, and, amazingly, it is not too different from some of the neuroscientific theories that are being put forward today. For example, a very loose analogy might be drawn between Alhazen's ideas of "pure perception" and "pure sensation" and what was said in the previous chapter about the nature of explicit memory, mediated primarily by the hippocampus and implicit memory, mediated primarily by the amygdala. It seems to echo as well LeDoux's idea on "the (explicit) memory of an emotion" versus "an (implicit) emotive memory".

Let us start with a basic question that is central to a study of "eyes on the page" reading: when one looks at an object, how does one perceive it? Neurobiologists, aided by advancements in neural scanning technology, now believe that they have a reasonable idea of how vision functions. Perception appears to begin in perceptor cells that are sensitive to external stimuli. In the case of vision, this external stimulus is, of course, light, which falls on the retina. Photons are then converted in the retina of the eye, which is part of the central nervous system, into electrical activity by photoreceptors at the back of the eye.

The process then flows from the retina to the thalamus, known as the sensory switchboard located in the mid-brain area. The thalamus is located at the top of the brain stem. It is believed to direct messages to the sensory receiving areas in the cortex and transmit replies to areas like the cerebellum and the medulla; two basic neural structures which regulate such fundamental processes like breathing and the heartbeat. This whole operation is thought to occur in parallel pathways, rather than in a single, serial one, which travel through both the sub-cortical and the higher cortical areas of the brain. These two routes are commonly known in cognitive neuroscience as "P" and "M" pathways. This is how Kandel and Wurtz (2000) describe the process. The "P" pathway travels from the retina via the thalamus to the posterior parietal cortex—this is the approximate area that Zull refers to as the integral back cortex—and then on to the primary visual cortex located at the back of the brain. This is a "higher" route, so to speak, that is thought to be responsible for the processing of such phenomena as motion, depth and spatial information. This area is therefore more concerned with spatial and locative relationships. On its "return" journey, as it were, from the primary visual cortex is thought to pass through the middle temporal region of the brain, which is concerned with motion and depth too. This return journey is known by a different name, namely the "dorsal" pathway, and can be said to pertain to the "where" and "how" of mental constructs. The "M" visual pathway also flows from the retina via the thalamus, but then goes on to an area known as the inferior temporal cortex before it arrives in the primary visual cortex. This is a "lower" pathway, as it were, that is more concerned with such phenomena as form and colour. This area is also thought to deal with recognition tasks of people, places and objects. On its "return" journey from the primary visual cortex, this route also takes on a new name, namely the "ventral" pathway and can be said to pertain to the "what" and "who" of mental constructs. It is important to note that even though these two pathways have different functions, there is now widely believed to be extensive interaction between them at all cortical levels. Exactly how this inter-modular interaction takes place is still largely unknown to neurobiologists. What is known is that perceptual integration is likely to be a multi-stage process, interacting with many other important visual areas such as the pre-frontal cortex (Kandel and Wurtz 2002: 505).

All vision must involve the primary visual or "striate" cortex, also known as the V1 area, and also the secondary visual cortex, known as the V2 area. However, as Semir Zeki has noted, there are other important "extrastriate" visual areas as well known as the V3, V4 and V5 respectively (1993: 104–5). When we see, we experience such things as colour, form and movement in a single perception. However, these categories are in fact processed in different areas of the visual cortex, as has been described in the fluvial-like journey above. More specifically, the aforementioned V3 area is concerned with the processing of dynamic form, the V4 area is dedicated to processing colour and form and the V5 area is given over to processing more general aspects of motion (see Zeki 1993: 94–112 and 166–70). These areas should not be seen as operating in isolation. For example, even though it is true that both V3 and V4 deal with different aspects of form and are processed differently, it would be a mistake to assume that the one is processed exclusively via the "P" system and the other through the "M" system. Instead, as Zeki points out, perception is an extensively distributed activity (1993: 189). What is essential to this entire account of neurobiological perception therefore is the notion of "distributed processing", namely that the processing of visual input is a procedure that involves many cortical areas of the brain. This mirrors what we have seen in the previous chapter with regard to memory systems. It is thus not a single *serial* procedure but rather a multiple *parallel* one that must, by its very nature, rely on interaction and ultimately on synthesis and confluence. As Kandel and Wurtz suggest there are multiple interconnections and interactions between the visual pathways at almost all cortical levels, as well as reciprocal interactions and connections from higher to lower levels both within pathways and between them (2000: 505). This observation suggests that the neural act of perception, which also includes the neural act of perceiving words on the page during reading, is a confluent, dynamic process.

As explained earlier, light falling on the retina is believed to be the primary bottom-up cue for the act of vision. By and large, this is in line with the aforementioned views of Epicurus and Aristotle. Perception, however, might also be triggered in part by internal input, as was argued by Empedocles, Euclid and Galen. This classical perspective on vision can also be observed in neurobiological research. Kandel and Wurtz, for example, state that "perception also is based on inferences about the nature of our world that are built into the wiring of the brain by genetic and developmental processes" (2000: 495).

Just as the Gestalt psychologists of the early twentieth century claimed, the act of seeing is therefore to some extent based on inferences and assumptions that our visual neural system makes as to what is "out there" in the world, rather than purely on what physically appears to be "out there" and gets triggered and channelled by light. This must be the case for reading too. How often, when reading certain phrases, clauses and sentences, do we read what we *expect* to be there, based on prior experience, rather than what actually is there. It should now be clear that vision is not a monodirectional process, be that bottom-up or top-down. Rather, although initial light input remains central, it is a creative activity that runs not just on external "reality" but also on assumptions and inferences that assist in transforming such patterns of light into the full magnificence of our three-dimensional world. As Kandel and Wurtz suggest, vision involves far more than just the information provided to the retina by any given stimulus event (2000: 493). Perception, as has been noted by Gerald Clore and Karen Gasper, is a continuous, ongoing process that involves "a constant interplay of top-down (belief-driven) and bottom-up (data-driven) processing" (2000: 40).

There is work done on neural aesthetics that focus mainly on vision related to emotion. In one prominent theory, neuroscientist Vilayanur S. Ramachandran (2005; 2006) sets out six "laws" of visual-neural aesthetics, all of which were originally grounded in our biological evolutionary survival system. These are (i) grouping (we first struggle to see that fragments belong to a whole, but once we do we experience an "aha" moment of gratification); (ii) symmetry; (iii) hypernormal stimuli (extended or multiplied patterns produce a big "aha" jolt); (iv) peak shift (how over-exaggeration or caricature leads to increased pleasure); (v) isolation (the "less is more" principle: outlines/sketches) and (vi) perceptual problem solving (whereby the search to solve the problem is as enjoyable as the final "aha" of recognition) (2006: 16–18).

The idea that perception is a creative process, mediated as much by top-down processes, i.e. what is *expected* to be seen, as it is by bottom-up processes, i.e. what patterns of light really reflect onto the retina, is not a recent technology-led discovery. As suggested above, the early Gestalt psychologists made similar observations at the beginning of the twentieth century, when they showed with their figure and ground visual experiments, based largely on form and distance, that the idea of an "observing" brain was in fact a fallacy, because the visual brain often assumes what is to be seen rather than just seeing it. As indicated in the previous chapter, this is also what Bartlett found in his literary reading experiments on remembering. Let us now move on and consider the biological act of reading.

It is generally accepted that when a person is reading his/her eyes are not in continuous motion over the page. Instead, the eyes move forward in a series of discrete movements known as saccades. This process can be seen most clearly in eye-tracking experiments. Cognitive psychologist Best describes the regular "jump-stop-jump-stop" rhythm in the following way:

> Once launched forward, the eye must come to rest at some point, however briefly, and the movement of the eye cannot be altered in mid-movement. During these motions, no information from the page can be gathered. Following the saccade, the reader fixates her eyes at one point on the page. During this fixation, the eyes are relatively motionless, and the work of reading is accomplished at this point. Typically, readers fixate for approximately 200 to 250 msec, and the saccade can be accomplished in about 5 to 10 msec. (1986: 354)

Reading is thus not just about vision but also fundamentally a question of motor skills, as Zull explains:

> To read, we must use the muscles in our eyes for focusing and for following the words on the page or screen. Each eye contains a small lens that is continually adjusted by small muscles in the eyeball, allowing us to focus on what we see. And, each eyeball is turned up, down, or sideways, by other small muscles, thus allowing us to follow the words along the page. The lens changes shape, and the eyeball moves as we read. Reading is an intense, focused use of the motor brain. Reading is action. (2002: 205)

Other studies, like that mentioned previously of Just and Carpenter (1980) have suggested that this "jump-stop" rhythm of reading can be more complex, and indeed often is, as readers appear to focus longer on what are termed "content" words than they do on "function" words. Readers appear as well to focus longer on words at the opening and closing of sentences. So, depending on the difficulty of the word and the importance of its positioning in the sentence, a reader can intervene in this automatic saccadic process and alter the rate—just as readers might also intervene in reading a much-enjoyed novel and slow down or even speed up. Just and Carpenter further point out that reverse saccades, known as regressions, are sometimes launched in order to aid the comprehension process. Fixations have been estimated at about three words. This is the equivalent of roughly ten characters either side of the fixation point. It is also widely believed that in normal situations cognitive rather than purely biological factors will largely determine the speed of processing, reading and comprehension.

In much of psycholinguistics, reading is traditionally thought to be limited to work done in the language processing areas of the brain, such as Broca's area and Wernicke's area. Broca's area is located in the left frontal lobe, which is thought to be principally responsible for directing muscle movements involved in speech. It has been noted how both visual and auditory pathways appear to converge in Broca's area (Kandel 2000: 14). Symptoms of Broca's aphasia include difficulty in speaking, defective syntax and a lack of function words and abstract nouns. Comprehension, however, is often good. Wernicke's area, on the other hand, is located in the left temporal lobe and is thought to be largely responsible for language comprehension. People suffering from Wernicke's aphasia have poor comprehension capacities. Their oral production, however, is by and large good. Their language is often syntactically complex and their vocabulary can be diverse, even if the nouns and verbs used are often simple.

The study of blood flow in the brain is also important for memory and cognition. Interestingly, fMRI-scans measure activity *later,* rather than when it actually occurs. This is because blood flow needs time to respond to a stimulus. In fact there is a 3–4 second delay in fMRI scanning—and the whole process of blood being redirected to a part of the brain to process information and then moving away again once the action has taken place can take up to 25 seconds in total. So what neurolinguistic researchers see on the monitor during language experiments using fMRI scanning equipment is not language being processed, but rather what we might see as the "shadow" or "echo" of those processes. Recent developments in brain-scan technology, monitoring blood-flow during language tasks, have shown, however, that language appears to be stored in different locations across the human brain. Neurolinguist Friedemann Pulvermüller, for example, claims that words are represented and processed in the brain by "strongly connected distributed neuron populations exhibiting specific topographies" (2002: 1). He adds that these neuron ensembles are more commonly known as "word webs" (2002: 1). At a more specific lexical level he explains how concrete words referring to objects and actions are thought to be organised as "widely distributed cell assemblies" in the sensory and motor areas, whereas abstract grammatical function words and grammatical affixes are thought to be housed in the left cortical areas, as well as in Broca's and Wernicke's areas (2002: 49). Similarly, grammar functions in the brain are thought of in terms of "neuronal assemblies", whose activity relates to the serial activation of other neurons (2002: 2). As Pulvermüller explains, these are called "sequence sets" (2002: 2). Neuronal sets are thus defined as functional webs that can have four states of activation, namely, (i) inactivity, (ii) ignition, (iii) reverberation, and, (iv) neighbour induced pre-activity (2002: 6). These serially ordered processes are known as "synfire chains" and also as "reverbatory synfire chains" (2002: 6). In support of this sense of reverberation during language processing, Pulvermüller speaks too of "fast oscillations" in the "rhythmic" brain (2002: 274). This notion of a rhythmic brain is an idea that was mentioned earlier in the recent work of Buzsáki. The work of neurolinguists suggest then that Broca's and Wernicke's areas are not solely responsible for the storage and processing of language, but are rather an important point of confluence that the tributaries of language flow through and converge in oral language production and reception.

PET-scan studies have shown conclusively that reading relies heavily on processing work done in the visual cortex. Zull alludes to this with his claim that "language is a tool to produce images" (2002: 169). It has also been suggested by Dronkers, Pinker and Damasio that "reading words and word-like shapes selectively activates extrastriate left cortical areas anterior to the visual cortex" (2000: 1184) and that "the processing of word shapes, like other complex visual qualities, requires that general region" (2000: 1184). Reading also requires the construction of mental imagery. As such, according to neuroscience, reading is, to a significant extent a visual act, in more than one way. It can be argued that one of the most potent and affective modes of language processing that relies on the construction of mental imagery is the reading of literature. Hence, the mental imagery produced by reading a literary text, or for that matter listening to one, is more likely to primarily involve the visual areas of the brain—perhaps more so than everyday language would.

Despite the convergence of visual and auditory pathways in Broca's area, relatively recent work has shown that both processes are fundamentally different. Saper, Iverson and Franckowiak describe an experiment that used PET-scan techniques involving two groups of subjects (2000: 379). The first group was asked to think about as many verbs as possible that would co-relate to a noun that they were presented with. This had to be done without vocalising the words. The second group was asked to do the same thing but to vocalise the words at the same time. The imaging showed that the patterns of activation were completely different. In the case of the group that generated verbs through silent thinking, Broca's area and supplementary motor areas came into play, whereas in the case of the group that vocalised their thought processes, the auditory and peri-auditory cortices were primarily activated. Indeed, Alan Baddeley's aforementioned work on a theoretical articulatory loop model shows how silent speech—or sub-vocal rehearsal systems—that can be accessed for example by reading words or numbers, made use of brain areas in rhyming tasks based on consonants that the vocalising of them from short-term memory did not use (see Saper, Iverson and Franckowiak, 2000: 360). Baddeley's experiments surprisingly showed that Broca's area was essentially non-vocal. These experiments strongly suggest that discussions on silent reading processes, as this study is, should not avoid a consideration of Broca's area.

The above-mentioned experiments are from the late 1980s. Today, there are several other theories with regard to reading processes that have been supported by brain scanning. One worth mentioning here is discussed in Stanislas Dehaene's article "Natural Born Readers". Here, Dehaene addresses the question as to why it is that we can read so well while the human brain evolved in a world without words. He is looking in more depth at what Kosslyn and Koenig had earlier called "an example of opportunistic processing" (1995: 168). Dehaene suggests that the brain's built-in flexibility diverts existing brain circuits to deal with the relatively new task of reading. More specifically he argues that "we are able to learn to read because the primate visual system evolved to do a different job that was sufficiently similar to allow it to be "recycled" into a reading machine" (2003: 30). His recent fMRI experiments have revealed that there is a vast network of cortical areas that are active in the different stages of reading. In fact, there appear to be about a dozen regions involved, spread across the entire brain (2003: 30). Imaging experiments have suggested that the region of the brain responsible for object recognition also plays an important role in word recognition, irrespective of the language or the alphabet/icon type employed. So even though we are not born with an area of the brain that is designed for reading, we all end up employing the same object recognition pathway on the left side of the brain to recognise words during reading procedures (2003: 30). This suggests perhaps that even in a language like English, the visual shape of a word may play an import role in the initial phase of reading. English words, therefore, are by no means icons, similar to those found in the Chinese and Japanese languages, but from a neurobiological perspective they appear to be treated in a somewhat similar way. Interestingly, as Dehaene suggests, in primates, the visual homologue region—which is part of the ventral visual pathway that humans use for word recognition—is still entirely dedicated to object recognition (2003: 30).

The foregoing discussion has focused on perception as a key sensory input for reading. However, it would be unwise to consider seeing as the be all and end all of reading from a sensory perspective, as there is much more to reading than a visual dimension. Two lesser-known sensory areas that I wish to touch on here are the vestibular function, located in the ear, and proprioception, which is part of the somatosensory system. As Gardner, Martin and Jessell explain (2000: 430–50), although the vestibular system is located in the ear, it has in fact little to do with the actual act of hearing. The so-called mechano-receptors that are involved in the hearing of regular sounds are located in the hair cells in the ear that pick up vibrations. However, the vestibular sensory system is grounded in the position of the body in the gravitational field. Hence, gravity, rather than sound, can be said to be its energy stimulus and balance is its modality. Like sound though, it has mechano-receptors. These are the hair cells located in the vestibular labyrinth. The second, equally unfamiliar sensory system is the aforementioned somatosensory aspect of proprioception. The type of modality that proprioception employs is concerned with posture and the movements of parts of the body, whereas its receptor class is based on the transitional notion of "displacement". The receptor cell types in proprioceptory displacement are "mechano" muscle and joint receptors. From all this, we can see that these two forms of sensory perception are linked. Sensory systems like proprioception and the vestibular function may not seem to be linked to reading, but as this work unfolds we will see that they indeed can be in specific emotive literary reading contexts.

As has already been alluded to, there are certain parts of the brain, such as the pre-frontal cortices and the amygdala, that represent information and feelings about a person's body. They also control the state of the body. Damasio refers to the feeling that we have about our body as "somatic markers" (1999: 40–42). It is believed that the body can indicate these changes back to other parts of the brain via the somatosensory cortex. This input then becomes part of the meaning-making appraisal maelstrom that is played out in working memory. Damasio notes that, amazingly, the role that the body plays may, at times, be temporarily "bypassed", as it were, so that the amygdala and the pre-frontal cortices can have a direct effect on the central processing parts of the brain. In other words, the affective areas of the brain can trick these processing parts into believing that the body is relaying information back that it is in a particular state, when it is not. (See

Damasio 1994 and Kintsch 1998). Recall from the previous chapter how Kintsch evaluated his own emotive and somatic reactions when looking out of a window. There we saw just how important Kintsch thought these implicit memory inputs were for processing procedures. In support of this, and moving the discussion more squarely into the domain of emotion and perception, Kintsch further states that "if somatic markers are always present in working memory, we must then modify our view of what is involved in perception" (1998: 410).

In sum therefore, one is indeed encouraged to conclude that perception is not merely a matter of what is "out there", i.e. what can be visually perceived and what is normally processed in a framework of beliefs, but also what is "in here", so to speak, with regard to feelings and an awareness of one's bodily states. Perception, as Damasio argues throughout *Descartes' Error* (1994) is more than mere sensual information: it has an intrinsic somatic component as well. Kintsch agrees:

> Perception is not only a cognitive process but also an emotional process. We react to the world not only with our sense organs but also with gut-level feelings. The things that excite us, please us, scare us are most closely linked to the somatic level. Our most central memories are the ones most intimately linked to our body. (1998: 412)

Although difficult to test empirically, this claim appears to cut down in one fell swoop many of the past philosophical claims that the mind is originally merely a *tabula rasa*. Such "blank slate" perspectives, including the philosopher John Locke's view that there is nothing in the mind before it is apprehended by the senses now seem implausible in the light of modern neuroscience, which, supported by imaging technology, shows the crucial role of both bodily and affective inputs in perception and meaning-making.

In the final four chapters of this work, and especially in the last chapter itself, I will argue that during certain phases of intensely emotive literary reading at closure, a reader is capable of experiencing a sense of felt movement. But how, one might ask, can a person possibly experience the feeling of motion without actually moving? The answer, in part, may lie in the proprioception and vestibular functions mentioned earlier, but it may also have something to do with a recently-discovered phenomenon called mirror neurons, which lends tangible, empirical weight to the cases of both proprioception, the vestibular function, as well as to similar theories like that of simulation, which can be described as people using their own cognitive and emotive processes to predict or understand the cognition and emotion of others.

The following description pertains to neurobiological research conducted on macaque monkeys completing a number of grasping tasks involving switches and knobs. There is evidence that the mirror system of macaques is not too dissimilar to that of humans. In fact, it might be even more flexible (Stamenov and Gallese 2002: 1–2). This is how Krakauer and Ghez explain mirror neurons:

> A unique type of neuron has been discovered in the lateral ventral premotor area. Like others, these neurons discharge when the monkey performs a specific grasping movement, but they also discharge when the monkey observes the same movement being made by another monkey or even by the experimenter. These neurons have been called *mirror neurons*. (2000: 778)[1]

Mirror neurons are located in the premotor area of the brain. More specifically, they fire in what is known as the F5 area of the ventral premotor region of the neo-cortex of macaque monkeys. Interestingly, this area is generally thought to be analogous to Broca's area in humans, an important area, as has been shown, to language production and silent reading (McGlone, Howard and Roberts, 2002: 125). Moreover, at the level of the individual neuron these visual responses are said to be matched with motor ones (Fogassi and Gallese, 2002: 18). Hence, there is a confluence of perception and movement at the level of the single mirror neuron: something Rizzolatti, Craighero and Fadiga refer to as "visuomotor neurons" (2002: 37). In light of the above, mirror neurons can be said to be quite a discovery. However, even more surprisingly is that not only do these neurons fire in the experiments when a monkey watched another monkey grasp a switch, or even when a monkey watched a lab researcher grasp the switch, but they fired as well when the monkey just looked at the switch, without grasping it or without seeing someone else grasp it. In light of the conjecture that "what works for grasping should also work for any other aspect of limb movement", and that "the motor systems in primates and humans are remarkably similar", this astonishing discovery reveals two things. First, if from a stationary position we visually perceive in the real world or on film or television someone making a limb movement such as waving, stretching out one's arms, jumping, dancing, etc., then we too, as observers, may somehow be capable of almost feeling the full sensory extent of that movement. If true, this would go some way toward explaining why we sometimes feel that we can jump fences with racehorses, while we are watching steeplechases on TV, or soar upward with eagles or perform dances with entertainers on stage—all while we are still seated. The second astonishing thing revealed by this discovery is that if we only visually focus on an object that we have previously interacted with—without the presence of the actor or agent—then we will still be able to "feel" or "experience" a similar movement. So, in effect, one does not actually have to see an eagle either on TV or in reality in order to feel a soaring sensation; one only needs look up at the sky or look into a valley and imagine. Hence, some kind of emotive or empathic "projection" appears to take place. This idea may seem somewhat fanciful. However, McGlone, Howard and Roberts have pointed to the covert nature of the working of mirror neurons: a position supported by Stamenov and Gallese's claims on the fundamentally unconscious nature of mirror neural activity (2002: 2). They also add a crucial, and to my mind essential, emotive dimension to mirror neural activity by claiming that this covertness provides a feeling of "empathy or familiarity in the observer" (2002: 133). Following Grafton et al. they suggest too that this must be the case, as the observed action has, by definition, to be one that is in the observer's behavioural or, just as importantly, *imagined* repertoire (2002: 133, my emphasis). This "imagined" category takes mirror neurons a step further as it opens them up to the domain of mental imagery.

Intriguingly, mirror neurons also have both a linguistic and a social dimension. With regard to the first, Stamenov and Gallese have suggested that mirror neurons may play a role in helping to sort out one of the main puzzles in linguistics, namely the emergence of the language faculty (2002: 2). This has also been claimed by Rizzolatti and Gallese and more recently by Oliver Gruber, who suggests that the evolution of the premotor cortices did not merely form the neuronal basis for language functions, but that it strongly affected working memory capacity and other higher cognitive functions too (2002: 77). In his experiments on the effects of articulatory suppression in memory performance he has also shown how Broca's area and other premotor areas are crucial to working memory (2002: 84). Gruber was, in part, able to make this claim exactly because the F5 area in macaque monkeys, where mirror neurons fire, is analogous to Broca's area in humans. Moreover, as we saw, not only is Broca's important for language production and silent reading, but it is essential too for some of the performance tasks in working memory.

Many current accounts of mirror neurons within a human framework tend to omit two issues that to my mind must be central to mirror neural activity: memory and emotion. One study that does not side-step these issues is India Morrison's neuro-social work on neuroscience and cultural transmission. In this work, Morrison observes that mirror neurons fire at an early visuomotor stage of processing. From this she concludes that "memory processing of this information probably occurs downstream from mirror perception" (2002: 335). In effect, Morrison is saying that the feeling of movement comes *before* the actual memory of the event. She continues by suggesting that "mirror perception more likely contributes at a relatively early stage to a cascade of responses which couple perception with action, and action disposition with memory" (2002: 338). Action disposition is concerned with emotion and more specifically with what Damasio has termed "somatically marked" emotions. Morrison also observes that mirror neurons probably play a role in cultural transmission and that the mirror system in humans probably does not have a single function but instead can contribute to "a gamut of social cognitive phenomena" (2002: 338). Mirror neurons, she concludes, hold great promise for knowledge on how the workings of the brain contribute to the workings of culture (2002: 339).

In light of the above work conducted by a range of neuroscientists it can be posited that mirror neurons can indeed be a fruitful phenomenon for studying literary language processing, and the notion that there may be a felt movement resulting from heightened emotive bodily response to that processing. Moreover, the physiological notion of mirror neurons also appears to give substance to much of the past theoretical work done on simulation. Indeed, Kai Vogeley and Albert Newen note that mirror neurons provide valid evidence for simulation theory (2002: 147). Additionally, mirror neurons might go some way to elucidating how the somatosensory system operates. As Damasio has claimed, somatic markers involve a number of brain regions including the prefrontal cortex, which is housed close to the pre-motor area (1994: 180–83). Perhaps one of the most enticing claims is Morrison's previously highlighted suggestion that mirror neurons fire at an early stage of visuo-motor processing and that, as a result, memory and the bulk of cognitive processing occurs "downstream", as she puts it. She implies that emotions have primacy here—in effect, that emotive processing takes places before the bulk of higher cognitive processing. This idea may seem novel, but it is not. In fact, the debate of what comes first, cognition or emotion, is one that takes us back to antiquity and in particular to Plato.

Let us begin with a definition. Cognitive appraisal, which is what we are essentially talking about, is said to be principally a linear process in which a stimulus is first perceived in the world, then a judgement or belief is cognitively constructed about the perception of that stimulus, and finally an emotion is experienced about the original stimulus based on one's beliefs or judgements. This is a doctrine that is still widely held in cognitive psychology. For example, in *Passion and Reason*, Richard S. Lazarus and Bernice N. Lazarus describe cognitive appraisal as follows:[2]

> An appraisal—on which emotions depend—is often a complex judgement about how we are doing in an encounter in the environment and with our lives overall, and how to deal with potential harms and benefits. Appraisal is not just passively receiving information about the environment. It must also actively negotiate between our personal agendas—that is, goals and beliefs. (1994: 144)

At first sight, this appears to be quite modern. However, modern psychology sometimes overlooks a very rich philosophical debate on this, which has been ongoing since antiquity. In *Philebus*, for example, Plato suggests that without thought, memory and a true belief there can be no awareness of pleasure, and hence no pleasure can take place (21-a–d). Similar viewpoints are also found in other works by Plato. In *Phaedo* for example, he recalls

Socrates's monologues which highlight one of his main beliefs, namely that the body is a hindrance to philosophical investigation (65-a/b):

> Surely the soul can reason best when it is free of all distractions such as hearing or sight or pleasure or pain of any kind—that is, when it leaves the body to its own devices, becomes as isolated as possible, and strives for reality while avoiding as much physical contact and association as it can (65-c).

For Socrates therefore, "flawless" comprehension had to be approached not with the body but with "unaided intellect" (65-e), i.e. "without taking account of any sense of sight in his thinking, or dragging any other sense into his reckoning" (66-a). His object of desire was the attainment of "truth". In order to achieve this one had to get rid of the contaminated body, because "the body fills us with loves and desires and fears and all sorts of fancies and a great deal of nonsense, with the result that we literally never get an opportunity to think at all about anything" (66-c). Socrates adds: "so long as we are alive, we shall keep as close as possible to knowledge if we avoid as much as we can all contact and association with the body; . . . " (67-a). What Plato appears to suggest is that emotions do not simply happen to us, rather we have to have a belief or indeed make a judgement before they can take place. In such views, emotion can be said to firmly operate under the exacting control of cool cognition, which is very similar to Lazarus's view cited above in which emotion "depends on" cognitive appraisal. This standpoint can be encapsulated by the maxim "every emotion must first be cognitively appraised by means of a belief or a judgement".

Following Plato, one of the most well-known philosophical devaluations of the body and the emotions was put forward by René Descartes, who thought that it was difficult to rely on our senses to tell us what is happening in the world and in our minds. In order to understand the world better, he wanted to start from zero by disregarding what had already been said in philosophy. Descartes's doubt in everything led him to his famed conclusion that nothing in the world can be true—except of course for his doubt. In effect, it can be suggested that he was not doing much more than echoing St. Augustine's dictum *Si fallor sum* (If I doubt, I exist). Descartes then extended his doubt to the place where "doubting" was formed and came to his celebrated conclusion that reason and the mind are all that can be trusted: in other words, *cogito ergo sum*. Lazarus's above-mentioned rational views on appraisal do not appear to be too dissimilar to these prominent views, stretching from antiquity to the seventeenth century. The only difference is that whereas almost all of these philosophers tended to see emotion as being separate from reason, Lazarus appears to see it as being included in cognition—albeit, as the quoted passage shows, always in a subservient position to reason and judgement.

We see from the above summary that quite a few of the major pre-twentieth century views in the emotion-cognition debate came down on the side of reason. This changed radically, however, with the advent of psychology in the late nineteenth century, which posed the questions "does one feel an emotion after one notices one's physiological response?" or "does one feel an emotion after one has realised that one is experiencing one?" Put differently, one could ask "does one feel sad because one is crying?" or "is one crying because one feels sad?" The main point here is whether one feels before one thinks or whether one thinks before one feels. Common sense tells us that we cry because we are sad and we hit out at somebody because we are angry, but the founding father of psychology, William James, suggested at the end of the nineteenth century that the reason we are sad is because we are crying and the reason that we are angry is because we have already hit out at someone. In other words, we can feel before we think, because to experience an emotion is to be aware of our physiological reaction.

James's theory of bodily superiority—also known as the James-Lange theory in recognition of similar parallel work done by the Danish psychologist Carl Lange—was soon challenged in the 1920s by the physiologist Walter B. Cannon, who made the telling comment that the body's responses are not distinct enough to evoke all the different emotions that we label linguistically. To show this Cannon posed the question: "what does a racing heart actually signal?" He concluded that yes it can indeed be fear, but it can be something completely different, like love. More importantly, Cannon noted that physiological changes, like perspiring or an increase of heart rate take a couple of seconds. Now, this may seem quite fast in everyday terms, but in neurobiological ones, where neural activity can take place in a thousandth of a second, it is very slow. Cannon thought that this was indeed the case and said that bodily changes occur far too slowly to trigger sudden emotion. Hence, he suggested that physiological arousal and emotional experience must occur simultaneously.[3] Technically, this viewpoint suggests that there is a simultaneous bodily and cortical interaction via the nervous system. So one's heart starts pounding exactly at the moment one experiences fear, not before or after it: so there is no real cause or effect. If James said that emotions can occur independently of cognition, Cannon responded that the emotions which we experience involve cognition too.

Following Cannon, in the early 1960s Stanley Schachter and Jerome Singer tried to move the discussion forward by suggesting that the experience of an emotion involves two ingredients: physiological arousal and a cognitive label for it. Both, they claimed, are needed to express an emotion. This contributed to the idea that an emotional experience always needs to be consciously interpreted, which, in turn, suggests that all emotions must be cognitively appraised, i.e. founded on a belief or judgement. The view is still widely held in certain quarters of mainstream cognitive science, as can be seen from the quoted passage from Lazarus. However, it is a perspective that is coming under increasing pressure.

In the 1980s and 1990s this debate was re-ignited as a result of advances made in neurobiological imaging technology. The Schachter and Singer position can be said to be roughly that of psychologists like Lazarus and his co-workers. Conversely, the James position is more clearly observed in the current theories of neurobiologists like Joseph LeDoux and Robert B. Zajonc. Proponents of both positions generally argue for the primacy of one of the two: cognition or emotion. Zajonc, for example, was one of the first brain scientists to suggest that emotion can precede cognition in cerebral processing activities. This is best seen in his two articles from the early 1980s: "Feeling and Thinking: Preferences Need no Inferences" and "On the Primacy of Affect". Rapidly evolving brain-scan technology allowed him to seriously question the accepted view that all primary processing takes place via the higher cognitive areas of the neo-cortex. Zajonc's insights have since been supported by LeDoux (1986), whose experiments have shown that in some cases a kind of "parallel processing" can take place when subjects are exposed to a stimulus. The first of these processing pathways—which should not be confused with the "P" and "M" visual pathways mentioned earlier—is purely cognitive and takes place essentially via the neo-cortical areas of the brain. The second processing pathway is seemingly more "affective" in nature, as it moves from the stimulus to the thalamus and the amygdala, located in the sub-cortex. This second route appears initially to bypass those cortical areas that are presumed to be given over to higher cognitive processing. LeDoux's most convincing finding is not that parallel processing indeed takes place, because the notion of cross-neural, multi-mapping was already becoming accepted at the time in neuroscience, but rather that this second affective processing pathway is consistently faster than the cognitive route. These neuropsychological findings have since been supported by further empirical evidence put forward by Murphy and Zajonc (1993), who suggest that when an emotive visual stimulus is presented subconsciously, it can have an effect on our impressions and judgements to a degree unequalled by stimuli presented in a fully conscious manner. So, one might conclude that this research suggests that initial affective processing can sometimes take place prior to higher cognitive processing when subjects are subconsciously exposed to visual stimuli that are thought to contain affect-prompting properties.

In his later work, *The Emotional Brain* LeDoux is more specific. Here he argues for a "high road" and a "low road" with regard to stimuli reaching the amygdala resulting in emotion. The high road takes the route: stimulus-thalamus-cortex amygdala, whereas the low road goes from stimulus to thalamus to amygdala. This thalamo-amygdala trajectory is not only shorter, but faster too. This is in part due to the fact that the cortical route has more connections to the amygdala. The lack of higher cortical intervention in the low-road route means that the amygdala is presented with crude representations of the stimulus; it is what LeDoux calls "the quick and dirty processing route", whereas the high road will give a much better quality of picture (1998: 164).

Employing this theory within a framework of aesthetic appreciation in literature and other arts, Patrick Colm Hogan asserts that although the subcortical arousal of the low road is ideal for film, it is not suited for literature (2003a: 176). He echoes this by stating "we will have (low road) emotional responses to film, theatre, photography and music—but not to literature" (2003a: 179). The attention and constant cognitive processing that is needed to read literature probably led Hogan to this seemingly logical conclusion. Literary emotion, it would appear, takes exclusively a "high road". However, is this always the case? I will return to this in the final chapter of this book.

It is worth noting that we often encounter this James/Zajonc/LeDoux perspective on affective primacy in cognitive processes in critical discussions on many of the arts. Consider, for example, the following text, which appeared at the entrance to the room where a number of Francis Bacon's paintings were exhibited at the Tate Modern in London in an exhibition that I visited in July 2000:

> Bacon believed that to communicate reality the painter has to capture not only the look of things but also the emotions that they arouse. In an attempt to generate images as accurately off his nervous system as he could, he sought to bypass reason in order to express feelings directly.

Although Bacon may not have been aware of it, his aim of trying to evoke feelings directly "off the nervous system", somehow circumventing cognitive reasoning, makes him a committed physiologist, as indeed many artists are—and understandably so. Comparable affective claims within sister aesthetic domains can also be found in abundance. From the literary domain, for instance, there is John Keats' famous yearning "for a life of sensations rather than thoughts" spelled out in a letter to his friend Benjamin Baily dated 22 November 1817 (ed. Rollins 1958). Similar sentiments have been made in the film world. For example, filmmaker and dramatist Ingmar Bergman observed the following in the introduction to his book *Four Screenplays*:

> When we experience a film, we consciously prime ourselves for illusion. Putting aside will and intellect, we make way for it in our imagination. The sequence of pictures plays directly on our feelings. Music works in the same fashion; I would say that there is no art form that has so much in common with film as music. Both affect our emotions directly, not via the intellect. (1960)

Bergman, like Bacon, Keats, and, indeed, many other artists before him, claims that emotion is prior to cognition for the person who engages with an art form.

All of these views fall broadly in line with James's claim about the primacy of physiology in thought processes and, to some extent, with the modern neurobiological claims of both Zajonc and LeDoux and with some of the recent findings from the field of mirror neuron research. Although these views may appear to lack solid grounding, they cannot be simply labelled erroneous. Instead, one may suggest that if they fall short, then this is because they lack a certain nuance. As we have seen, all visual processing, whether it be of literary words on the page or art objects in space, requires, at the very least, activation of the visual cortex, which is a core cognitive system. We have also seen how external information can only reach the visual cortex by travelling from the retina via the thalamus. These processes cannot entirely bypass cognition, nor does internal visual input that gets activated from a person's memory systems located throughout the brain as seen in the previous chapter. What these artists seem to be alluding to here is not non-cognitive emotion but rather what I like to call "affective cognition", which is similar in some ways to Alhazen's perception views on "pure sensation", or what LeDoux referred to as "an emotional memory" and the "low road" to emotion. Affective cognition is undoubtedly a cognitive process, but one where emotion plays a dominant role. This is something that will be explored in depth within the context of literary reading in the coming chapters.

To return to my discussion, works of art may therefore activate in viewers and readers certain affective cognitive structures, perhaps even mirror neurons, in implicit, emotive and somatic ways. The result is a completely different kind of initial cognitive processing, not the kind that is based on beliefs or judgements or reason, such as that described by appraisal theorists, but rather one based on an affective cognition special to personal encounters with works of art. To conclude this discussion for the time being: both the Lazarus and Zajonc positions, in their most absolutist forms, seem to pose more questions than they answer. To my mind there must be a way of arguing that emotion is part of cognition without becoming a pure judgement-based rationalist. A way to get more clarity on this is to find out more about what psychologists say about what an emotion is.

Many psychological accounts of emotions seem to focus on what can or what cannot be classified as a "basic" emotion. One such account, and a prominent one, is that of Oatley and Johnson-Laird (1987), who claim that there are five basic emotions, namely, happiness, sadness, fear, anger and disgust. This is a popular division in the field. However, it is perhaps best to heed Oatley's later comments in *Best Laid Schemes* that there is no absolute taxonomy of emotive words (1992: 83) and, as such, "the most prudent course is to be agnostic as to exactly how many basic emotions there are" (1992: 61). I will follow this sound advice here. In addition to categorising basic emotions, psychologists often classify types of emotion labels. Oatley and Jenkins, for example, make the following basic distinction (1996: 375–81):

*Emotion:* A state usually caused by an event of importance to the subject. It typically includes (a) a conscious mental state with recognisable quality of feeling and directed towards some object, (b) a bodily perturbation of some kind, (c) recognisable expressions of the face, and, (d) a readiness for certain kinds of action.

*Affect:* A general term used to include emotions, moods and preferences.

*Mood:* A maintained state of emotion or a disposition to respond emotionally in a particular way that may last for hours, days or even weeks, perhaps at a low level and perhaps without the person knowing what started the mood.

The main distinguishing factor here appears to depend on intensity, however; to judge emotions this way alone would be too simplistic. In *The Emotions* Frijda argues that a distinction ought to be made between concepts like feeling and emotion based not simply on intensity but rather on nature. Fear, for instance, is not necessarily always more intense than something like apprehension. Frijda describes emotion as "felt action tendency", while feeling, he says, is a sense of "enhanced" or "impeded" functioning, adding that "certain objects or situations elicit "feelings"; (while) opportunities and risks in obtaining or avoiding those objects or situations elicit emotions" (1986: 244–45). "Feeling", Frijda further suggests, has many meanings (1986: 251). However, it does not simply refer to emotions of a "lesser" intensity, because weak emotions, e.g. milder cases of happiness, can be inferior to more powerful feelings, like indignation or disgust. Like Frijda, Damasio sets out a long discussion on feelings and emotions in *Descartes' Error*, in which he claims that "although some feelings relate to emotions, there are many that do not", adding "not all feelings originate in emotions" (1994: 143). He is referring here to something important he calls "background feeling", which he differentiates from mood, because it corresponds to the body state prevailing *between* emotions, calling it the "image of the body landscape" (1994: 150).

In addition to feelings and emotion, Frijda also speaks of concepts like sentiment, passion and mood. Sentiments, he says, "are feelings in which object evaluation is the major situational meaning component" (1966: 253). He adds, "passions, are goals, springing from action tendency" (1986: 253), in which a current or desired situation is of great importance. Mood he claims is used to refer to an affective state, often of longer duration than emotion, feeling, passion or sentiment (1986: 252). He further points out that mood is often elicited by some biochemical activity, i.e. an internal rather than an external event (1986: 252–53). Despite these classifications one should take heed of Frijda's advice that "emotions, moods, feelings, sentiments and passions are not sharply separate classes of experience ( . . . ) Feelings may turn into emotions ( . . . ) Moods and passions may form the background for emotions" (1986: 253).

Above, Frijda links passions to goals, in which a current or desired situation is of great importance. Cognitive science informs us that emotions are heavily reliant on goals and the plans that lead to goals (Oatley 1992: 98). But how does all this pertain to the reading of literature, if at all? It is thought that when we read literature we do not have any goals, in the emotive sense, or rather "the goals and plans that bear on emotions are not ours" (Hogan 2003a: 148). This hypothetical postulation is correct if we view the plot and characters as channelling our emotions, but it becomes problematic if we approach it from the macro-level of readers looking to be emoted by an art object. In acts of literary reading therefore, there appear to be two sets of plans. First, our own individual goal as a reader to become emoted in some way by a text—this is akin to a desire and can be active long before the eyes meet the page—and second, the goals of characters with which we become involved and emoted because of our ability to empathise and simulate: in Aristotelian terms, we *pity* their misfortunes and in doing so *fear* for our own situation as we project those fictive events onto our own lives and loved ones. My concern in this study, however, is with the first of these: the "real" reader. It is true that twists and turns in the plot and the fate of the protagonist or narrator do create emotions in readers and that this is a primary source of literary emotions. However, I want to look at more than such phenomena. I want to see what effect other processes might have on such text-based events.

Ed Tan has argued that film viewers have goals. In his work *Emotion and the Structure of Narrative Film: Film as an Emotion Machine* he suggests (i) that viewers have expectations that concern envisioning a number of possible structures that can come about as a result of the ongoing narrative, (ii) that they continually test those structures, and (iii) that they hope to feel during that testing that some kind of progress is being made towards closure or a favoured closure. In Tan's own words this is "a preferred final outcome" (1996: 98). If film viewers have goals, which they clearly do, literary readers must have them too and, as I suggest above, these start long before the reader engages with the text. Hogan engages in an insightful dialogue with Tan's work (2003a: 149–50) and poses a probing question in an endnote to that discussion: "why do we formulate this "preferred final outcome" then care so much about it when the events are fictional and we have no egocentric involvement in them" (2003a: 223). My provisional answer to this would be that even though the events are fictive, our commitment as readers to become emoted by the chosen literary work of art most definitely makes literary reading an egocentric process from the level of the reader's macro-goals. Hogan believes something similar:

If we add Tan's account to Oatley's we see that the audience member's response to a narrative may appear to be a direct function of the protagonist's goals. But it is in fact the reader's formulation of a goal (the preferred final outcome), even though that is a goal for the characters rather than for the reader him/herself. Thus our emotional experience of a literary work is a function of junctural evaluation of narrative events in relation to our own goals—specifically our preferred final outcome, a goal that need not be the same as that of the protagonist. (2003a: 149)

Hogan adds that a reader's emotion at such junctures need not coincide with that of the character, even when we share his/her goals. Several issues may have a bearing on this: not least the literary critical notion of dramatic irony, where, due to the elected mode of narrative presentation, the reader or viewer knows far more about the ensuing fate of the characters than the characters do themselves.

In the course of his 2003 work on *Cognitive Science, Literature and the Arts* Hogan (re)introduces a Medieval Sanskrit theory on art reception and emotion called *dhvani*, put forward by the philosopher Abhinavagupta. The general principle of classical Indian aesthetics is that all works of art communicate emotion through their *dhvani* or "suggestiveness". He continues:

> *Dhvani* includes all the associations that cluster around anything that a reader encounters in a work of literature or a viewer encounters in a performance. It derives from individual words, patterns of imagery, scenes, characters, narrative sequences and so on. The suggestions themselves comprise not only other words, but a wide range of non-verbal associations. (2003a: 156)

In literary theoretical terms this is akin to Bakhtin's notion of intertextuality, and in cognitive psychological terms it bears traces of Rumelhart's theory of parallel-distributed processing. Abhinavagupta, Hogan informs us, wondered how all these associations can produce emotions in readers. His answer was that all experiences leave traces in the mind, and that these traces are encoded with the emotions that were felt at the time. The traces are then used to process and contextualise each new aesthetic experience. This is not necessarily a one-to-one mapping that leads to explicit recall: after all, we are talking about cognitive traces interacting with textual and contextual suggestiveness. Although particular suggestions can be understood as matching up with particular memory traces, suggestiveness can also connect to a memory in more implicit ways that does not lead to explicit conscious recall (2003a: 156). Hogan equates these "intermediate states of semi activation" in cognitive terms as "priming", namely, an item in memory that is activated to a high degree but nonetheless is just below a level of accessibility (2003a: 158). However, Hogan makes the modified claim as well "that relevant memories are *continually* primed in our experience of literature", adding that "the suggestions of literary works keep the emotion-laden memories primed for long stretches of time. Thus their cumulative effect may be strong" (my emphasis, 2003a: 158). In sum, "personal memories are crucial to our emotional response to literature" (2003a: 158).

Hogan draws on Oatley's four-part model of literary cognition: story, discourse, suggestion structure and realisation structure. In doing so he observes that the third of these is in fact *dhvani* and that the fourth, the realisation structure, i.e. 'the story as we imagine it', is "entirely personal to the reader and it is to a great extent the result of recruiting personal memories" (2003a: 158). In other words Oatley's fourth stage results from his third. So, details of textual entities prime certain emotive memories in a reader's head. Hogan adds that, like the story itself, these memories involve "persons setting and events" (2003a: 160). It seems clear then that in filling out the background knowledge while reading, it is these person-based and place-based affective memories that are continually primed, and hence it will be these that get launched into the confluence of meaning-making first. This, indeed, is a conclusion that Hogan comes to later, when he suggests that not only does reading lead to the priming of such personal memories but also to their activation (2003a: 162). He further points out the cyclical nature of this affective process:

> As our emotional response to a work develops out of a particular set of primed personal memories, those memories begin to guide our realization or concretization of that work. As a result of this concretization, the memories themselves are reprimed and thus our emotional response is reinforced or enhanced (2003a: 161).

He reinforces the emotive goals of the engaged reader as opposed to those of characters in the text, when he summarises the whole process of affective reading:

> Fragmentary memories complete or fill in our imagination of a work and simultaneously give rise to our emotional response. In keeping with our general tendency to explain emotions by reference to salient experiences, we attribute that emotional response to the events of the work, which are the objects of our attentional focus. This is in part a misattribution. But it is not entirely a misattribution for our imagination of these literary events incorporates elements from the actual, biographical source of our emotions (2003a: 162).

Hogan shows us as well how Abhinavagupta too had a clear view on the relationship between emotions and reading literature. Evaluating the Sanskrit philosopher's work he writes "literary emotions are the result of emotion-laden memories that have been triggered by literary events, characters and so on, but are not self-consciously recalled" (2003a: 157). This, for him, appears to possess a highly plausible account with great explanatory potential (2003a: 157–58). I agree. Hogan himself adopts this idea in an earlier article and comes to the conclusion that *dhvani* is "all the elements of any memory system that receive activation as a result of the experience of the literary work" (2003a: 157). A central idea in his theory is that episodic memory does not just record facts about emotion, but can give rise to emotions as well.

The work done on intense or heightened emotion will be particularly relevant for this study. Intensity, as Frijda has pointed out, is not a straightforward concept (1986: 32). A key factor in emotive intensity is tension and the subsequent release of built up tensions. In discussing this, one can go back as far as Aristotle's ideas on *katharsis*, which focused on drama: in effect, on narrative writing. Classical theatre-goers, going back to the sixth century BC, were moved to empathise with the characters on the stage while at the same time reflecting on their own lives. This is the "fear" and "pity" that made up cathartic responses.

One twentieth-century theory proposed by Daniel E. Berlyne (1960; 1974), is appealing for my study, because like Aristotle's theory, his too is interested in charting intense emotive responses to art, including literature. His theory of aesthetic response, which is concerned with "hedonic value", claims that a subject's interest in an object will grow with increased complexity until it reaches an optimal level. This is known as the "arousal-boost". After reaching a crescendo it will fall with increasing complexity. This is the "arousal jag". The arousal boost-jag theory was expressed by means of a Wundt Curve by which the hedonic value/pleasure was represented by an inverted U curve while the arousal potential/complexity was expressed by a rising line. The notions of highly emoted tension, arousal and release were all at the core of this theory. Tension involves activation: the readiness to respond emotionally or attentionally (Frijda 1986: 51). Frijda suggests that the term "relax" is perhaps appropriate to refer to the drop in heightened emotion described by Berlyne (1986: 51). He says further that because long exposure to high levels of arousal is not pleasant there is a kind of drive to regain homeostasis. He calls this feeling pleasurable and seems to suggest that people might even seek thrills not necessarily to experience the "assent", but rather the "descent" (1986: 346). This, in effect, is Berlyne's arousal jag. Frijda adds that arousal is concurrently both pleasant and unpleasant and that the question of which of the two dominates, and when, depends on the intensity of the arousal (1986: 346). However, he suggests too that being moved by aesthetic objects should not be seen in mere terms of "tension release" but rather as "surrendering to something greater than oneself" (1986: 358). In that same discussion he turns to another aspect of aesthetic emotion that he says "is distinctly of less cognitive nature", one that has a "relevance to desire, to join and to possess"; highlighting further the notion of "losing oneself" as an aspect of the aesthetic process (1986: 358).

Tension can be said to go hand in hand with anticipation, and both involve some sense of movement. Frijda suggests that anticipation intensifies emotional experience in that "it considerably extends the time period over which a given event exerts emotional influence; the event casts its shadow . . . forward" (292). He adds that anticipation affects the response to the emotional event when it comes (1986: 293). For example, it permits preparatory actions like "relaxing and bracing" and it gives one opportunity for "advance coding or recoding of events"(1986: 293). Similarly, Zull has recently argued that there is a neural basis for a strong connection between movement and happiness: "play, sex, dance, music, games, eating, talking and many other pleasures all involve movement" (2002: 61). He goes on to suggest that we get enjoyment not merely by anticipating movement but also by anticipating imagined movement. His key example is literature: "we see it in stories that lead our minds towards a goal. In fact, this is probably the most important thing that keeps us reading a good book or watching a movie. We want something to happen" (2002: 62).

Euphoric emotions are also something discussed by Hogan within the context of literary reading. He observes that "the effects of emotional intensity on the central executive are not merely continuous. They involve stages or thresholds" (2003a: 171). The three stages are the orientation threshold, the expressive threshold and the control threshold. With regard to the first of these Hogan notes how this narrowing of attentional focus, once an emotion has passed this threshold, is what Gordon Bower and Joseph Forgas (2001) have referred to as "mood congruent processing": a coming together of the relevant information with one's "prevailing emotional state". At this orientation stage there is still an aspect of volition on the part of the readers: they can restrain and alter the intensity of the emotion. The second stage, the expressive threshold, is registered as having been passed when one cannot control one's expression of emotions any longer. Tears and laughter are common features at this stage, though a person is still able to suppress actional impulses. The third stage, the control threshold, is where we lose control, even over actional responses (Hogan 2003a: 172). In the case of fear this would be akin to freezing rabbit-like in the headlights, whereas in joy this takes on the form of hedonistic states of euphoria. Such states can also be said to blend sometimes excessive joy with excessive sadness. This for me is reminiscent of "agreeable melancholy", a term coined by the eighteenth-century philosopher David Hume in his essay "Of the Delicacy of Taste and Passion" (1757/1965), written while working on emotive responses to art objects.

> Nothing is so improving to the temper as the study of the beauties either of poetry, eloquence, music or painting. They give a certain elegance of sentiment to which the rest of mankind are strangers. The emotions which they excite are soft and tender. They draw off the mind from the hurry of business and interest; cherish reflection; dispose to tranquility and produce an agreeable melancholy. (1965: 27)

Hogan ends his discussion by noting how "this distinction on thresholds has a considerable bearing on literary study" (2003a: 172). It should further be noted that there is also emotion under the level of orientation, which we usually call moods or feelings. Hogan points out that such subordination-level emotions do have a bearing on our experience of art (200a3: 173). However, he then restricts this by saying that this can only occur in contexts where attentional focus in not required. So in Hogan's view it would work with background music but probably not with literature, because literature would demand continuous, rather than sporadic attention. In summing up his position on emotion and literature, Hogan makes a number of important assertions, including that emotional memories are implicit and almost certainly play a major role in literary experience. He adds that their activation, rather than their priming, is the main source of literary emotion (2003a: 183). We respond emotionally to literature because of three essential things: trigger perception, concrete imagination and emotional memory (2003a: 185). A number of variables such as proximity, speed, vividness and expectedness will affect the intensity of emotive responses and thus our response to literature (2003a: 185). He also draws some important intersubjective conclusions: although the particulars of individual memories will differ, many emotional memories share some common features (2003a: 185).

Let us return now to my central discussion on the neurobiology of emotion. Emotive processing, like all processing, is known to be a cross-cortical affair. The sub-cortical limbic system, where much of the initial emotive activity takes place, is known too as the visceral brain— "visceral" in the traditional sense of "relating to inner feelings" rather than conscious reasoning. This general region contains the aforementioned amygdala, hippocampus and (anterior) thalamus. The latter area, we recall, is a brain structure through which visual information must travel before it arrives in the primary visual cortex. At a "lower" level, the generation of emotions relies on neurotransmitters called endorphins which are of great importance for feeling and mood. They are essentially hormones secreted in the brain and the nervous system. Certain endorphins can be said to lead to pleasurable experiences and even states of euphoria, whereas others can have more elementary soothing effects. From a neurobiological perspective, emotions and emotion processes are dynamic and fluvial. This has also been found to be the case with regard to studies on literary emotion. For example, in their psychological work on literary text processing de Vega and Díaz have suggested that "emotions are dynamic states", adding "and so their mental representations should also be dynamic" (1996: 303).

Similarly, at a psychological level emotion is increasingly understood not as static, perennially and irrevocably subordinate to cognition, but rather as a dynamic, integrated aspect of cognition. Writing on the interaction between emotions and beliefs, Frijda, Manstead and Bem have claimed that "emotions can awaken, intrude into and shape beliefs, by creating them, amplifying them or altering them" (2000: 5). In this view, emotions are an integral and crucial part of beliefs, rather than merely being dependent on them. Indeed in *The Emotions* Frijda had already argued that the appraisal process was distinctly unconscious (1986: 464). This is seemingly the opposite of what Lazarus and other cognitive appraisal theorists are saying. The crucial role that feelings can play in influencing beliefs, judgements and thoughts has been highlighted too by many other cognitive psychologists. For example, Herbert A. Simon first proposed back in the 1960s that emotions can alter processing priorities. He spoke too of "hot cognition", i.e. emotive information leading to deeper impressions, rather than the somewhat cooler category of "cognitive emotion".

More recently, a whole host of psychologists have emphasised the role that emotions have on beliefs and judgements. For example, Clore and Gasper have done work that looked at how moods and emotions influence beliefs, and they concluded that "feelings arising from moods can become donors of credibility to any associated beliefs" (2000: 39). In other words, emotions guide attention and are often prior to beliefs. Similarly, Frijda and Mesquita state that "emotions influence beliefs" (2000: 45), adding they can give rise to beliefs where none existed, change existing beliefs or enhance or decrease the strength with which a belief is held (2000: 45). They aptly speak of an "emotion-belief spiral" (2000: 49) and go on to turn the equation on its head by claiming that beliefs, rather than being a prerequisite for emotions, are actually a part of emotions (2000: 52). Indeed, they suggest that not only do emotions influence beliefs but they influence thinking in general (2000: 64). Similarly, Joseph Forgas has argued "affective states can also influence the processing strategies people employ when constructing a belief" (2000: 130). He backs this up with earlier work which describes how affect infuses beliefs (1995).

We can conclude therefore that not all cognitive scientists believe in the primacy of beliefs and judgements, with emotions, feeling and moods always coming second. Oatley perhaps hits the nail on the head in *Best Laid Schemes*, his cognitive-psychological work on literary reading, when he says "emotions are not on the periphery but at the centre of human cognition" (1992: 3). Emotions then are not merely the beneficiaries of beliefs; rather, in some cases, they can be their benefactors. I would argue that this is especially the case in situations where the embodied mind engages with an aesthetic object like a literary text. In this sense, therefore, beliefs, by their very nature, must almost always be to a significant extent emotive, because they are not grounded in a pure objective sense of world knowledge. Indeed, our beliefs are often outlandish for they are infused with our emotions, feelings, desires and moods. Such affective states are thus at the core of beliefs as Frijda and others have convincingly shown. Indeed, emotions can be said to be the very ebb and flow of higher cognitive processes, like beliefs and judgements.

Let us now step back and recap. From the works mentioned in this chapter, it is evident that advances in neurobiological imaging techniques have revealed the veritable multi-mapping, cross-neural nature of all kinds of cerebral processes. If the biology of thought, in the form of brain-based neurotransmitters flooding across synapses, has a confluvial, undulating, non-linear nature to it, as empirical neural testing seems to be suggesting with increasing force, then why should the abstraction of thought, in the form of mind-based cognitive appraisal models, not function in a similar fashion? Discussions in this chapter suggest that beliefs are part of inter-personal background knowledge: as Oatley and Jenkins suggest, judgements combine what we know with how we feel (1996: 278). I believe that such subconscious mind-fed inputs are unavoidably drenched in fragmentary emotive remembrances of the self, our loved ones and our lost childhood homes. This is especially the case, I believe, when we bring beliefs to bear on objects and texts designed to aesthetically emote us, and especially the less directly visual objects like literature and music, as will become clear in the forthcoming chapters. It appears that beliefs by default carry strong emotive resonances. As Forgas rightly says, beliefs are "intensely personal, idiosyncratic creations" (2000: 108). An increasing number of cognitive neuroscientists are coming to appreciate the importance of emotion for our cognitive functioning. For example, Alice Isen writes "cognition itself is profoundly affected by feelings, even mild feelings" (1984: 227); Mark Turner has stated that "feelings can affect intellect and vice versa" (1987: 44); whereas Antonio Damasio has asserted that the influence of feelings on cognition is immense (1994: 160). It is not impossible, but most unlikely, that all these cognitive scientists, working independently, are mistaken.

If we were to continue to believe in rigid, reason-based appraisal processes, we would be supporting an idea similar to the traditional one of a mechanical or computational view of mind and brain processes. As Damasio suggests, one must exert caution when using the "brain as computer" metaphor because "the metaphor is inadequate" (1999: 321). Not only, however, is it figuratively inadequate, but recent neuroscientific research has started to show how flawed it is in literal terms too. Spivey, Grosjean and Knoblich (2005), for example, have shown in their recent experiments that not just spoken language, which was the focus of their research, but also many cognitive and perceptual processes involve continuous uptake of sensory input, leading to dynamic competition between simultaneously active representations. In other words, processes in the brain do not work computer-like in distinct stages, rather the brain is continually awash with processing activities. The result of this is that sensory input is continually cascading back and forth in the mind. This idea of ebbing and flowing is echoed by neuroscientist Zull: "many, if not most, pathways of signalling in the brain include a combination of neurons that send signals in one direction and neurons that send signals in the other direction"(2002: 193). This general position was observable as well in my earlier discussion of how the amygdala continuously sends and receives information. However, perhaps the clearest description of the fluvial processes of the mind is given by Kosslyn and Koenig. These authors say towards the end of their influential work on "the new cognitive neuroscience" entitled *The Wet Mind* that if they were to be given the chance to revise their work they would adopt a slightly different approach to thinking and neural computation. Instead, they would choose "a hydraulic metaphor", as this metaphor "stresses the complex, interactive nature of the brain's computation, and it encourages us to think about how emotion and motivation can alter information processing" (1995: 447–48):

> Imagine an above ground swimming pool with a hole in the wall just at water level; if the water laps against the sides, a series of pulses of water slosh through the hole. This sequence of sloshes is the output. Also imagine rocks, of different sizes and shapes, dropping into the pool and causing patterns of waves to spread. The rocks correspond to the input from the senses, and piles of rocks on the bottom correspond to memories; it is clear that the precise pattern of ripples will change as the rocks begin to alter the topography of the bottom. When ripples are modulated by the rocks on the bottom and bounce off the walls, complex patterns of interaction will develop. Indeed, this complexity will be exaggerated when rocks are dropping in multiple places, corresponding to input in multiple sensory modalities. Places where wavelets meet and interact may correspond to the functional subsystems we have proposed here (and to Damasio's "convergence zones"). (1995: 448)

Here, mind and brain processes are expressed as wave interaction. Together with other views, it points forward to my notion of oceanic cognitive processes, to be discussed later. Such views can no longer be seen as outlandish or fanciful; rather they are rich and, more importantly, close to describing in actual terms, as well as metaphorical ones, how the mind and brain are now thought to function.

The cognitive and neurological background against which the main arguments of this book will be set have now been discussed in these two opening chapters. This primarily involved unpacking some of the mysteries that lie behind the secret, private act of reading and the human memory systems that are needed to facilitate it. In the next five chapters I turn towards the main subject of this book—the literary reading experience—and explore the elements that go into what can be called the optimum rhetorical situation of literary reading. In order, these are literary reading-induced mental imagery (Chapter 3), the mood of the reader prior to reading and the location of the reading event (Chapter 4), the themes in the text (Chapter 5) and the style and rhetoric of the text (Chapter 6). In Chapter 7, I will tie up these five affective inputs by setting out a preliminary theoretical model as to how the notions of memory, cognition and emotion interact with all these "affective inputs of reading" to produce that unique and cherished emotive feeling of reading.

# 3 Literary Reading-Induced Mental Imagery

Robert Louis Stevenson, one of the finest storytellers in the English language, wrote a novel called *The Ebb Tide* (1894/2007), together with his stepson Lloyd Osbourne, about a character who gets shipwrecked on an island. Marooned with him is a copy of Virgil's complete works. Stevenson describes how the castaway reads the book incessantly to pass the time. He also tells about something that might be deemed as rather odd. During the reading process, the images of the places and locations that are created in the mind of the castaway are not those that Virgil directly describes in his book, as one might expect, but something completely different. In Stevenson's words "a phrase of Virgil speaks not so much of Mantua or Augustus, but of English places and the student's own irrevocable youth" (2007: 2). Expanding on this he writes:

> Visions of England at least would throng upon the exile's memory: the busy schoolroom, the green playing-fields, holidays at home, and the perennial roar of London, and the fireside, and the white head of his father. (2007: 2)

What is happening here? The character in the novel appears to "ignore" or "bypass" the physical locations described by Virgil and somehow replaces them with his own idiosyncratic and fragmented imagery of places, people and events from his own youth; more specifically, images of his childhood home and of a primary caregiver. Why does this occur? What process is at work here? Does this also occur when real people read works of literature? These are the questions that I will seek to address in this chapter which will be on the nature of "perception" with regard to mental images that are produced in the minds of people when they read literature. For the sake of ease, I will call this phenomenon Literary Reading Imagery (LRI).

In the previous chapter I explained how the perception of clearly defined objects in the world relies to a significant extent on light stimuli that are picked up by the cones of the photoreceptors in the retina. LRI, however, has a less direct stimulus. There is no immediate, ready-formed image "out there" in the world: just words on the page. This means that there must be a profound difference between the perception of real objects in the world—even artistic objects, which undoubtedly require far more affective processing than everyday objects—and culturally-determined, linguistic symbols. Instead of being primarily ready-formed and hence relying to a large extent on the bottom-up process of patterns of light striking the retina, reading-induced "vision" must be grounded in something else. It is highly plausible that the elementary base for this kind of visual input comes from our emotive and somatically infused long-term memory. As a result, the kind of imagery that gets channelled is quite possibly grounded in the indistinct, unconscious remembrance of past events, past locations and past loved ones: not too dissimilar to what Stevenson describes in the above literary citation.

I will argue in this chapter that because our childhood memories—i.e. the important places and people from our personal pasts—are the most emotive and most enduring kind, they are most prone to unconscious activation while reading literature in order to flesh out all kinds of situations in novels. Of course, not only childhood memories will be activated, highly emotive memories are not limited to childhood, but I believe they will generally dominate for reasons that will become clear in later chapters.

Mental imagery that is produced while reading literature is a robust phenomenon. You can easily test this yourself. Recall, if you can, a moment in your life when you realised that one of your favourite novels was being made into a film. Can you remember the excitement and the anticipation you felt? Perhaps, though you can also recall your disappointment once you were in the cinema and confronted with those opening images. Some of you may have thought, as indeed I have on several occasions, "that is not her", and "that is not him", and "they do not live there". Seem familiar? If not, consider the thoughts of one of the foremost scholars of literary reading in the twentieth century: Wolfgang Iser. The quote below if from his book *The Act of Reading*:

> If, for instance, I see the film of *Tom Jones*, and try to summon up my past images of the character, they will seem strangely diffuse, but this impression will not necessarily make me prefer the optical picture. If I ask whether my imaginary Tom Jones was big or small, blue-eyed or dark-haired, the optical poverty of my images will become all too evident, but it is precisely this openness that will make me resent the determinacy of the film version. (1978: 138)

Iser suggests here that the optical poverty of the images induced by reading literature paradoxically leads to a sense of directness. Why, one might ask, is it that our LRI is so robust? What are those characters and locations that we subconsciously call up when reading literature? Why do they seem to be so important to us as individuals? And why will this impoverished mental imagery not give way to the visually far superior, vivid delights that the movie industry has to offer us?

I tend to agree with Iser when he says "in reading literary texts, we always have to form mental images" (1978: 137). This is borne out in psychology by the "radical-imagery hypothesis" which states that subjects convert visual and verbal stimuli to images that are then stored in memory. Zull supports this when he says "comprehension often requires us to make images out of language" (2002: 171). Iser suggests something more complex, namely that "our mental images do not serve to make the character physically visible; their optical poverty is an indication of the fact that they illuminate the character, not as an object, but as a bearer of meaning" (1978: 138). If we were to think about this statement in psychological terms for a moment, we could suggest that characters are optically poor because our subconscious mind somehow wishes us to downplay the details and to focus on more fundamental aspects of meaning. But what is that meaning? Why do LRI take on such seemingly profound status? Is this also why they remain so forceful and show such longevity when they are confronted with corresponding real images in cinema theatres? I believe that the imagery produced while reading literature is so powerful, in part, because aspects of it are fundamental to who we are as individuals and where we came from. The "meaning" that participants and indeed locations and activities carry in the mental imagery of literary readers appears to be bound to those three most fundamental philosophical questions: Who are we? Where did we come from? Where are we going?

There are different kinds of images that are formed in the brain. First, in the real world, there are everyday visual images which can be perceived. This includes objects such as houses, trees, people, etc. There are aesthetic visual images in the real world too such as sculpture, architecture, figurative painting, film, etc. We might for a moment make a distinction here by thinking of them in Alhazen's terms of "pure perception" for everyday objects in the world and "pure sensation" for art objects. For both of these, initial neural processing probably takes place in broadly the same way: light carrying the image strikes the retina and then the information travels via the central areas of the brain on to the visual cortex. Second, there is the mental imagery of thinking and reflection on the one hand, which is largely conscious, and that produced while dreaming, day dreaming, reading literature, etc., which is largely unconscious. My emphasis here will be solely on the last of these: literary discourse processing.

There is thus a basic difference between processing of literature and film. There are arguably certain aspects of "givenness" in visual objects that have been fashioned to evoke aesthetic and emotive responses in viewers: elements like form, colour, depth, duration, etc. These are already to a large extent present in the work. Of course, there is no one-to-one mapping, but there is a relatively concrete source. Literature is different. In literature there are only the black marks on the page. So if the mental images produced while reading literature rely on vision as its primary pictorial input only inasmuch as it involves apprehending the words, where do those images come from? The answer must have something to do with the mnemonic, somatic, visual and affective parts of the brain.

Let us start with the admission that literary reading is not purely a visual act. The literary critic M. H. Abrams says of such literature-induced mental images that their apprehension is not just a question of visual but also of "auditory, tactile, thermal, olfactory, gustatory and kinaesthetic qualities" (1988: 81). Manguel echoes this:

> The act of reading establishes an intimate, physical relationship in which all the senses have a part: the eyes drawing the words from the page, the ears echoing the sounds being read, the nose inhaling the familiar scent of paper, glue, ink, cardboard or leather, the touch caressing the soft or rough page, the smooth or hard binding, even the taste at times, when the reader's fingers are lifted to the tongue (1996: 244).

However, notwithstanding this, let our focus here be on vision, or paradoxically the lack of it, but before moving on to object of our study, first see how the natural and social sciences account for mental imagery.

A mental image can be defined in neurological terms as "a reassembled or unified set of neuronal connections" (Zull 2002: 165). This much we know, even if neuroscience does not yet have a complete explanation of mental imagery, as Zull suggests (2002: 144). Notwithstanding, many things are known about this phenomenon. For example, it is widely acknowledged that mental imagery makes use of the visual cortex just like the perception system does. Experiments charting both cerebral blood flow and electronic activity in the brain have confirmed this (see, for example, Farrah 1985; 1988). Hence, the two forms of imagery, real and mental, are similar in that they make use of the visual cortex. The great dissimilarity, of course, is that the one largely relies on direct stimuli from the outside world whereas the other depends mainly on mind-based input. The latter must come from long-term memory. These must be episodes that were first experienced as visual input, perhaps many years earlier. A key question is where and how this information is stored? Two other questions that pertain particularly to LRI are: why and how does mental imagery get "triggered"? And what is the nature and make-up of this imagery?

Before proceeding, let us first briefly revisit some of the discussion on memory from Chapter 1. We will recall that retrieval is important for the formation of mental images and that it is a constructive process bringing information together from lots of different anatomical sites. Bartlett's words that "affective attitudes influence recall" are important, as is his observation that, in particular, the nature of the recalled event may tend to produce "stereotyped and conventional reproductions which adequately serve all normal needs, though they are very unfaithful to their originals" (1995: 55). From this we may deduce that mental imagery seems to be of a distorted yet conventional kind. A plausible link from the core cognitive act of reading words on the page to the emotive act of experiencing LRI, might be found in the earlier-mentioned notion of "retrieval structures". In *Comprehension* Kintsch claimed that these retrieval structures are activated by cues in short-term memory that communicate with long-term memory and that just one cue can activate a whole event or episode in a relatively wholesale manner. The conclusion drawn from this was that all of our memories are potentially just one step away. In the first chapter a division was also made between explicit and implicit memory. There, we saw how implicit memory involves little conscious effort and flows automatically, whereas explicit memory must be retrieved deliberately. We learned too how implicitly processed stimuli activate the amygdala without activating explicit memories or otherwise being represented in consciousness (LeDoux 1998: 203). In light of this, it can be proposed that LRI is primarily concerned with implicit rather than explicit memory.

The parts of the brain that are active when we experience mental images from the fragmented parts of our memory are located in the integrative cortex, just in front of the visual cortex (Zull 2002: 166). Its position means that it is very close to other core sensory areas such as the auditory cortex and the somatic area. As such, to quote the neuroscientist Zull, "it is a short journey for signals to travel from these sensory regions to the integrative back cortex" (2002: 155). It is here where the pieces of information come together and where a lot of mental image processing is believed to occur. As we saw, there are two pathways which take information out of the visual cortex during visual processing. The upper pathway deals with spatial arrangement, whereas the lower one deals with object recognition. A rough analogy here may be made between episodic and semantic memory.

To the best of my knowledge there has been no neurobiological research done specifically on the nature of LRI. The difficulty in finding an appropriate testing methodology has no doubt been a major hindrance to this. Therefore, I need to look at a similar notion in order to draw some plausible analogies. Writing on the nature of mental images that occur during moments of reflection, rather than reading, Zull remarks that "whatever the topic, my brain has vague but identifiable images of it. These images slip by in a flash sometimes, and if I try to focus on them, they may disappear [ . . . ] when we reflect, we bring up images from our past experience" (2002: 165). Reflection is more often than not a conscious act, whereas experiencing imagery while reading literature is wholly a subconscious one. Notwithstanding, it seems plausible that LRI would be at least as identifiable, albeit fleetingly. What we have learned about the nature of implicit memory in Chapter 1 also seems to support my intuitions.

In an early study on the characteristics of visual imagery Kosslyn (1975) argues that the notion of focus in mental imagery, just like focus in visual imagery, is crucial to "seeing": if objects in mental imagery were pictured too close up, then, like visual imagery, they would get out of focus, as it were, and could not be apprehended appropriately. The term he uses to

describe the very moment when an object in mental imagery begins to dissi-
pate and become indistinct is "overflow". The same general ideas are echoed
by psychologist Ronald A. Finke in his *Principles of Mental Imagery* where
he discusses the non-photographic and spatial, rather than visual, nature
of images (1989: 16–21). In a later study conducted by the psychologist
Martin A. Conway (1990), subjects were asked to generate a mental image
in response to an emotion word. It was found that more than sixty percent
of the images related to specific incidents that had occurred in a particular
time in their life that had an emotional significance for them. This was not
the case for other words that subjects were exposed to, like abstract words.
From this experiment it would appear that the idea of emotional words
leading to the generation of mental images that are tied up with an emotional event in a person's individual past is quite plausible.

A further relevant psychological experiment on this topic was conducted
by Uffe Seilman and Steen F. Larsen (1989). In their empirical study of
"remindings while reading" they put forward their "personal resonance
theory". In their experiment they explored the experience of personal relat-
edness to literary works by studying the recall of specific experiences that
occurred during reading. They devised a method of "self-probed retrospec-
tion" whereby subjects read a text and marked it where they experienced
personal remindings. These were then discussed after the reading. One
group was given a literary text and the other one an expository text. The
authors hypothesised two things: (i) that the literary texts would produce
mental imagery, involving the reader as an active participant, and (ii) that
this imagery would occur early in the story because the reader would have
to construct a representation of the text world; once this was done, the text
world would be able to run on its own (1989: 171). The research discovered that both texts produced a similar number of occurrences of personal
remindings, but that the literary text produced twice as many remindings
of experiences where the reader is an active participant in his/her mental
imagery. The expository texts appeared to produce far more remindings
where the reader was playing a more passive, observer-type role. In the
words of the authors:

> Probably, the prototypical instance of remembering to most people
> is precisely their personally experienced autobiographical memories.
> The subcategory of a person's knowledge of specific occurrences and
> facts that involve himself in some way may be considered the person's
> *empirical past*. It is the knowledge he has of what he has done, who
> he knows, how they have reacted to him, where he has been, what
> events he has witnessed, what places he has lived in, and so forth (1989:
> 168—69; emphasis as in original).

In addition, Seilman and Larsen found that much of this imagery occurred
at the beginning of the story rather than in the middle or at the end. The

mobilisation of this knowledge need not result in conscious remembering (1989: 169). It would seem that it remains, for a large part, a subconscious process. They also sought to look at the age, vividness and importance of the source of the reminded experience in relation to both types of text: literary and expository (1989: 172). However, this was not discussed in any detail in their study apart from the cursory remark that the data "did not disclose any striking differences" (1989: 174). Based on this research two things may be posited: (i) that mental images of the self during LRI are active or, in motion, and (ii) that LRI appear to be more prominent at the beginning of stories. The authors conclude that such personal resonances are a particularly important ingredient of "great" literary experiences (1989: 167). The idea that the autobiographical memories of the reader play an important role in the literary reading process is also expressed in J. M. Black and C. M. Seifert's (1985) experiment-led proposal that good literature is that which maximises reminding from the life of the reader (cited in Seilman and Larsen 1989: 169).

There are several other persuasive empirical arguments from the social sciences that the nature of mental imagery is likely to be indistinct rather than vivid. The psychologists Oatley and Jenkins note that "there is no evidence that people can remember scenes in perfect detail, and with perfect accuracy, as if they were stored in some internal video recording" (1996: 269). This echoes Bartlett's observation that remembering "is an imaginative reconstruction, built out of the relation of our attitude towards a whole active mass of organised past reactions or experience, and to a little outstanding detail [ . . . ] It is thus hardly ever really exact [ . . . ] and it is not at all important that it should be so" (1995: 213).

Lawrence W. Barsalou's theories on mental imagery and memory are substantial and thus warrant a longer discussion. Several detailed empirical studies have suggested that the notion of activity is a dominant feature in the organisation of autobiographical memories and that activities act as cues for these dynamic memories (e.g. Reisner, Black and Abelson 1985). Barsalou (1988a) expanded on this by investigating the content and organisation of autobiographical memories. This resulted in his "activity dominance hypothesis", which states that event type forms the dominant organisation of event memories (1988a: 199). He also looked at the organisation of those events and distinguished three activity-based categories: (i) location (e.g. going out in your hometown), (ii) participants (e.g. travelling by train with friends) and (iii) time (e.g. partying at Christmas). He found that subjects often recall several different events involving the same person (1988a: 205). He conducted a number of experiments which produced mixed results. However, in one cued recall experiment he found that subjects generated more participants than any other type of cue: the category of activities was also prominent followed closely by location. The category of time stood out as being the least frequent by far (1988a: 208).

This participant and activity-dominant pattern, that includes some evidence for location as well, has also been supported in subsequent experiments by other psychologists. For instance, in a presentation of their ongoing work Katinka Dijkstra and Mine Misirlisoy conducted tests as to the validity of the activity-dominance hypothesis.[1] In an experiment on initial verbal reports of memory it was shown that the activity and participant components dominate. In another experiment that tested for retrieval cues, these two were also found to be dominant, as was location. It was found that temporality appeared to play no meaningful role. The experimenters concluded that because the organisation of memories occurs around activities in interaction with the environment, namely participants and locations, this may lend support for an embodied account of cognition, as formulated in Barsalou's theory of "Perceptual Symbol Systems" (PSS) and in the work of the cognitive linguistics (see, for example, Gibbs 2006).

In similar experiments, Brewer (1987a) has shown how remembering an event is often accompanied by mental imagery that can extend across a number of modalities, including the sense of movement. Because this information must once have been apprehended physically in some past act of perception, the sense itself is central to the memory. Given the re-usability of such imagery, this may explain in part how people have stored what Brewer terms "perceptual generic knowledge" of events. Barsalou, like others before him, suggests that events are often recalled in a fragmented way. He proposes that the reason for this might be that certain elements in the memory, for example, people, places, times or objects, get lost in event recall. This he defines under the headings "event fragmentation" and "event confusion" (1988b: 230–32). Writing on the relative instability of knowledge, Barsalou has argued that people create representations all the time from loosely organised knowledge in order to meet the parameters of specific contexts (1987, 1988b: 236). So even if the final product is different, it is nonetheless made up from the same familiar components.

More recently, Barsalou has developed a persuasively modern account of mental perception in his theory of perceptual symbols systems (1999). This theory was developed in opposition to the sign-fed theories on language and thought processing such as those found in fields like logic. In his PSS theory Barsalou argues, as the empirical philosophers Locke and Hume had done before him, that perception and cognition share the same neural systems. He deduced that as a result of this, cognitive processes are engaged immediately. During the act of seeing, it appears that certain "association areas" in the brain capture bottom-up patterns of activation in sensory-motor areas. Later, these association areas partially reactivate sensory-motor areas to implement perceptual symbols. The storage and retrieval of these perceptual symbols operate at the level of what Barsalou terms perceptual "components". So perceptual experiences are stored in memory that later get activated (1999: 577). This process allows memories of the same component to cluster around a common "frame": defined by Barsalou as an integrated system of perceptual symbols that is used to construct specific simulations of a category (1999: 590). All this leads to the implementation of what he terms a "simulator", which can produce infinite simulations of the component. Hence, as Barsalou himself puts it "related symbols become organized into a simulator that allows the cognitive system to construct specific simulations of an entity or event in its absence" (1999: 586).

It is important to note that perceptual symbols have a number of characteristics. Six of the most important of these are that they: (i) function unconsciously; (ii) reside at the neural level; (iii) are dynamic in nature; (iv) produce componential images rather than holistic ones; (v) produce simulators "that are *always* partial and sketchy, *never* complete" (emphasis in original); and (vi) are multimodal not just visual, including introspection (1999: 583–86). Barsalou explains further that mental images in his PSS theory are componential and sketchy because "as selective attention extracts perceptual symbols from perception, it never extracts all of the information that is potentially available. As a result, a frame is impoverished relative to the perceptions that produced it, as are the simulations constructed from it" (1999: 586). Drawing on Gestalt psychology, he also explains why simulations are likely to be biased and distorted and how they are grounded in both experiential and genetic components.

According to Barsalou, linguistic symbols operate like perceptual symbols in that they are schematic memories of a perceived event (spoken or written). More specifically he says:

> As selective attention focuses on spoken or written words, schematic memories extracted from perceptual states become integrated into simulators that later produce simulations of these words in recognition, imagination and production. As simulators for words develop in memory, they become associated with simulators for the entries and events to which they refer. Whereas some simulators for words become linked to simulators for entire entries or events, others become linked to subregions and specializations. . . . Within the simulator for a concept, large numbers of simulators for words become associated with its various aspects to produce a semantic field that mirrors the underlying conceptual field . . . Once simulators for words become linked to simulators for concepts, they can control simulation. On recognizing a word the cognitive system activates the simulator for the associated concept to assimilate a possible referent. On parsing the sentences in a text, surface syntax provides instructions for building perceptual simulations. (1999: 592)

A number of things become clear from this, not least that PSS is not just about mental representations of prior experiences but also of imagination. It is the very schematicity of perceptual symbols that allows them to combine in creative ways and simulate imaginary images. This may sound strange, but as Barsalou himself observes, children's films, cartoons and books frequently employ this capacity to alter the laws of the physical world by mixing and matching all kinds of structurally similar objects for all kinds of functions. Sharing past experiences with others and planning together for the future involve imagination and conceptualisation as well. Although Barsalou makes no mention of it in his 1999 article, the reading of literary fiction—the central focus of this work—demands a similar fluid capacity for simulation, creativity and imagination, as I shall show as the forthcoming chapters unfold.

Writing on memory systems, Barsalou claims that working memory runs perceptual simulations.

> The articulatory loop [Baddeley 1986] simulates language just heard or about to be spoken. The visual short-term buffer simulates visual experience just seen or currently imagined. The motor short-term buffer simulates movements just performed or about to be performed . . . Not only do these working memory systems operate during perception, movement and problem-solving, they can also be used to simulate these activities offline. (1999: 604)

From a PSS perspective, short-term and long-term memory share neural systems with perception. As Barsalou explains, long-term memory harbours the simulators while working memory implements specific simulations (1999: 604). Barsalou adds that "memory retrieval is another form of perceptual simulation, with fluent simulations producing attributions of remembrance" (1999: 605), and he describes how these simulations can either become active unconsciously, in implicit memory, or consciously, in explicit memory, and the process of retrieval itself:

> As a memory is retrieved, it produces a simulation of the earlier event. As the simulation becomes active, it may differ somewhat from the original perception, perhaps because of less bottom-up constraint. To the extent that the remembered event's features have become inaccessible, the simulator converges on its default simulation. (1999: 605)

Barsalou's idea that perceptual simulation underlies comprehension is persuasive, although it says nothing about the PSS nature of literary discourse processing and far too little about the involvement of emotion: a topic that would seem to be of crucial importance to any contemporary model of the mind. This becomes evident if we recall Damasio's claim that "virtually every image actually perceived or recalled is accompanied by some reaction from the apparatus of emotion" (1999: 58).

Barsalou's basic PSS ideas—that abstract concepts and conceptual processing have perceptual, sensorimotor and embodied influences—share common ground with a number of other theories: (i) the general philosophy of embodied cognition put forward by cognitive linguists (e.g. Langacker 1991; Gibbs 2006), (ii) some of the ideas I discussed earlier on mirror neurons, and (iii) Damasio's notion of convergence zones discussed in his 1999 work. Here Damasio constructs a model for the basis of the "neuroanatomical autobiographical self" based on his experiments and observations in experimental and clinical neuropsychology, physiology and anatomy. In this model, which brings together neural networks and mental images, he posits two specific locations: an "image space" and a "dispositional space". In the image space, imagery of all sensory types occurs consciously and explicitly. Damasio suggest that the neural centres and patterns likely to be responsible for these images are located in the early sensory cortices of varied modalities (1999: 219). Dispositional space is the domain of unconscious, implicit knowledge. Here, images can be reconstructed and processed in recall. Movement can also be generated. Moreover, previously perceived memories are held here and similar images can be reconstructed. They can help as well in processing real images. Higher-order cortical neural areas as well as subcortical nuclei are thought to be the main centres involved. These dispositions are held in neuron assemblies, which Damasio terms "convergence zones" (1999: 219). Damasio stresses that the true content of dispositions can never be directly known due to their unconscious state and dormant form and that dispositions are not words but abstract records of "potentialities", which can fleetingly come to life, "Brigadoon-like", as mental images before they wane again into imperceptibility (1999: 332).

This final comment completes this scientific overview of mental imagery. Next, I will consider the more literary and philosophical components of this topic. Several of these psychologists have been referring to conscious recall and explicit memory. In light of this, the premise can be put forward that if this kind of mental imagery is often imperfect, imaginative, emotional and inexact as is claimed, then subconscious recall, employing implicit memory, as must occur during LRI, is at least as fragmentary and incomplete, if not more so. This is the hypothesis that I will now take forward as we look at some evidence provided from the domains of literature and philosophy.

In his work on psychology and the twentieth century novel *Out of the Maelstrom*, Keith M. May has argued in the context of his reading of Proust's work, that "since memories are distorted, our self-images must be correspondingly inaccurate"(1977: 65). Following up on this in a discussion on subconscious recall, he states that "in a moment of involuntary memory the past is made to encroach upon the present so the subject fleetingly exists out of time. He cannot be deluding himself, because he has discovered this extra temporal dimension by accident, not through wishful thinking" (1977: 65). Echoing the basic precepts of Alhazen's theory on perception that we discussed earlier, he also makes a distinction between "the sense impressions of a thing" and "the image that we form of it" (1977: 65). May concludes by suggesting that the epiphany-like impressions of involuntary memory that Proust's protagonist undergoes "precisely matched the sense-impression of childhood" (1977: 66). Bringing this phenomenon from the fictional world into the real world of the individual reader he concludes that "a succession of such moments would be the ideal psychoanalysis, the means to perfect self-understanding" (1977: 66). This point is not unimportant. As such, we shall return to it in Chapter 11, the final episode of this work.

Moving more centrally into the literary theoretical domain, in *The Act of Reading* Iser argues that there are "blanks" (*Leerstellen*) in a literary text left by the author either consciously or subconsciously, and that these blanks "make the reader bring the story itself to life" (1978: 192). This is not exactly a new idea. The implied author in Laurence Sterne's *Tristram Shandy* (1759/1956) says that "the truest respect you can pay to the reader's understanding, is to half this matter amicably, and leave him something to imagine" (1956: 79). It is these blanks, Iser argues, that "hinder" the reading experience and general textual cohesion and in doing so they become "stimuli for acts of ideation [ . . . ] what they suspend turns into a propellant for the reader's imagination, making him supply what has been withheld" (1978: 194). He suggests that the shifting nature of the blanks in a text is responsible "for a sequence of colliding images" (1978: 203). Iser thought that these images influenced each other in the flow of reading:

> The discarded image imprints itself on its successor, even though the latter is meant to resolve the deficiencies of the former. In this respect the images hang together in a sequence and it is by this sequence that the meaning of the text comes alive in the reader's imagination. (1978: 203)

This idea does not wholly correspond to the majority of observations by psychologists. Iser is echoing the philosophy of Edmund Husserl and it is here I momentarily part company with him. I agree that there appears to be a definite motion aspect to LRI but I wonder why reading should involve a whole sequence of differing images triggered by the content of the text. Recall from the beginning of this chapter that Stevenson's fictive reader did not use Italian vistas to flesh out his Virgil, but rather the scenes from his London childhood. If we were to follow Stevenson's character for a moment, we would have to say that LRI appears to be based on indistinct, semi-familiar locations, the essence of which gets repeatedly activated when reading a novel, though it is uncertain what effects on LRI the subject matter of the text and the mode of narrative telling may have.

Iser also claims that "the structure of the text sets off a sequence of mental images which lead to the text translating itself into the reader's consciousness" (1978: 38). This view of literary reading attributes a strong initial sign-fed aspect to reading, which can be observed in Iser's choice of the phrase "sets off". Although a ground-breaking claim in the 1970s, such an assertion seems one-sided from a twenty-first century perspective. Far more interesting is what Iser writes in that same discussion: "the actual content of these mental images will be colored by the reader's existing stock of experience, which acts as a referential background against which the unfamiliar can be conceived and processed" (1978: 38).

A further interesting point that Iser makes is that "the significance of the work, then, does not lie in the meaning sealed within a text but in the fact that the meaning brings out what had previously been sealed within us" (1978: 157). Can the same be extended to mental imagery? If we think about it for a moment, the only thing that can be "sealed within us" is our own personal past, grounded in our own experience. Does literature bring out the indistinct images of our past, as some of the previously discussed psychological theories have suggested? Iser notes further that as the reader's conscious mind is activated by the textual stimulus "the remembered apparition returns as a background" (1978: 117). In essence, he claims that lexical and syntactic triggers in the text, and their stylistic arrangement, channel remembered apparitions, i.e. memory-based mental imagery, which is deployed as a backdrop. This might very well entail indistinct, i.e. "backgrounded", representations of locations and places from an individual reader's past. The idea of a location-based contextualisation of literature-induced mental imagery emerges as well in Iser's associated claim that "if a reader is prodded into recalling something already sunk into memory, he will bring it back not in isolation but embedded in a particular context" (1978: 116). So when a word "prods", or better still, subconsciously "channels" the deployment of LRI, the imagery that is evoked may very well be grounded in the mentioned locations and places of our own personal pasts.

More recently, Elaine Scarry has argued in *Dreaming by the Book* for both the indistinct and dynamic nature of LRI. Although her work is primarily literary-theoretical, she draws on the neuroscientific work of Kosslyn (1994). An important point of departure for her is that poems or novels are in fact a set of instructions for mental composition (Scarry 1999: 224). She supports her claims for LRI with somewhat opaque observations such as "the imagination has a special expertise in producing two-dimensional gauzy images" (1999: 59), and that some images of persons induced by reading literature can be "gossamer" in nature (1999: 111). However, she also says that focussing in mentally on objects is likely to produce vivid rather than indistinct images (1999: 53). Drawing on the neuroscience of Kosslyn's mental imagery she highlights the dynamism of such LRI by speaking of the cognitive phenomena of "mental skating" (1999: 211) and asserting that we "somatically mime the motion" (1999: 216). She speaks further of "radiant ignition", which, she says, "helps make apprehensible the interior motion of fictional persons" (1999: 86). She adds, mental images tend to "float around" (1999: 92) and "flex and throb" (1999: 151); our mental composition of even a still picture has, she claims, "motion in it" (1999: 137).

Several years before these literary theoretical observations were made, the philosopher Gaston Bachelard, had said that images evoked through reading are "hardly perceptible" (1958: 124). In his classic work *The Poetics*

*of Space*, Bachelard poses the question as to why it is that childhood locations, and especially interior locations of the childhood home, should play
such an important role when filling out mental models of new situations
encountered while reading poetic language. Bachelard's basic philosophical premise pertains to the mnemonic, image-based importance of familiar
childhood locations that are evoked during the reading of poetic language
in order to infuse the reading experience. He calls his work a study of
"topophilia", an investigation "to determine the human value of the sorts
of space that may be grasped" (1958: xxxv). The work poses the essential question as to why it is that readers can access the mental imagery of
familiar childhood locations through reading, even when those locations
have long since been demolished or redeveloped. In essence, what he is
asking is why and how it is the case that books can be portals to our pasts
when engaged with in the optimum affective mode. Bachelard also discusses some felt physiological effects that may arise from reading: that the
creation of mental imagery can make us feel a kind of poetic power rising
within us, adding "after the original reverberation we are able to experience resonances, sentimental repercussions, reminders of our past" (1958:
xxiii). He later adds, the state of poetic reverie "must always set the waves
of the imagination radiating" (1958: 36).

Some of Bachelard's other observations that are relevant for this work
include the idea that in reading we comfort ourselves by reliving memories
of protection (1958: 6). The reason we "encounter" such childhood locations, like the house we were born in, is to re-participate in its original
intimacy and warmth of the place where the protective beings lived.[2] Blending the notion of the primary caregiver with that of the location of childhood memory, Bachelard terms this phenomenon "the maternal features
of the house" (1958: 7). At the very first word that prompts the childhood
home, at the very first poetic overture, the reader "leaves off reading and
starts to think of some place in his own past" (1958: 14).[3] These highly
affective, locative childhood spaces, that must substantially influence the
reading experience itself, are unequivocally and irrevocably blended with
the notion of the parental protector or primary caregiver.[4] According to
Bachelard, these "values of intimacy" are so absorbing that a reader ceases
to read the description of the childhood locative space presented by the
text. Instead, "he is already far off, listening to the recollections of a father
or a grandmother, of a mother or a servant . . . in short, of the human
being who dominates the corner of his most cherished memories" (1958:
14). Here then, the memory of the protector and the memory of the protective space meet and merge.

This final observation, which mirrors the previously mentioned visions
of Stevenson's castaway reader, concludes my discussion on the nature of
LRI. The combined body of the mentioned empirical and theoretical evidence from across the academic disciplines has gone some way towards
providing a rationale for the following theoretical assumptions pertaining

to LRI, which I shall now explore in a number of rudimentary surveys of my own.

- While reading literature readers experience LRI
- LRI is indistinct/fragmented
- LRI involves movement/activity/dynamic scenes
- In that movement in LRI the reader is an active participant
- LRI is linked to (idealised) childhood memories/images
- Aspects of our primary caregivers appear in LRI
- Childhood locations occur in LRI
- LRI will relate to specific incidents in a person's life with emotional significance

The evidence of LRI might be grouped into three categories: (i) literary theoretical, i.e. the claims of Bachelard, Iser, Scarry, Hogan and May; (ii) literary discourse analytic, i.e. the empirical research evidence of Conway, Seilman and Larsen and Seifert and Black, and (iii) general psychological studies pertaining to the broader nature of mental imagery in event recall, i.e. Barsalou, Zull, Brewer and Dijkstra and Misirlisoy. In what follows, I present and discuss the data from some very basic tests. The purpose of these surveys is not to establish proof—the numbers of subjects involved and the types of experiments are not set up for that purpose. Rather, it is to look at the quality of some of the responses and see where these views might show aspects of similarity with what has been suggested so far from the empirical and theoretical studies already discussed in this chapter.

The tests below employ broad qualitative methods by means of a number of reader-response questionnaires. I carried out three different sets of reader-response surveys pertaining to the subject matter of this chapter. These were conducted over a three-year period with student subjects from four institutes of higher education in the Netherlands: the Free University Amsterdam (VU); Utrecht University (UU) and her two liberal arts and sciences honours colleges: University College Utrecht (UCU) and Roosevelt Academy, Middelburg (RA). The first survey involves one small group of UU student subjects. It pertains primarily to the notion "first memories", i.e. what a subject's earliest recollection of an event was and which three objects could the subjects recall from that early phase of their lives. The purpose of this was just to generate some response material: I wanted to know whether certain objects were more common than others. I also wanted to know what role, if any, people, places and activities played. The second survey pertained to the vividness or indistinctness of LRI and was conducted among a small group of UCU students. The third survey involved two groups of subjects from two different Dutch universities (VU and RA). It focused on a single question. This question was number 14 from my own Novel-Reading Questionnaire (henceforth, NRQ). It pertained to the nature and form of LRI. Below are the responses to all three of these surveys (numbers 1, 2 and 3), followed by short discussions.

**1. Earliest memories survey:** This survey was conducted in 2002 on a group of twenty second-year undergraduate English majors who were studying at Utrecht University. They were all Dutch nationals and their average age was nineteen. They all attended my course, which was a rhetoric and stylistics approach to creative writing. The subjects were asked to provide open answers to two questions. I conducted this survey at the very beginning of the semester while I was still unknown to the students in order to try to minimise my effect on the group. I also embedded the two questions in a list of six. Four of these then, which were about creative writing pedagogy, were in effect "dummies" that tried to draw attention away from what I was doing.

The first question asked the subjects to reflect for a moment and then write down what they believed their earliest memory to be. In the second question subjects were asked to recall three objects from their earliest childhood memories. I wanted to see if these first memories supported any of the evidence I have discussed in this chapter from across the sciences pertaining to LRI. Based on that evidence I made three predictions, of which the first was perhaps obvious, the other two less so. In parentheses are the names of the researchers whose work is either directly addressed by the statement or whose findings are associatively relevant

- 1. That the earliest memories of a childhood object would be related to the home: i.e. an object in the house or near it—(Bachelard)
- 2. That a sense of action or movement would be present in the recollection of that first event—(Scarry, Seilman and Larsen; Barsalou, Brewer, Dijkstra and Misirlisoy)
- 3. That these first memories would either involve a view of themselves playing or a view of themselves with a caregiver/parent/older sibling, i.e. a recognisable participant—(Bachelard, Hogan, Black and Seifert, Conway, Seilman and Larsen, Barsalou, Brewer, Dijkstra and Misirlisoy)

The twenty responses about the earliest remembered event are listed below. I have numbered them 1 to 20 so that they can be referred to in subsequent lists without having to reproduce the responses again. These responses are not reproduced verbatim as they were quite long. I have synopsised them in the clearest and fairest way I thought possible—attempting at all times to remain faithful to their claims.

1. Moving house
2. Being in hospital
3. Looking up at someone sitting in a chair
4. Being at home and noticing the colour of the furniture and wallpaper

5. Being in a swing in the backyard
6. Mum and dad telling me bedtime stories and singing songs
7. Going to my grandparents' house by train
8. Riding my bicycle indoors and crashing
9. Sitting in front of my mom on her bicycle
10. Playing with toys with my mother
11. Walking with my grandmother in the park
12. Jumping into a swimming pool and yelling at my mother to look
13. Being on a swing with my little brother in the garden being pushed by dad
14. Me and my sister playing in a pile of courgettes that my father has just brought in from the garden
15. Playing outside with my brother
16. Running to my grandmother to ask for candy
17. Playing on my bed
18. Falling down the stairs and my parents being mad at me
19. Watching my mother vacuum cleaning
20. Falling asleep on my father's chest and then waking as he put me in bed

With regard to prediction number one (home-related memories), twelve responses appear to concur (numbers 1, 3, 4, 5, 6, 8, 10, 13, 17, 18, 19 and 20) With regard to prediction 2 (action in memories), sixteen responses appear to concur (numbers 1, 5, 7, 8, 9, 10, 11, 12, 13, 14, 15, 16, 17, 18, 19 and 20). Here, two of the responses can be said to be perhaps less convincing examples: they are the two that refer to "moving house". However, by and large, the others give a palpable sense of the movement of the remembered child. With prediction three I report the data in three sections: a first that focuses on play, a second that picks out being in the presence of a parent/caregiver/older sibling and a third that mentions both these. With regard to playing, eight responses appear to concur. Even though some do not mention the word "play" they are quite clearly ludic events (numbers 5, 8, 10, 12, 13, 14, 15 and 17). On the idea of being in the presence of a parent/caregiver/older sibling, fourteen responses agree (numbers 3, 6, 7, 9, 10, 11, 12, 13, 14, 15, 16, 18, 19 and 20). The only real debatable response is "looking up at someone sitting on a chair". I take this in all likelihood to be a primary caregiver and/or family member. Lastly, five of the responses appear to incorporate aspects of both playing and the presence of a caregiver or loved one (numbers 10, 12, 13, 14 and 15). Looking back at the actual written data, only one response did not fall into any of the three categories, number 2: "being in hospital".

In order to get a better insight into the nature of the earliest objects that subjects remembered, I asked them to list three specific ones. There were nineteen responses to this question (one student failed to complete this question and two students did not write down three objects). In total therefore, there were just fifty-five objects mentioned instead of sixty. These were:

| Cuddly toy (8) | Dolly | Spoon |
| --- | --- | --- |
| Fish tank | Wallpaper (2) | Curtains (2) |
| Old desk | Garden fence | Old storage box |
| Brown furniture | My bed (2) | Stairs (2) |
| Couch (4) | Playpen | Lamp |
| Toys | Piano (3) | Wardrobe |
| Swing (2) | Kitchen cupboard | Plant |
| Clock (2) | Bicycle (4) | Music box |
| Book read to child (2) | Floor covering (tiles) | Carpet |
| Tractor tyre | First pair of shoes (brown) | Photograph |
| Fireplace | Bookcase | Pillow |

One "western universal" category that can be said to be of lesser interest here, because of its predictability, is the cuddly toy. It is mentioned here eight times and thus will be excluded from the discussion. All other responses will be considered, including the "bicycle", though it is a predictable Dutch cultural object, owing to the geographic make-up of The Netherlands. The objects that received more than one response were: couch and bicycle (four mentions each), piano (three mentions) and bed, swing, clock, stairs, curtains, wallpaper and a book read to a child (all mentioned twice each). Several of these objects have an inherent aspect of movement or action, be it explicit or implicit. These include the curtains, with their back and forth opening and closing movement, the swing, with its similar ebb and flow movement and, less explicitly, the stairs, with their implied action of an object ascending and descending them. The bicycle also clearly falls into this action/movement category.

To conclude this earliest memories survey, clearly no conclusions can be drawn or even begin to be drawn. However, some responses, and the ways in which they tally in some ways with some of the previously discussed theories and experiments, certainly encourage further investigation.

**2. Vividness and indistinctness survey:** For this second survey, I put six written questions to eighteen second-year students taking another stylistics and rhetoric-driven creative writing course I was teaching at University College Utrecht in the spring semester of 2002. The students had backgrounds in the sciences, social sciences and humanities. They had mixed nationalities: one Polish, one Slovakian, one Nigerian, one Italian, four American and ten Dutch. In total there were eleven females and seven males. I gave them thirty minutes to answer the questions (approximately 5 minutes for each), which involved a simple yes/no part and, most importantly of all, a space to elaborate should a student wish to do so. I again attempted to give the test as early as possible in the semester so that these students, whom I had not previously taught, might complete the test without having been exposed too much to my own explicit and implicit pedagogical views and expectations. Almost unavoidably, like the questions highlighted in the previous experiment, these too are loaded to some greater or lesser extent. The questions were:

- 1. Are you an avid reader of literature?
- 2. When you read literature do you experience mental imagery?
- 3. If so, does that imagery differ from film imagery?
- 4. Do you think that memories of your childhood have something to do with this literary imagery?
- 5. Do your childhood locations appear in your mental imagery?
- 6. Do you think that literary reading has anything to do with spirituality?

Based on these questions, I made five predictions pertaining to questions 2 through 6. From a practical perspective, questions 2, 4 and 5 are the most significant for this study. Question 3 is also relevant, as I was trying to indirectly access responses pertaining to either the clarity or indistinct nature of LRI. Question number 1 is not much more than a filler question. Question 6 is not relevant here but will be for a later discussion in the final chapter of this work. Our main focus therefore is on the responses to questions 2, 3, 4 and 5. Below are five propositions. They all relate in different ways to the theories and studies that have been discussed in this chapter by, for example, Bartlett, Iser, Bachelard, Scarry, Zull, Hogan , Conway, Barsalou, Seilman and Larsen, Dijkstra and Misirlisoy, Seifert and Black, etc.

- 2. LRI is produced while reading literature
- 3. LRI differs significantly from the imagery experienced in a film or on TV
- 4. A link will be observed between childhood memories and LRI
- 5. Childhood locations will appear in LRI
- 6. Literary reading is linked to spirituality

## Question 1: Are You an Avid Reader of Literature?

Fifteen of the eighteen subjects responded affirmatively. One responded negatively and two wrote that they mostly read non-fiction. There was no qualitative data requested. As stated this was an opening (filler) question to see whether the subjects considered themselves avid readers. It seems I was dealing with readers who perceived themselves as such, irrespective of how they defined it.

## Question 2: When You Read Literature Do You Experience Mental Imagery?

All eighteen subjects responded affirmatively. Nine opted to add a comment.

1. Especially descriptions of setting become vivid
2. In the sense that I sort of imagine what the people look like or where they are. Not incredibly detailed though
3. When I don't I think it is a bad book. Also when I reread a book without knowing I've read it before the mental imagery will be familiar where I have forgotten the storyline, title or characters
4. It is more imagery like a feeling of faces and surroundings
5. Very strongly especially when it's good writing
6. I frequently have intense mental images with literary works. Quite often I find the dialogue provokes the most images for me, scenery and the like usually don't give a vivid image
7. Descriptions that I read become "pictures"
8. However, it often happens that it is an image very distantly related to the story, so it's often based on one expression (word)
9. I think I automatically do. Literature is more than words. Right? Mental imagery is an essential part of the connection a reader makes with a text, I think

Interestingly, it can be seen from the responses that there seemed to be a split at this stage as to whether this imagery was indistinct or vivid. Indistinct claims included responses 2, 4 and 6 and were best represented by the observations "in the sense that I sort of imagine what the people look like or where they are. Not incredibly detailed though" and also "it is more imagery like a feeling of faces and surroundings". This second response expresses distinct emotive and somatic aspects of perception in LRI. However, there is also strong evidence for vividness too in responses such as "descriptions that I read become pictures" (number 7).

## Question 3: If So, Does that Imagery Differ from Film Imagery?

Seventeen of the eighteen subjects responded affirmatively. One subject had not circled the negative or positive options, but instead had written "sometimes". Fourteen students had added the following optional comments:

1. Not as explicit: I think most mental imagery is "unpronounced", underdeveloped, undefined in the sense that it is a process that mostly takes place subconsciously. On a screen, there is a thought-out picture, without "gaps". Text allows for more subtlety (esp. in detail) and symbolism
2. Often includes myself, which I don't really get in film
3. It is less clear, the image is not that sharp because a description always misses some pieces that a "picture" does include
4. Film imagery usually evokes emotion in me rather than a full mental image. They usually don't stick very long either, whereas book induced images can come back very often
5. Usually somewhat more hazy; the action or description is very clear, background is harder to define.
6. Mental imagery can change faster and is more personal
7. Very much so. It is less complete and therefore more interesting
8. Yes, but the more films I see the more I imagine things that way. If it is a movie from a book and I read the book after, I picture the book like the movie
9. No background music
10. More fragmentary
11. You choose literary imagery, film imagery is the director's choice
12. The difference between film and literary imagery is the difference between film and literary thoughts and feelings. In film they have to be very clear, even spoken, whereas in literature you can easily hint at them with some well-chosen words. Often film misses the subtlety literature can have
13. Sometimes it is like film imagery. And sometimes after I've seen a movie before reading it, I'm kind of "biased" when I get to read it in the end
14. It depends on what the imagery is. There are times where I imagine some things that I read and view a movie that shows completely different depictions from what I imagined

A number of observations can be made here. First, the claim that LRI is more indistinct than TV or film imagery can be observed in a significant number of responses. These include numbers 1, 3, 5, 7, 10 and 12. Second, an image of the self is also often seen in LRI. Interesting responses that pertain to this include 2 and 6. Such observations comply with Seilman and Larsen's personal resonance theory and perhaps too with Black and Seifert's ideas that good literature maximises remindings from the life of the reader. Other, more general yet interesting responses include "you choose literary imagery; film imagery is the director's choice" and "there are times where I imagine some things that I read and view a movie that shows completely different depictions from what I imagined". Finally, the longevity and repetitive nature of LRI was alluded to in response number

4: "book induced images can come back very often". This idea echoes Bartlett's claim with respect to his empirical study of reading processes that memories tend to produce "stereotyped and conventional" reproductions even though they may be unfaithful to their originals.

## Question 4: Do You Think that Memories of Your Childhood have Something to do with this Literary Imagery?

Eleven of the eighteen subjects responded affirmatively and seven responded negatively. Ten opted to add a comment:

1. Many memories are etched in someone's mind beginning in childhood. When one reads literature it is very common to picture these images that are made early in life
2. It usually has to do with the book not external images generated in childhood
3. Not that I would have ever realised
4. Memory plays a role in making the picture
5. Sometimes, not often
6. To some extent yes, but not predominantly
7. It gives you a basis for your imagination
8. Your childhood shaped you, made you into what you are now. You could say almost all you think has to do with your childhood, so it's only logical that it also shapes the way you read
9. I think that books that I read when I was little have an influence on how I imagine what I read now
10. From life, not specifically from childhood. I often subconsciously form imagery that resembles familiar places/faces/images, and especially how they feel/felt if that makes any sense. I only realise this (the use of familiar image) when the text or the film made after it for that matter conflicts with what I had in mind. I want to stress it has as much to do with *feelings* connected to places/people, as the usual images

The responses are rich, if mixed. Several reject the earlier-stated proposition out of hand, for example, responses 2 and 3. Others, however, seem not to: for example numbers 1, 4, 7 and 8. Response number 1 is intriguing: "many memories are etched in someone's mind beginning in childhood." He/she continues "when one reads literature it is very common to picture these images that are made early in life". I will return to this later. Response number 10 is also interesting as it seems to agree with almost everything that has been discussed in this chapter on the nature of LRI with the one significant exception that it is not specifically from childhood but from other significant moments in a person's life as well.

## Question 5: Do Your Childhood Locations Appear in Your Mental Imagery?

Ten of the eighteen subjects responded affirmatively and eight responded negatively. Eight opted to add a comment:

1. Depends on the context and its similarity to what I'm reading
2. But not only physical locations also things you read or heard about as a child
3. It happens but mostly inside locations (I grew up in Amsterdam, so I did not really spend a lot of time playing on the street)
4. Sometimes places where I've been play a role
5. If they do, they would be outside
6. Reconfigured imagery, pieces of things, but not direct transfer
7. Not specifically from childhood. Locations are more prominent than people, situations
8. Homes, schools, nature and forests I have seen

Some of the qualitative data here is quite rich. Responses in support of the prediction include numbers 2, 3, 4, 6 and 8. Response number 3, with its focus on inside locations, provides some evidence for Bachelard's "interior" claim; response number six reinforces the idea of indistinct LRI pertaining to childhood locations; and response number 8 with its schools and home mirrors parts of the LRI-induced reflection that we saw at the beginning of this chapter experienced by Stevenson's marooned reader. Other responses also warrant some discussion. These include response number 5 which goes against Bachelard's "interior" claim and response number 7 which, in high-lighting location, argues against Barsalou's (and Dijkstra and Misirlisoy's) ideas on the dominance of activity and participants in mental imagery. Response number 7 is interesting as well: in stating "not specifically from childhood" it is echoing a similar response from the previous question.

## Question 6: Do You Think that Literary Reading has Anything to do with Spirituality?

Nine of the eighteen subjects responded affirmatively and four responded negatively. Two wrote "it depends", one wrote "could be" and two did not respond at all. Eight subjects opted to add a comment. This final question is quite different from the rest. As already stated, I posed it for a later chapter where the final discussion will come together. I will therefore only repro-duce the eight responses here without any discussion.

1. I believe it does but all spiritual moments I ever had were restrained to moments when I was reading
2. What you believe shapes how you see things

3. Yes, mental imagery and spirituality are both really personal and both mental. Somebody's spiritual life influences mental images

4. Sometimes. Depends on the narrative of the book—if book addresses spirituality it does

5. Your interpretation of the characters and their actors has a lot to do with it

6. For the most part, when one is spiritual, it seems that an individual seems to relate more to literary images than someone who is not spiritual. The spirituality I am referring to is the level in which someone can be in touch with their emotions themselves and senses

7. Yes, I sometimes get spiritual experiences when a book is very captivating

8. Depends on the content of the book

In conclusion of this survey on vividness and indistinctness, it can be said that some of the data are interesting. However, it should not be forgotten that the way I posed the questions will have affected the way students responded even though, as reported, these responses were given (i) anonymously, (ii) while I was out of the classroom, and (iii) early in the course, i.e. before they knew what my own ideas were. Taken as a whole, these responses can be said to broadly favour some of the predictions especially those pertaining to the indistinct nature of LRI, and that LRI appear during reading (questions 2 and 3). They also appear to provide some evidence for some of the theories and research studies presented earlier in this chapter from across the disciplines.

**3. Vividness and indistinctness (revisited) survey:** The third and final survey in this chapter is a question in three parts from my Novel-Reading Questionnaire (NRQ). It focuses on just one question from that questionnaire: number 14. The testing, conducted in 2004, was the most recent of all the studies in this chapter and involved the largest number of subjects: thirty-six. Though these numbers are a welcome improvement, doubling the total from the previous survey, they are still quite low for data collection. Once again the focus will be on the qualitative data rather than the simple yes/no responses. Of the thirty-six students who responded by completing the questionnaire twenty-seven were from the Free University Amsterdam (henceforth, VU) and nine were from the Roosevelt Academy, Middelburg (henceforth, RA). All of the subjects were undergraduates working towards various BA degrees. In contrast to the previous two experiments, not all of the subjects were from my classes. Rather, the questionnaires were distributed to subjects by e-mail in the case of the VU students, and via colleagues in the case of RA students. This added an aspect of randomness to the responses, which helped counter some of the methodological weakness of the survey. No students were paid and all took part on a voluntary basis. In the case of the VU group an e-mail was sent to all students in three humanities departments: literature, cultural studies and communication and information studies. There were approximately 150 students on those mailing lists from all year levels; the response rate (twenty-seven subjects) was approximately eighteen percent. I took a completely different approach at RA. All subjects were first-year students in the first month of their first semester taking a course entitled "Great Literary Works". All subject were taking a liberal arts and sciences degree and were going to major either in the humanities, the social sciences or the sciences. Participation in the experiment was again optional. One thing perhaps worth noting at this stage is that while the VU students were approached to fill in this NRQ in their own time during the summer of 2004, the RA students were approached immediately after having read *The Great Gatsby* for a class assignment in September 2004, and had approximately two weeks.[5] Also, whereas all twenty-seven students from the VU were arts and humanities students, and thus all had some affinity and experience with literary reading, only four of the nine RA students who took part were: the others were scientists. Whereas the blending of two such different data collection systems in the same experiment might be problematic in statistical surveys, for my main goal, namely the acquisition of as much written qualitative feedback as possible, this system has its benefits.

### NRQ—Q.14a When You Read, Can You Readily Visualise the Persons and Places Described in a Novel or Short Story?

I purposely used the expression "readily visualise" to refer to whether or not mental imagery occurs and to avoid leading terms at this stage like "vividness" and "indistinctness". My very basic prediction with regard to this very general first question was that most students would answer affirmatively. They did (see the following). The response data of these thirty-two respondents will now be taken into consideration in the remaining two questions.

- VU          Yes = 23          No = 4
- RA          Yes = 9           No = 0
- Total        Yes = 32          No = 4

### NRQ—14b   Do those Persons and Places more Often than not Appear Clearly in your Mind or are those Images More Often than not Indistinct?

By using the both terms "clearly" and "indistinct" I hoped to achieve some methodological balance in the question. My very basic prediction was that most students would choose the "indistinct" option, thus supporting the direct and associative claims some of the scholars and scientists cited in this chapter.

- VU          Clear = 9          Indistinct = 14
- RA          Clear = 7          Indistinct = 2
- Total        Clear = 16        Indistinct = 16

The total responses were equal and thus appear to reject the basic prediction I made. This outcome also questions some of the data from questions two and three of the previous survey which appeared to favour an indistinct option in LRI. It will be noticed, however, that the responses from the two institutions are mixed here. The ones from the larger group of VU students broadly concur with the prediction, whereas the smaller RA group result clearly rejects it. There are some structural reasons that might help account for this. What might have affected the RA result was that all students in that group were in the first month of their academic lives. Another reason is that whereas all of the VU students were humanities majors, of whom it would be perhaps expected that they read literature regularly, less than half of the RA students were humanities majors. The majority of students in the RA group were science students (four social science majors and one life science major). These reasons, however, do not explain fully the nature of the responses from the RA group, nor those responses from the VU group either.

**NRQ—14c Since You Have Never Physically Seen these Fictional Settings and Characters Before, What and Who is it Then That You actually see? And Also, Where Are Those Locations and Settings, i.e. Where/What are they Based On? (Please Expand on These Two Central Questions Below. Please Also Try Not to Think of a Book That You First Saw as a TV Adaptation or as a Film in the Cinema. Instead, Choose a Book Which You Read Without the Aid of Film Imagery).**

In this third question, which I deem to be the most significant of the three because of its far more open nature, my basic prediction is that childhood locations and primary caregivers will be prominent. This broadly concurs with some of the claims of a number of scholars and scientists mentioned in this chapter pertaining to their own work. This third question could not be answered with a simple yes/no and therefore I do not know how many of the subjects explicitly agreed or disagreed. More important was that sixteen open responses were given, some of which contained rich qualitative data.

1. I think that the images I make in my mind are a mix of things I remember in life. It is not that I really recognise them, but I think that this is the way the mind works. I make images I want to see and to make them I must have seen them or things that look like it or a combination of things I have experienced in life

2. The surroundings are normally based on places I have been to, especially in American and British novels, because I would kind of know what it would have to look like. It totally depends on the books where these settings are of course. But mostly, if the setting would be American, I would base it on the way my home town looked when I lived there. e.g. I just read a Japanese book and the houses and alleys looked a bit American in my imagination

3. Normally when reading a novel I only have a vague impression of how a character is supposed to look. The name for instance would call up a vague impression of colours, mostly. I tend to get the details wrong too. (For example, until seeing the Harry Potter film I was absolutely convinced that Draco Malfoy's hair colour was dark, like Harry's. After seeing the film, I went back to the text and found evidence that his hair really was fair all along, I just missed it)

4. I never see anything while reading. Reading for me is more abstract than that. I feel, I know and I feel close to the places and persons in the book but they never mature into something physical, just an abstract experience of the narrative and the story

5. If I read something that reminds me of something in my childhood for example that theme gets evoked in my head

6. They are probably made up of characters and body parts of people I know. Similarly, locations are probably based on places I've been before or I have seen before in a picture or something. I think that it is impossible to not recall places or people you know or you have seen while reading literature. That is your field of reference, your experience. I should also say that I never actually see the exact faces, probably just the silhouette. Perhaps this sounds a bit far-fetched but it is almost like those pointillist paintings, where you cannot immediately see what is in the picture. You just see little parts

7. I think that in visualising we tend to put emphasis on that which is known and familiar to us, both people-wise and location-wise. What we see is a mix of memories and internal knowledge about certain places and types of people

8. The location and setting might have something to do with the place from my childhood, but that's all very subconscious . . . when I think of a lake, I always see the same lake, unless the author describes it in detail

9. Sometimes I see people who are similar to somebody I know

10. I often find that when I am reading a book where people are in a certain house I actually visualise a house where I have been before, but with a lot of alterations. I've got the same thing with people and landscapes, the whole visual image is actually made up out of several pieces of people and places I've seen

11. I think I take the description an author gives of a character and the scenery and then I combine that with people and places I know myself that fit into the picture to make the picture complete

12. It is like dreaming, when you think you see the same thing. When you look back on dreams you see that persons and locations are composed of multiple parts. When I was younger I remember that most books I read were based in my house
13. When the passage describes something that is familiar to you because you have experienced it in your childhood, you will go back to this when you need it in the novel, even if it is not specifically about your childhood in the story/passage
14. I always picture the houses of friends or family when I read about houses in novels, which for me is the most peculiar thing. Also I have no idea as to why with certain novels I also picture our old house we used to live in and with others the flat my father used to live in and even sometimes my grandmother's house. I think that it is based on the descriptions from the text but I can't pinpoint what exactly
15. Location and setting: very often any house or domestic setting becomes my grandmother's house and/or neighbourhood. Sometimes this mental image is so strong that I can't change it even though the novel gives clear description of locations and settings. If it doesn't fit into the picture I have of it, I will soon forget and need constant reminders (if it is something that is important somehow and recurs often). However, I will not adjust my mental image
16. Fictional characters: usually remain indistinct. I know what they look like but I could not really describe them if I had to I think. If the novel turns into a movie this can sometimes collide: the character and his/her appearance are not what I imagined them to be

Some of these responses are interesting for the prediction that childhood locations and primary caregivers will be prominent. These include response numbers 5, 6, 7, 8, 10, 12, 13, 14, 15 and 16 and might be best summed up with the comment from response number 7 that states "I think that in visualising we tend to put emphasis on that which is known and familiar to us, both people-wise and location-wise". Response 14 is representative as well: "I always picture the houses of friends or family when I read about houses in novels", and he/she continues, "I have no idea as to why with certain novels I also picture our old house we used to live in and with others the flat my father used to live in and even sometimes my grandmother's house".

In addition to these responses, there were other interesting ones. These include number 2 that, like a previous response, seems to echo an aspect of what Stevenson's character felt when he read Virgil, described at the beginning of this chapter. This subject respondent, seemingly raised in the USA, observed that even though he/she had just read a Japanese novel "the houses and alleys looked a bit American in my imagination". Was he/she perhaps doing what Bartlett has predicted, as we have seen in an earlier response: showing that memories tend to produce "stereotyped and conventional reproductions" even though they may be unfaithful to their originals? The suggestion is plausible. Another intriguing response was number 3, which serves as support for another of Bartlett's claims discussed in an earlier chapter that we bring our personal and cultural expectations to a text that are so strong that they will override the actual textual detail. This is a main claim of schema theory too. In this case, the writer referred to, J. K. Rowling, has chosen to go against strong cultural conventions, i.e. that a wicked character in a book about a struggle between good and evil should have dark hair in a western cultural framework, not light. The author, of course, may have played with this convention purposely. In any event, the reader who responded "read over" this; such was the strength of his/her culturally-driven, mental expectations and LRI.

A further interesting observation was made in response 6 that LRI is like a pointillistic painting. This lends weight to the indistinct claims of LRI including Iser's claims of "optical poverty" and is all summed up in response 16 that "fictional characters usually remain indistinct". Response 6 also made the somewhat macabre, yet plausible, observation that characters in novels are made up of "the body parts" of people whom the reader knows. This same idea was echoed in response 12 that referred to persons and places being composed of "multiple parts".

Are these then a quite literal interpretation of the "fragmentary memories" that fill the imagination when reading of which Hogan spoke earlier? In sum, the overriding idea that memories and LRI are not vivid was locatable in much of the feedback including the very first respondent who claimed that the images he/she made in his/her mind "are a mix of things I remember in life. It is not that I really recognise them, but I think that this is the way the mind works". Such "gossamer" reflections, to use Scarry's term, are persuasive. Response 6 also implicitly refers to a theme that has come up in previous experiments when he/she says that LRI locations are probably based on places he/she has been before or has seen images of. One could deduce from this that he/she is not just speaking of childhood as this is not explicitly mentioned. Having highlighted all this, it should not be forgotten that several responses clearly rejected the prediction. This might be best summed up by response number 4 who claimed that he/she "never sees anything while reading". Let us now sum up the theories and surveys discussed in this chapter.

At the beginning of this chapter I proposed that because our childhood memories—i.e. the important places and people from our personal pasts—are the most emotive and most enduring kind, they are most prone to activation while reading literature in order to flesh out all kinds of situations in novels. We can now review this LRI hypothesis based on the rudimentary surveys I conducted. This might best be done by reviewing the eight general statements I set out before the testing was discussed as these cover the most import aspects of the questions. After each statement in parenthesis I will draw a very brief and very provisional conclusion. One should not forget that given the methodological paucity of the three surveys, these conclusions are indeed of an interim nature.

- While reading literature readers experience LRI ... (*highly plausible*)
- LRI is indistinct/fragmented ... (*plausible*)
- LRI involves movement/activity/dynamic scenes ... (*highly plausible*)
- In that movement in LRI the reader is an active participant ... (*highly plausible*)
- LRI is linked to (idealised) childhood memories/images ... (*unconfirmed*)
- Aspects of our primary caregivers appear in LRI ... (*unconfirmed*)
- Childhood locations occur in LRI ... (*unconfirmed*)
- LRI will relate to specific incidents in a person's life with emotional significance ... (*unconfirmed*)

In light of the above, a repositioning is necessary. Thus far I have emphasised exclusively that LRI is based on events, locations and participants from a reader's childhood. Although I have found some engaging qualitative evidence for this, I think that in light of some of the contradictory qualitative data I need to provisionally review this standpoint. I will now assume that even though much of the emotive content of LRI is based on events, locations and participants from a reader's childhood, other imagery can be evoked too from important emotive events that took place later in a reader's life.

Now that my discussion on the nature of LRI is concluded, we can return to the beginning of this chapter to address a question posed there, namely, why it is that while reading Virgil, Stevenson's character saw locations and primary caregivers from his own personal English childhood rather than Italian vistas. In light of this chapter, my explanation is not that the author has conjured up some literary fancy, rather, I believe that Stevenson, like many accomplished authors, was drawing on his own experience as a reader, and in doing so was touching on something that many engaged readers of literature appear to share, to a greater or lesser extent. This is arguably an innate ability to produce mental imagery while reading literature of sketchy, undulating, fragmented images based on some idealised form of our individual childhood locations and primary caregivers or those of some later period. Vision is a creative process, and reading, especially literary reading, involves a flood of mental perceptions as we have seen.

We have now looked in detail at LRI. In the next chapter, we will explore two further plausible affective inputs that go into the literary reading adventure: the mood of the reader and the location in which a reader chooses to place his/her body prior to and during the literary reading experience.

# 4   Reading Moods and Reading Places

In this chapter we will focus on two pre-reading, mind-fed, affective cognitive factors called "mood" and "location". The first pertains to all of the, as yet, unfocused thinking that takes place once a person "decides" to read literature. The second concerns the place in which a person chooses to position his or her body in anticipation of the literary reading experience: this is usually the final stage of the pre-reading situation just prior to the hands opening the book and the eyes meeting the page. Both mood and location have been largely neglected in previous analytic accounts of literary discourse processing. They should be properly explored because their role in literary meaning construction can be crucial. The addition and proper consideration of two such factors will enhance the range and depth of contextualised stylistic analysis and will better validate the claims of empirical scholars of literature. Let us first look at mood.

Literature, one could say, is all about words and sentences. From my position as a university lecturer in rhetoric and English, I believe, however, that literary reading is about far more than just lexis and syntax. This is not an easy admission for a stylistician to make—equivalent perhaps to a barrister saying that justice is about more than just laws and statutes. Nonetheless, I believe it to be true. Readers create meaning not solely by perceiving and processing words on the page; they are also affected by a whole scale of interactive, largely non-textual, phenomena that constitute important inputs that go into the meaning-making confluence of literary discourse processing. This is what this chapter will show, beginning with the phenomenon of "mood".

When I use the term "mood" in this work I do not mean it entirely in the strict psychological sense of the word as it was described in a previous chapter, namely, affective states of relatively long duration often elicited by an internal event (Frijda 1986: 252–53). Rather, by mood I mean a primarily subconscious and somatic pre-reading state that plays a distinctive role in the reading process. In effect, mood is a positive kind of feeling that a reader can get once a mainly subconscious "decision" has been made to engage with a literary work. This is not a simple process. Manguel confirms this when he suggests that meaning in literary reading comes about "through a vastly entangled method of learned significances, social conventions, previous readings, personal experiences and private tastes" (1996: 37). The diversity of pre-reading mood is described by the twentieth-century novelist and academic Harold Brodkey in his 1985 essay *Reading, the Most Dangerous Game*:

> The act of reading as it really occurs is obscure; the decision to read a book in a real minute, how one selects the book, how one flirts with the choice, how one dawdles on the odd path of getting it read and then reread, the oddities of rereading, the extreme oddities of the procedures of continuing with or without interruptions to read, getting ready to read a middle chapter in its turn after going off for a while, then getting hold of the book physically, having it in one's hand, letting one's mind fill with thoughts in a sort of warm-up for the exercise of mind to come—one riffles through remembered scenes from this and other books, one diddles with half-memories and other pleasures and usefulnesses, one wonders if one can afford to read, one considers the limitations and possibilities of this book, one is humiliated in anticipation or superior (*sic*) or thrilled in anticipation, or nauseated in retrospect or as one reads. One has a sense of talk and of reviews and essays and of anticipation or dread and the will to be affected by the thing of reading, affected lightly or seriously. One settles one's body to some varying degree and then one enters on the altered tempos of reading, the subjection to being played upon, one passes through phases, starting with reacting to or ignoring the cover of the book and the opening lines. (Reproduced in Gilbar 1995: 101–2).

As an avid reader of fiction, I too recognise such flirting with choices in book selection; the dawdling on the pathway to the reading event; the getting hold of a book physically and letting my mind fill with thoughts in a warm-up for the mental exercises to come. I can also recognise a kind of automatic riffling through remembered scenes from previously read books and playing with half-memories. I too have felt thrilled in anticipation and have had a sense of talk, reviews and essays. And perhaps most important of all, I have had the subconscious desire to be affected intensely by the very act of reading literature. This description by Brodkey comes very close to capturing what I mean by mood as it touches on all the important, often unconscious, preparatory affective and somatic issues; all of which are grounded to some extent in prior experience. These include the pre-decision-making processes, the mental projection of states of satisfaction and the flashbacks before moving toward the physical preparation of "settling one's body", as Brodkey puts it.

Let us return to mainstream cognitive psychology for the moment. The general principle that emotion comes into being as a result of an interaction between many associated physical and mental phenomena is, as we saw, a view also held in the social sciences. As Frijda puts it:

Emotions are rarely, if ever, elicited by an isolated stimulus. Rather, the emotional effectiveness of sensory stimuli depends upon the spatial, temporal, and meaning context in which they occur, the adaptation level upon which they impinge, and the expectations with which they clash or correspond. (1986: 267)

From the previous chapters we learned a number of things specifically about mood in its default psychological sense. These included the notion of "mood congruity effects": if a person feels happy, then that person is more likely to remember things learned and stored while in a happy state of mind, than things learned and stored in a negative one (Frijda 1986: 121). We also saw that positive affective states lead to better retrieval of positive material. This is essentially what is known as mood-state-dependent retrieval. Isen expanded on this by claiming that if affective states are essentially retrieval cues, then the events and experiences that are stored in memory must be tagged according to the feelings that are associated with them (1984: 218). Oatley and Jenkins echo this in their assertion that "moods are specific modes of brain organization, and so specific moods preferentially give access to memories of incidents experienced in the same emotional state" (1996: 277). From this, Oatley and Jenkins concluded that "emotions are heuristics" (1996: 280), something Aristotle noted in his discussion on pathos in *The Art of Rhetoric*.

In the previous discussion we also saw how a person's mood affects the style and performance of how he/she cognitively processes objects in the world (Forgas 2000: 130; Fiedler and Bless 2000: 163) and how moods can influence beliefs (Clore and Gasper 2000: 39). I also briefly touched on Damasio's notion of "background feeling", which he differentiates from mood because it is what he calls a body state that exists *between* emotions, namely, "the image of the body landscape" (1994: 151). In addition to these previously mentioned mood-based cognitive phenomena there are also other relevant cognitive concepts. One of these is known as mental "set", which can be defined as "any preparatory cognitive activity that precedes thinking and perception" (Solso 1995: 522). The idea of "set" allows us to pose two relevant questions. First, can literary reading involve a kind of mental set that can be defined as an anterior, embodied, neural process? Second, are there processes active before, or even long before, the full flood of affective cognition arrives in consciousness and working memory? The idea that much unconscious cognitive work takes place before conscious cognitive processing may seem far-fetched, but several experiments in neurobiology have supported this general principle. One famous experiment conducted by Benjamin Libet showed that the intention to do something takes place *after* the brain has actually started doing it. Libet's consciousness experiments in the early 1980s showed how the decision to act comes nearly a whole second after the motor areas have started preparing themselves for action (see Libet 1981). This is a very long time in neurobiology for a stimulus to be made conscious. Fellow neuroscientist Susan Greenfield has referred to the enormous social implications of these findings with use of the word "staggering" (2000: 184). Even that seems to be an understatement.

Mood, as a pre-literary reading input, must also be linked to such notions as desire and anticipation. From the perspective of the first of these, mood can be said to be a kind of primarily, but not exclusively, subconscious desire: a longing to become emoted through the abstract, yet seemingly deeply personal, medium of fiction. In this sense, reading fiction is addictive in neuro-chemical terms. But what is the nature of this desire?

I believe that it is not simply a desire to be "transported" to other worlds as Richard J. Gerrig has cogently argued in *Experiencing Narrative Worlds*, although this is undoubtedly and important motive for many readers to read fiction (see Gerrig 1993: 157–95). Nor, do I believe, as Thomas J. Scheff has maintained in his work *Catharsis in Healing Ritual and Drama* that it is simply to experience emotion at "a safe aesthetic distance" (1979: 13).

> When we cry over the fate of Romeo and Juliet, we are reliving our own personal experiences of overwhelming loss, but under new and less severe conditions. The experience of vicarious loss, in a properly designed drama, is sufficiently distressful to awaken the old distress. It is also sufficiently vicarious, however, so that the emotion does not feel overwhelming. (1979: 13)

Rather, in addition to these literary psychological ideas, I believe that this desire is also something more fundamental and philosophical, as will become evident in the discussions I will hold in later chapters.

Mood can also be viewed as an emotive form of anticipation. Anticipation may seem to be at the threshold of emotion rather than being a full-blown emotion itself. Evidence, however, would suggest otherwise. Frijda and Mesquita, for example, have argued that emotion anticipations are real felt emotions (2000: 58). In order to be maximally affected in the course of reading literature I believe it is beneficial to first have experienced such affective anticipation of the reading event itself. It will be recalled from an earlier chapter how Frijda suggested that anticipation intensifies emotional experience in that it "considerably extends the time period over which a given event exerts emotional influence"; he added that it "casts its shadow forward" (1986: 292). He also stated that anticipation affects an emotional response when it comes, because it permits, among other things, preparatory actions like "relaxing and bracing", giving one the opportunity for advance coding or recoding of events (1986: 292–93). In a similar vein, Zull writes that we get enjoyment from anticipating imagined movement. The apt example he uses to illustrate his point is literary discourse processing: in his own words "[anticipation] is probably

the most important thing that keeps us reading a good book" (2002: 61).
Exactly what that anticipation entails is unresolved. One recent study has
suggested that readers rely to a substantial degree on character description in order to generate expectations pertaining to how that character
might behave and how the story around him/her might evolve (Rapp,
Gerrig and Prentice 2001).

Anticipation in the domain of literary reading was also an important concept in the reception studies of the 1970s, also known as reception aesthetics. It featured prominently in the work of Hans Robert Jauss, who wrote
on the phenomenon of readers' "horizon of expectations".[1] The basic idea is
grounded in the idea of "assumptions". There is a predominant social side
to the theory, but an individual aspect is also present. The former involves
readers having shared assumptions about such things as genres, structure
conventions and culture in texts. If the text activates these in a reader, this
will lead to a kind of reformulation of those expectations. Similarly, at an
individual level, a reader can be said to bring his/her assumptions to a text.
The discovery of them in that text can help to bring about better personal
understanding. Jauss also said that a text will be different for every reader
both cross-culturally and historically through time. But whereas Jauss's
"horizon of expectations" only comes into play once the text has been
engaged with, I argue that those expectations and assumptions are already
having their "shadows cast forward", to paraphrase Frijda. In short, the
anticipation of textual meaning based on prior experience, and all the full-
blown emotion that comes with it, will already be active before the first lexical item of the text is visually processed. Just how this works will become
evident in Chapter 7.

Addressing the role of prior mood and the affective expectations of certain literary genres, discourse psychologists van den Broek et al. say:

> Activation of a schema results in top-down processes, that is, the gen-
> eration of extensive expectations and inferences. For example, when a
> reader is told that he or she will read a fairy tale, general knowledge
> about the content and structure of fairy tales may be activated and in-
> fluence the interpretation of the text that follows. (1999: 89)

It seems likely to me that this situation will be the case for many experienced readers of literature as can be seen from the earlier Brodkey quote,
which lends substance to van den Broek et al.'s claims of "extensive expectations and inferences". Somewhat similarly, recent work in psycholinguistics claims that language users continuously anticipate lots of things
depending on whatever language internal or external cues they happen to
have at their disposal (see, for example, van Berkum et al. 2005 and Otten
and van Berkum 2008). It seems that all kinds of things can plausibly be
anticipated: upcoming, words, themes, turns, topics, arguments and indeed
meaning itself.

Since this discussion on pre-reading mood has now landed in the domain of discourse psychology it is pertinent to reconsider how language appears to be processed. It will be recalled from Chapter 1 how discourse processing is often considered either immediate or cumulative/incremental. What I am suggesting with my concept of mood is that in certain affective literary discourse processing situations, an important aspect of that processing takes place before the immediacy of first eye contact with the words on the page. In effect, there is plausibly a notion of *pre*-immediacy in such anticipated emotive encounters with fiction. However, if the starting point of affective literary reading is not when light strikes the retina after being reflected off the semiotic symbols on the page, then what is? In short, what floods the mind first? I believe it is inferences, memories and expectations, all of which are saturated with emotion while pouring into working memory and the buffer-zones that support and feed it. In effect, these are Manguel's "previous readings", "personal experiences" and "private tastes"; they are Brodkey's "remembered scenes from previously read books", "half-memories" and "the sense of talk, reviews and essays"; and they are Jauss's "horizon of expectations for the individual reader". This is also the "generation of extensive expectations" that van den Broek et al. spoke of in the context of particularly the literary discourse processing of fairly tales. Hence, mood, in contexts of affective literary discourse processing, can be "pre-immediate". The inferences are not minimalist as Ratcliff and McKoon thought, nor are they limitless as Graesser has argued; rather, I like to see them as "flexible, yet predictable, patterns". This may seem counterintuitive and somewhat oxymoronic, but I am doing no more here than echoing Bartlett's sound claims on "conventionality in recall".

In sum, therefore, mood is, in its initial state, a mind-fed affective input. It is initially mind-fed in that affective cognition is flooding through the embodied mind long before hands are brought into contact with the book and eyes with words on the page. This act of "letting one's mind fill with thoughts in a warm-up for the exercise of mind to come", to echo Brodkey, is a top-down process. However, all those visions, images and anticipations are based on previous physical and perceptual experiences, albeit ones that are now significantly altered through the diffuse storage system that long-term human memory employs. During the actual literary reading process, mood will, of course, be affected by styles and themes, but it can also, in turn, affect them.

I have shown above how both the humanities and the social sciences seem to offer support for the idea that expectations and mood that occur prior to the actual reading event can influence the interpretation, meaning-making and reading experience itself. But how might such claims stand up to responses from a group of readers? The next section will seek to address this question. Question 8 of my NRQ had two parts. The first asked for simple yes/no responses while in the second, more important, section subjects were asked to elaborate. Less than half the subjects chose to do so. My

basic prediction was that a good majority of responses would react affirmatively to the statement and that this would be reflected in the qualitative
data inasmuch as tangible references to my claim, and the theories upon
which I have based it, would be present.[2]

## NRQ—Q.8   Prior to Starting to Read a Novel do you Think That Your Mood has ever Affected the Actual Reading Event Itself?

Twenty-nine of the thirty-six subjects responded affirmatively. Thirteen
subjects opted to give a written response.

1. When I'm very happy it's easier to see the happy/positive side of a story. When I'm feeling a bit down, it's easier to just notice the negative/depressing side of a story. So my mood can really influence the way I read a novel and it can also influence the way I think about the story
2. If I am in a good mood, I have less trouble appreciating a novel
3. I think that the mood has a big effect——maybe not on reading as such, but definitely on what I remember from the book
4. For instance, I was once in a very happy and energetic mood when I started to read a book that was rather serious and dramatic. For me, my mood didn't go together with the moods of the people in the book. So I put the book down because I couldn't identify with the book's characters. However, when I picked it up at a later time, when I was in a more serious and calm mood, I found the book to be wonderfully written and I found it very interesting and gripping
5. My mood influences which book I read. It can also account for why I stop reading a book after just a couple of pages because it doesn't match the way I am feeling at that moment in time
6. I think one's mood always affects the reading somewhat, mine certainly does, although the effect tends to turn around very quickly, i.e. the reading will have a stronger effect on my mood than the other way around
7. There is always more than one reading of a text possible and my gut feeling tells me that my mood could very well influence this
8. Sometimes you have to be in the mood to read something. It is not that you can read anything in any mood. I have read the same book more than once in the same period and it turned out that I could appreciate the book more in a certain period than another and vice versa
9. Sometimes I know I mustn't start in a certain book, because my state of mind isn't right. For example, in *The Discovery of Heaven* I must have a certain state of mind to start that book. Otherwise, I can't enjoy it, and I can't even read the book properly
10. If I don't feel right when I start to read a book, I will just stop because I won't be able to get into it. If I read a book I am usually on vacation or at least do not have a lot of studying to do, my mind is clear and the book will help me to relax even more

11. If I am in an emotional mood, it's more likely I get emotional because of tragic or unhappy events in the book. If I'm very happy, I tend to laugh easier at jokes in the book

12. When I feel stressed out or sad/bad about something, then I cannot concentrate properly. My mind wanders off to what's bothering me. That's why I probably never was any good at obligatory reading. I did read the books, but not as well as I wanted to. Simply because I had to finish the book in a certain number of hours. I think I tend to read best when I'm happy and won't get distracted by a sad thought

13. To be in the mood to read, feeling energetic, but always a little lonely, works for me

There is some evidence for the mood-congruency effect, especially in responses 1, 2 and 4. Also Forgas's claim that the processing effects of mood may influence how observed information is attended to seems to be confirmed in a number of responses and is perhaps best represented in response number one. Also Fiedler and Bless's claim that mood and feeling states can influence cognitive performance appears to be supported by response number 2 as well as some others. There is also evidence for the cognitive psychological phenomenon of "set", i.e. "any preparatory cognitive activity that precedes thinking and perception", in responses 8, 9 and 10. Two responses appear to resonate Jauss's horizon of expectation theory. The first is number 8, which suggests that reading the same book in different periods of one's life can lead to different levels of appreciation. The second, response number 7, added a more personal aspect to Jauss's theory by saying his/her gut feeling was that his/her mood could influence the kind and number of readings that a text might offer.

Several respondents spoke of mood in the more general sense: response number six is a prime example of this. Some responses seemed to fall in between what I described and the more general sense of mood. These included respondent ten who indicated "if I don't feel right when I start to read a book, I will just stop because I won't be able to get into it". Another respondent stressed the importance of mood by saying that it has a "big effect on what he/she remembers from a book. The subject who provided response number 5 confided that his/her mood influences which books he/she reads, suggesting that the book must fit the mood and not the other way around. Respondent nine confessed that he/she cannot start a certain book until his/her state of mind is in the appropriate mode. Perhaps the most quixotic yet paradoxically pertinent response was number 13. That reader confided that he/she needed to be both "energetic" and "lonely" in order to read literature. It is this state of what we might term "fluvial nostalgia" that perhaps best embodies the underlying concept of what I mean by pre-reading mood. It also has a similar somatic profile to Damasio's notion of "background feelings".

From these responses, we can provisionally conclude, as response 6 indicates, that "one's mood always affects the reading somewhat". So despite the mixed nature of the qualitative feedback, I hold that during literary discourse comprehension, meaning-making starts long before a reader's eyes encounter the words on the page. In order to explore this further I now wish to focus on what might be seen as a key aspect of pre-reading mood that occurs at the end of the preparatory "cline", so to speak. I am referring to the moment just before the eyes meet the page and engage with the text. Brodkey alluded to it when he spoke of "settling one's body to some varying degree": it is the essentially mind-fed affective input of "location".

A central concern that can influence mood is the physical location that a reader chooses to place his or her body in when reading. The place, time, and reasons for reading are of great importance. Consider the following claim by Manguel:

> Some books seem to demand particular positions for reading, postures of the reader's body that in turn require reading places appropriate for those postures . . . Often, the pleasure derived from reading largely depends on the bodily comfort of the reader. (1996: 151)

Before starting to read for pleasure one often makes some kind of loose plan. Whether one reads at home or on vacation; at night or during the day; in the summer or in the winter, readers are wont to try and match the subject matter of the book with a designated place of reading, and sometimes even vice versa. This can occur consciously or subconsciously. When people are about to go on vacation, for example, they will try to "select" books that may match both their mood and destination. It seems that finding the right place to read for pleasure is important. This also includes securing conventional criteria like comfort, silence, solitude and good light. Indeed, much of what I have said here about reading largely holds for writing, editing and correcting too, as many teachers, scholars and writers will confirm. But let us backtrack and first review some facts about reading locations.

It may seem counterintuitive but the act of literary reading as we know it today is largely socially constructed. For a long time reading was always done indoors. Until the seventeenth and eighteenth century, books in Europe were generally produced as leather-bound tomes to be read in libraries or in a person's study. All this changed in the nineteenth century when certain editions of books became light enough to be read outdoors or while travelling. In the mid-nineteenth century the bookseller W. H. Smith and Son set up the first railway bookshop at Euston station in London. There, novels and short stories were sold from the "Routledge Railway Library" series. But full reader mobility only came with the "invention" of the pocket paperback, which was first launched by Penguin in 1935. Only ten books were chosen to be marketed in this format and at first it was far from a success: sales remained well under break-even levels. It was only when Woolworth's stepped in and sold them in their chain of general stores alongside the tea, vegetables and biscuits that sales rose and the publishers became convinced that there was a profitable future in pocket paperbacks.[3] This story shows that the idea of curling up snugly with a book in a place of one's choice in order to try to create comfortable reading conditions of one's own making only very recently became possible. This illustrates again how much the affective cognitive act of reading is just as culturally and socially constructed as it is biologically and genetically engendered. We could even go further and suggest that the literary reading mind is a blend of our neurobiological nature and our social nurture.

I believe that when readers sit down in a comfortable location of their own choosing to read a book, they experience subconscious echoes of where they came from and what made them. These are implicit, somatic, affective memory prompts. Manguel suggest something similar when he says the manner in which he personally interacts with the words on the page when he starts reading depends on who he is and how he became who he is (1996: 38). Hence, literary reading does not start with a *tabula rasa*; rather, it is a process, which is common and yet personal to the process of reconstruction (Manguel 1996: 39). This inter-subjective idea of "the common yet personal" is something that has been tested and confirmed in discourse psychology. Indeed, there have been several studies that have highlighted the existence of inter-subjective affective responses in specific situations. For example, Martin A. Conway and Debra A. Bekerian have shown in their experiments from the 1980s that members of the same culture share a high degree of consensus over what affective states are readily associated with particular situational contexts. There seems to be no reason why a situational context of a literary reading experience should be any different. In light of this research it might be argued that readers know beforehand what kinds of affective states are achievable during literary reading situations.

Criteria like the size, the colour or the form of a book might seem to be completely superfluous to the facilitation and realisation of emotion during reading. But is this the case? Consider the following account:

> My hands, choosing a book to take to bed or to the reading desk, for the train or for a gift, consider the form as much as the content. Depending on the occasion, depending on the place where I have chosen to read, I prefer something small and cosy or ample and substantial. Books declare themselves through their titles, their authors, their places in a catalogue or on a bookshelf, the illustrations on their jackets; books also declare themselves through their size. At different times and in different places I have come to expect certain books to look a certain

way, and, and, as in all fashions, these changing features fix a precise quality onto a book's definition. I judge a book by its cover. I judge a book
by its shape. (Manguel 1996: 125)

From this perspective, reading literature appears to have far more than a
visual sensory dimension. The tactile gripping and bending and folding of
a book are also of importance. There are most certainly readers who will
refuse to engage with a novel produced in hardback, because this "flexibility deprivation" would take away from their overall reading experience.
In the above statement there is also an implicit acknowledgment of the
somatic role that the body plays in literary reading. Judging by their earlier comments, scientists like Kintsch and Damasio might very well concur
with a description like this.

The location of reading is important, not only for everyday readers
like ourselves, but also for many writers when they read. For example, as
a girl, the French writer Colette read in bed in order to create a safe and
comforting haven for her reading experience. Reading in her bedroom,
however, would not just remain a childhood preoccupation, as Manguel
notes:

> Throughout her adult life, Colette would seek out this solitary reading-
> space . . . she would set aside (not always successfully) an area in which
> the only intrusions would be those she invited herself. Now, stretched
> out in the muffled bed, holding the treasured book in both hands and
> propping it up on her stomach she has established not only her own
> space but her own measure of time. (1996: 150)

Reflecting on his own reading experience Manguel notes that he too read in
a long succession of beds from those in his childhood home, through those
of hotel rooms, the bedrooms of strange houses in towns or by the sea and
the homes of his recent adult life. No matter where he was, he could always
read in bed, and that act had a kind of intangible sense of continuity to it.
Reflecting on this, he says "the combination of bed and book granted me a
sort of home, which I could go back to night after night, under whichever
skies" (1996: 150). The very location involved in the cognitive act of reading was for Manguel, from the very beginning, inscribed with an aspect of
being able to return to a sense of his childhood. Perhaps other literary readers will be able to identify with some of the things Manguel says about his
own reading habits and those of Colette, as I do. I believe that like Colette
we too may "seek out a solitary reading-space", an area that has been "set
aside (not always successfully) in which the only intrusions would be those
we invite ourselves". There, like her, we can establish not only our own
space but also our own measure of time. Similarly, the combination of bed
and book—or even favourite chair and book—might grant us, like it did

Manguel, "a kind of home" to which we can return, no matter where we are or how old we become.

These ideas are not as fanciful as they may first appear. There are many more examples of writers with special locative reading habits. For instance, Henry Miller confessed that all his best reading was done in the toilet, adding "there are certain passages of *Ulysses* which can be read only in the toilet, if one wants to extract the full flavour of them", whereas Marguerite Duras did not like to read outdoors, especially on beaches or in gardens (Manguel 1996: 152). A final example concerns the writer and academic Stanley Elkin, who wrote in his essay "Where I Read, What I Read" that when he was younger he spent the whole 1958/1959 academic year reading in bed.[4] He was not ill. He was in fact preparing to take his preliminary exams for his Ph.D. and he only left his bed for reasons of personal hygiene or to teach rhetoric to first-year undergraduates. This was the place he could best read all the novels on the required reading list for his examinations. Elkin was not reading for pleasure, but as a kind of side-effect of his year spent reading in bed he found that in later life he could read nowhere else: not at the beach, nor on park benches, nor on airplanes or trains, nor in waiting rooms and not even in libraries—which, in later life as a professor of modern literature must have been something of a handicap. Thus it seems that for many readers the location of the reading event is far from a trivial matter. Perhaps there is some locative and bodily reason as to why only certain books can be read in certain places? Judging by several of these self-reflective accounts, that reason must involve to some extent satisfaction and emotional gratification. As Manguel observes: "there are books I read in armchairs, there are books I read at desks, there are books I read in subways, on streetcars and on buses" (1996: 151).

The majority of the above accounts come from literature and literary theory. However, cognitive psychology also has something to say about the role of bodily comfort in processing situations. Frijda, for example, suggests that bodily comfort is seen as one of the unlearned stimuli for positive emotions that can often be seen as an elicitor of desire (1986: 275). So, contrary to what one might think, one does not need to be tense in order to be ready for emotion. As Frijda has also pointed out, muscle tension and action readiness can be uncoupled, as indeed they are in various Eastern martial arts (1986: 91). This physiological state appears to fit the optimum condition needed for affective acts of literary reading. I believe that just as animals make a warm, safe nest for themselves, so too do we often go in search of the comfortable chair or snug bed when we want to create the optimal conditions both before and while reading literature. The desire to be emoted during literary reading therefore appears to go hand in hand with the preparatory need to position one's body in an optimally favoured space or location. In his *Poetics of Space* Bachelard writes of the physical pleasure experienced when we consider withdrawing into a favourite corner or space. He alludes as well to the primal, animal-like nature of this procedure (1958: 91).

The significance of the physical position and location of one's body in all kinds of acts of perception and remembering is something that has been highlighted in the text processing work of Walter Kintsch. In *Comprehension* Kintsch reflects on how the self is represented in working memory. He says that this "sense of self" is not fixed or vivid, rather it is being constantly reconstructed. More specifically, Kintsch also suggests that a person's memory content is determined by his/her physical location: "the memories that make up myself are probably not entirely the same when I am at home with my family or when I am speaking at a professional meeting" (1998: 411). If this is true, then LRI in a place of comfort will differ from LRI in an ad hoc reading environment. In order for all this to work, short-term memory must also have somatic markers continually present together with other more loadable and re-loadable cognitive ones (1998: 410). This is something I believe is true and will attempt to model in the final chapter of this work.

Kintsch also points out that the sense that we have of our own body is context-dependent: "there is the constant background feeling of one's body—its position, tone and feeling. There is the self that is reading" (1998: 411). This is essentially Damasio's notion of "somatic markers": the idea that the body develops specific feelings associated with certain cognitive tasks. Of course, if we assume that somatic markers are an essential aspect of working memory, then we must also conclude that bodily feeling becomes an important aspect of knowledge, beliefs, perception and language, as Damasio cogently argues throughout *Descartes' Error*. Convincing evidence that language and the body are linked is provided by cognitive linguistics, not least by the works of Lakoff and Johnson (1980; 1999), Johnson (1987) and Gibbs (2006). If we were to take this and apply it, not just to everyday occurrences of discourse comprehension, as Kintsch does, but also to literary ones, this would show how the location of a reading event will help determine which somatic nodes in long-term memory are primed for activation. For example, reading while sitting in a favourite comfortable chair in a trusted environment will in all probability lead to quite different mind-fed inputs from reading in a sterile, unfamiliar setting. These affective cognitive, somatic inputs, which may change the affective content of a reading experience, will have their own form and content irrespective of the genre, content and style of the literary text that is to follow. So reading a novel, for example, as part of an experiment in a laboratory or classroom is unlikely to produce the same LRI content, and all the affective and somatic aspects that go into it, that reading at home would. In sum, bodily comfort appears to be a significant component of affective cognition in literary reading processes. But how valid is this claim? Let us look at some reader responses on the matter of location.

**NRQ—Q.6    If You Want to Read a Novel That You Have
Very Much Looked Forward to Reading, Does it Matter to You,
and to the Quality of Your Subsequent Reading Experience,
Where You Actually Read it, i.e. Where You Decided to
Physically Put/Position your Body for the Reading Process?**

Twenty-seven of the thirty-six subjects responded affirmatively. Twenty-two subjects opted to give a written response.

1. If I want to read a book I've really looked forward to I find myself a quiet place where I can sit comfortably and where I will not be disturbed. I would never read such a book for instance on the train because then I am not really able to "dive" into the book

2. When I am in a comfortable situation (not too much noise, etc) I can concentrate much better which makes me enjoy reading more

3. I would not be able to concentrate on reading a book elsewhere than in my room. Especially if it is a book I have been looking forward to reading. I am even used to locking my door while reading

4. The place where I decide to sit should be somewhere comfortable where I can curl up and read the book in peace; for instance, a couch or a big deep chair. Also, the spot should be in the sunlight; in natural light

5. I would want to read that novel in either a very comfy chair or love seat or in bed at night. I cannot just sit down in the train and read it. I get too distracted to be able to fully enjoy the novel

6. It has to be somewhere reasonably comfortable and for me it is also important that I know I'll have plenty of time to read (that I don't have something urgent to do or have be somewhere in an hour or so). That also has to do with the place; it's nice when it's somewhere where I'm not very likely to be interrupted, somewhere not very crowded or loud

7. I have experienced that I can't read in places where there is a lot of noise as good as I can in silent places. Also reading in bed or in hot/sunny places makes me feel tired and decreases my attention

8. It is more relaxed to read a book sitting on the couch, than it is when you are sitting in a car. I always prefer reading a book in the garden when the sun shines, this makes it possible for me to really "get into" the book

9. I cannot start reading a book that I have looked forward to just anywhere. I need to be at home and also need to have some time so that I can read at least the first few chapters before having to put it down again

10. I always wonder how people can read in trains, busses and aeroplanes. I have tried doing so many times but have never really enjoyed it. I tend to be easily distracted by people and things around me and then

I need to reread parts of what I have read because I cannot continue reading while knowing that I have not completely absorbed those parts. I always have the fear of having missed something that is crucial for the story. I do like reading outside, for instance at the beach, but then early in the morning or late at night—again to make sure that there are not too many people there to invade my reading experience. In the U.S. I used to love reading in the college church and in the stacks of the library. Also, at the fountain, because the constant sound of water had a soothing effect

11. The place I always do all my reading is in bed. I like to make it comfy and cosy and cuddle up big time with lots of pillows and blankets/ covers and hot chocolate

12. If I look forward to reading a book, I want to take the time to read it. I probably won't start reading it in the metro or something, or somewhere very noisy, where I will get distracted but somewhere I can pay all my attention to the book. Probably my couch or my bed

13. I like to read when I am on vacation in quiet places with not too many people bothering me. I also like to read at home, alone, in bed. Some people I know read when they take the tram to work or to the university but for me that's not quiet enough

14. When I look forward to reading a book, let's say the new Harry Potter, I want to give it my full attention. I don't want to miss a thing. So I read it when I'm alone. I probably won't answer the phone when I want to spend a couple of hours reading. I don't want to be disturbed

15. I love to read in bed or in a place where I feel safe. But I do read in planes and on trains as well. These last two probably out of boredom, and to keep my mind busy to prevent thinking about "what will happen if" scenarios. I definitely prefer the former: in bed and places where I feel safe

16. It has to be quiet and comfortable, i.e. a sofa

17. I read best when I am alone with some very soft music in the background, either in a comfortable chair or on the balcony in the sun. Sometimes I can enjoy reading on the train but there is often too much noise and talk to concentrate for long

18. I like to lie down on the sofa or in bed with lots of cushions. I need to be nice and comfortable. And have my feet up

19. I read best when I am at home on the sofa or in bed. When I start reading a novel that I really want to read then I almost always start at home. When I am sitting for example in a metro/train, I can't concentrate that well. With a really good novel I want to be able to concentrate really well, because I don't want to miss one word of it

20. I usually read in or on my bed, either in the evening before going to sleep or during the day (for lack of a chair or couch). I tend to really "install" myself, complete with a cup of tea, cushions at my back, feet up and music on

22. When I read I prefer to lie on my bed or sit in a comfy chair where I can relax
23. I think when starting to read a novel that I have been looking forward to I would like to be in a place where I feel comfortable and peaceful. I have to be able to focus my attention and let go the ego to become part of a story which is different to mine

Embodied in the central question to which my subjects responded was my assumption that the place a person decides to position their body in prior to reading literature would be of importance to the reading event itself. From my subsequent observations, it became clear that especially the notions of comfort, solitude, silence and good light would play a significant role in the positioning of the body. Several of the responses above seemed to agree with this. My comfort claims, echoing the personal experiences of Manguel, and the writer Colette, in her *bateau-lit*, and Frijda's ideas on bodily comfort as a stimulus of positive emotion and desire, might be divided into two categories: comfort in the sense of relaxation and comfort in the sense of consolation. Several subjects appeared to support this in their responses. Some of the better examples included responses 15, 18, 19 and 20.

I also suggested that in addition to the bed, the "comfortable chair" would also be a popular place of reading. Responses in support of this included numbers 4, 5, and 21. Further, some readers exhibited what might be termed "Elkin-like obsessiveness" with their acts of reading in bed, for example, responses 3, 9 and 11. Implicitly the role of the "locative body" in language processing suggested in several of these responses also lends weight to both Kintsch's fluvial sense of self and Damasio's observations on the importance of somatic markers. My solitude prediction, echoing Colette that readers would "seek out a solitary space" found some support too. The response data, however, was not as compelling as I had anticipated, although there were some comments that did appear to support my claim. Some of the better examples include numbers 6, 7 and 14. Some responses even combined both notions of comfort and solitude; these included numbers 1, 2, 4, 13, 16 and 22.

In conclusion of this section, some support has been found for my assumptions. Of course, there were also responses that rejected them. These included subjects who read "on planes and trains" (response 15) and "with the music on" (response 20). By and large though, these appear to be in the minority, in this group at least. Hence, we can make a tentative suggestion, as in the case for mood, that location might very well be a key affective cognitive pre-reading input in the literary reading experience that can influence meaning-making and the reception process as a whole. I therefore I go some way towards agreeing with Manguel that "often, the pleasure derived from reading, largely depends on the bodily comfort of the reader" (1996: 151).

It is proper, however, to end this section on a note of caution, because there is counter evidence out there in the world that should not be ignored.

For example, comfort and solitude might not have to fit the reading location for an appropriate reading experience to take place. Moreover, what most of us consider as "comfortable" will not be the same for everyone. This can be individually or culturally determined. For instance, I was recently confronted with two cases of "bicycle-reading", which, although they are perhaps anomalies, have had some impact on my thinking with regard to comfort and location. I spotted my first bicycle reader in May 2006 in Zeeland in The Netherlands while looking out of the window of a train. There was a bicycle path parallel to the rails where a cyclist was reading a book in the afternoon sun—while cycling. I was very surprised, but on reflection convinced myself that he probably knew that no-one would be travelling in the opposite direction and that if he just kept cycling in a straight line while reading he would be safe. I therefore discounted this incongruity. However, later that same year in December I saw a young woman in the east end of Amsterdam cycling along a busy road in the cold and rain engrossed in a book. Although these are oddities—and perhaps even cultural oddities related to the prevalence of cycling in a flat country like the Netherlands— the reality of the "bicycle reader" shows that my comments and findings on the reading location in this chapter are neither absolute nor exclusive.

Somewhat similarly, the tactile aspect of grasping, bending and folding a book may also be but a temporary or cultural phenomenon, because we appear to be on the threshold of a hardware e-book revolution. In a 2006 newspaper article by Robert McCrum, he maintained that world of publishing stands on the cusp of the greatest innovation since Guttenberg. He posed the telling question that with cheap, portable electronic readers just around the corner, what is the future for the printed book? Similarly, in November 2007 the world's largest on-line bookseller Amazon launched the *Kindle*: an e-reader that, according to the makers "disappears in your hands, like a real book and does not get in the way of the reading".[5] Amazon is also in the process of reissuing many books in digital/e-form to run on its hardware, and the Kindle has already gone through a couple of upgrades since 2007. Are we at the start of a slow beginning, leading to a rapid evolution, before e-readers become ubiquitous? The battle lines have been drawn but at the end of the first decade of the twenty-first century the outcome regarding the rise of the e-reader is still uncertain. Developments in the next ten years will determine (a) whether digital books will dominate the market, (b) whether they will share it with hard copy analogue versions or (c) whether the e-reader will disappear as quickly as it arrived. In spite of my own current beliefs and preferences, as can be gleaned from this chapter, the latter of these, it has to be said, is least likely of all.

# 5 The Affective Nature of Literary Themes

In our journey so far, we have looked at LRI, mood and location, all of which are primarily non-textual phenomena. It is now time to focus more on the text itself and in particular on literary themes and their affective nature. We might start by posing the question, how important are literary themes to the process of meaning making? Themes such as (i) childhood, (ii) primary caregivers (i.e. the mother), (iii) the home, and (iv) death. We might also ask about the affective nature of other, less obvious, literary themes, such as (v) a sense of nostalgia / a feeling of distance, and (vi) the notion of incommunicability. We might even pose a far more challenging question, namely, are such themes always triggered from the page, bottom-up, while reading, or can they also come from the mind in a top-down fashion? Before addressing these questions, let us start with a story, and perhaps unexpectedly, a non-fictive one.

There used to be a popular BBC Sunday morning television programme called *Heaven and Earth*, which had a weekly spot called "sacred places". British celebrities were invited to go back to a location in their lives that meant a lot to them. Despite the religious connotations of the word "sacred" all of the celebrities chose secular locations, ranging from old houses to football stadiums. However, almost all of these locations were places that the celebrities remembered from their childhood; a time when mortality was still largely unknown to them. One particular week the guest was the actor Frances Barber, who took a camera crew to Portmeirion in Wales, where she used to spend her annual summer vacation with her parents.[1] The piece began with Barber conducting an interview in which she told about lots of things including how as a nine-year-old girl she remembered thinking that God lived in the large house in the centre of the village. Then, with the camera still running and still in the middle of her narrative, she stopped speaking. Her mind appeared to focus on more immediate matters: the kind of dilemmas that many adults experience at some stage of their life. The camera continued to roll as she remained silent. After a while Barber said she wished she were back in Portmeirion again, not as an adult, as she is now, but rather as a nine-year-old girl. The reason behind this desire, she went on to say, was not to be young again and have her life over, but rather so that she could once again hold the hand of her long-dead mother. She then started to weep. When she had stopped, the reporter asked her when she would return to her "sacred place" again. Barber answered, not for a long while, if indeed ever.

This anecdote may seem insignificant or even somewhat trite, but it touches on a deeply philosophical question: could it be that no matter how old we are we may at times long to return to familiar and trusted locations of our childhood? This is something that, barring a traumatic childhood, might be felt by many adults. It may especially the case in adults who read literature or who engage regularly with other indistinct art forms that impinge less on the visual sense and more on the somatic ones and even auditory ones such as music. In the above example, we see how Barber's heightened sense of emotion, triggered by a physical return to a favourite childhood location, brought with it the memory of the primary caregiver, in this case the mother. The childhood location and primary caregiver appear to blend into a single concept. This is, as we saw, what Bachelard suggested, especially with regard to memories and mental images associated with poetic reading. Perhaps, not so coincidentally, the word "mother" topped a list of most beautiful words in the English language.[2]

Memories of childhood locations, like the ones experienced in LRI, whether they be holiday or home, interior or exterior, appear somehow to be locked into a perennial blend with our primary caregivers and protectors. In the above example this conscious "longing to return" came out in a television interview. I argue throughout this work that the place *par excellence* where this phenomenon frequently occurs is during engaged acts of literary reading, while immersed in the affective maelstrom of the subconscious mind, and especially during heightened emotive moments of literary reading. It is the visually-indirect nature of literature that helps facilitate this. When I speak of a mnemonic "return" to childhood locations in the framework of literary reading, I do not mean specific, concrete places, for as we saw in Chapter 3 on LRI, the nature of human memory makes this impossible. Instead, during such "recollections" readers may be able to see themselves in their mind's eye, perhaps together with their mother or some other caregiver. Often, they will be in some form of rhythmic motion: running, skipping, climbing, or swinging: a kind of activity dominance hypothesis for literary reading. Indeed, one may recall some of the comments in the response data in Chapter 3 when students were asked to consider their first memories. These events can be any activity from rocking in a familiar chair or playing on a swing to walking along a familiar footpath, either alone or with some primary caregiver.

There is a link between what I have set out earlier on childhood and some findings in clinical neurology. The workings of the brain might not immediately seem to be central to childhood, but sometimes in adulthood we can gain fascinating neurobiological insights into its fundamental nature. In clinical psychology it has been observed that both damage to, and degeneration of, the brain can lead to a longing to return to the mother or primary caregiver and the locations of childhood. The result of this, as I will show later, is similar in some ways to the effects that literary reading, and especially heightened "epiphanic" emotive states of literary reading, can sometimes have on a reader.

Clinical neurologist, Oliver Sacks tells a story of a patient he once had called Mrs O'C. This lady lived in an old people's home in New York. As her brain degenerated, she started to suffer from something called ana-mnestic seizures, which, according to Sacks, "took her somewhere else". "I know you are there Dr. Sacks", she would say, "I know that I am an old woman with a stroke in an old people's home, but I feel I'm a child in Ireland again—I feel my mother's arms, I see her; I hear her voice singing" (Sachs 1985: 130). Another eminent clinical neurologist, Wilder Penfield said that such episodes are not hallucinations but "memories of the most precious kind, accompanied by the emotions which accompanied the origi-nal experience" (Sachs 1985: 130; see also Penfield and Perot 1963). Pen-field believed that the brain retained powerful emotive episodes throughout a person's life, which they were capable of evoking and re-experiencing under special circumstances in later life. I believe that highly emotive epi-sodes of literary reading are capable of tapping into this neural capacity. Somewhat similarly to Penfield, Esther Salaman has written in her 1970s work about "the necessity to preserve or recapture the sacred and precious memories of childhood" (Sachs 136–37; see also Salaman 1970). Speaking of the deep joys that such experiences can create, she also mentions how impoverished and ungrounded life can be without them: "we are all exiles from our lives" she says, "we need to recapture it" (cited in Sachs 137; see also Salaman 1970). Salaman, I believe, is alluding to the need to discover other means to reach such a state. One way in which it might be recaptured is to read literature, that most skeletal and affective-cognitive of art forms; for in doing so we experience intense emotive episodes through interac-tion with texts which are purposely designed, consciously or otherwise, to emote. The childhood home, whether it be the lack of one, the desire to have one or the longing to return to one, is a strong affective theme.

The notion of "the mother" in literary reading can refer to a mother, but it does not have to. It can refer to another primary caregiver like a father, grandparent or elder sibling. It can even go beyond this. There is an example in the literary work of the nineteenth-century Russian novelist Nikolai Leskov. In his famous essay "The Storyteller", Walter Benjamin speaks of how Leskov's numerous and varied characters "are unmistakably suffused with the imago of his mother" (1968: 103). Ben-jamin's claim here is that Leskov's mother was recognisable in all the characters in his works, whether they were male or female; young or old. Feeling the proximity of the mother, as we saw in the Barber episode, can often induce a sense of comfort. An associated idea can be found in psy-chology, where Frijda suggests the presence of the mother, together with comforting actions like rocking, can decrease fearfulness and distress in infants (1986: 284).

In cognitive linguistics, attention has been given to the related notion of "kinship". In *Death is the Mother of Beauty*, the cognitive linguist Mark Turner lists ways in which we routinely project stories of birth onto other stories in everyday language. He claims that "locations and situations give birth to occupants" and further that these locations have conditions "from which their occupants can spring" (1987: 28–29). Here, Turner sees location and mother as being two entities that under certain conditions can lose their boundaries and blend into one single concept. In effect, Barsalou's categories of "participant" and "location" become momentarily one. Indeed, Turner suggests that the idea of "mother" is usually employed to refer to a number of things, including "places" (1987: 56–57). He also notes that the dominant component of all these kinship metaphors is "feeling" (1987: 41), adding that at the heart of them "mother and child overwhelmingly dominate" (1987: 55).

In addition to the themes already discussed, the topic of death is also of significance in literature. In her literary critical work *Stabat Mater*, Julia Kristeva says that "man overcomes the unthinkable of death by postulating maternal love in its place—in the place and stead of death and thought. . . . Such a love is in fact, logically speaking, a surge of anguish at the very moment when the identity of thought and living body collapses" (1987: 170–72). So at the point of death, it is perhaps the mother, and the accompanying notion of childhood that the mind longs to return to. Similarly, Benjamin wrote "death is the sanction of everything that the storyteller can tell" (1968: 94); he adds: "what draws the reader to the novel is the hope of warming his shivering life with the death he reads about" (1968: 101). Can reading about the death of a literary character have a kind of preparatory function? Harold Bloom in *How to Read and Why* appears to think so when he suggests that "one of the uses of reading is to prepare ourselves for change, and the final change alas is universal" (2000: 21). In light of all the aforementioned, literary reading might be seen as both the midwife and mortician of human emotion. But what do real readers think about these themes and their affective power in literary reading? Let us look at the first group of four I introduced in the opening paragraph to this chapter, namely childhood, the home, the mother and death, and let us call them "primary" literary themes.

## NRQ—Q.12   Have the Themes of Childhood/Home/Mother/Death ever Affected You During Your Novel-reading Experiences?

The numerical outcome of the thirty-six subjects in the survey was as follows:

- Childhood = thirty-three affirmative responses

- The home = nineteen affirmative responses
- The mother = twenty-one affirmative responses
- Death = twenty-six affirmative responses

Before we discuss these, let us first look at the two other themes mentioned at the start of the chapter: (i) nostalgia/a sense of distance and (ii) the notion of incommunicability, and let us call these "secondary level" affective literary themes. Both of these embody a feeling of indistinctness, so let us begin there.

A sense of the indistinct can be said to be intrinsic to many aspects of literature. Consider, for instance, Grace Paley's short story "A Conversation with My Father". This text is about a woman, who, like Paley, is a writer. After a life of limited conversation with her father she is trying to break down that communicative barrier at the end of his life. At the beginning of the story, the old man is on his deathbed. Suddenly, he breaks the silence between them by making a final request of his daughter. Inverting the roles of the parent storyteller and the child listener, he asks his daughter to create for him "a simple story". He continues, "you know, the kind de Maupassant wrote, or Chekhov, the kind you used to write. Just recognizable people and then write down what happened to them next" (1981: 162). In writing this episode, Paley hits an appropriate note with regard to generating emotion in this reader at least, through some of the themes mentioned earlier.

Another similar affective narrative strategy that writers sometimes use is to present a death of such a "just recognisable" character in what can be called insert stories. Characters in these narrative asides often burst into the main narrative of the text in an unexpected and surprising manner. These embedded texts, which can be viewed as stories within stories, can have a prominent emotive effect on my reading and perhaps on that of other engaged readers too. This is perhaps because they are generally brief and often involve the death of the protagonist. An example that comes to mind is the Captain Brierly episode in Chapter 6 of Joseph Conrad's *Lord Jim* (1900/1983), where the seemingly well-respected officer inexplicably steps off the back of his ship one night while on watch. Another is the "wild child" episode in Alice Walker's *Meridian* about the poor parentless girl, who, while trying to cross the road after her first real meal in a long time, is slowed down by the unexpected weight of her stomach and is hit and killed by a speeding car (1976, 23–25). Another is the "tramp episode" in Willa Cather's *My Ántonia* (1918/1994) about the man who has just started working on the threshing machine when suddenly he stops his labour, waves to the other agrarians in the field and throws himself into the thresher (1994, 142–45). These insert stories and other like them can be said to have a similar pattern: a window is briefly opened onto a new story and just enough information is given to make a reader feel concerned about the well-being of certain "barely recognisable", micro-level protagonists; then, suddenly, that character is killed or kills himself/herself. It seems to me that the brevity, the fleetingness and the "just-recognisability" of such characters contributes to heightened emotive responses from engaged readers.

It is but a short step from the notion of the indistinct to that of distance—even if distant things are always indistinct, yet not all indistinct things are distant. Distance is a complex term in the context of art and philosophy. For instance, there is the traditional aesthetic notion of distance in the Kantian sense, i.e. as a disinterested contemplation supposedly independent of our personal feelings. There is also Wayne Booth's notion that authors manipulate readers with regard to character concerns as seen in his discussion of "the control of distance" in Jane Austen's *Emma* in Chapter 9 of *The Rhetoric of Fiction* (1961: 243–66). Further, there is Bertolt Brecht's *Verfremdung* technique in "Epic Theatre", pertaining to alienation and estrangement, the aim of which is more or less the opposite of Booth's idea, i.e. to make the familiar seem strange and in doing so prevent the audience from emotionally identifying with the characters on stage, thus producing a critical attitude that may lead to action. And there is T.S. Eliot's idea of the "objective correlative" from his 1919 essay "Hamlet and His Problems", at the heart of which lies the claim that in order to express an emotion in art the artist must first find an "objective correlative", i.e. a set of objects, a situation, a chain of events, which is the formula of that particular emotion. This is claimed to have the capacity to evoke the same emotion in the reader that the writer feels or wishes to convey.

What I mean by distance is something more akin to nostalgia and a sense of returning, as well as something that links it to the concepts of childhood, home, mother and death. In cognitive psychology, nostalgia is seen as:

> Awareness that something past, while desired, cannot be regained, except by maintaining proximity in thought. If search tendency nevertheless gets the upper hand, it turns into recurring grief; if impotence with respect to desire is added, it turns into belated painful suffering. (Frijda 1986: 76)

Linked to this distal theme is the notion of "stretching out", reaching out for something/somebody in order to be (re)united. Such episodes are also very often textually represented in literature. The stretching can be manual, but also visual or cognitive. A stock example is a character who does not want to die or be left alone. Even a dead person can long to return, as in Virgil's *The Aeneid*, where the throng of the dead in Hades on the bank of the river "stretch[ing] out their arms in longing for the further shore. But the grim boatman takes some here and some there, and others he pushes away far back from the sandy shore" (1990: Book VI, lines 314–18). Many aspects of stretching bear echoes of the famous story of Tantalus: a man bound to a post for his sins against the gods; "tantalisingly" just out of reach of food and water.

Certain aspects of my notion of distance also have some links to Scheff's previously mentioned work on catharsis. Particularly relevant is his idea that powerful emotions in the real world may be too overwhelming for us to cope with, and the best place to experience them therefore is in prose, poetry and drama, or other arts: this is the best or safest aesthetic distance. Some writers appear to share the essence of this idea. For example, as his sister Caroline lay dying, Gustave Flaubert wrote a letter dated 15 March 1846 to his friend Maxine du Camp saying "my own eyes are as dry as marble. It is strange how sorrows in fiction make me open up and overflow with feeling, whereas real sorrows remain hard and bitter in my heart, turning to crystal as soon as they arise" (cited in Unwin 2004). Another example of what Scheff means can be found in Benjamin's aforementioned essay "The Storyteller". There he ponders Michel de Montaigne's reflections on Herodotus's story of the Egyptian king Psammenitus who did not weep when his son was led away to be executed by Cambyses and his Persians. But when he noticed his old, faithful servant in the ranks of the prisoners, he "gave all the signs of deepest mourning—beat[ing] his fists against his head" (1954, Book Three, section fourteen). According to Herodotus, the great King Croesus—i.e. the legendary affluent Lydian ruler who famously ignored Solon's advice and then misinterpreted the oracle and as a result destroyed his own kingdom—also wept upon hearing this, as did the Persians who were present (1954, Book Three, section fourteen). Quoting de Montaigne's reflections, Benjamin comments that "since he was already overfull with grief, it only took the smallest increase for it to burst through its dams", adding "great grief is pent up and breaks forth only with relaxation" (1968: 90). Hence, having seen his son led away to be murdered, the sight of the servant was for the king a kind of "relaxation". Echoing de Montaigne, Benjamin writes: "we are moved by much on the stage that does not move us in real life" (1968: 90).

The seeming denial of emotion, which bears traces of Stoicism, leads to empathy, as we realise through experience that a person who cannot grieve openly is a person who is hurting inwardly. On the face of it, in emotive terms, Stoicism also represents a form of distance taking, which seems quite affective in its very denial of emotion. Think, for example, of the very stoic, yet still very emotive, butler, Stevens in Kazuo Ishiguro's novel *The Remains of the Day* (and also Anthony Hopkins's portrayal this character in the film adaptation), who refuses to grieve, even when his father dies, and instead continues with his duties. It seems that it is the lack of communication that creates the distance.

A sense of incommunicability emerges when words cannot express the true affective content of that which we wish to convey. In some sense it is akin to the style figure aposiopesis. The idea of being "lost for words" is something that is often played on in highly emotive episodes in novels. Below is an example of how this works in F. Scott Fitzgerald's *The Great Gatsby* (1925/1992). This example also shows how the theme of the incommunicable can blend with those of distance, reaching out and the indistinct:

> Through all he said, even through his appalling sentimentality, I was reminded of something—an elusive rhythm, a fragment of lost words, that I had heard somewhere a long time ago. For a moment a phrase tried to take shape in my mouth and my lips parted like a dumb man's, as though there was more struggling upon them than a wisp of startled air. But they made no sound, and what I had almost remembered was uncommunicable forever. (1992: 107)

This is not unique. Here is a similar example, this time from Willa Cather's *My Ántonia* (1918/1994):

> The feelings of that night were so near that I could reach out and touch them with my hand. I had the sense of coming home to myself, and having found out what a little circle man's experience is. For Ántonia and for me, this had been the road of Destiny; had taken us to those early accidents of fortune which predetermined for us all that we can ever be. Now I understood that the same road was to bring us together again. Whatever we had missed, we possessed together the precious, the incommunicable past. (1994: 288–89)

I should say at this juncture that these two examples were for me initially sign-fed, i.e. I learned about them from the page. This is not remarkable. However, I have come to know them so well that they now somehow occupy an in between space: caught between words on the page and text fragments in my mind. Of course, when I read them again it is primarily a sign-fed procedure, as I process the discourse with my saccadic-driven eye movement. However, when I am reading new novels and similar themes to these are evoked, either by textual elements or by emotive and somatic inputs in my mind, the skeletal themes of such acts of incommunicability somehow get projected into my literary comprehension maelstrom. Exactly how this is possible and what is happening in cognitive and neural terms I shall try to explain in Chapter 7 of this work. For now, let us look at what other readers think of the affective power of this second set of literary themes that we have been discussing here.

## NRQ—Q.12   Have the Themes of Incommunicability, Distance or Sense of Returning/Nostalgia Ever Affected You During Your Novel Reading Experiences?

The numerical outcome of the thirty-six subjects in the survey was as follows:

- Distance/a sense of returning/nostalgia = twenty-nine affirmative responses
- Incommunicability = sixteen affirmative responses

In referring to these themes as "secondary", my general expectation was that there would be far fewer affirmative responses than occurred in the previous "primary" themes group. The topic of incommunicability has affirmed this expectation, but the theme of distance/returning/nostalgia has not. Before we look further at this, let us consider the response results to some further related thematic literary categories that I also put to the group of thirty-six readers. If the first group of four were termed primary, and the second group of two, secondary, let us simply call these extra four categories "other". They are (vii) exterior childhood locations, (viii) the father figure, (ix) siblings, and (x) the literary notion of "promises".

- Exterior childhood locations = nineteen affirmative responses
- Fathers = nineteen affirmative responses
- Siblings = thirteen affirmative responses
- Promises = twelve affirmative responses

Let us now view at all ten thematic categories that we called primary, secondary and other (marked with a P, S or O below). They have been place in the number of affirmative responses received from the group of readers. For clarity, I have also placed a percentage next to the total.

| | | |
|---|---|---|
| 1. Childhood (P) | 33/36 | 91% |
| 2. Distance/a sense of returning/nostalgia) (S) | 29/36 | 81% |
| 3. Death (P) | 26/36 | 72% |
| 4. The mother (P) | 21/36 | 58% |
| 5. The childhood home (inside) (P) | 19/36 | 53% |
| 6. The childhood home (outside) (O) | 19/36 | 53% |
| 7. The father (O) | 19/36 | 53% |
| 8. The incommunicable (S) | 16/36 | 44% |
| 9. Siblings (O) | 13/36 | 36% |
| 10. Promises (O) | 12/36 | 33% |

This work does not rely on any kind of quantitative methods, so I will not dwell on these numbers, but will instead move on to view the qualitative data. All we can say about the above is that very generally speaking my "primary", "secondary" and "other" categories do not appear to be absurdly wide of the mark when compared with the affective thematic choices of this group of thirty-six readers. The notion of childhood seems most important for this group of readers. One noticeable thing, however, is that the secondary category of distance/a sense of returning/nostalgia is much more prominent than I had anticipated.

A very important aspect of this question was that the subjects were also invited, indeed encouraged, to list as many affective themes as they wanted that were not in my three lists that they had received in the questionnaire. There were twenty-three, quite varied, new categories supplied by the readers. I will not discuss them all here, just the ones that received more than one mention. The highest were the literary thematic categories of "love" and "friendship", both with six mentions each out of thirty-six. These were followed by "loss" and "lovers" with three mentions each. Lastly, the three themes of "war", "illness" and "religion" all received two mentions. Also, a small number of subjects (just three) opted to add an additional comment, which was not explicitly asked for in the NRQ at this stage.

1. I think that any theme that is close to me will affect me, as long as it is well written
2. Sickness is important for me because I spent a great deal of time in hospitals when I was young because my mother was ill. This theme can make me forget about what I am reading and can make me drift away to think about old memories
3. Most of the themes above that I have answered with "yes" have affected me, especially when in the novel the themes were surrounded with sad events, e.g. a mother's death, not being able to go back home, etc.

It is time now to move on from this discussion about possible primary and secondary themes and look at other aspects of the affective nature of literary topics and get some more feedback from my group of literary readers on what they feel and think about literary themes as affective prompts. We have two sets of response data below that may suggest some further lines of enquiry on sign-fed (bottom-up) and mind-fed (top-down) thematic prompts.

## NRQ—Q. 11 Do You Think That Certain Themes in a Novel, That Appear both Throughout a Novel and at the Closure of a Novel, Can Affect Your Emotional Mood During the Actual Reading Process Itself?

Thirty of the thirty-six subjects responded affirmatively. Twenty-two of those subjects also opted chose to supply a comment.

1. Maybe it is not themes as such but the way themes are portrayed
2. If it is a theme that you already know a lot about, you know how it feels, and you feel the same emotions that you felt when you had that experience
3. If a certain theme really affects you, then it affects your mood during the reading process

4. Only themes I can relate to

5. The more I can relate to a theme or the more the author draws me into a theme, the more I get involved in a novel and this naturally affects my emotions. When I'm involved I start to feel with the characters

6. Of course I have preferences for themes that touch my heart or my mind and even put me in the mood for reading

7. A theme that maybe I have experienced or find interesting will affect my mood. I get back the memory or feeling that belongs with my mood. A theme can speak to you; you can get more in the book because of the theme

8. A book that tells a love story can trigger feelings or ideas about love. It is the memories or ideas that are derived from a certain theme that can alter the mood of a reader. Projection of the story onto the past experiences of the reader can direct the reader's emotions

9. Reading a novel will make me feel calm. The atmosphere of a book may act as an example; one may find oneself trying to recreate an atmosphere from a novel in your own life

10. They show what is important in a novel. As a reader, they make me think more deeply about a novel. This evokes memories as well as emotions that are triggered by the same themes in books I've read in the past. I have thoughts like, yes, this is important, this is what it's about, this is where it all comes together

11. If the themes are very important in your life, it will affect your reading because you feel a strong emotion towards it. Especially if that theme comes back at the end of the book, because that's usually the conclusion, and you'll remember that best

12. Themes in novels can definitely affect my emotional mood. When the theme is funny, it makes me happy. When the theme is sad (e.g. about death, loss, etc.) it can certainly make me feel sad too. This emotion is never long lasting though

13. Books can make me cry and laugh out loud. A theme would remind me of certain things in my own life, so in that sense it is different from just laughing because something funny is happening. It would be more emotional because if that happens; it's not something that is over and done with quickly. It will make me reflect on what's happened in my own life as well

14. Certain themes may trigger memories and therefore affect my emotional mood

15. If you read a book, themes can change your mood

16. If a theme keeps on returning, it's bound to linger in your head. Some themes can also make you change the way you see things or want to see things. They make you think about life

17. Especially if these themes are present in your own life as well. You will read it with more personal interest. Reflect on it more

18. It depends on the theme. Some themes that are important in a novel and are central to the story will affect me, but it does not depend on the place in the novel, either throughout or at the end of the novel. A change of sad themes and happy themes also make me feel sad at one moment and happy at another. Quick changes between themes that differ cause quick changes in emotion during the reading process

19. If a theme is obvious, it annoys me, like with some Disney films, when you can see the morals dripping from the narrative. If it is done subtly, I'm usually not annoyed by it. If it's a good theme, I'll even like it

20. A theme might remind you of something that has happened to you or some emotion you are struggling with, and in my experience your mood will then definitely change while still reading the novel

21. Especially when a theme is close to home, it tends to get me in an emotional state. It may remind me of past experiences, people I knew, places I have visited, etc.

Many of these responses suggest that the sign-fed aspect of themes can affect a person's mood and thus the reading experience as a whole. Two of the best examples are response number 8 "a book that tells a love story can trigger feelings or ideas about love" and number 13 "themes in novels can definitely affect my emotional mood". However, consider response 11, which states "themes show what is important in a novel. As a reader, they make me think more deeply about a novel. This evokes memories as well as emotions that are triggered by the same themes in books I've read in the past". This is clearly a kind of intertextuality. However, what is remarkable is that a number of book-related themes seem already primed in the working memory of this reader, plausibly ready to flow into conscious meaning-making. If there are, these will in all likelihood be themes that have affected this person before while reading literature. This sentiment is echoed in the words of respondent seventeen, who says "if a theme keeps on returning, it's bound to linger in your head". However, if affective, book-related themes "linger in your head", to cite the respondent, then might those affect-laden themes not get subconsciously loaded in the buffer-zones of working memory prior to a new act of reading? And further, might they not on occasion get deployed *in anticipation of* textual themes, as well as in response to them? I believe they can.

There were other interesting responses in this data. Respondent four, for instance, claimed he/she could become emoted "only with themes he/she can relate to", which highlights the importance of themes in the mind for "best emotive fit". Response number two appears to link themes to a kind of mood-congruity effect. Bartlett's idea that personal past experiences help determine new ones seems to appear in responses 2, 4 and 5, whereas response number 12 stressed the importance of affective themes at the end of a novel. Others suggested (i) how affective themes can alter moods during reading (responses 5, 8 and 21); (ii) how themes can prepare the way for affective reading (response 6); (iii) how themes can help match memory to mood (response 7) and, (iv) how the whole process can channel certain emotions (response 8).

What I earlier referred to as primary affective themes are also visible in some responses. For example, respondent twenty-two writes: "especially when a theme is close to home, it tends to get me in an emotional state. It may remind me of past experiences, people I knew, places I have visited, etc." In addition, the sheer power of affective themes as a meaning-making input during reading is evident in many different ways. Three of these are (i) the power to induce full and observable emotions of laughing and crying (response 14); (ii) the power to evoke contemplation (response eighteen), and (iii) the power to quickly register alternating affective themes in literature (response nineteen). In sum, and paraphrasing the words in response number 13, themes in novels can definitely affect the emotional mood of readers. With this data in mind, and the idea that themes might not be entirely textual, let us now look at the responses to a second question I posed.

## NRQ—Q. 13 Do You Think That Any of the Above Themes Can be Evoked in a Reader's Mind Even if They are not Mentioned Directly in the Text? (For Example, is it Possible That a Novel Can Invoke in you Memories of Your Childhood, Even if the Passage You are Reading is not Specifically About a Child or a Childhood Event?)[3]

Thirty-four of the thirty-six subjects responded affirmatively. Twenty-nine subjects chose to respond. Three questions are of interest here. First, is there support in this data for the kind of themes mentioned in this chapter operating in an anticipatory, top-down-first fashion? Second, can thematic issues be evoked during literary reading independent of matching textual cues? And third, might themes somehow be permanently active in the subconscious mind of the avid reader? Here is the raw data.

1. It can be anything. Even one word can trigger a memory. Everyone has different memories and experiences so for everyone it is different
2. I associate certain distinct emotions for example with childhood; the similarity between the two would make me remember
3. I think that it triggers you subconsciously, even though you are not aware of it
4. It works because you connect it to other things that are happening and from there you make another link e.g. to a childhood event
5. I don't think that memory works in the sense that when you read about something that you've experienced yourself, you immediately think about it. It's more certain feelings, details, moods, weather conditions and stuff like that that make you remember things

6. I think that when a book describes places or even meals or nature it evokes a feeling. For example, when a reader reads about some special thing, which he then immediately associates with a memory

7. It might be even colours, sounds, music or smells that can evoke a certain memory

8. I believe that anything that is directly or indirectly hinted at in a text can have an impact because everything is there for a reason. Any well-seasoned reader should recognise his

9. I think that the atmosphere described, or even smaller things in the text, can invoke emotions and memories that on the surface have nothing to do with the text

10. It works by association. This could be anything. The description of a smell or a specific place or building can evoke some event that has occurred in that same place or in the period that the place was visited. The text is merely a trigger to free association

11. I think when a situation, conversation, location or other things are described in a novel it can remind you of something. Maybe because of what someone says, what someone is wearing, how someone looks, a feeling, just about anything. In daily life, it works the same. When somebody is mentioning something it can remind you of something that has nothing to do with it or what looks like nothing to do with it. But many things in life can remind you of your own experiences, and I think that this is the same way it works in novels. A feeling or person or whatever can remind you of a lot of things, of memories

12. If what is described triggers a memory or a chain of memories then it brings you further back

13. Even little things that happen in a book can evoke memories of other things

14. If I read something that reminds me of something that theme gets evoked in my head. Every theme can be evoked in a person's head if one gets reminded of it somehow. It can happen because of all sorts of "links"

15. I think that small things can evoke certain memories or associations, which have nothing to do with the thing that started the first memory

16. Idiosyncratic associations. It can't be explained how the mind works

17. Certain parts of books can remind you about your childhood even if they are not about childhood

18. Maybe through word association, i.e. a certain word in a text makes you think of something else, etc. and then you end up, for example, at some event from your childhood

19. I think that as a reader you connect to a lot of emotions experienced by characters in a novel, and you don't compartmentalise, so to speak. If an emotion that a character is feeling is not connected to their childhood, or there is no childhood involved, then that doesn't stop you

as a reader from connecting it to your own childhood or an emotion experienced by you as a child

20. All a text has to do is present you with the right kind of circumstances or the right situation
21. Human beings have a great gift of being able to use "free association" whenever they feel like it. About places and people in novels, there are always aspects that we can identify with, and that makes us think of places and people that we ourselves have known or still know
22. When reading the passage something is triggered in your memory, by means of a word or the feeling it gives you while reading it
23. Maybe because of one trying to get into the story, to feel what is supposed to be felt, but sometimes it fails and you think something else
24. Definitely. The smallest word or utterance might recall an event or an experience from a long time ago. For example, if a character utters a word that your mum always used in her conversations (or perhaps only once), it might make you think of her, even though mums are not in any way present in the book. That's how the mind works—through weird associations
24. If a novel gives the reader a certain feeling about something he/she is reading, this feeling can be the same as you've experienced before, like in your childhood
26. Anything can make you think of your childhood. A direct link is not necessary. It can be a thought, an occasion, anything really
27. Sometimes you just associate random things with each other. I don't know how it works. I think that it is probably specific words that trigger certain memories. Or maybe in a more roundabout way, e.g. when a specific song is mentioned in a novel, you might think about where you heard it first. I also think that reading books in a language that you didn't grow up with makes it more difficult to get childhood memories triggered
28. I think that when you read a book you reflect on your own experience to understand the book, to follow the story and the characters. So when a theme or an event in a novel is much like something you have gone through yourself, you reflect on that experience even if it is not explicit in the text itself
29. When a passage describes something that is familiar to you because you have experienced it in your childhood, you will go back to this when you read it in the novel, even if it is not specifically about childhood in the passage/story

In response to my first question is there indeed support in this data of the kind of themes mentioned in this chapter operating in an anticipatory, top-down-first fashion? If there were, this would go against much of the received wisdom in discourse processing. The data are inconclusive but there are some interesting remarks for us to consider. For instance, response five mentions meteorological conditions prior to the reading as a possible determining factor. This respondent also goes on to mention "feelings, details and moods". Respondent nine emphasises the role that "the atmosphere" can play, as well as "smaller things in the text". Although such "smaller elements" are still sign-fed prompts, the distance seems to be closing.

In response to my second question, did any specific themes play a role as mind-based top-down inputs? Again, the data are inconclusive. However, places, locations and buildings are mentioned in responses 6, 10, 11 and 21. The last of these also mentions "clothing" and "(facial) features", perhaps of a loved one; of a past primary caregiver, and perhaps not. Response twenty-one also refers to "people that we ourselves have known or still know" being evoked by "free association" while reading. The "mother" (mum) and "'her conversations" is mentioned explicitly in response 24, even when "mums are not in any way present in the book". Conversations are also mentioned in response 11. Responses 17, 26 and 29 contain rich data pertaining to childhood and do suggest that linguistic prompts might not be necessary. However, we must be very careful about jumping to conclusions here as the example given in the question to help the subjects in the survey might very well have subconsciously prompted aspects of their responses.

So can thematic issues be evoked during literary reading independent of matching textual cues? In asking this I am trying to draw a link to Bartlett, Kintsch, van den Broek et al., etc. As we saw in Chapters 2 and 3, all these scholars ask how concepts can be evoked in the reading process independent of direct textual cues. Indeed Chapter 1 established an important link between long-term memory and short-term memory in terms of "retrieval structures". As we saw, Kintsch argues that retrieval structures are activated by cues in short-term memory so that one such cue can activate a whole event or episode in a relatively wholesale manner. In this sense, as he explains, all of our memories are potentially just one step away: they can be retrieved in one operation by a single cue. Kintsch also points out that such structures do not occur naturally, but have to be learned through repetition and practice. He also suggests that in a familiar domain the expert reader does not even need inferences from the text for a familiar retrieval structure to be activated immediately. Not only does such information not have to be inferred, it does not even have to be installed in short-term memory or consciousness.

At least nine of the responses are interesting in this respect. Response 22, for example, speaks of how the "feeling" a word imparts can trigger things in memory rather than the word itself, while response 14 speaks of "reminders" in a similar way. "Associations" that are "idiosyncratic" (response 16) or "small"/"little" (responses 13 and 15) can also trigger memories. Response 8 suggests further that anything either "directly or indirectly hinted at in a text can have an impact". This respondent goes on to suggest that the avid ("well-seasoned") reader should recognise this.

Response 9 focuses on the evocative power of the "atmosphere" in a text for evoking "emotions and memories that on the surface have nothing to do with the text". Finally, response 10 reports the text "as a mere trigger to free association". This associative aspect is also prominent in responses 18, 21 and 24. So perhaps literary texts may not always need words and themes as prompts? Maybe all they need to do is to "provide you with the right kind of circumstances and situation", as respondent twenty in the data set notes.

Lastly, let me move to my third and final question in this section, namely, might themes somehow be permanently active in the subconscious mind of the avid reader? This might be seen to be a kind of preparatory reading mode. Such themes might not just get cued when a subconscious decision is "taken" to engage with art, whether it be an indirect form like literature or music, or a more direct one like visual art or film, but rather they are continually cued. Indeed, they might even already be being channelled into the subconscious mind as we saw was the case in Libet's previously mentioned psychological experiments. In practice it is difficult to answer yes or no because it is hard to gather valid data owing to the subtleness and elusiveness of the topic, and that fact that we are not aware of what our subconscious mind is doing. The data thus tells us little on this point, although one respondent wrote "I think that it triggers you subconsciously, even though you are not aware of it". Whether he/she can be sure of this, we cannot yet know. What we do know, with increasing certainty, is that themes matter; that they form real affective inputs in the literary reading adventure and, that unlike what we might think, themes are not just about words on the page, but also about neurons in the brain.

# 6    From Style on the Page to Style in the Mind

Style is the fifth and final affective input in literary reading that we will look at. Of all the phenomena discussed thus far, style can be said to be the most textual, or sign-fed, of all. The main questions that I will explore in this chapter include: (i) Can literary style evoke and channel emotion? (ii) Are there certain style and grammar elements that can be termed "distal" that might help this process? And, most perhaps contentious of all, (iii) Can certain aspects of style be viewed as initially mind-fed. By this, I mean can highly skeletal echoes of previous styles, structures and rhythms that have affected a reader in the past be subconsciously channelled and brought to bear on concrete sign-fed, textual aspects of style during engaged acts of literary reading. In order to explore all this, let us first set out some background by looking at emotion in three related contexts, namely, those of general linguistics, stylistics and rhythm.

Emotion has figured prominently in a number of recent linguistic theories. In systemic functional linguistics, for example, emotion, in the guise of feeling, plays a role in the mental category of Michael Halliday's grammar of experience, together with thinking and seeing (1994: 108). It also plays a part in his discussion of the ideational metafunction of language (1994: 179). Similarly, emotion is viewed in discourse analysis as a key communicative concept. The expression of feelings and attitudes is deemed to be a significant component in both verbal and written communication, especially within a framework of subjectivity and interpersonal discourse functions. One such component is *intensity markers*, which can be defined as affective linguistic devices. Randolph S. Quirk, et al. list these words in three groups: "hedges" (e.g. rather, perhaps, etc.), "emphasisers" (e.g. primarily, certainly, etc.), and "amplifiers" (e.g. extremely and absolutely). According to Georgakopoulou and Goutsos, intensity markers can include verbs, adjectives and adverbs that encode the speaker's emotions, feelings, moods and general dispositions (1997: 138). In addition to intensity markers there is also the phenomenon of *involvement strategies*, initially developed by Wallace Chafe in his work on discourse types. Chafe suggests a number of categories that show how speakers/writers can enthral their listeners/readers by affecting their inner states. These strategies include "detail and imagery", "first and second person pronouns", "action and agents", "hedges", "direct speech" and "aggravated signals" (see Chafe 1980). Chafe's work on emotions has since been developed and expanded by Deborah Tannen in her book *Talking Voices* (1989), which makes a distinction in involvement strategies: the first based on sound; the second on linguistic interaction with an audience. Sound involves rhythmic voice patterns based on repetition. Such repetition helps to create a shared discourse world between the speaker/writer and his/her audience. Moreover, as Georgakopoulou and Goutsos put it, it contributes to the emotional experience of connectedness between the discourse participants (1997: 135). Tannen's second category, linguistics interaction with the audience, consists of four aspects: "imagery and detail", "constructed dialogue" (i.e. the representation of characters' speech as direct quotation), "ellipsis" and "tropes". The four tropes she highlights are metaphor, metonymy, synecdoche and irony. In addition to involvement features/strategies there is the notion of *performance features* set out by Wolfson, which includes "expressive sounds", "motions and gestures", "repetition", "direct speech", "the historic present" and "asides". There's also Polanyi's *evaluation devices*, which include "negation", "repetition", "character speech" and "the mental and emotive states of characters". Other important discourse analytic concepts are Claudia Caffi and Richard Janney's work on *affective keys* (1994) and Douglas Biber and Edward Finnegan's notion of *affective stance* (1988; 1989). This latter concept refers to the use of language to convey all kinds of emotions and judgements with regard to the particular linguistic utterance that is being expressed at that moment. Looking at syntactic and lexical markers across different registers, Biber and Finnegan placed fiction, and in particular romance fiction, in the category of "emphatic expression of affect" (cited in Wales 2001: 366).

Furthermore, emotion plays an increasingly important role in cognitive linguistics. At the very beginning of his influential work *Concept, Image, and Symbol*, the cognitive grammarian Ronald Langacker argues that meaning is conceptualisation. He adds that "conceptualization is interpreted quite broadly: it encompasses novel conceptions as well as fixed concepts; sensory, kinaesthetic, and emotive experience; recognition of the immediate context (social, physical, and linguistic); and so on" (1991: 2). Here, at the very centre of cognitive grammar and linguistic-semantics, we find the realisation that meaning is equal to conceptualisation and that both rely heavily on the immediate physical and cerebral context of human emotion. Later in this introductory section Langacker reinforces this idea by discussing the basic categories in conceptual hierarchies. He mentions our understanding of time, space, colour, perception and temperature, adding that "emotive domains must also be assumed" (1991: 4). Clearly, then, emotion is an important contributory factor to cognitive linguistics.

Emotion is becoming increasingly significant in George Lakoff and Mark Johnson's work on cognitive metaphors as well. In *Philosophy in the Flesh* they frequently mention of the role that emotion plays in cognition. The groundwork for this is arguably set out on the very first page, where they state that "thought is mostly unconscious" (1999: 3). As I have discussed in Chapter 2, it is unlikely that unconscious thought is grounded exclusively in explicit belief-based, cognitive appraisal systems; it must rather be based on something less tangible and, in all likelihood, more affective. Lakoff and Johnson say further that "reason is not dispassionate, but emotionally engaged" (1999: 4), adding that "the mind is not merely corporeal but also passionate, desiring and social" (1999: 565). Zoltán Kövecses is another cognitive linguist whose work has primarily focused on emotion. One of the central claims of his *Metaphor and Emotion* is that emotions are to a large extent constructed by embodied experience and by different cultural settings rather than merely by biology. He convincingly shows how different languages represent emotions and how those emotion concepts can correspond to relatively broad patterns of thought. Referring to Len Talmy's 1988 cognitive work on force dynamics, Kövecses highlights a single "master metaphor", namely EMOTIONS ARE FORCES,[1] which, he says, organises much of our thinking about emotion (2000: xiv). Two such forces are what we might term internal and external pressure. Kövecses deals with the first of these chiefly in relation to "anger": a force that builds up inside our container-like bodies until the pressure becomes too much and it spills out (2000: 21–23). Indeed, Lakoff and Turner also discuss THE BODY IS A CONTAINER metaphoric theme in the context of "life is fluid in the body" and "death is the loss of fluid" (1989: 19–20). The second force that Kövecses discusses is in relation to the concept of love, which, like natural external forces such as wind, water, floods and waves, can sweep us away (2000: 87–113). In sum, he illustrates how cultural, biological and metaphorical-linguistic aspects of emotions are all crucial parts of a single integrated system. In doing so he rejects the absolutist claims of both biological reductionism and social constructionism. A somewhat similar claim has been made in general linguistics by Anna Wierzbicka. In *Emotions Across Languages and Cultures* (1999) she sets out to identify the universals of human emotions in different social environments, by combining psychological and anthropological insights with linguistic ones, to help us understand how emotions are expressed and experienced in different cultures. Here, as with Kövecses, we see the importance of local culture in local emotive linguistic universals. In effect, what we have is a blend of the universal and the particular; of nature and nurture.

With regard specifically to literary discourse, the narratologist and cultural analyst Mieke Bal has highlighted the potentially emotive nature of linguistic structures in literary fiction (1997: 44–52). In her book *Narratology* she shows how certain linguistic units at the level of character speech, such as "declarative sentences", "declarative verbs", "verbless sentences", might lead to emotion in a reader (1997: 43–44). She also makes a distinction between emotion types occurring in language exchanged between a speaker and hearer (I/you), and language about others (he/she/they). Thereafter, she divides these into "personal" and "impersonal" language situations, specifying language forms that best fit into these categories (47–48). In the *personal* section of her table of emotive textual signals, she includes "1st and 2nd personal pronouns", "(proximal) deixis", "emotive words", "conatives", "modal verbs" and "adverbs that indicate uncertainty in the speaker (e.g. perhaps)". She then sets out an *impersonal* column, which includes "3rd person forms (pronouns, etc.)", "all past tenses", and "a more distal sense of deixis". In effect, she is listing linguistic features that create either intimacy or linguistic distance in character, or ethos-creating, situations between a speaker or writer and his/her hearers or readers.

Miall and Kuiken have also conducted some interesting empirical studies on literary foregrounding and emotion (1994; 1995) whereby they claim that linguistic foregrounding and unexpected narrative events prompt a kind of uncertainty in the reader and thus lead to the arousal of feeling in the reader (1995: 282). Or, as they conclude in their 1994 study, foregrounding leads to de familiarisation which evokes affect in a reader and finally this emotion leads to "refamiliarising" interpretative efforts (1994: 404). This is a linear, bottom up process, following a characteristic line. However, in that same study, they also suggest a follow-up affective, cognitive process:

> As de Sousa (1987, p. 196) has argued, accentuated feelings set the "patterns of salience among objects of attention". Thus, the feelings accentuated while reading foregrounded passages sensitize the reader to other passages having similar affective connotations. Furthermore, such accentuated feelings sensitize the reader to other "texts" (e.g., personal memories, world knowledge) having similar affective connotations . . . With such affectively congruent intra- and extra-textual resources, the reader "refamiliarizes or "thematizes" the textual subject matter (1994: 395).

There is evidence here for the primacy of affective style in the mind which is something we shall return to later. The authors also look at reading times in this article and conclude that literary foregrounding leads to attentional pauses and thus slower reading times of such foregrounded elements (1994: 394). Also, a "reattentional" procedure or refamilairisation can take place at such junctures.

Let us now move on and look at emotion in the field of stylistics. Stylistics is the study of style in language, i.e. the analysis of distinctive linguistic expression and the description of its purpose and effect (Verdonk 2002: 4). It is descended from classical rhetoric, in particular, from the third canon, known in Roman times as *elocutio*. Moreover, it spans the divide between language studies and literary studies, and for this reason is also known as "literary linguistics". Stylistics can also be taught for language proficiency ends (Clark and Zyngier 2003) and even for more specific pedagogical purposes such as teaching methods in cognitive stylistics (Burke 2004; 2006). A significant part of stylistics concerns foregrounding, that is, deviation on the one hand and repetition and parallelism on the other. These are essentially macro-level figurative schemes of structure. Foregrounding can be internal, relating to the immediate linguistic environment or it can be external, relating to all kinds of contextual and intertextual phenomena. One of the core functions of foregrounding in literary environments is to bring about emotions in readers. These emotions do not emerge from the apprehension of new textual phenomena, i.e. we do not perceive something totally new; rather, readers apprehend something seemingly novel yet subconsciously recognisable from interactions with similar stylistic structures from comparable past reading experiences. Stylistic analysis itself seeks to bring to light such foregrounded phenomena and then describe their effects within a linguistically-grounded literary criticism. Such an analysis should seek to take into consideration all of the levels of language and discourse, which include phonology (sounds, rhythm, rhyme, etc,), graphology (typological features), morphology (the construction of words), lexis (vocabulary), syntax/grammar (sentence structure, the use of tenses, etc.) semantics (considerations of textual meaning) and pragmatics/discourse (features of external context and the communicative situation). Foregrounding, i.e. the making and breaking of textual patterns, is an affective phenomenon. As Barbara Herrnstein Smith puts it "every disruption in our expectations causes some kind of emotion" (1968: 14). Such unexpected twists and turns she suggests "is a major source of our excitement—that is, our pleasure in literature" (1968: 14). In this view, to which I subscribe, rhetoric and stylistics are inextricably about emotion: both the prediction and the reception thereof.

The roots of stylistics-related affective criticism can be traced back to classical times. Aristotle's earlier-mentioned theory of catharsis in *On the Art of Poetry*, which refers to the "purging" or "cleansing" of emotion from the body, was one of the first physiological, reception-based accounts of narrative emotion. The modern history of emotion in stylistic-orientated criticism, however, emerged in the 1940s and 1950s. In this period, the New Critics opposed subjective approaches to literary criticism. In their theory of the "affective fallacy" discussed in *The Verbal Icon* William Wimsatt and Monroe Beardsley highlighted what they saw as the inappropriateness of evaluating literature by its emotive effect on readers. The New Critics essentially espoused an objectivist view towards literary interpretation and reception, which, by its very nature, had to exclude emotion as a factor in reception. Such anti-subjective views that echo Plato's and Socrates' attempts to cast off the body in order to engage in emotion-free contemplation are questioned today, owing to what is now known about the crucial role that mind-fed processing plays in reading procedures and the embodied nature of the human mind.

Certain aspects of text-based formalism, set out in work of the New Critics, were continued by Roman Jakobson in the 1960s by relying on formal linguistic criteria in identifying stylistic patterns in texts. His famous "speech event", for example, included six categories, none of which concerned emotion. However, in addition to describing those six constituents of communication, he also identified six corresponding functions, one of which was "the emotive function". This emotive capacity, often called "the expressive function", referred to the emotive role of language that communicates the addresser's emotions and attitudes. Thus Jakobson did not entirely deny that emotion was a relevant factor in human communication, although his account of emotive discourse is concerned solely with production.

This changed in the 1970s and early 1980s, when emotion became an important factor in stylistics-oriented criticism, especially in some of the reader-response theories of the time. Not the emotion produced by writers but that experienced by readers became the object of study in stylistics, even if these "readers" initially were almost always theoretically constructed ones rather than real ones. A main figure in this period was Stanley Fish, who was interested not only in the physiological aspects of emotive response, such as those that classical catharsis professes, but also in the mental or cognitive aspects of such responses in stylistics. The main tenets of Fish's "affective stylistics", as it was called, involved a rejection of the pure Jakobsonian author-based textualism in favour of reader involvement. It viewed stylistic effects as being in the reader rather than in the text. His approach therefore involved a theoretical account of interpretative processes, assumptions and expectations in the reader. However, for all the advantages of Fish's affective stylistics, it was not primarily concerned with either real emotion or real affect in reading; rather, it focused on the role that context in general plays in literary interpretation.

For quite a while after Fish's affective stylistics, emotion played a less prominent role in stylistic analysis. This is somewhat surprising, given that the study of emotion and affective language was gaining increasing popularity in functional linguistics and discourse analysis, two areas from which stylistics traditionally takes its cues. More recently, however, emotion has once again started to take on an increasingly important role in a developing field that has become known as "cognitive stylistics", which attempts to look not just at sign-fed textual phenomena in literary reading situations but at mind-fed cognitive-emotive inputs too. This move from literary to cognitive stylistics is a natural development in the ever-expanding study of context in stylistic study as I have also argued elsewhere (see Burke 2005: 2007). Some recent affective studies in cognitive stylistics concern: narrative comprehension, with regard to character empathy and foregrounding (Emmott 1997); a poetic theory of emotion (van Peer 1997); the emotional function of reading literature (van Peer 1994); iconicity and emotion (Burke 2001), the feeling of reading (Stockwell 2002c); and reading for pleasure

(Emmott 2003). Thus in stylistics, as in linguistics, emotion has played a role. This is especially the case over the past thirty years, as the reader has become acknowledged as an important component in the meaning-making matrix. Emotion has also started to play a significant role with the advent of cognitive stylistics.

I will now start to look more specifically at a small number of "distal" sign-fed phenomena that may evoke emotion in the engaged reader. My first and most detailed discussion will be on the elusive notion of rhythm and in particular prose rhythm. I will outline the domains of rhythm in prose and in everyday language and explore the idea of embodied rhythm. Linguistically and etymologically rhythm is a fluvial phenomenon: the word rhythm derives from the Greek word *rhuthmós* meaning "to flow". In addition, it is an important aspect of style and a potent emotive concept: as Corbett and Connors suggest "the euphony and rhythm of sentences undoubtedly play a part in the communicative and persuasive process—especially in producing emotional effects" (1999: 363). They allude further to the distal character of rhythm: "the rhythms of our sentences . . . exert an influence on the emotions that is no less real for being all but unnoticeable" (1999: 290). Before embarking on this discussion of rhythm in literary discourse we should first stop and briefly consider rhythm in everyday spoken language.

At a basic level, features of pitch, speed, loudness and silence combine to produce the effect known as rhythm. Our sense of rhythm is based on the perception that there are noticeable or prominent units that occur at regular intervals of time. According to phonologist and cognitive psychologist Peter Roach, the English language is rhythmical (1983: 120). In phonology and prosody, rhythm usually finds form in perceptual patterns of stressed or unstressed syllables, sometimes referred to as "accented" or "unaccented". The English language is commonly known as a "stress-timed" language, so called because stressed syllables tend to come at equal intervals. One must not, however, think of the English language as being rhythmic in an absolute sense; rather, as Quirk et al. note, the natural rhythm of English has a regular beat, although not an absolutely regular one (1985: II.10. 1597). Rhythm also helps in the comprehension process in oral production, because it allows listeners to project forward and anticipate stressed syllables. Intonation in rhythm appears to assist this as well. David Crystal lists several functions of intonation: emotional, grammatical informational, textual, psychological and indexical (1995: 249). Several of these help in identifying, processing and even predicting rhythm. It seems reasonable to postulate that what holds for rhythm in speech should also hold for the memory of speech in silent literary reading procedures.

Rhythm and metre are obviously an integral part of poetic language and subsequent meaning-making. However, in the words of Mick Short "rhythm is not special to poetry" (1996: 125). For instance, rhythm is essential to the persuasive discourses of advertising, political speeches, and legal discourses, and many style figures, especially schemes, are constructed with this in mind. This was something that the rhetoricians knew all too well. Aristotle and Quintilian both emphasised the importance of rhythm in their respective works *The Art of Rhetoric* and *The Institutes of Oratory*, as, in more recent times, did Hugh Blair in his *Lectures on Rhetoric* (1783). Aristotle, referring to his native ancient Greek language, thought that diction should be neither fully metrical nor completely without rhythm, whereas speeches should produce loftiness which will lead to a sense of elevation in an audience (1991: 230–31). Arguably, much the same can be said about modern English. Quintilian said that rhythm pervades the whole area of every text and that it is especially prominent at the close of a discourse. He further stressed the embodied aspects of rhythm saying that while metre was a matter of words, rhythm included body movements (1922: IX. vi. 189 and 195). Mirroring much of the pedagogy of Quintilian, Hugh Blair devoted a whole chapter from his *Lectures on Rhetoric* to the "harmony of sentence structure", in which he drew clear links between rhetoric and music. This was quite logical. Approximately one hundred years earlier, the Baroque composers were experimenting with musical composition based on classical rhetorical structure. Indeed, as Sadie and Tyrell argue, starting from the seventeenth century, analogies between rhetoric and music permeated every level of musical thought.[2] In his illuminating discussion on rhetoric and music John Neubauer deals with a number of examples which show "that music helps language to persuade and to transport the listener into the desired emotional state" (1986: 31). Indeed, in that same work, Neubauer also discusses issues related to rhetoric and music such as "music and language", "affect theory" and "musical mimesis".

Rhythm is also important for prose fiction. Unlike poetry, with its patterns of regular stresses, prose is dependent on more subtle variations. This is the view of literary scholar Marjorie Boulton who suggests that what differentiates good prose from mediocre prose is that the former must have fine rhythm (1980: 49). Katie Wales supports the idea that rhythm is crucial to prose by suggesting that prose works posses an undeniable regularity of rhythm that can be used by novelists to foreground expressive or iconic effects (2001: 348). Geoffrey Leech and Mick Short agree, claiming in their book *Style in Fiction* that written prose "has an implicit 'unspoken' intonation of which punctuation marks are written indicators" (1981: 215). In that same discussion they skilfully show how rhythm in graphic units can heighten tension. Rhythm is thus important to prose. Moreover, because the final lines of any artistic piece are in a highly foregrounded position, prose rhythm at the close of a novel may, as Quintilian noted above, be able to produce even stronger emotive effects in a reader.

Rhythm can affect literary readers in other cognitive ways too. In her book *Art Objects* the writer and critic Jeanette Winterson speaks of words "in rhythmic motion in and out, preoccupying, echoing, leaving a trail across the mind" (1995: 94). Winterson is not only speaking here of rhythm in her own work only, but also of that in the works of other writers. For example, she says that in Virginia Woolf's writing "rhythm underpins her thought" (1995: 76). This echoes Coleridge's earlier poetic claim that there is "rhythm in all thought" (from his poem, "The Eolian Harp" 1.26).

From what has been described here, it would seem that experienced writers can often "feel" the music and rhythm of the text they wish to write even before they consider the words that are to fill those syllabic slots. But what about readers? Consider the following. If you regard yourself to be an avid reader, you may have experienced that you can vaguely remember the rhythms of a text before you can recall the words. This is probably most prevalent in poetry but it is possible in prose as well. Perhaps this has occurred especially at the end of a short story or novella. To use a musical analogy again, it is as though you had a grasp of the melody, but not the lyrics. If this is recognisable to you, as it is to me, then you may ask what is happening here. I believe that what Winterson describes from the perspective of the author is not too different from the experience of the engaged, literary reader. This process must find form in some kind of subconscious automatic channelling of highly schematic lines of prose from memory prior to the actual physical interface with the text. As to exactly what this may be is something I will explain later in this chapter.

In addition to there being rhythm in prose and everyday language there is embodied rhythm too in our very being. The literary critic and poet William Empson noted in his classic work *Seven Types of Ambiguity* (1931/1966) that the direct effect of rhythm appears to be a matter of physiology (1966: 30). Similarly, in her aforementioned discussion Boulton says that such is the unconscious nature of prose rhythm that great prose probably came to writers by some inner, unbidden, barely felt pressure (1980: 68). She goes on to relate these processes to physical sensations associated with strong emotions: "the rate of breathing, the heartbeat, the frantic, eager or apathetic movements of the body" (1980: 69). To my mind these embodied phenomena that a writer experiences cannot be too dissimilar to those that affect the engaged reader. This general idea of literary rhythm and embodied affective cognition has been dealt with within a stylistic framework in Richard Cureton's observation that "rhythmic cognition is one of our most basic mental capacities" (1993: 71). It seems therefore that we do not simply feel rhythm, nor do we merely produce it, rather, in many senses, we "are" rhythm. Applied linguist, Guy Cook appears to agree with this in his work *Language Play and Learning* when he points out that in addition to rhythm being important for music, dance and verse, it is also "an intrinsic part of our internal and external lives. It is with us pre-natally in the regularity of our mothers' heartbeats, and immediately post-natally in the rhythms of sucking and rocking" (2000: 22). He adds that "in later life, it continues in the rhythms of heartbeat, breathing, sexual climax, and giving birth (all rhythms which indicate or originate life)" (2000: 22). He concludes by suggesting that such intrinsic rhythms seem to have been exploited to evolutionary advantage. In light of the above it seems obvious, in the words of Short, that "rhythm is a fundamental human ability" (1996: 125).

This concludes our discussion on rhythm. Let us now look at some examples of distal affective style features in literary language. It will be recalled from the previous chapter that the notion of distance proved to be an affective theme in literary reading. It is now time to expand this further at the level of language with a number of stylistic phenomena. The list below is not exhaustive, as embarking on establishing one would be as fallacious as it would be superfluous. Instead, I just consider a number of arguably seldom-highlighted stylistic properties as means of exemplification. In particular, I will look at the distal grammatical categories of (i) mood (the subjunctive), (ii) deixis (distal, 2nd person), (iii) style figures (aposiopesis, erotema), (iv) punctuation (ellipsis marks), (v) style (plain), (vi) adverbs (perhaps, maybe), (vii) rhythm, (viii) repetition, (ix) asides (insert stories), and (x) gesture (e.g. "stretching out"). What these have in common is that they were all listed above as prominent style markers either by the ancient rhetoricians and/or by modern language theorists. These include, for example, Bal's emotive levels of narration, Quirk's intensity markers, Tannen's involvement strategies, Polyani's evaluation devices and Wolfson's performance features. I will now conduct a short discussion with the aid of literary examples of what can be viewed as "distal affective style features in literary discourse processing".

A first distal affect style figures is mood. In its grammatical sense mood is the name given to represent the subjective attitude of the speaker towards the state of affairs described by the utterance. Distinctions of mood appear to be linguistically universal and they are variously expressed, for example, by verbal forms or by the use of special grammatical items such as modal auxiliaries. My focus here will be on the subjunctive, as I believe that this distal aspect of grammatical mood can trigger affect in a literary reader because it expresses a sense of desirability and remoteness, which seems to be not just a matter of grammar, but also one of cognition and emotion. Such grammatical aspects of distance, particularly when combined with the notion of desire, can form a powerful concoction. Consider the emotive force of the italicised subjunctive forms, modal verbs and hypotheticals in the following closing lines to Thomas Wolfe's autobiographical novel *Look Homeward Angel* (1929). Note as well the direct references to two of the emotive themes I discussed in the previous chapter, distance and home, as well as a visual sense of "stretching out".

> And the angels on Gant's porch were frozen in hard marble silence, and at a distance life awoke, and there was a rattle of lean wheels, a slow clangor of shod hoofs. And he heard the whistle wail along the river. Yet, as he stood for the last time by the angels of his father's porch, it seemed *as if* the Square already *were* far and lost; or, *should* I say, he was like a man who stands upon a hill above the town he has left, yet

does not say "The town is near," but turns his eyes upon the distant soaring ranges. (1973: 544)

Numerous tropes and figures other than the ones I have discussed are also capable of prompting or channelling emotion in hearers and reader. In the text above we can observe the oxymoronic "hard marble silence", the auditory-vivid "rattling lean wheels" and the alliterative "wailing whistle". The fact that style figures produce emotional effects in listeners and readers is something that has been consistently shown by rhetoric throughout history and therefore needs no further elucidation here. I would, however, like to focus on what I believe to be potentially some of the more affective tropes and figures that can occur in literary reading contexts, particularly because of their distal nature. One of these is the earlier-mentioned aposiopesis. According to Demetrius in his work *On Style* "in certain cases conciseness, and especially aposiopesis, produce elevation, since some things seem to be more significant when not expressed but only hinted at" (Chapter 2, 103–5). Aposiopesis, I suggest, does not only produce elevation, but it is capable of bringing into existence the most powerful of affective-contemplative emotions. In formal terms, as we saw earlier, aposiopesis is the sudden breaking off of a piece of discourse by failing to provide the final words of a clause or sentence. One might see it as "the rhetoric of silence" echoing the Greek word *aposiōpan* which literally means "to be silent". Thomas O. Sloane says such a figure "can simulate the impression of a person so overwhelmed by emotions that he or she is unable to continue speaking" (2001: 29). Similarly, Wales notes that "in the normal flow of literary discourse aposiopesis is rare, but marked when it appears" (2001: 27). To my mind, aposiopesis is a powerful affect-channelling rhetorical tool in literature, and especially when it occurs at literary closure, as it makes clear its verbal intent through its paradoxical rhetoric of silence. In formal terms this figure is often alluded to by punctuation and in particular by ellipsis marks. Work done on ellipsis marks appears to point to the affective capabilities of punctuation in literature. In her work on punctuation and ellipsis, Anne Henry speaks of the "subtlety" and "discretion" of the three dots (2001: 153). In this study she also shows how trends and influences in dots, dashes and asterisks have changed and evolved throughout literary history. Consider the following example from the closing lines of F. Scott Fitzgerald's *This Side of Paradise* (1920) to see how aposiopesis can work to great affective ends at closure in literature.

> But—oh, Roselind! Roselind! . . .
> "It's all a poor substitute at best," he said sadly. And he could not tell why the struggle was worth while, why he had determined to use to the utmost himself and his heritage from the personalities he has passed . . .
> He stretched out his arms to the crystalline radiant sky.
> "I know myself" he cried. "But that is all." (1995: 304)

The elliptic dots and exclamation marks are one of the main generators of emotion here. The literary fragment also has a manual "stretching out" gesture at the close of the novel, as opposed to the visual one shown earlier, just as in the Willa Cather example in the previous chapter: "the feelings of that night were so near that I could reach out and touch them with my hand" (*My Ántonia*). Perhaps not coincidentally, this appears to happen at the close of several novels. Consider, for instance, the case of Mrs. March in Louise May Alcott's *Little Women*, who stretches out her arms at the close of the novel, as if to gather children and grandchildren, or indeed Josef K. in Kafka's *The Trial* who raises his hands and spreads out his fingers at the end of the book just moments before his death. You might also recall how Stein in Joseph Conrad's *Lord Jim* stretches out to wave his hand sadly at his butterflies at the close of the novel. To return to ellipsis marks and aposiopesis, a similar phenomenon in the form of a dash, rather than dots, can be observed at the close of Carson McCullers's novel *The Member of the Wedding*:

> Francis turned back to the window. It was almost five o'clock and the geranium glow had faded from the sky. The last pale colours were crushed and cold on the horizon. Dark, when it came, would probably come quickly, as it does in wintertime. I'm simply mad about—. But the sentence was left unfinished for the hush was shattered when, with an instant shock of happiness, she heard the ringing of the bell. (1946: 190)

Punctuation employed in this fashion, and especially at the close of a novel, as here, can, I believe, enact a kind of pathos or poignancy. Of course, this is not the only formal emotive function of ellipsis marks, punctuation can have comedic effects as readers of Sterne's *Tristram Shandy* can attest. However, here, in such thematic contexts, poignancy seems to be appropriate.

So far I have started to highlight a number of linguistic and stylistic phenomena linked to the notion of distance, which, as we saw in the previous chapter, turned out to be one of the most emotive concepts that the thirty-six readers highlighted. Thus far, these have been fragmentary and somewhat *ad hoc* analyses. I shall now conduct a longer stylistic analysis of a text fragment at the close of a novel. In doing so, I will be looking for a greater number of these distal affective style figures, as well as a number of theme-based distal affective features that have been discussed in the previous chapter. In this analysis I will consider the potential emotive effects of designated stylistic and thematic features on myself as an engaged reader, i.e. this is my stylistic reading. Some other readers might identify either fully, or in part with some of my observations. Others might not at all.

I wish to return to an episode in Walter Benjamin's earlier-mentioned essay, "The Storyteller", to which he only devoted two short paragraphs. I will elaborate on this short discussion and will highlight the affective themes and language present in it. I want to show how this piece includes key themes such as "distance", "closure" and "incommunicability" and how they might affect other readers the way they do me. I will start here to deal with my somewhat contentious proposition, set out at the start of this chapter that style may be in the mind as well as on the page.

At one stage in his essay, Benjamin ponders the effect of the final words of Gustav Flaubert's novel *Éducation Sentimentale* (99–100).[3] The final scene of this novel occurs in Chapter 7 of Part III, which is just four pages long. The scene concerns two boyhood friends, Frédéric and Deslauriers, who are looking back and discussing an incident of their childhood in which they picked a bunch of flowers from their garden and took it to a brothel in their home town to present to the *patronne*. The novel then ends with the two men contemplating that deed:

> "That may have been", said Frédéric, when they had finished, "the finest thing in our lives". "Yes, you may be right", said Deslauriers, "that was perhaps the finest thing in our lives".[4]

Benjamin appears overwhelmed by this ending and praises its profundity, discussing the meaning of life in the context of such a sudden, yet paradoxically languid, closure. What he does not do though is look at the language and themes for clues as to why he is so overwhelmed. That is what I will do. I believe that there is a combination of theme, language and rhythm at work here that might not only make the text appear emotive to readers once they reach the end of the novel, but combine as well to somehow appear to project beyond the text, back onto fresh reading experiences.

With regard to the thematic content of the piece, these two aging men appear to stop time for a moment and reflect on a joint incident of their childhood. This, on its own, is a powerful emotive theme that is often employed in literature to great effect: think, for example, of Wordsworth reflecting in the "First Book" of *The Prelude* (1799) on his "act of stealth and troubled pleasure" (lines 361–62) as he stole away in a rowing boat. As boys, Frédéric and Deslauriers picked flowers from their garden and took them to a prostitute. If you do not know the story and just read Benjamin's critical account, you will not be able to tell from this text fragment alone whether the boys know she is a prostitute or whether they think she is just a pretty lady: or even both. Perhaps they have fallen in love with her or perhaps they know what her profession is and have taken pity on her. Any of these alternatives could potentially produce emotive material in a work of fiction. Giving flowers is an act of human compassion by the children toward an adult who has fallen on unfortunate times in her life as a prostitute. It is, as William Wordsworth wrote in "Lines Composed a Few Miles above Tintern Abbey" (1798), one of those "little, nameless, unremembered acts of kindness and of love" (ll. 34–35). As we saw, even if this theme of unacknowledged, spontaneous sympathy were to appear on its own, it could elicit reader emotion, because human minds would be drawn into engaging with such a humanistic, empathetic topic. In sum, childhood and the distance of the event are perhaps the two most prominent themes here. It may be recalled how "childhood" and "distance" were designated as the two most emotive literary themes by the thirty-six subjects in the previous chapter. Together, they can be said to combine to produce poignant nostalgic subject matter.

With regard to the rhythm and indeed tone of this text, there seems to me to be a languid, pre-industrial feeling to such a flashback, where time seems to move more slowly than it does nowadays. This finds form in two phenomena both of which are based on a kind of mirroring. Let me restructure the English version of the text that I, as a reader, have been exposed to. As you can see in endnote #4, much of the linguistic parallelism is observable in the original French version.

> "That may have been", said Frédéric, when they had finished, "the finest thing in our lives".
> "Yes, you may be right", said Deslauriers, "that was perhaps the finest thing in our lives".

A number of things are immediately noticeable. A first is that both sentences are roughly of equal length, although Deslauriers has slightly more text. Additionally, both spoken parts are split in two by the direct speech markers. The direct speech is mainly iambic in metre—it may be recalled how such character speech was labelled a marker of affect in Polanyi's "evaluation devices". Even more noticeable is the literal, linguistic repetition. Here, broken down, we see just how prevalent the mirroring is:

| may (have) been | vs. | may be |
|---|---|---|
| said Frédéric | vs. | said Deslauriers |
| the finest thing | vs. | (perhaps) the finest thing |
| in our lives | vs. | in our lives |

This undulating repetition, a distal affective style category I mentioned earlier, can slow down the reading. Recall also how both Wolfson and Polanyi identified repetition as an emotive marker. When I read these lines they appear to trigger in me an intertextual echo of the close of James Joyce's story *The Dead*, in particular the chiasmic "faintly falling, falling fainting" style figure he employs to great effect there. It feels too like I have similar memories of such rhetorical structures; as though they have somehow been primed in me by my subconscious and are now on the verge of entering my working memory to meet the incoming text. Although this is a discursive exchange, the second part of Deslauriers's response seems to be literary language rather than everyday usage, because a real interlocutor in a real discourse situation would be unlikely to repeat the entire final phrase "(perhaps) the finest thing in our lives" uttered in full by the first interlocutor. It is thus a rhetorical device of echo: a repetitive parallelism. I cannot say how this might affect other readers, but when I read this I experience a number of multi-sensual intertextual echoes. These include a long southern drawl, the heat of a Mississippi summer, a vague semblance of some Huckleberry Finn who is perhaps sitting on a fence or wall, legs dangling as he is exchanging platitudes with an equally opaque Tom Sawyer. These are for me distal yet strong echoes that somehow get projected into my maelstrom of ongoing affective meaning making. They also appear to be somehow based on vaguely familiar people and places from my own childhood past. Moreover, if I experience emotive mind-based inputs, rather than purely text triggered ones, these will get projected too. And if they impinge on my own experience, or my sense of my own mortality or those of my loved ones, they will have a strong emotive quality. For example, if we return to the main reflection at the close of the story, we can assume that most children go through a stage when they are infatuated with an older person—more often than not, for both boys and girls, with a primary school teacher, somebody who has shown much love and care for them in the temporary absence of parents. These are just some of my own associative echoes that the text has prompted in my memory that will be added to my ongoing interpretation of the last few lines of this text.

To return to the text itself, it is written in a matter-of-fact plain style that uses no florid language. This, perhaps paradoxically, increases the emotion for me. Plain style in ancient times was not meant to move or please, but rather to instruct: Quintilian, that great, erudite Roman professor of rhetoric, saw it as the language of the classroom. However, this need not always be the case. Writing on the works of Horace, Corbett and Connors say that "it is possible to feel an emotion without displaying it extravagantly. In fact there will be times when the more dispassionate the emotion-provoking description is, the more intense will be the emotion aroused" (1999: 79). Benjamin's remarks on the written style of Herodotus seem to confirm this: "his report is the driest", yet thousands of years later his stories are still capable of arousing astonishment and thoughtfulness in a reader (1968: 90). Such dry reports in a literary context, rather than a narrative-historical one, often pertain to the death of a character; they can be the most emotive of all the passages in the story.

A powerfully emotive linguistic feature in this piece is the use of the demonstrative "that". This distal deictic marker not only sets up the nostalgic reflection but also keeps the event away from the I-speakers. The event that they appear to so cherish and long to experience again will always be a "that" and never a "this". As we saw earlier, Bal pointed to distal deixis as a potential site of linguistic emotion, albeit in the third rather than second person, as I do: third person deixis might be seen as "extra distal", e.g. here-there-"yonder". Let me now consider a core aspect of the language of this Flaubert text. I feel that two words dominate the tone here. The ones in question are the two occurrences of the modal auxiliary "may" uttered by Frédéric and Deslauriers, and the adverb "perhaps" uttered by Deslauriers. "May", in the sense of "possibility" is often used interchangeably with "might", although "might" is somewhat more tentative. Here then we see how Deslauriers's modal adverbial "perhaps", said after echoing Frédéric's "may", is close in meaning to "may". The "mayness" and the "perhapsness" of these statements at the end of Flaubert's story are two of the distal categories I mentioned earlier. These were also alluded to by Bal as a site of affective language use.

The majority of things discussed so far have involved sign-fed stylistic phenomena. However, I have started to introduce the idea of how mind-fed style might operate, especially in my analysis of the Flaubert text. But what does mind-fed style actually mean? Consider the following remark on the act of literary reading by contemporary writer Lynne Sharon Schwartz: "these inky marks . . . even give the illusion of containing emotion, while it is we who contribute the emotion. Yet it was there in advance too, in the writer" (cited in Gilbar 1995: 133). So, according to Schwartz, emotion is mainly in the author and thereafter in the reader. In that same essay, entitled *True Confessions of a Reader*, Schwartz goes on to suggest that, unlike painting and music, literary reading does not rely solely on transference through the inanimate medium of language, rather "intricate neural transactions take place *before* words find their elusive target" (1995: 133, my emphasis). What does this mean? How can the mind have a role in determining style? Later in this chapter I will seek to shed some light on this by suggesting that although writers choose the vocabulary, the syntactic structure, the punctuation, the rhetorical and stylistic devices (whether consciously or subconsciously), it is nonetheless the reader who ultimately makes the meaning in text processing. In hindsight it might be suggested that all of the above-mentioned literary devices act to *channel* rather than just "trigger" meaning and especially the more affective aspects of meaning. They do not, and indeed cannot, ever constitute complete meaning. As I have shown in Chapters 2 and 3, text comprehension, and especially literary text comprehension, is far more than the mere semantic decoding of words.

Before engaging in a discussion on the idea that style may be mind-fed in literary meaning making, as well as mainly sign-fed, it is useful to look at what some of my fellow readers thought. I decided not simply to ask the subjects whether they felt that there is more to affect in style than just language, as I wanted to try and have as little influence on their responses as possible. Instead, I posed a general question about sign-fed style and emotion in language. What I hoped to find in the responses were traces of references to mind-fed aspects of style, even though I had not asked for them. Moreover, I hoped to find fleeting references to the some of the affective style features I have been discussing.

## NRQ—Q. 10  Do You Think That a Well-structured Literary Style Can Alter or Affect Your Emotions?

Twenty-eight subjects out of thirty-six responded affirmatively. There were twenty-three open responses.

1. I am sure it can but I don't know exactly how. It might be that if a book is written in a rather "loose" style, and then suddenly you get a very structured style, say at the end, you are sort of distanced from the characters, and you become more serious and you can start to think about what you've just read in the novel
2. I think that it is more psychological
3. The more in touch I am with a text, the greater the chance is that the text has an emotional impact on me
4. If an author carefully chose the style of his writing it will evoke emotions even stronger in me because when the style is well structured it's easier to "dive" into the story. This is also the case at the end of novels I believe because at the end of a novel I read extra carefully and if the author then chooses his literary style carefully that will make it easier to really "get into the story" and feel and see and think the way the characters do
5. Specific lexical choices and the use of metaphor can enhance the strength of certain emotions in the novel, which affects your own emotions as well
6. When the language is a bit poetic, but still realistic and well structured, that for me makes the novel blissful to read which affects my emotions. This is for me a sign that I am reading a good novel, so it also has a similar effect at the end of the novel, when it's well structured
7. I think that the right turn of phrase or positioning of information in a sentence can definitely affect emotions. Sometimes it might "hit" you much harder if it has been put in the right place in a sentence, and this is especially true I think for the ending of novels. I am always curious as to what the ending of a novel is going to be like, not just because I want to know how the story ends but also because I want to see how the author has chosen to close his or her novel; what is going to be the last sentence, the very last word. I think an ending written in a bad style can ruin a novel, at least a little bit, and a great ending can definitely enhance any emotion you are feeling when reading the last page of a novel
8. Yes, if I really don't like somebody's literary style, then most likely there are too many adjectives, too many adverbs and too many descriptive relative clauses. Sometimes I don't bother finishing a book
9. If metaphors are employed in a very good way, it adds to your emotional reactions to the contents of the story. Punctuation also has

a great effect on this for it may cause you to slow down at those moments when a second longer of reflecting may cause you to become emotional about something. I think that the same thing goes for the closure of a story

10. To turn the question around, an ill-structure style can be really annoying and distracting

11. A well-structured style may keep on surprising you; sometimes you only discover the structure at the end of a novel and sometimes while reading it, then you can actually experience little mini epiphanies every time you are surprised by the book's set up

12. When a book is written in a rotten style or is ill-structured, it irritates me and affects my emotions

13. I much prefer stylistically well-written novels. If the closing line is crap or insignificant, I'll definitely be disappointed. If the style is good, it makes me happy, especially if I can spot the grammatical structures that I wasn't sure about or the words that I know I have seen before but never knew the meaning of. For me, the pleasure of reading English novels lies in understanding and learning English vocabulary, not so much plot or emotions

14. I have cried about things I have read in books, like for example if my favourite character dies at the end. I also won't be able to forget that quickly

15. If the sentences are easier to read, I will get more "caught" in the book, and then I am much more susceptible to emotions

16. In a book with a "mysterious" atmosphere sentences need to be long and poetic. This way I get more gloomy or romantic. If the style doesn't correspond with the nature of the story, or if I don't get the style, I tend to get irritated with the book and stop reading it

17. Style can guide emotions. If something mundane is mentioned in the text, then it can get more meaning if it is stylised

18. If something is written beautifully, with certain metaphors, etc., it can have an influence on how you experience it and also how you feel about it afterwards

19. Yes, it can influence my enjoyment of the book. When I like a certain sentence very much, for example, I will re-read it a few times so that I can really enjoy it

20. Yes, I think too that the end of the book should be the "climax", not only in the story but also in the language. If this is not the case, I would be disappointed

21. A good novelist can alter mood and manner of reading through stylistic elements

22. Style can affect my feelings. It affects the intensity of how I read something

23. If it is especially good, my appreciation for it will be enhanced. If it is bad, then it will annoy and distract me

First, many responses appear to lend some weight to the general claim that style can influence emotion; they included responses 4, 5, 7, 9 and 15. In light of this one might be persuaded to agree with a comment in response 17 that "style can guide emotions". Second, with regard to my distal emotive elements none were directly referred to. Of course, we have to remember that the question did not ask for them directly or otherwise. Some interesting associative observations were made by the writer of response 9 who wrote "if metaphors are employed in a very good way, it adds to your emotional reactions to the contents of the story". He/she went on to add that "punctuation also has a great effect on this, for it may cause you to slow down at those moments when a second longer of reflecting may cause you to become emotional about something". This seems to be close to what we discussed earlier on the subject of ellipsis marks. The final comment of this person was "I think that the same thing goes for the closure of a story". Other responses that made mention of metaphor included numbers 5 and 18. Respondent five noted as well the importance of "specific lexical choices" without going into any detail. Respondent eight found too many adjectives and adverbs unbearable. Something else that was seen by some of the respondents, especially sixteen and twenty, is that style is not an ornament but an integral part of meaning. Other interesting responses included number 19, which indicated that re-reading affective well-structured sentences was needed in order to get the full enjoyment out of them. The first response suggested that a sudden change in style at closure might induce emotions. This was echoed to some extent by respondents four and six, who said that they read the end of a novel extra carefully. Another intriguing response was number 7, which, in addition to closure, referred to a kind of epiphanic reading event: "sometimes it might 'hit' you much harder if it has been put in the right place in a sentence". Response number 11 went further to make a literal reference to experiencing "mini epiphanies".

All in all the responses confirmed that style is a sign-fed phenomenon. But some seemed to question the claim about the exclusive textual role of style in creating or guiding reader emotion. One interesting comment came from respondent number two, who indicated "I think it is more psychological". But what exactly did this respondent mean? How can style be more psychological than linguistic? In addition, respondent three said that the more "in touch" he/she was with a text, the greater the chance that the text had of having an emotional impact on him/her. But what does it mean to be "in touch" with a text prior to being exposed to its style? Does it mean in touch somatically or emotionally, perhaps? In a somewhat similar vein, respondent ten chose not to answer my question, but instead turned it around saying "an ill-structured style can be really annoying and distracting". Respondent twelve did something similar.

A question we might pose at this stage is why did these subjects choose to allude to something other than the style as a text-based trigger? Does the engaged literary reader expect something else? If so, might that expectation be based on fragments of affective style that are already being processed and brought into working memory in an engaged reader? Is this why the disappointment is all the more palpable? Is it because the expected sign-fed "prompts" do not live up to the emotive expectations of the fragmentary mind-fed input? Consider as well response sixteen. This subject says that when sitting down to engage with a book that has a "mysterious atmosphere" the sentences need to be "long and poetic". Only this way can he/she become more "gloomy or romantic". The respondent adds that "if the style doesn't correspond with the nature of the story, then this leads to irritation" and he/she will stop reading the book. Is cognition affecting linguistic form here?

Let us reflect for a moment on the above. For a small number of these readers fragmentary mind-fed aspects of style appear to be brought to bear on the style of the text and if this results in a mismatch, the reading stops. There appear further to be stylistic expectations and anticipations at literary closure. The writer of response twenty, for example, says that the end of a book should be a climax, not just story-wise but also style-wise, and if this does not happen then the result will be disappointment. Respondent twenty-three makes a similar observation. So these readers, it seems, somehow subconsciously project fragments of highly stylised language that have affected them in previous readings onto the text in search of an emotive match. For some engaged readers in certain situations specific aspects of style appear to be in the mind and already in the meaning-making fusion of affective cognition long before eyes meet the style on the page. In light of such responses, I would like to explore further—from a more theoretical perspective—the suggestion that something "more psychological" may be going on when a reader encounters style on the literary page. Schwartz's earlier claim that intricate neural transactions, based on style fragments of previous affective reading situations, take place *before* the words on the page find their target seems to be becoming gradually more plausible. Let us look more closely at what might be called mind-fed aspects of style.

The linguistic, surface structure of a text plays a dominant role in its processing. This is arguably even more so the case in texts that are written to delight and persuade: the fields of classical rhetoric, stylistics, creative writing and critical discourse analysis all attest to this. Hence, in literary discourse processing, style is most definitely not a question of "mind over matter". This is aptly summed up in Wales's observation that "stylistic features are basically features of language" (2001: 371). This is completely true. However, I am interested too in what Wales is alluding to with the modifier "basically". I quoted a similar observation by Best in an earlier chapter of this work. According to him, decoding is "largely" a bottom-up process. What aspect of meaning-making with regard to style is outside the direct domain of processing from the page or screen? I believe that the answer must have something to do with what I have been calling affective cognition. In the final part of this chapter I will explore more closely the idea that style is in the mind as well as on the page. In doing so, I will reactivate a number of views discussed in the first chapters of this work from the domain of cognitive psychology. Let us start though with linguistics.

In her discourse studies Deborah Tannen has written about "that mysterious moving force that creeps in between the words and in between the lines, sparking ideas, images and emotions that are not contained in any of the words in any one time" (1988: xi). This is akin to Iser's earlier-mentioned *Leerstellen*. Consider too the perhaps more relevant remarks of the stylistician, Peter Verdonk that "style is concerned with the mutually creative interplay between perceptible form and intangible content" (2006: 197). In that same discussion he also speaks of the "deep conceptual significance" and "assumed intrinsic value" of style (2006: 197). Perhaps, then, in light of such views, style does not merely persuade, delight, instruct and even deceive us from "out there" in the world waiting to be perceived and processed. Instead, because it is reliant on emotion, and emotion is a mind-fed process, style may rely to some extent on what is brought to bear onto text or discourse. By this I mean an echo of some schematic template, a distant feeling, a lost rhythm, a reverberating line. Such "just recognisable" distal echoes of styles and themes that have affected a reader in the past will, I believe, be subconsciously primed and channelled into the meaning-making current of affective cognition once a reader sits down in an emotive and committed frame of mind to read literature. Form, rhythm, metre and syntax must somehow have a neural as well as linguistic base: a kind of re-usable subconscious imprint that starts to pour down onto a text once a reader "discovers" that he/she is about to engage with literature. But how is this possible? Where is the hard scientific evidence for such a claim? Let us recall some of the things that were cited and discussed in Chapters 1 and 2 of this book.

Schank said that expectations are the key to understanding and in a great many instances these expectations are sitting in a particular spot in memory, awaiting the call to action. Bartlett proposed that readers' expectations produce powerful interpretations of a text that can override the semantic content, and that those expectations will be based not just on prior experience but on emotions. Kintsch made a similar point: lexis, syntax and semantics are overridden by mind-fed input in retrieval structures, where no sign-fed prompt is even needed nor indeed does information have to be channelled into short-term memory. Let me try and make this more concrete by quoting Schank once more. When we re-read it, we should think of "style in the mind" as an apt example of such a mode of outcome-driven memory:

> More often we do try to figure out what will happen in a situation we encounter . . . In attempting to imagine what will happen next we must construct a model of how things will turn out. (This model can often be quite wrong of course). Sometimes during the construction of the model, we come across memories that embody exactly the same state of

affairs that we are constructing; this is an instance of outcome-driven reminding. (1999: 80)

We can do something similar with Barsalou's earlier remarks on simulations from Chapter 3. Imagine below that when he is speaking of memory, he is actually referring to the notion of a style fragment. I have inserted parenthetic references to help the general comprehension process:

> As a memory (*of a style fragment*) is retrieved, it produces a simulation of the earlier (*stylistic/rhetorical*) event. As the (*style*) simulation becomes active, it may differ somewhat from the original (*linguistic*) perception, perhaps because of less bottom-up constraint. (based on Barsalou 1999: 605)

Such perceptual simulations operate in working memory. We recall that Kintsch described short term memory as "a dynamically changing stream" awash with "changing patterns of activation" (1998: 411). Earlier Barsalou explained that the articulatory loop simulates language just heard or "about to be spoken". Similarly, the visual short-term buffer simulates visual experience just seen or "that which is being currently imagined". The motor short-term buffer simulates movements just performed or "those which are about to be performed". So, not only do these working memory systems operate during perception, movement and problem solving, they are also operational in simulating these activities off-line (1999: 604). In other words, predictions, anticipations and expectations are all real and primary in working memory *prior to* textual engagement. It seems probable that these kinds of style fragments are subconsciously channelled into the buffer zones of working memory.

It might seem excessive to relate style to neurobiology, but this is not as far-fetched as it once seemed. Recently, there have been experiment-led claims made about the neural basis of the rhetorical figure of irony: a figure that Tannen identified earlier in this chapter as an emotive involvement strategy (see Shamay-Tsoory, Tomer and Aharon-Peretz: 2005). Additionally, there have been studies conducted on neural research into literary metaphor processing and the areas where that processing takes place (See Hoorn 1997; Danesi 1989). Hence, I am optimistic that there must be as yet undiscovered areas of the brain that also recognise affective style and can store, in a distributed manner, fragmentary memories of such styles that have affected individuals as literary readers. These could be repetitions, parallelisms, deviations of either a graphological or rhythmic nature. The graphological features will require extensive processing in the visual cortex during subconscious retrieval during recall, wheras rhythmic ones will require quite some processing in the auditory cortex. In view of the somatic inputs required in text processing, and especially in literary text processing, both will undoubtedly also activate the sensory motor-systems.

For me, as an avid and competent reader of literature, these stylistic fragments will include the essences of a number of my favourite lines, rhythms
or structures. But how does all this work? Before I address this head on,
let us look at some views on how style in the world and style in the mind
operate in relation to narrative works of art.

In *Cognitive Science, Literature and the Arts* Hogan speaks of "style
motifs" in music: a riff or trill in a stretch of music that is recognisable as
a hallmark of the artist or a group of artists to the avid listener (2003a:
19–23). According to Hogan, these style motifs get stored in long term
memory and in buffer regions. When triggered, motifs get activated with
all the memories and emotions of the previous times they were experienced.
Echoing the claims of the mood-congruency effect, once stored again, they
are strengthened and reappear in a more elaborate and stable form. Because
of their constant reactivation we subconsciously come to understand that
there is a pattern at work in art. We can extend this and realise that there
are themes and patterns (in all musical pieces)—"thematic phases and variations" (2003a: 21) as Hogan calls them. The cognitive work is largely done
with "procedural schemas" (2003a: 23) that are employed subconsciously
to channel thematic phrases or to map variations onto stored thematic
phrases. Here, style motifs are stable, powerful and instantly available for
recall (2003a: 23). The question is, can this be mapped from style motifs
in music to rhetorical textual ones, produced by the parallelism, repetition
and deviations of style figure and style fragments? In spite of my earlier
discussion on rhythm, there are huge differences between musical composition and rhetorical structure, at least at the level of production rather
than reception, so it would seem unlikely. As Neubauer states when paraphrasing Brian Vickers writing on figures of music and figures of rhetoric, "all comparisons of the arts are made at the peril of overlooking their
differences" (1986: 40). The link therefore seems unlikely, but it would
be unwise to conclude at this stage that the cognitive processing of style
motifs in music has no structural connection whatsoever with the cognitive processing of style figures in literary reading until we have completed
our exploration; not least because reading and music have in common that
they are relatively abstract arts, compared to the full vision of pictorial art,
and both have interconnected auditory and visual buffer zones or "slave
systems" in working memory.

Consider for example the comments of Barbara Herrnstein Smith, who
claims "our expectations regarding any particular poem will be at least
partly determined by our previous experience with poetry" (1968: 29). To
sum all this up: it seems that style moves through experience from the world
of words to the world of the mind. Once stored there, in highly schematic
form, it can be spontaneously deployed in future literary reading situations
in waves of affective cognition that are subconsciously brought to bear on
a literary text. Hence style, the most sign-fed of all the affective inputs that
I discussed in this chapter, can sometimes function in a mind-fed manner.

This may also occur when a reader engages with any text that is designed to emote (advertisements, editorials, obituaries, written versions of political or legal speeches, etc.), where a reader, or even listener, has a broad idea of what he/she can expect. So, the styles and themes we have read will shape the style and themes we are yet to read. In short, as Manguel puts it, "reading is cumulative . . . each new reading builds upon whatever the reader has read before" (1996: 19). This happens to me as a reader and I know that it can happen to other expert readers too, as I have recently observed.

At the start of his plenary lecture at the 2006 annual conference of the Poetics and Linguistics Association an eminent stylistician, Mick Short, admitted to his audience that he was unable to read a book of Robert Frost's poetry without the influence and interference of the spy thriller that he had just finished. It must have been confusing for him to stop by woods on a snowy evening only to watch spies come in from the cold. This, however, should not come as a surprise to us because it is an everyday occurrence that avid readers regularly and repeatedly undergo, and it is the themes and styles of past reading events, and not just the most recent one, that I believe get projected onto current ones.

It has even been suggested that in some literary reading situations it is possible to recall events that have not been memorised at all. Mark Turner, looking at the rhythms that underlie such memory, suggests this in *Reading Minds* when he speaks of "remembering the unmemorized with regard to literature" (1991: 90–91). In this discussion, Turner mentions that we intuitively know what will come next in a poetic text, based on metrical, rhythmic, grammatical and conceptual symmetry. Turner is to some extent correct here, even if a significant amount of prose fiction seeks to challenge and purposely disappoint such expectations. What Turner appears to suggest is that a kind of "embodied intuition of symmetry" exists with regard to literary texts that can give us direct access to appropriate parts of our cognitive unconscious, thus allowing us to recall that which has not been memorised.

Let me now return to my promise and try to explain how this often works for me as an engaged, committed individual reader. Because reading is an intersubjective activity, in the sense described by Iser, analogous aspects of what I will say about my reading experiences may be recognisable to other readers: readers like you. Of course, other readers may disagree completely. When reading a novel that I am emotively engaged with and cognitively committed to in a location and at a time of my own choosing, I find that if I stop for a moment near the end of the text and try to reflect on what my mind is doing I notice different projections taking place. One type of projection pertains to similar question-like structures that somehow appear to drift in and out of my working memory. This is the case even if there seems to be nothing linguistically similar on the page that might have subconsciously triggered them. This happens most frequently when I am at the end of a book. In fact it occurred again very recently when I was reading the closing pages of Haruki Murakami's *Kafka on the Shore* (2005). The following are some of the question-like style fragments I noted at the time. I recalled Virginia Woolf's tripartite "What is this terror? What is this ecstasy? What is it that fills me with extraordinary excitement?" from the end of *Mrs Dalloway,* as well as Thackery's "Which of us is happy in this world?" from *Vanity Fair,* a book I last read more than twenty years ago. These philosophical-rhetorical questions that get almost spontaneously projected into my working memory at literary closure are not just limited to prose. I regularly experience what might be termed "the essence" of W. B. Yeats's enigmatic "How can we know the dancer from the dance"? ("Among School Children") and his "Did she put on his knowledge with his power / Before the indifferent beak could let her drop?" ("Leda and the Swan"). Phillip Larkin's philosophical pondering are similarly often part of my affective stylistic pre-cognition, especially lines like "Where is the tree gone, that locked sky to earth? What is under my hands that I cannot feel? What loads my hands down?" ("Going"). Wales says that such juxtaposed questions can lead to heightened emotion (2001: 328). I would not disagree.

So what is happening here and how unique is this to me? Let me start by saying that although this experience I describe relates solely to rhetorical/ philosophical questions, it can also pertain to other style and theme elements. For example, I am particularly susceptible to episodes of stretching out at literary closure, manually, physically, visually or cognitively. We saw several literary examples of this earlier. These, and indeed many others, are somehow and for some reason seemingly important to me. Am I really unique in this?

To return to my example, upon reflection I realise that the suggestive power of these questions appears to always be with me, lightly activated on the background swell of my sense of self. This is especially the case when I choose a comfortable space to engage with a novel. For me, these questions—and indeed many more not recalled here through this conscious method—feel as if they are almost always primed in me, albeit in unconscious and somatic ways, and that they somehow start up in earnest once I start to ponder the idea of reading literature. Hence, when deployed subconsciously in real reading situations such style fragments are never whole or complete or concrete, rather they are skeletal, indistinct and distal. At the same time, however, they are often predictable. What I am trying to describe here is something I have already dealt with above, in the many views on anticipation, expectation and priming. More evidence of this is to be found in Ulric Neisser's 1976 "perceptual anticipation hypothesis", which focuses on pre-visual priming mechanisms and perceptual anticipations. His basic claim is that before perceiving an object a person's mental imagery gets primed. This "imagining" of what the physical object will be like has the function of speeding up actual processing of the object once it arrives in the visual field. One can see how this would have evolutionary advantages in preparing for a flight or fight response.

Let us try to bring this closer to style and language. In linguistic terms this anticipation would be a bit like an impatient person finishing your sentences for you when he/she knows roughly what you are going to say. What is interesting is that the mental content only becomes really noticeable when there is a mismatch, a bit like my reading of the Murakami novel, where no rhetorical-philosophical questions occurred at the end of the book and therefore I noticed more readily the questions that I had been projecting onto the text. If there is a match or near-match, then the mind-fed input goes largely undetected. In sum, what Neisser proposed for mental imagery in acts of visual apprehension, I propose for stylistic and thematic text fragments in literary discourse processing. Some work has in fact already been done on written language, so the leap is not that great. Martha J. Farrah (1985), for example, conducted research with regard to letters of the alphabet that supports the perceptual anticipation hypothesis (see also Finke 1989: 50–52).

We can now take this further. Because images and words are processed (a) in broadly similar ways at the level of the visual cortex, as Kosslyn has argued in his work *Image and Brain* (1994: 295), and (b) in the sensory motor system through simulation, as was seen in my discussion on mirror neurons in Chapter 2, the same might be said of linguistic style. This is the case because style also has a visual aspect to it at many linguistic levels, not just at the graphological one. I claim therefore that style is not only about motivated choice on the part of the writer, be it conscious or subconscious, but on the part of committed literary readers too, especially if they are expert readers, i.e. ones who have a basic sense of the workings of rhetoric, style or narrative, etc., who are *expecting* this motivated choice to take place. It is readily acknowledged in discourse psychology that avid readers are in possession of knowledge about the structure/text schemata and even sometimes the content of stories before they start to read. This resembles what van Dijk and Kintsch have called "rhetorical superstructures". Such knowledge allows readers to form anticipatory schemata; i.e. the textual equivalent of Hogan's "procedural schemas".[5] Indeed, in Chapter 4 I have already cited from van den Broek et al. In that discussion they mention this pre-processing phenomenon in the context of the literary genre of fairy tales.

Story structure in novels is often far more complex than in fairy tales, but are they really so innovative as to be unrecognisable? Moreover, readers do not only *expect* such events to unfold, they expect foregrounding to take place as well, which will result in their being emoted and enchanted by lexis, syntax and rhythm. This is especially the case once the reader has made a conscious decision to set aside some time and space in which he/she can sit down in a comfortable, isolated location and affectively engage with a much-longed-for book. In this pre-reading mode of expectation, highly schematic stylistic structures are unconsciously primed, as echoes of affective memories, ready to be channelled into the undertow of the oceanic literary reading mind. Of course, there will be no exact stylistic match between what is channelled down to what flows up, but that is not necessary, and the nature of human memory makes this more or less impossible anyhow. All this was cogently argued by Bartlett when he states "style seems to be one of those factors which are extremely readily responded to but extremely rarely produced with any fidelity" (1995: 81). So what we bring cognitively to bear on a certain stylistic feature in a text is only the skeletal echo of some other stylistic feature that has delighted us as readers in our literary reading past. It will have little real resemblance to what it once was or what it is being channelled down to meet on the page. The partial and diffuse nature of such "figures of the mind" is quite natural; as Sanford and Garrod observed earlier: human language processing may often be incomplete. So, just as I argued in a previous chapter that LRI are blurred and indistinct, I now say that memories of affective stylistic schemata, and indeed of themes, are indistinct too. In some literary reading situations, dependent on the affective context, style might even be as much construed by the mind as it is given by the text.

Style in literature is therefore not always just a linguistic "trigger" to the deep well of the mind, although this is sometimes the case, especially when a reader is surprised by the text. Additionally, style can be represented by mind-fed input first. What style does not do, however, under any circumstances, is to determine affective meaning on its own. Style can never wholly be a sign-fed phenomenon. Affective meaning does not reside in texts but is instead to be found in the embodied minds of individual readers in a socially-constructed, highly dynamic and malleable form. In short, style is of course *techné*, a skill, an art, a technique, it is about words and clauses and sentences; about choice and also motivated choice, but for an engaged literary reader it is about memory too; the distant subconscious memory of half-forgotten rhythms, half-remembered lines and half-felt syntactic structures.

Writing on reader reception, Iser suggests that the structure of the text acts as a kind of "indicator to the imagination" (1978: 9). In the twenty-first century, cognitive stylisticians should also start to think about the ways imagination can be an indicator to the structure of the text as well. Hence, although sign-fed processes are dominant in affective reading, it is the coming together of "sign and mind", and the confluent ebbing and flowing of affective memory between them that is perhaps of most significance. In light of this, explorations of the role of the reader in the twenty-first-century should not be focused solely on the contents on the page; they should, in addition, try to capture what a reader might subconsciously "bring" to a text: cognitively, emotionally, somatically and culturally. In light of my short discussion in Chapter 4 on the limitations of methodology in this area, this will not be a simple task. Readers are of paramount importance to interpretation because they infuse embodied affective meaning into a text; they do not merely *receive* linguistic and stylistic data. From what is known about the embodied human mind, readers do not merely read "off", but also read "in". Hence, it may be advantageous to think of reception study as literary reception and anticipation study along the lines suggested by Jauss in his work on "horizon of expectations". This, in time, will facilitate the real study of affect in stylistics, because anticipation, as we have seen Frijda and Mesquita argue in a previous chapter, is a real, full emotion.

In conclusion, Bakhtin's famous theory of intertextuality can be expanded. What most of the cognitive and neurobiological evidence discussed in this chapter suggests is that intertextual echoes of fragmentary themes and styles, and even LRI, are being activated and channelled into the buffers-zones of short-term memory, ready for full deployment into an upcoming literary reading event long *before* we have commenced reading. Here, it is the fragments of *expected* and/or *desired* themes and styles that are primary, not the concrete linguistic prompting. This final comment concludes our discussion here. It is now time to try and bring together LRI, mood, location, themes and styles discussed in previous chapters and ground them in a framework of affective cognition that will point forward to the oceanic workings of the affectively engaged literary reading mind.

# 7 Towards a Model of Emotion in Literary Reading

In this chapter, I will pull together all that has been discussed thus far on the topic of affective inputs in literary reading. In doing so, I am moving towards constructing a model of emotion in literary reading. By means of schematic modelling, I will also attempt to show how the five inputs (LRI, mood, location, themes and style) interact and how they relate to what I have termed affective cognition. Previously, I labelled these five inputs sign-fed and mind-fed. As I explained at the end of Chapter 1, these are merely temporary terms of convenience. In this chapter, I will start to show just how difficult it is to keep using these definitions once one describes the actual process of engaged literary reading, because their borders become fluvial, as cognition, emotion and language work on each other and coalesce. Additionally, I will start to explain how the affective cognition in a literary reading experience connects to the macro processes of the oceanic mind.

Let us start by returning to the passage by F. Scott Fitzgerald about literary reading, quoted at the very beginning of this work. In a letter to his fellow writer Ernest Hemingway dated 1 June 1934, Fitzgerald claims there that "the purpose of a work of fiction is to appeal to the lingering after-effects in the reader's mind" (cited in Turnbull 1964). If we presume for a moment that this is true, a number of questions arise:

- 1. What are those "after-effects" and what are they made up of?
- 2. Where do they "linger" in the reader's mind?
- 3. How does a work of fiction "appeal" to them?
- 4. Why do they linger in the reader's mind?

The first two will be answered here in the body of this chapter. The answers to questions 3 and 4 must wait until Chapter 11. Below are my four working hypotheses. Our focus for now should be on the first two.

- 1. Those after-effects are often a blend of the five affective inputs or fragments of individual ones that have emoted us during past literary readings

- 2. They linger in long-term memory spread throughout the brain and flow towards buffer-zones in working memory once a "decision" has been made to read literature. During and after use they flow back either because they have not made it into meaning or because they have already been employed and are returning into storage re-primed
- 3. Works of fiction appeal to these after-effects in an act of desire, arising out of a need to experience artistic pleasure, in this case literary pleasure, which is a powerful process. In this sense, art is an addiction, and fiction the appropriate fix
- 4. They linger in a reader's mind because they appear to fill a lacuna left by our primary caregivers. In doing so, they act to comfort us in our ephemeral, largely secular, modern existence

Fitzgerald's words may seem like literary critical fancy but they are not. There is real psychological substance to this observation on post-reading and pre-reading after-effects. For example, van den Broek et al. agree with this. As discussed, their landscape model of discourse processing states that the mental representations that get translated from individual sentences "linger far after the reader has put down the book" (1999: 71). The focus here is admittedly on LRI, but, as we will see later, in such subconscious processing they are often difficult to separate from style, mood, theme and location. Perhaps then we can no longer speak of reading events that start with the opening of a book and end with its closing. It may be the case that mind-based residues of the themes and styles and LRI of a book never truly go away but continue to hover in the background, ready to be deployed. In this sense they would be fluctuating between inactivity and activation on the point of being deployed, as van den Broek et al. have suggested in their discussion of textual elements. Viewed this way, literary reading, like many communicative linguistic events, is an ongoing process: it is not a series of finite linear events but rather a perpetual circular procedure, what I see as "a literary reading loop", continuing, arguably, even while we sleep and dream.

One might see this as a situation whereby the oceanic reading mind of an individual is on a kind of low swell for much of the period when physical reading events are distal in time. But once a new reading event approaches, textual and non-textual elements in the mind start to undulate, moving in and out of working memory, occupying the buffer zones and then receding into longer-term holding areas until the actual text processing is in full flow. Here there is a steady increase in tension. Thereafter the ebb and flow of textual, cognitive and somatic elements takes on a more rhythmic pattern, somewhat like the physical subconscious act of breathing. The tempo changes when approaching the end of the novel as the intensity of the reading increases. The post-reading phase is similar to pre-reading, only that tension decreases. This, in time, settles back into the low swell of a text-inactive reading state.

How plausible is all this? We recall that Hogan addressed the case of literature head on. He starts by saying that in everyday discourse the notion of priming is about intermediate states of semi activation: an item in memory is activated to a high degree but remains just below access. In the case of literary discourse, however, things are more enduring, because relevant memories are continually primed in our experience of literature. The reason for this ongoing activation is due to the suggestiveness of literary works. It is this that keeps the emotion-laden memories primed for long stretches of time and this makes their cumulative effect strong. As Hogan puts it:

> As our emotional response to a work develops out of a particular set of primed personal memories, those memories begin to guide our realization or concretization of that work. As a result of this concretization, the memories themselves are reprimed and thus our emotional response is reinforced or enhanced. (2003a: 161)

Here, the guiding role of LRI is made prominent. It is also those fragmentary memories that flood our imagination that give rise to our emotional responses (2003a: 162).

So, in addition to the existing discourse psychological notions of the cumulative and the immediate in the processing of everyday discourse, a case can be made for extending this when we are referring to engaged acts of processing literary discourse. This might be widened even further, to include any discourse processing that is recognisable to the reader and where one of the main goals is the attainment of pleasure. The new categorisations would be (i) a kind of pre-immediate processing that starts long before the eyes reach the page or computer screen, and (ii) a cumulative unconscious processing that takes place long after the physical act of reading has ended. As I have suggested earlier, in literary discourse processing, inferencing is most certainly not unlimited, contrary to what Graesser has claimed. However, nor is it limited either, reliant on mere local bridging elements, as the proponents of the minimal hypothesis, Ratcliff and McKoon, argued. Rather, in acts of committed literary reading, one might say that inferences are to some extent broadly conventional, even if this is a non-definitive kind of expectedness.

This claim should not come as a surprise, because Bartlett said more or less the same thing: affective attitudes influence recall and as a result this will produce representations that are "stereotyped and conventional". Schank agrees with this when he said recall is not a random process. All LRI, styles, themes, moods and locations are in the main "stereotyped and conventional". This suggests that implicit, rather than explicit, memory is involved in acts of emotive literary reading, because it is inflexible and non-conscious. We may recall a number of key characteristics of implicit memory: (i) they strengthen the older we become; (ii) they flow automatically; (iii) they make use of the amygdala, and, (iv) they sometimes operate together with explicit memory. It seems clear too that much of the work done in acts of literary reading employs episodic rather than semantic memory. My arguments in Chapters 4 and 5 on the semi-autobiographical nature of many of the themes and LRI employed in literary discourse comprehension and appreciation appear to support this. We recall that, according to LeDoux, episodic knowledge is situated in the pre-frontal cortex, where much of working memory takes place, whereas semantic knowledge is located throughout the neo-cortex in distributed fashion. Let us put this discussion on hold for a moment while we look at a number of schematic representations of engaged literary reading. This should help clarify some of the arguments I have made previously in this work.

In the following table located on the next page, I set out the seven "stages" of reading according to the five designated affective inputs. I am aware that tables of this kind cannot indicate the fluvial nature of the inputs, but this may help to initially define the stages of engaged literary reading.

This table shows seven linear stages, though, as we saw in the previous section, they are circularly interconnected. A first preliminary observation we might make is that there are essentially four main states: non-reading, pre-reading, reading and post-reading and all four of these involve aspects of literary discourse processing to some lesser or greater extent. A second observation concerns the actual text-processing phase itself. At the start of a novel there is a strong focus on lexical elements: readers tend to overcompensate in order to get "into" the story and have an idea of the newly introduced characters, and their relation to each other (stage 3). This moves to a more balanced and natural flow of varied affective inputs during reading (stage 4). As a reader approaches the end of a novel, however, the sign-fed and mind-fed information accumulates (stage 5). The sign-fed information increases as a reader may slow down to take in every word—or rushes to the end, perhaps to return and slow down to savour the text—whereas the mind-fed occurs as subconscious expectations and anticipations go into overdrive in an attempt to achieve what Tan referred to as "a preferred final outcome" when we engage with narrative art.

Perhaps most importantly, in the final column of the chart one can see just how problematic my sign-fed/mind-fed division has become, especially during the actual physical reading event itself (stages 3–5). Indeed, such a chart is far from ideal in representing a confluent event like engaged literary discourse processing. Schank's words, quoted in my first section, support this: we should not break down the tasks of understanding language into small components because language is an integrated process. Van Dijk echoes this too when he states that the distinction we draw between text and context is only an analytic one (1999: 132).

It is time therefore to discard the mind-fed/sign-fed terminology and replace it with a more general term that I used in the title of this section: affective inputs. The Venn diagram (Fig. 7.1 on page 153), although far from perfect, comes much closer to representing the circular interconnection of

*Table 7.1*   The "Stages" of Reading

| Stages | Inputs | Main medium | Sign-fed/ mind-fed |
|---|---|---|---|
| **Stage 1:** Long before the reading event | - Previous reading experiences - Subconscious themes, style, LRI and other affective elements | - The subconscious mind- Implicit memory- Affective cognition | - Mind-fed |
| **Stage 2:** Shortly before the reading event | - Location - Mood - Occasion - History | - *Kairos* | - Mind-fed |
| **Stage 3:** During reading (at the start) | - Styles - Themes (and also to a lesser extent mood, location and LRI) | - Text (and mind) | - Sign-fed (and some mind-fed) |
| **Stage 4:** During reading | - Styles - Themes (and also to a lesser extent mood, location and LRI) | - Intertextual echoes - Memory input - Narrative structure - Rhetorical style | - Sign-fed and some mind-fed |
| **Stage 5:** During reading (at closure) | - Location - Mood - Styles - Themes - LRI | - Strong text focus and strong mind focus | - Sign-fed - Mind-fed (both more intense) |
| **Stage 6:** After reading | - Location - Mood - Styles - Themes - LRI | Mind - (Meaning and Interpretation) | - Mind-fed |
| **Stage 7/Stage 1:** After reading / Before reading | - Previous reading experiences - Subconscious themes, style, LRI and other affective elements | - The subconscious mind - Implicit memory - Affective cognition | - Mind-fed |

pre-reading, reading, post-reading and non-reading. I have indicated this in the previous section. In this fourth state of non-reading, emotive-cognitive processes will involve distal, non-conscious memories of style and theme fragments, as well as LRI and mood echoes. All these are located in long-term memory spread across the basin of the oceanic reading mind and will be undulating on a low swell ready for priming in order to infuse working memory for the next literary reading event. This non-reading stage can be accounted for in part by the established cognitive notion of "set". In my discussion on mood in Chapter 4 I have introduced set as "any preparatory cognitive activity that precedes thinking and perception". What I describe now as the non-reading stage is a kind of "literary reading set".

In setting out these four confluvial stages of literary reading I am accounting for the entire literary reading process. Writing on the topic of the reading occasion, Balz Engler claims that "as we always encounter texts as part of a particular occasion, and never in isolation, there is no way in distinguishing between what has been contributed to the result ( ... ) by the as yet uninterpreted black marks on the page ( ... ), and what by other factors of the occasion" (1993: 162). What we see in this confluent model goes some way towards accounting for this. Henceforth, I shall refer to this constant undercurrent of literary reading as *the literary reading loop*.

In the same vein we may consider the five main affective inputs (see Fig. 7.2) listed in the first main column of the chart. Clearly, such a description is

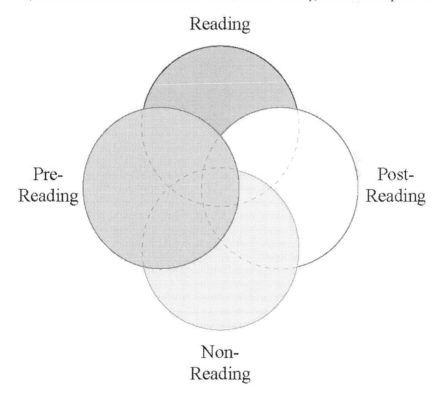

*Figure 7.1* The four confluvial stages of literary reading.

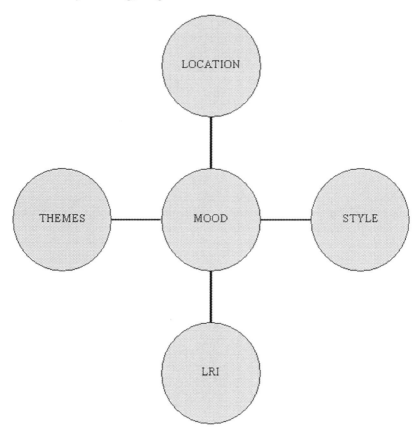

*Figure 7.2*   The five affective inputs in literary reading.

wholly inadequate. Let us then look at this anew, proceeding from the premise that mood will be to some lesser or greater extent responsible for the governing of the other inputs. If we model this, we see the following (see Fig. 7.3):

Once again, this is not entirely accurate, because phenomena like location and LRI are more dependent on mood than themes and style. Upon reflection, then, the following Venn diagram represents more completely how affective inputs plausibly interact.

Here mood is still at the top but has a greater influence on location and LRI. Its effect on themes and style is present, though not dominant. We also see that themes and LRI greatly overlap, just as I have indicated in my discussion of them. Although far from perfect, this model offers a better representation of how the affective inputs I have thus far discussed operate in emotive, engaged acts of literary reading. A question that remains is how do affective inputs in literary reading link to what I call affective cognition?

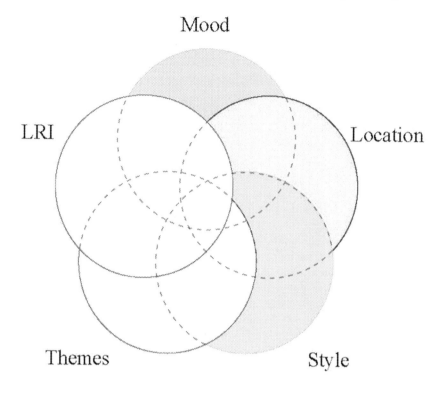

*Figure 7.3* How the five affective inputs in literary reading might interact.

I have called mood, location, themes, style and LRI "affective inputs". But why are they affective and what is their relationship to what I have been calling affective cognition? First, in the previous chapters I have explained in detail why these literary reading phenomena can be considered emotive, hence there is no real need to repeat this in detail here again. In short though, what makes them affective is (a) the personal fragmentary remembrances of LRI; (b) the preparatory excitement and projection of mood; (c) the somatic pleasures of location, (d) the sentimental, cultural universals of themes and (e) the pleasurable balance and rhythm and the breaking thereof in style. Second, affective inputs are linked to affective cognition in the following way: while style and themes are more cognitively emotive during normal emotive episodes of literary discourse processing, the other three, namely LRI, location and mood, are primarily concerned with affective cognition. However, there are implicit links between cognitive emotion and affective cognition at the reading stage and there will therefore be an ebb and flow of emotive information exchange between them. We can assume this in part because my distinction between affective cognition and cognitive emotion mirrors, in some way, the distinctions drawn by LeDoux (a memory of an emotion vs. an emotive memory) and Damasio (image space vs. dispositional space), as well as the general idea of explicit and implicit memory. In all these cases we saw that although each concept is clearly distinct, all had implicit neural connections that caused them to flow into each other. Because an engaged act of literary reading is a largely non-conscious activity, and given that literary reading crucially involves emotion and the body, we must conclude that much of the memory active during such episodes of reading is implicit, and much of the emotion has an affective cognitive nature. This is supported by the evidence that implicit memories are robust and stereotypical, as we saw in the case of LRI, style and theme fragments in the mind.

Below we see how during regular emotive literary reading episodes—as opposed to highly emotive ones—the non-reading, pre-reading and post-reading phases of all five inputs rely most on affective cognition (Table 7.2). These will be strong in the case of pre-reading and post-reading and weak in the case of non-reading:

Because what I term "cognitive emotion" is akin to explicit memory, it shares many characteristics with previously mentioned neurobiological theories, including LeDoux's notion of "the high road" and his "memory of an emotion", Damasio's "image space", and even Alhazen's idea of "pure perception". In effect it is akin to an appraisal theorist's view of emotion: that emotion follows reason. Such text-driven emotive events are processed through the higher route via the thalamus and then the higher cortical areas, before moving onto the emotive centres of the brain. Affective cognition, however, is akin to implicit memory. It is therefore close to what LeDoux described as "the low road" and "emotive memory"; what Damasio defines as "dispositional space"; and in visual terms what Alhazen called "pure sensation". Like Damasio's idea of "somatic markers", it involves emotive, sensor-motor, somatosensory and higher cognitive areas. It shares characteristics with emotion, as we saw in the particular psychological tradition from James to Zajonc. This kind of somatic emotion comes in under the higher cortical radar, so to speak, and is processed first via the thalamus and then directly on to the amygdala, milliseconds before the higher cortical

*Table 7.2* Affective Cognition during the Stages of Reading

|  | *During reading* | *Pre-reading and Post-reading* | *Non-reading* |
|---|---|---|---|
| Cognitive emotion | styles, themes | XXXXXXXXXXXX | XXXXXXXXXXXX |
| Affective cognition | LRI, mood, location | (strong) styles, themes, LRI, mood, location | (weak) styles, themes, LRI, mood, location |

areas are involved. As LeDoux states, because it bypasses higher cognitive areas, it provides the amygdala with the mere impression of the original stimulus (1998: 164). It is not a simple task to map out exactly how this works. It may be recalled that according to Damasio dispositions are held in neuron assemblies, which he called "convergence zones". He holds that the true content of dispositions can never be directly known, due to their unconscious state and dormant form, and that dispositions are not words but abstract records of "potentialities", which can fleetingly come to life, "Brigadoon-like", before they wane again into imperceptibility (1999: 332). The same can be said of affective cognition. Let us revisit a memory flow chart I employed in Chapter 1 (Figure 1.1), but let us now add a number of extra categories that I have discussed in the meantime: cognitive emotion, affective cognition and, tentatively at this stage, oceanic cognition.

Below in Figure 7.4 we see, among other things, how cognitive emotion comes primarily from the more explicit side of memory, whereas affective cognition stems from the implicit part of long-term memory. We also see that working memory has a direct link to both cognitive emotion and affective cognition and that this ebbs and flows in both directions. Most clearly, however, we see that oceanic cognition constitutes a kind of back and forth interaction between explicit memory, cognitive emotion, implicit memory and affective cognition. This is combined with the ebbing and flowing of

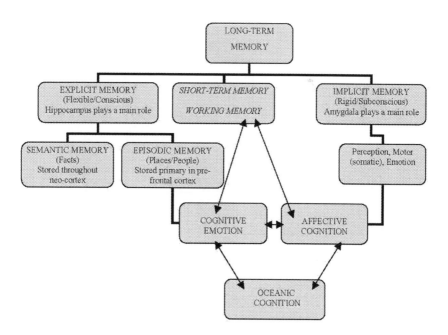

*Figure 7.4*   Oceanic cognition in memory functions.

this information from long-term storage areas—the pre-frontal cortex in the case of episodic memory, and, distributed throughout, the neo-cortex in the case of semantic memory—to buffer-zones in working memory. Let us now model a neurobiological, rather than cognitive psychological, figure (Fig. 7.5) based on discussions here and also earlier in Chapter 2.

The primary thing we notice here is that affective cognition is reached more quickly through the implicit memory route and that, as a result, the affective aspects of neural and cognitive ebbing and flowing start sooner. The model, however, is still somewhat static and does not do justice to affective cognition, even though I have inserted weaker links that connect affective cognition and cognitive emotion. Oceanic cognition is represented here as two blocks, though it should be seen as a single, potentially border-less macro-category into which all inputs lead and flow out of. In effect, all of the above stages, as well as those in the previous diagram, also fall *under* the heading of oceanic affective cognitive processing. This is the paradox: oceanic mind processes operate at a macro and micro level in literary reading situations.

We now need to turn to yet another Venn diagram (Fig. 7.6) to get a better insight as to how affective cognition and cognitive emotion work within their respective domains of implicit and explicit memory. The confluent nature of these four phenomena starts to show the oceanic processing nature of the human mind.

Affective cognition overlaps here more with cognitive emotion and implicit memory than it does with explicit memory. Likewise, cognitive emotion has stronger links to affective cognition and explicit memory than it has to implicit memory. Similarly, implicit memory has a larger overlap with affective cognition and explicit memory than it does with cognition

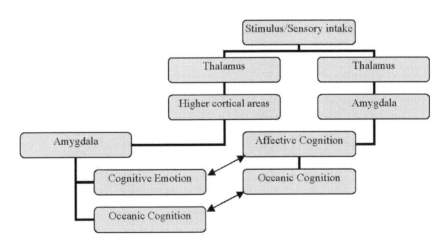

*Figure 7.5*   Oceanic cognition and neuro-cognitive brain functions.

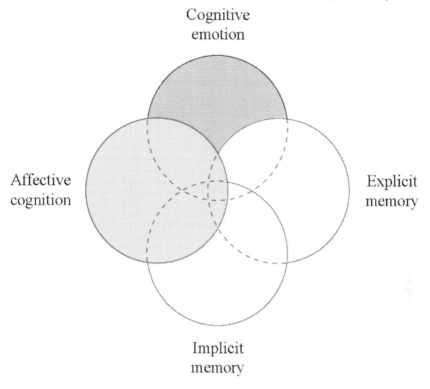

Cognitive
emotion

Affective
cognition

Explicit
memory

Implicit
memory

*Figure 7.6*   The oceanic processing nature of the literary reading mind.

emotion, whereas explicit memory shares more features with implicit memory and cognitive emotion. The important thing, however, is that they are all linked in some greater or lesser way: cognitive emotion has a modest overlap with implicit memory, and explicit memory with affective cognition. In this model we see the main abstract components of oceanic cognition. Though this is a more fluvial account of how these aspects operate, this final model is still far from ideal. Much thinking and testing must be done still to strengthen its validity. It is difficult to make an accurate and complete diagram of what happens when one reads. We saw earlier in Dehaene's assessment, based on his fMRI experiments, that "there is a vast network of cortical areas that are active in the different stages of reading: at least a dozen regions spread across the entire brain" (2003: 30). Zull went even further, suggesting that during emotive and cognitive episodes many parts of the human brain can be active at once "in neuronal networks of incomprehensible complexity" (2002: 100). In spite of this daunting prospect, I believe that these diagrams, figures and flow charts, despite being rudimentary and restricted owing to their elemental design, start to shed some light on these processes and, by default, on my main arguments.

The main aim of this short chapter is to pull together all that has been discussed thus far in this work in order to lay the groundwork upon which a later theory of emotion in literary reading might be built. By means of a number of schematic models and Venn diagrams I have shown how my five affective inputs interact and relate to what I have termed affective cognition. Further, I have started to show how the affective cognition of a literary reading experience might connect to the macro processes of the oceanic mind. This discussion will be continued in the final four chapters. Before then, let us recap the main points of the book thus far:

- Style and themes are in the mind as well as on the page
- In the pre-reading stage themes, style fragments and LRI are already drifting in and out of working memory before a reader's eyes have met the page, suggesting that intertextuality is active much earlier than we might think
- During engaged acts of literary reading it is impossible to separate sign-fed and mind-fed sources due to their constant ebbing, flowing and coalescing, and as such they should henceforth be just known as *affective inputs* when discussing literary discourse processing
- Literary reading is not just about the actual text interface. There are instead four confluvial parts that make up what is the *literary reading loop*
- *Affective cognition* in literary reading is made up of *affective inputs*
- *Oceanic cognition* is to some extent the interactive, ever-fluvial combination of explicit and implicit memory together with cognitive emotion and affective cognition
- Engaged acts of reading at literary closure involve an intensification of all affective inputs

To understand more fully what I mean by oceanic cognition we need to look not just at the emotive events encountered while reading literature but also at those intense emotive moments that come about while reading fiction. It may be recalled from one of the surveys in an earlier chapter that one subject wrote that one is "hit" while reading when affective style and cognitive input come together at the close of a novel. This very real phenomenon is loosely known as "reader epiphany". It is the neuro-cognitive basis of this literary phenomenon that will now be investigated in the final four chapters of this book.

# 8 Literary Closure and Reader Epiphany

Can you recall a time that you were reading a novel that you were very much enjoying and, as a result, were in the process of becoming very much emotionally attached to? If the answer is yes, then consider the following idealised reader scenario. Our reader is in an optimum mood and in a comfortable location of her own choosing. The themes in the book are to her liking and the style is well-crafted and engaging. The mental imagery that is being deployed in her mind to flesh out events in that novel bear echoes of her indistinct childhood home and of a sense of her primary caregivers. Now imagine that she is approaching the end of the book which she promptly finishes. At the moment of conclusion, where the physical text ends, and at the point where her eyes stop reading, she suddenly realises that something strange is happening to her. She experiences a sense of motion, a kind of forward movement, even thought she is not really moving. By the time she has gathered herself she notices that she has stopped reading; her book has fallen away; she is staring blankly into space; a tear is rolling from her eye down her left cheek and down onto her pullover. As stated, this is an idealised account, but some avid readers may recognise aspects of it in some of their own past reading experiences. What this is, is a description of reader epiphany and in this chapter, and the ones that follow, I aim to start to uncover some of its neuro-cognitive, emotive and philosophical aspects which will lead me to my working theory of "reader disportation". Before this can take place, however, we need to review some of the basics, and this is what this chapter will solely focus on doing. The fundamentals are two-fold: the notion of literary epiphany as we currently know it and the idea of reading at the end of a novel: literary closure. First, though, let us look at the background of the text selected for analysis in the forthcoming three chapters. For the sake of continuity, it is the work that was mentioned on the very first page of this book: *The Great Gatsby* by F. Scott Fitzgerald. The author, you may recall, believed in the "after effects" of literary reading.

A text fragment from a single book has been chosen for analysis here simply for pragmatic purposes. Had this study been of an empirical, quantitative nature, then more texts and indeed control groups would have been necessary. This particular novel was selected because I wanted to use a story in the survey that is both well known and relatively short, so that it could be read at one long sitting. I also wanted the text to be critically acclaimed. These three constraints, I believed, would all prove to be beneficial when asking for qualitative responses from real readers, as I do in the next chapter, Chapter 9.

*The Great Gatsby* is indeed still well known. It still sells over 300,000 copies every year (Prigozy 1998: vii). Further, it is manageable; the novel is less than 200 pages in length and can be read in a single day, plausibly at a single sitting. Lastly, it is renowned for its style; for example, Tony Tanner has described it as "the most perfectly crafted work of fiction to have come out of America" (2000: lv), and *The New Yorker* has called it "one of the most scrupulously observed and beautifully written of American novels" (cited in Prigozy 1998: viii). This stylistic praise is echoed by Matthew J. Bruccoli who has said of the novel that "Fitzgerald sought to convey, by means of language and style, the emotions associated with the actual and fictional settings" (1992: 193). An important question that still remains is why am I looking at a fragment from the end of the text rather than a piece from another part of the book? This question leads us into a longer discussion that must take place on the first of the two main themes in this chapter: literary closure.

Why choose to focus on the closing lines of a novel? One reason is redrafting. It is well known that several writers have been known to spend considerable time paying close attention to redrafting the closing lines of their novels. One of Fitzgerald's contemporaries, Ernest Hemingway, once told an interviewer that he rewrote the last page of *A Farewell to Arms* thirty-nine times before he was satisfied. When asked whether there was some technical problem hindering him, he replied that he was just trying to get the words right (Newman, Cusick and Tourette 2000: 163). Such authorial anecdotes are not uncommon, as we saw in previous chapters. Style is of central importance to closing lines, perhaps more so than in any other part of the text. This claim is also supported in the domain of literary instruction. When teaching budding creative writers how to become successful novelists, Josep Novakovich offers the following advice: "no matter what type of ending you use, you must end skilfully and gracefully because this is the reader's last impression of your piece which will cast light on the whole piece retroactively" (1995: 171). It is prevalent too in the domain of classical rhetoric, for instance in Aristotle's advice that speeches should be rounded off not just with recapitulation but also by "bringing the listener to emotions" (1991: 260, ed. Lawson-Tancred). Quintilian would later echo this in his comments on the essential role of stylistic affect (*affectus*) at discourse closure.

A second reason for focusing on closure, as opposed to any another part of a text, is that readers work towards the ending and, although the journey itself should be seen as the most valuable part of reading, it is the terminus that is all too often given primary importance. The closing lines occupy a highly foregrounded position in this respect. A third reason pertains to analytic pragmatism. When using real readers in experiments it is easy to let them read poems or very short stories and then comment on them. Novels, however, by their very length, pose something of a methodological challenge. When using novels in reader response experiments, I believe that the beginning or the ending of a story poses fewer contextualising problems than a piece of text taken from the middle of a novel might. Indeed, endings might be even more suitable for study than beginnings, because the closing lines of a novel often embody the content of the whole text that has gone before. Herrnstein Smith appears to lend support to this in her book *Poetic Closure*, when she claims that "the sense of conclusiveness in the last lines of a poem, like the finality of the last chords of a sonata, seems to confirm retrospectively, as if with a final stamp of approval, the valued qualities of the entire experience we have just sustained" (1968: 4). Although this comment pertains to poetry, I believe that the same can be said about closure in novels. There are, of course, many ways to end a novel. Newman, Cusick and Tourette, for example, list four main types (i) the protagonist gets what he/she wants and lives happily ever after, (ii) he/she does not get what he/she wants and lives unhappily ever after, (iii) he/she realises that the goal was not worth it, and (iv) he/she discovers that he/she was better off without it in the first place (2000: 55). In short, an ending can be happy or sad; it can involve death or birth or even rebirth; it may be ironic or surprising, linear or circular. Moreover, some endings even provide, or appear to provide, no resolution at all.

The notion of "control" is also important to reading at the close of a novel. Readers have control at all times during the reading process but this somehow seems more important at closure, when readers may try to optimise the affective input in their reading experience. For example, when reading at closure, readers can choose to stop and prolong the enjoyment. In doing so, they opt to save the best bit for later as they might some candy or chocolate treat. Something similar is seen in Manguel's reflections on his own reading behaviour when reaching the end of a novel: "I don't think I can remember a greater comprehensive joy than that of coming to the last few pages and setting a book down, so that the end would not take place until at least tomorrow, and sinking back into my pillow with the sense of having actually stopped time" (1996: 151).

Interesting work related to the notion of literary closure has been done by Susan Lohafer and especially on her notion of pre-closure in short stories. In her experiments subjects were asked to indicate where they thought a story should have optimally ended, and why. She concluded from her results that readers are capable of tapping into a deeply ingrained ability to recognise narrative wholeness (2003: 3). She calls this "storyness", a phenomenon concerned more with what a story reveals, than with story structure or story grammar. "Storying", as she calls it, thus is an elemental cognitive process that makes experience intelligible (2003: 3). So while pre-closure points are always textual, they also give insights into the basic narrative workings of the human mind.

A further reason for me choosing closure as an appropriate place for the analysis and testing of reader responses is that many readers seem to be in a more affective mood at the close of a novel. Herrnstein Smith suggests that "the sources of our gratification in closure probably lie in the most fundamental aspects of our psychological and physiological organization" (1968: 2–3). Interestingly, she appears to be alluding here to what is known these days as "embodiment", which refers to the grounding of meaning in the nature and make-up of our human bodies, especially in the way we perceive and interact with the world around us: a process that is as cultural as it is biological. Cognitive psychologist and embodiment specialist Raymond Gibbs Jr. has stressed the importance of the cultural basis of embodiment, especially in metaphor, by claiming that "recognizing that what is cognitive and embodied is inherently cultural [and] should be a fundamental part of how we do our work as cognitive psychologists, linguists and anthropologists" (1999b: 156; see also Gibbs 2006). There are crucial embodied aspects to endings in novels. Readers know when a story is ending. Their sensual input, both visual and tactile, will tell them this. There is thus a subconscious, visual-somatic preparation for the final lines which are to come. As Novakovich points out, "in a novel it is clear when the end will occur—the book ends physically. You can't hide it, unlike in movies, in theatre, in symphony" (1995: 164–65). There are stylistic reasons as well for looking more closely at closure. This is highlighted again by Herrnstein Smith when she argues that poetic convention and styles in the study of closure are important for many reasons. One of these is that formal and thematic elements that typically appear at closure may activate conventional past experiences of similar discourses. For example, a repeated final line in a poem can seem familiar to a Western reader because such repetitions are found in nursery rhymes, which are more often than not experienced in childhood (1968: 30).

The closing lines of *The Great Gatsby* have not only been remarked upon for their stylistic eloquence, but for the embodied effects that they have on a reader too. Prigozy, for example, says of the final lines, "Nick's soaring language at the end is the triumph of style" (1998: xxxii), later adding that "the charged prose lifts it above the first-person narrative pattern of the rest of the book" (1998: xxxiv). Comments like "soaring language" and "charged prose" seem to suggest that a reader might become emoted at the end of this novel by a combination of various inputs that will most certainly include the language and style of the piece, as well other mind-based affective-cognitive phenomena discussed in the previous chapters. There is an underlying suggestion here that some kind of epiphany, a felt sense of movement and elevation, may take place in a reader. I will explore this intuition in Chapters 10 and 11.

Let us now briefly look at how readers read. There have been very few good empirical experiments conducted on literary reading times, and where and why readers might speed up and slow down when reading a literary text. One exception is Cupchik and László's 1994 article. In this experiment the authors examined the responses to short story excerpts that either focussed on the experience of the character or on action. They also looked at levels of subject involvement and objective detachment. They then measured scale ratings and reading times. The forty subjects (twenty male and twenty female) read six tests each. Drawing on preset data obtained for each fragment, they found that segments which "provided insight" were read more slowly, whereas surprising segments were read more quickly. Regarding subject involvement, they observed how readers slowed their pace of reading if they judged the text to be rich in meaning about life. In the object set, stories that were adjudged to have evoked images were also read more slowly. Female readers found stories to be richer in meaning and to be more personally relevant, i.e. females were more responsive to subject involvement. Females also slowed down more often while reading pieces of text that they judged to be rich in meaning about life, whereas males slowed down more often when the text evoked images in their minds. Another similar study has, for example, found that readers consistently read longer segments of text faster, per syllable, than shorter text segments, which are read slower (Miall and Kuiken 1994: 399).

With this in mind let us turn to our thirty-six readers in the NRQ survey. I wanted to find out a number of things. A first was whether readers thought they read more slowly at closure. A second was whether readers go back to re-read the final lines more slowly if they have initially read quickly at closure. A third was whether language and style have an effect on their reading speed, be this during the first reading or a subsequent (more or less immediate) rereading of the closing lines. With regard to the first of these one might expect that when readers are coming to the end of a novel they will read more slowly. There is evidence that slow reading is generally beneficial. A basic principle, according to the literary critic and essayist Anatoyle Broyard in "Rereading and Other Excesses", is that the more one likes a book the more likely one is to take one's time with it. In modern discourse psychology there is a phenomenon known as "wrap-up", first described by Just and Carpenter (1980), which implies a slowing or even pausing at sentential, clausal and discourse endings. P. David Pearson describes it as follows:

> In the sentence wrap-up stage the reader attempts to resolve any inconsistencies within the sentence and to search for referents that have not been assigned. The ends of sentences indicate that one thought has ended and another is to begin. Thus the reader knows that this is an appropriate place to attempt integration. Readers may also do some wrap up at the ends of clauses or at the end of units longer than a sentence. (2000: 215).

The notions of "attempting to resolve inconsistencies and integration" during the reading of the wrap-up stage of a syntactic unit suggests a slowing down, perhaps leading to a brief pause. This in turn supports the general idea of a reduced reading speed at sentence endings and at the end of larger stretches of text as Pearson alludes to. In a discussion on the diverse contradictions, ambiguities and inconsistencies that a reader can come across while reading, van den Broek et al. state with regard to their landscape model of reading:

> Once an inconsistency is detected, the reader needs to restructure the mental representation to re-establish coherence. This process, similar to that observed during wrap-up at the end of a text or sentence, takes time and hence reading slows down. (1999: 87)

Very little of this research pertains to reading literature. It focuses instead on artificial texts manufactured for use in eye-tracking experiments. This is understandable given the experimental context, yet unfortunate because "inconsistencies" and "ambiguities" are the very essence of literary discourse, with its frequent use of style figures and foregrounded syntax and lexis. Let us now turn to my own group of readers. Remember that these responses do not pertain to reading *The Great Gatsby*, even though I have started to discuss that book, rather they refer to reading experiences in general.

### NRQ—Q.2   When You Feel/Realise That You are Reaching the End of a Much-enjoyed Novel Does your Default Reading speed Tend to Alter, i.e. Does it Tend to (a) Slow Down, (b) Speed Up, or (c) Remain the Same?

Eleven respondents said that they slowed down, twenty-four said that they speeded up, and one said it remains the same. A few of the twenty-four subjects who chose the "speed up" option opted chose to supply an additional comment. Many of these were broadly the same in content and can be represented by the response of one subject who said "I often get so excited and curious that I can't stop until I am finished". Some, however, rejected the idea out of hand, whereas others were more reflective. One subject said "Yes, I often speed up, but after I have finished the novel I then regret I didn't slow down". Below are six comments from those eleven subjects who claimed that their reading speed slowed down at closure.

1. When I like the novel I slow down at the end because I want to stay "in the story"
2. My reading slows down because I feel if I slow down then there is less of a chance that I will miss something important, something meaningful. I also slow down to avoid having to reread

3. I tend to slow down tremendously and read a sentence word for word instead of scanning it
4. As I realise that I am coming to the end of a good novel I slow down so that I fully understand everything that is happening, so that I can absorb it completely and enjoy it till the final letter
5. I don't like finishing a book I like, so I slow down my reading
6. When I read a favourite novel I always have to cry near the end and my thoughts wander off, slowing down the reading process

Let us now return to the majority: the group of twenty-four subjects who believed that they speed up at closure, and let us pose them a related question.

### NRQ.—Q.3   Once You Have Finished Reading a Much-enjoyed Novel Do You Tend to go Back and Reread the Final Few Pages or Paragraphs?

The responses from the twenty-four subjects were split here, twelve–twelve. Looking at the overall reading habits at closure of the thirty-six subjects, we can see that approximately one-third slowed down at closure, a second third read quickly and then went back and reread the closing lines, and a final third read quickly and that was that. With regard to the second group, the re-readers, we can perhaps assume that their second act of reading was conducted with more attention and less speed. We cannot, however, be sure of this. Nine of the twelve subjects who admitted to re-reading also chose to add additional comment. Perhaps these will shed more light on this matter.

1. I usually read it a couple of times to understand the message of the book. It always touches me when the end of a book is very good
2. Because the ending of a much-loved novel is usually one of the most important aspects of a book, and when I speed up at the end I don't really enjoy it. So I reread it
3. I think it's because there is always something about an ending which makes you think—A good end to a novel always leaves me with a kind of hangover, especially when the ending is surprising or difficult to deal with. Therefore I tend to reread certain parts in an attempt to fully understand it
4. Yes, I reread it more carefully and definitely at a slower pace
5. Slower. To enjoy the "ride" once more
6. When I go back I reread more concentrated. I try to let the last words of the book resonate a little longer so that I can remember them better
7. I read slower. A more normal tempo. But I don't reread all the last pages I just look for the most exciting passages

8. Speed-reading means I lose some detail. That's why I go back; to "savour"
9. Sometimes do this because I don't want the book to be over. I then read slowly

We see that while reading at closure, some readers in this survey are "touched", "given hangovers", "enjoy the ride", "allow the book to resonate in them", "go in search of exciting passages", "go back in order to 'savour'", etc. The raw data from the survey are interesting, but they do not provide solid evidence for my general intuition that readers slow down their reading speed at literary closure. However, it may be recalled that the empirical study conducted by Cupchik and László suggests that segments which "provided insight" were read more slowly. Hence, perhaps the type of book that a reader had in mind would affect the content of his/her response.

A third and final question with regard to reading at closure asks whether the actual written style of closing lines can affect the reading speed and the way a person reads. Less explicitly, it also asks readers to reflect on how they process the language that they are reading. One would expect the way people read at closure is affected by the style of the written piece and that this in turn impinges on the reading speed. Let us see what our readers thought. Below is the question, which I will break down into three parts when looking at the response data. The parts pertain to (a) general style at closure, (b) whether reading speed can be affected by literary style at closure, and (c) whether or not readers processes the text in "chunks" at literary closure.

## NRQ—Q.9   Do You Think the Way in Which the Closing Lines of a Novel are Written, i.e. the Style (e.g. Lexical Choices, Syntax Structure, Clause Structure, Punctuation, Use of Metaphor, etc.) Can Affect the Way You Read (i.e. Your Reading Speed and the Chunks of Text You Read in One Go, as it Were, i.e. Words, Clauses, Sentences)?

Twenty-nine of the thirty-six subjects responded affirmatively that style at closure can affect they way they read. Let us look at a section of the response data. These eight all comment on general style at closure, which is the first part of the question I wish to focus on.

1. If the closing lines of a novel consist of long and complicated sentences, I believe this affects my reading experience. I might have to re-read one or two sentences or parts of sentences in order to get the full gist of what is being said
2. Sure, the way something is written has everything to do with how it is read. An author can choose to make the ending a thoughtful piece of reading because the reader is likely to want to read and fully understand it anyway

3. If the sentences are very long and the writer uses a lot of "difficult" words then it takes me longer to read the sentences. If the sentences are relatively simple, I do not have to think about the grammar and it is easier for me to get "caught up" in the book

4. An author should make his closing lines more complicated so that reader will think about them more

5. If the closing lines of a novel are completely out of style with the rest of the novel, it annoys me. I don't like overly long, intricate sentences as closing lines because you have to go back and puzzle them out, which is not what I want in closing lines. They are in my opinion supposed to finish the narrative. I prefer short, one-liner kind of sentences, preferably with a sort of punch-line effect. If a novel ends in a very difficult kind of paragraph, it can make me actively dislike the novel, even if I had been enjoying it up to that moment

6. Yes, style at closure affects the readability of a book

7. I think it only influences your reading style if the writer changes his style dramatically from what he has used in the rest of the book. The ending is always special, but if it is the same style as the rest of the book I don't know if you would notice it as much

8. When an author uses dots like these. . . . It makes me think about it immediately. If he uses open sentences or incomplete sentences or questions, it has the same effect on me

These data show a variety of things with regard to the importance of style at closure. For instance, they include the idea that "ellipsis dots make readers think about their possible meaning", which echoes the significance of ellipsis in such literary contexts. They further allude to the idea that longer sentences seem to take longer to read and, therefore, can cause irritation in a reader, although sometimes they may make the reader "think more". On the other hand, shorter sentences may cause readers "to get caught up in the book", while yet another respondent likes "one-liner sentences" that can produce "punch-line effects". Other respondents comment on the necessity of stylistic change at closure, a shifting down of a gear, as it were, or, as one respondent puts it, "the ending is always special, but if it is the same style as the rest of the book I don't know if you would notice it as much". Others, such as respondent five, expresses contempt for such stylistic strategies, irrespective of whether they be conscious on the part of the author or not. Two others state "the way something is written has everything to do with how it is read" and "style at closure affects the readability of a book".

Let us now look at a second part of the above question: whether reading speed can be affected by style at closure. There are eight responses pertaining to this.

1. Sentence structure, etc. always affects how fast you read. If at the end of a novel the sentences are long, with lots of sub-clauses and

metaphors, then you can't read fast (even if you want to because you want to know how it ends). If I read fast, then I'll miss half of what is being said (this is especially the case for me when I read in English, especially nineteenth century novels like Austen, Hardy, Gaskell) so I have to read slowly

2. If it's complicated and more philosophical, you'll have to read slower and will have to think about it more to process your thoughts about it

3. If the style is in such a way that it adds to the pleasure of reading, then the reading speed will change. It may speed up because the language is as fast flowing as the story itself, but it may also slow down because you may wish to absorb every single word of the final part of that book you loved so much

4. Short sentences, for example, make one read faster. I think a good author is someone who can direct readers like this in subliminal ways. So style can affect the way I read very much

5. When something is written in a certain way, especially at the end of a book, it really can affect your speed of reading and how much you remember at the end

6. I guess if a sentence is written fluently, i.e. there are no weird constructions that break up the sentence or force you to pause, it's much easier to read. Perhaps if there are difficult metaphors in the closing lines you slow down because you need to concentrate even better. Punctuation is essential for reading speed. A long sentence, without punctuation, can make you stumble over words or a construction

7. Endings with action make me read faster whereas endings with contemplation make me read slower

8. Long sentences with many short words make me read fast, whereas short sentences can get me to stand still for a moment and think about their meaning

There is some consensus about the idea that style can alter reading speed, even if different readers think different things. One of the respondents suggested that "the style *adds* to the pleasure of reading". Hence, other aspects, likes themes, and cognitive input, as alluded to in responses 2 and 7, are important as well. Affective literary reading, especially at closure, therefore might very well depend on a selection of blended affective input; perhaps one not too dissimilar to those I discussed in previous chapters.

Let us now look at a third and final part of the above question that asks how readers think they read at closure. I asked them whether or not they felt that as they slowed down they processed the text in kind of "chunks". This is not an easy question to formulate. The mixed nature of the five responses below appears to bear this out.

1. Sometimes when a writer uses a lot of stylistic devices in the closing lines it makes it difficult to really get the ending and understand what

the conclusion is, so that makes my reading speed go down. It will also decrease the chunks of text I read in one go

2. Lots of adjectives can slow down my reading and make me reread certain phrases

3. I tend to read more slowly at the close of a novel, but I don't stammer. I get the feeling I'm getting sucked into the end of the story

4. The end of a novel has extra meaning, it has to offer closure and also give a feeling of satisfaction. I always hold my breath when I am reading the end of a novel, and I like to see this tension reflected in the language that is used. The more elegant, direct or meaningful and heavy the ending is, the better. Punctuation is always something that can determine speed at which you read. Also metaphors that seem to sum up the book

5. Metaphors and disrupting style at the end always pull me into the novel and affect how I read it

These responses give no evidence that because of a slow-down in reading speed at closure subjects would be inclined to read closing lines in textual chunks. Only the first respondent appears to say anything directly relevant when he/she notes that stylistic devices not only make his/her reading speed slow down but also "decrease" the chunks of text he/she reads in one go. Further, there is respondent two who claims that adjectival clusters can cause him/her to slow down.

There were, however, some very interesting comments in these responses about the role that the body and bodily processes play during affective, slow reading at literary closure. These comments are all the more interesting as they were not requested directly but came about indirectly. Some focused on the body and on movement. For example, the third respondent speaks of reading more slowly at closure but not stuttering ("stammer") in his/her reading patterns. Rather he/she gets the feeling of being "sucked into the end of the story". Somewhat similarly, the fourth respondent admits to always holding his/her breath when reading the end of a novel in order to see if the tension caused by not breathing is reflected in the language that is used. Furthermore, respondent five speaks of "being pulled along into a novel at closure" by such things as metaphor and deviant ("disrupting") style. These last three responses seem to be touching on something that is real for them, even if they do not have the terminology to explain what is happening to them. What is described here can, I believe, be discussed and labelled in cognitive linguistic and cognitive stylistic ways. In particular, this kind of highly-emoted text-processing at closure can be discussed in embodied image-schematic terms. In Chapter 10 I will attempt to show in depth how this may work.

To summarise, the discussion thus far language and style at closure appear to have some importance for affecting some readers, and that some readers are aware of this. Further, few readers appeared to slow down initially at closure when reading a much-enjoyed novel, but several more appear to go back and reread almost immediately if they had originally read quickly. Lastly, there were no reports that engaged readers read in "chunks" of discourse at closure, even if some respondents made intriguing comments about movement, the body and being "pulled in".

Despite the outcomes of this raw data, I believe that a major reason for slowing down at the close of a much-enjoyed novel is not just to "savour" the language and style, as one subject claimed, although this is extremely important, but also to prepare for savouring their mind-fed cognitive "output" too. In such situations at closure, all of the earlier mentioned affective inputs—LRI, the mood, the location, the themes, the style and language—come together in a confluence of affective, oceanic cognition to produce the kind of feeling that some readers can, and do, experience. Furthermore, this event is on the cusp of the "reading—post reading" stages described in Chapter 7, where the dominance of language in affective literary discourse processing situations gives way to the ascendancy of the affective mind. Perhaps it is when this blend of affective cognitive inputs is at its optimum state that the embodied mind takes that one extra step that leads to what is known as reader epiphany, a sense of felt movement? Let us investigate the phenomenon of literary epiphany further.

Epiphany has several meanings. First, in its biblical sense it refers to a Christian feast day, 6 January, which commemorates the manifestation of the newborn Christ to the three Magi. The etymological root of the word means "showing" or more figuratively "bringing to light". The notion of vision is thus paramount. Moreover, there is a clear classical precursor in the Greek term *epiphaneia*, which was a recurring event involving the ancient gods swooping down from their mountain domains to appear before mortal men and women. In this sense, although the focus is still on "showing", as seen in the etymology of the word, there is movement and apparition involved. In the literary, character-based notion of the word, epiphany involves a sudden manifestation or perception of the essence or meaning of something. This is the sense of the term most frequently used in mainstream twentieth-century literary scholarship to refer to heightened character emotion. The most-cited example from English literature takes place in James Joyce's *A Portrait of the Artist as a Young Man* (1914–15/1992) and concerns the protagonist Stephen Dedalus's revelation while watching a young girl wade in the ocean surf (1992: 185–86). An equally famous yet much earlier episode is William Wordsworth's reference to "spots of time" in his *Prelude* (1799: II. 258). Such character epiphanies are usually triggered by a seemingly trivial incident that is often linked in some way to childhood or the memory of childhood locations.

Attempts have been made in the last thirty years to theorise epiphany. For instance, Morris Beja introduced the two terms "incongruity" and "insignificance" in the early 1970s. The first of the essentially philosophical terms indicates that an epiphany is irrelevant to the object or incident that triggers it. The second term suggests that an epiphany is triggered by a trivial object or incident (1971: 16–17). More recently, Robert Langbaum has added to these two criteria another four, which appear to be more relevant to the kind of cognitive description of epiphany that I am attempting to explore. The first of these is *psychological association*, which asserts that "the epiphany is not an incursion of God from outside; it is a psychological phenomenon arising from a real sensuous experience, either present or recollected" (1999: 44). The second, *momentousness*, suggests that "the epiphany lasts only a moment, but leaves an enduring effect" (1999: 44). The third pertains to *suddenness*, which entails "a sudden change in external conditions cause[ing] a shift in sensuous perception that sensitizes the observer for epiphany" (1999: 44). The fourth, *fragmentation*, suggests that "the text never quite equals the epiphany" (1999: 44). This final category is also referred to as the "epiphanic leap" (1999: 44). Langbaum makes some interesting observations here by emphasising the embodied and emotive reality of epiphany and by suggesting that epiphany is about far more than just what happens to characters.

I am interested in what happens to readers while reading literature, not in what happens to characters in stories. It is more akin to the emotive reading experience described in the opening paragraph of this chapter about an idealised reader. Such a process involves Langbaum's notion of a momentary psychological phenomenon arising from sensuous experience and leaving a lasting effect; a felt shift in sensual perception.

The following two real accounts of reader epiphany show what it is I am trying to describe. The first pertains to poetry and the second to prose. The first example involves the twentieth-century beat generation poet Allen Ginsberg reflecting on his reading of "Ah Sunflower" by William Blake back in the 1940s, and how he felt at the end of the poem (this event is also cited in Gibbs 2002, where I first came across it). Below, Ginsberg reflects on how during his reading of the closing lines he suddenly went into some altered state.

> My body suddenly felt light, and a sense of cosmic consciousness, vibrations, understanding, awe, and wonder and surprise. Kind of like the top of my head coming off, letting in the rest of the universe connected to my own brain. (1966: 40)

I believe this to be an example of reader epiphany at poetic closure. If epiphanies owe part of their attraction to "felt aesthetic impact" (1999: 179), as Phillipp Wolf has claimed, then physiological aspects of such an epiphany are observable in Ginsberg's account of "vibrations" and "his body suddenly feeling light". Reading is cognitive processing but there is a tsunami of affective cognition at work here that defies the rationalising label of pure cognitive processing. Jay Losey suggests accordingly that "epiphany describes a powerfully felt moment which occurs non-rationally" (1999:

379). This type of cognition even appears to go beyond the affective cognition discussed in the previous chapter. It warrants a categorisation of its own.

A second example of what might be seen as a reader epiphany involves the reading of the closing lines of *The Great Gatsby*. Looking back on her life from the position of an established writer and scholar, Alice Kaplan shares an intimate literary reading experience in her autobiography.

> It was afternoon, and the sun was coming through an especially large window that looked out towards the mountains. I looked up towards the window and let the sun shine right in my eyes. The sunshine made me realize I was crying. I put the book on the table, spine down, to wipe away my tears. (1993: 58)

Here, Kaplan recalls how she was emotionally overwhelmed. Similar accounts appeared in my NRQ data, even though these were not expert readers. For example, one subject said "it always touches me when the end of a book is very good", while another, almost echoing Kaplan, reported: "when I read a favourite novel I always have to cry near the end and my thoughts wander off, slowing down the reading process". Interestingly, Kaplan's gaze gets diverted from the book: she is staring up at a window as the sun streams onto her face. She is crying, something that she does not immediately realise. She has quite plausibly undergone a reader epiphany at closure. She reflects here on a childhood reading experience, but she is apparently unable to let go of it as an adult.

In light of this we can wonder how other readers feel when they have just finished reading a much-enjoyed novel and also whether specific memories get triggered, and further, if so, what is the content of those recollections. Let us take these three questions one at a time. Before we look at the data I should say that although presented as a whole originally, there are really two questions in NRQ 4. I, therefore, break them up here into 4a and 4b for ease of discussion. NRQ 5, which follows, also projects back to question NRQ 4.

## NRQ—Q. 4a   Try to Recall the Moment When You Had Just Finished Reading a Much-loved Novel. Can You Remember the Feeling at That Moment? If So, Can You Say Something About That Feeling?

All thirty-six subjects produced a written response to this question. Several subjects, however, only made very short, one-word, references to the kinds of emotions they remember having felt at the close of a much-enjoyed novel. These included "happy", "sad", "disappointed", "satisfied", "baffled", "tearful", "reflective", "overwhelmed" and "empty". Some had more than one mention. Broadly speaking, these responses can be summed up under the heading "sad but satisfied": sad at having finished the novel, but satisfied for having read it. There were eighteen more detailed responses as well, which are listed below. I have grouped them in three sections to aid the discussion.

1. I felt a sense of dread the novel was over because I now had to find a new one
2. I was really sad—a mood that could last for a couple of days actually
3. When I finish one of my most-enjoyed novels I always feel strange. I always wait a moment, close my eyes and think of the meaning of it. It feels like having a secret that nobody knows about
4. I feel content and usually stay seated for a time afterwards. I think about the book but also other things
5. It was like I was still living in the story. I usually have a great feeling of satisfaction
6. I am often in an accomplished mood. I feel kind of sad, but also content. The emotions I feel are strong, but I don't know how exactly
7. I felt the same emotion that the last few sentence contained
8. I felt happy about what had happened, and happy about myself
9. It is sort of coming out of a novel and back into reality. It's a feeling of having to redefine myself with the new experience of the book

There are some through-provoking comments made here in this first group of nine responses. Perhaps the most interesting one is made by respondent five, who claims to be still "living in the story" after he/she has finished reading. This reader is in the post-reading phase that I described in Chapter 7 when I was discussing my four confluvial stages of reading. Perhaps he/she might continue at a lower level of intensity into the non-reading stage and form intertextual material for deployment in new engaged reading situations?

Other responses were emotive in a philosophical sense, which suggests that the ending of literary texts can be concerned with far more than mere emotional gratification. There are four of these:

10. Peaceful, with a clear mind, feeling good about what I had read and contemplating the content of the story
11. I felt like I had understood the world
12. When I finish a novel I always reflect on life in general. It gives me a positive feeling and also enriches my inner life
13. I felt as if I had reached a higher level of understanding

The most interesting responses for this experiment were, however, those that suggested heightened emotion combined with epiphanic aspects.

14. Quite excited. Climactic (in the reading sense). Just like waking from a vivid dream or coming off a roller-coaster
15. Very emotional. Disappointed and euphoric at the same time. But also calm and focused (in a Zen sort of way)—taking it slow
16. I felt a sort of release
17. Thrilled. Heightened attention. Intense experiences and excited expectation
18. Excited, euphoric—Somehow I am still reading in my mind.

These responses and references to "reaching a higher level", "climactic", "euphoric", "feeling a sort of release" and "intense experiences" are all quite intriguing and will be discussed later, when I reflect on my own epiphanic reading experiences. Moving on, the second part of question 4 is presented below.

## NRQ—Q.4b   Were Any Specific Memories Triggered by this Reading Experience?

Eighteen of the thirty-six subjects responded affirmatively to this question. I had anticipated a higher number. Perhaps the word "specific" in the question may have been too constraining and too confusing, but on the other hand, perhaps it was the case that no memories were triggered at all.

The third and final question therefore, which is question five in the NRQ, is only directed at the eighteen subjects who answered "yes" to the above question:

## NRQ—Q. 5   If You Have Answered "Yes" to the Above Question (4b), Could You Please Add Some Detail.

There were eleven responses from the eighteen who answered affirmatively. I present these data in two groups below for ease of discussion. Here are the first seven.

1. It was a bit of a blend. Some memories were concerned with a specific location, but also with my friends and a specific event was taking place. We were saying goodbye
2. Some novels remind me of summer and being on holiday like earlier. The smell of the grass and the water is very intense
3. It reminded me of myself, when I was young (8–12 years old).
4. The memories are blends of special persons and special events from my past
5. I just read a novel about Jewish boys and it made me think of my childhood. I am not Jewish though
6. Things you recognise, like relationships. Also descriptions of places I have been, locations that I remember. Sometimes my attention goes

straight to that place instead of staying with the novel. That happens at the end of a novel but I am not sure that this is the only place it happens

7. The novel I read seemed to describe very graphically a number of existing locations and buildings that I have visited. These memories were triggered quite extensively as well

These responses provide examples of the kinds of LRI and themes I have discussed such as childhood, locations (annual holiday and closer to home), special persons from one's past, etc. Response number 6 is very rich in that it shows how remembrances of childhood locations can flesh out a reading experience, overriding the imagery and detail being prescribed by the words in the text, just as happened to Stevenson's marooned Virgil reader that we read about in Chapter 3. While these seven responses were rich, others tended to be more general.

8. This is quite hard to remember but it reminded me of a mood I was in during a specific period of my life. I would like to tell you more about this but I just can't remember

9. It made me think of my boyfriend. Of times when I had not quite understood why he did certain things

10. Any novel will trigger memories at the end and I tend to identify with (at least some) of the (main) characters. These memories are most often just flashes, along the lines of "hey, that happened to me" or "boy, do I know how he/she feels" or sometimes "geez, is the author way off here". It depends very much on the novel

11. I read a book about London recently (*Hawksmoor*) and it reminded me of when I was there on holiday

We have to conclude that the raw data is clearly mixed. Up until now I have presented reader epiphany mainly within a literary context. However, I will now introduce associated neurobiological, cognitive, psychoanalytic and linguistic aspects of epiphany-like phenomena in order for me to be able to draw links later. In short we need to look at epiphany in the cognitive age.

It is one of the aims of the following chapter to take the literary notion of reader epiphany and ground it in a more cognitive-affective embodied framework. This shift from the epiphany of character events to that of reading phenomena might seem whimsical, but significant steps have already been made in cognitive linguistics, cognitive psychology and psychoanalysis to describe the phenomenon of felt motion in the embodied human mind. I am thus attempting to show how cognitive stylistic analysis can in part account for felt motion in episodes of emotive literary reading at closure. In attempting to ground reader epiphany in cognitive stylistics, I am to some extent carrying out the claim of literary scholar Ashton Nichols that "cognitive studies can illuminate our understanding of a concept like literary epiphany" (1999: 472). I will briefly discuss some relevant theories, several of which will return in the subsequent discussion section.

In cognitive linguistics, Lakoff and Johnson have started to develop an idea they term "empathic projection", which is in some ways similar to felt movement during reader epiphany. In *Philosophy in the Flesh* the authors put forward an account of what empathic projection is:

> In preparing to imitate, we empathetically imagine ourselves in the body of another, cognitively stimulating the movements of the other. That cognitive stimulation, when "vivid", is the actual activation of motor programs with input to the muscles inhibited, which results in the "feel" of movement without moving. The experience of such a "feel" is a form of empathic projection. (1999: 565)

Drawing on the earlier-mentioned simulation theory, as well as the workings of mirror neurons and proprioception that I set out in Chapter 2, Lakoff and Johnson show how we can feel a definite yet discrete sense movement without moving at all. This is just what happens during reader epiphany. Another cognitive psychological account of felt movement in the framework of general emotional experience is put forward by Gibbs:

> Our way of characterizing the felt dimension of emotional experience is in terms of "affective space" or the space we move through as we experience distinct emotions . . . Affective space has a sensuous feel to it, a texture that makes it neither purely mental, nor reducible to the physiological body. (2002: 20)

Here, drawing on the previous work of Cataldi (1996), Gibbs emphasises a sense of movement, as well as the space we move through, when emotions are experienced. In this same discussion Gibbs also speaks of the effect and sensation of travelling through this affective space: "moving through affective space has a textured palpitably felt dimension just in the way that we can feel different textures and substances we touch with our skin" (2002: 20). According to Gibbs, skin-deep textures are thus capable of distinguishing different emotions when moving through affective space. He adds that the work done on this "suggests that emotion is conceived of, and experienced in terms of, embodied movement through affective space in dimensions that are textured and have depth" (2002: 26). The felt sense of movement through affective space that Gibbs describes also might be valid for intense emotive episodes of literary reading: the kind of felt reader epiphanies that I will explore later.

What Gibbs describes with emphasis on emotive distance and emotive movement is in some ways reminiscent of D. W. Winnicott's psychoanalytic notion of "transitional objects" and "transitional phenomena". Winnicott's research, most of which is based on a blend of clinical observations and theoretical conjecture, mainly focused on the concepts of "projection", "travelling", "creativity" and "child–parent relationship". This is analysed in depth in *Playing and Reality* (1971), the roots of which lie in Winnicott's 1951 paper, "Transitional Objects and Transitional Phenomena". A central concern in his work was the extremely personal intermediate space between internal and external reality, largely grounded in a person's childhood experiences. The transitional object is the space between the infant and the mother, or, more specifically, between the unweaned baby and the mother's breast. Winnicott claims that this space will remain important throughout the life of an individual, as it is "a neutral area of experience which will not be challenged" (1971: 12). It often symbolises the union of baby and mother. As the infant grows, the mother and her breast fade in its consciousness into a state of limbo and are replaced by a favourite soft toy or piece of material on which the infant continues to suckle. A similar transition takes place in childhood, whereby play takes the place of the object of attention. Finally, in early adulthood phenomena like "artistic creativity and appreciation" take on the role of play (1971: 5). As Winnicott himself put it, these latter phenomena are retained in adult life "in the intense experiencing that belongs to the arts and to religion and to imaginative living, and to creative scientific work" (1971: 14). To my mind, it is the most abstract and hence most personal of the arts—like music and, above all, literature—that best facilitates the transitional phenomenon of adult life.

Felt epiphanic movement in literary reading also ties into what Roland Barthes described in relation to the visual perception of photographs. In *Camera Lucida* (1980) he discusses a phenomenon he calls *punctum*, which concerns a sudden, unexpected recognition of hidden meaning that shoots out of the photograph like an arrow to pierce the viewer. In theorising this, Barthes draws primarily on his own experience. The image that triggered his own personal *punctum* while rifling through a pile of old photographs was one of his long-dead mother. When he started, Barthes had no idea which photograph he was searching for but when he found it he recognised it immediately. Although there are clear modality differences, Barthes's search for his emotive release mechanism can be said to be similar to a reader's search for heightened emotion while engaged with a literary text. For instance, literary readers attempt to first set out the appropriate conditions that match optimum place to optimum time to optimum mode. Thereafter, like Barthes's reader they commence "looking/reading" with only partial knowledge of what they actually hope to encounter. The photograph of Barthes's mother as a child was in many ways unexpected, because he had no guarantee of experiencing his *punctum*, just as there is no guarantee that a reader will become highly emoted by reading a specific novel in a specific location under specific conditions. However, the nature of the projectile, the *punctum*, is perhaps not really what is of central importance in this process, because the focus is never purely on style or themes. In a neurocognitive approach to reading, the projectile's origin and composition are also relevant. In the context of a heightened emotive state of literary reading these include the five aspects of affective cognition: LRI, mood, location, themes and style.

We have now looked more closely at the notions of literary closure and literary epiphany. The scene has now been set for the three chapters to come. The importance of reader epiphany will become clear in the next chapter, which will be primarily of an analytic nature. There, I will investigate how the thirty-six readers in my experiment read the closing lines of *The Great Gatsby*.

# 9 Reading the Closing Lines of *The Great Gatsby*

*The Great Gatsby* was Fitzgerald's fourth major novel. He was twenty-eight when he started writing it and he would work just ten months on the project. While writing, he remarked to his editor Maxwell Perkins: "I want to write something *new*—something extraordinary and beautiful and simple and intricately patterned" (Prigozy 1998: ix). In this quest, Fitzgerald made alteration after alteration. Indeed, it has been noted that "Gatsby achieved its greatness in proof" (Prigozy 1998: x). Matthew J. Bruccoli goes even further by saying that the art of Fitzgerald's fiction is rewriting (1992: ix). On its completion, aware of its stylistic quality, Fitzgerald told Perkins "I've found my line—from now on this comes first" (Prigozy 1998: xii). *The Great Gatsby* became Fitzgerald's most successful novel, but initially it was a commercial flop. The first print run sold just 20,000 copies, far fewer than the 70,000 that were hoped for. A second print run was commissioned, but by the time Fitzgerald died fifteen years later it had stopped selling. The apotheosis of the novel began after Gatsby's death. In the 1950s it boomed, and by 1960 it had, as mentioned, reached the top of the Scribner bestseller list, where it has remained unchallenged ever since (Bruccoli 1992: 203–05).

The novel is often cited as embodying the Jazz Age, a triumph of the art deco period. It is, as Bruccoli claims, the defining novel of the 1920s (1992: ix). Some themes in the book include nostalgia, intangibility and distance. All of these are, of course, intertwined. The concept of time is central to the novel too, both stylistically and thematically: Bruccoli claims that this short novel contains 450 expressions of time (1992: xiv). He suggests further that the notions of "mutability" and "loss" are prominent in these time references (1992: xiv). Gatsby thinks he can control time because he is now rich: "Can't repeat the past? Why, of course you can", he incredulously claims at one stage in the story, during his quest to reclaim his old love, Daisy. Critics also attribute an "elusive quality" to the story. As Prigozy notes, "the story is powerful as much for what is suggested as for what is told" (1998: xi). She adds that "the characters in *The Great Gatsby* are presented in as fragmented and sketchy a manner as the narrative" (1998: xxvi). This distal dimension, which I discussed in Chapter 5, adds to their emotive elusiveness. It seems likely that much of this sense of intangibility is achieved by conscious uses of themes like incommunicability, a longing to return and childhood. The distal use of language also plays a significant role. Prigozy speaks of a vocabulary of "impermanence and evanescence", citing words like "whisperings", "drift", "relentless" and "murmurings" as examples (1998: xxxi). Neither is Nick's narration of events ever proximal; it is almost always distal. As Tanner notes "his account is constantly marked by such words and phrases as the following: 'I suppose', 'I suspect', 'I think', 'possibly', 'probably', 'perhaps', 'I've heard it said', 'he seemed to say', 'there must have been', 'I have an idea that', 'I always had the impression', etc." (2000: xxii). According to Tanner, the words "as though" and "as if" are used over sixty times (2000: xxii). All this elusiveness makes the novel a kind of mystery story, albeit one that is told through the somewhat moral filter of its young narrator.

Tanner speaks further of "regressive yearnings" and "hints of nostalgia for the pleasure of childhood" that manifest themselves in the novel (2000: xxxi). This then is a story about yearning, a yearning to go west and return home. From an abstract spatial perspective this involves a movement from right to left, something that from a Western cultural cognitive understanding of space and movement seems appropriate within the framework of "returning". In cognitive linguistic terms, we live our Western lives largely from left to right, as we observe it (i.e. from west to east) in a SOURCE-PATH-GOAL type fashion. This is echoed, for example, in the way westerners these days read and write. This has not always been the case in the Western world. For example, the direction of early Greek inscriptions was unstable (Robinson 1995: 167). Sometimes they would write from left to right, sometimes from right to left and sometimes in a back-and forth style known as *boustrophedon* (from the Greek *bous* "ox" and *strophos* "turning": quite literally "as the ox turns when ploughing". Most important of all, the example in the main text shows how cognition is not only tied synchronically to culture but also diachronically to history. "Returning" in a right to left (east to west) fashion in Western terms appears to take one back to a sense of one's source. As Nick says near the end of the novel: "I now see why this has been a story of the West, after all Tom and Gatsby, Daisy and Jordan and I were all Westerners". In effect then, *The Great Gatsby* is not a story about being home, but perhaps one about a desire to return home.

In this story, desirable objects are at a distance and characters have to stretch out, either manually or mnemonically, in order to come close to them. On its very opening page, for instance, Nick says, "an intimate revelation was quivering on the horizon" (Fitzgerald 1992: 7). As Nick notes soon afterwards, "instead of being the warm centre of the world, the Middle West now seemed like the ragged edge of the universe" (9). Further, distal objects are also sometimes blended with characters in the novel. Tanner notes, for instance, alluding to a blend of the famous elusive green light in the novel and Daisy, how lights have to be kept at a distance. His reasoning is that lights that come too close will all too soon lose their lustre and their appeal (2000: viii). Daisy too has something illuminating about her, as her cousin Nick observes: "her face was sad and lovely with bright things in it" (Fitzgerald 1992: 14).

Tangibility and intangibility are thus common themes in the book. According to Tanner, Nick sees Gatsby in gestural terms" (2000: xxiv). Nick also equates Gatsby's personality with "an unbroken series of successful gestures" on the second page of the novel already. But what exactly does Tanner mean? The main gesture in the book appears to be a kind of Tantalus-like stretching out towards something. This is mostly a manual act but occasionally a visual one too, either ongoing or recalled in the memory of the narrator, Nick. There are many examples of these stretchings in the novel. From the manual perspective, there is Gatsby's stretching out to grasp the elusive green light at the end of Daisy's dock. This is a lasting image in the novel. As Tanner notes:

> Seen from across the water and everything else that separates him from Daisy, the green light offers Gatsby a suitably inaccessible focus for his yearnings, something to give definition to desire while indefinitely deferring consummation, something to stretch his arms towards, as he does, rather than circle his arms around, as he tries to. (2000: viii)

Gatsby points across the sound on other occasions too. One time he sees a small yacht and follows it with his eyes. Just as it is disappearing out of sight he raises his hand and points across the bay (Fitzgerald 1992: 112). Intangibility also plays a role at the very moment when Gatsby loses Daisy: "but with every word she was drawing further and further into herself, so he gave her up, and only the dead dream fought on as the afternoon slipped away, trying to touch what was no longer tangible" (128). He is left "clutching at some last hope" (141). During a flashback, when Gatsby is leaving Louisville, having vainly searched for Daisy in the place they both used to frequent, he tries to grasp the essence of what he so desires. In doing so he stretches out his hand, grasping at the air to somehow save a piece of her, but he knows there is nothing for him to clutch at and he has thus lost her forever (145–46). Nick first sees Gatsby as he comes out of his mansion. It is night and he is standing alone on his lawn. Nick wants to shout across the garden to him when he notices Gatsby make a move: "He stretched out his arms toward the dark water in a curious way" (25). Nick then looks seaward and apprehend the green light "minute and far away, that might have been the end of a dock."(25). When his glance turns back to where Gatsby was stood, he has vanished. There are even figurative occurrences of stretching. Reflecting on his life on his thirtieth birthday "as he drives towards death in the cooling twilight" (129), Nick notes: "before me stretched the portentous, menacing road of a new decade" (129). When, as quoted earlier, Gatsby incredulously tells Nick that he can and will repeat the past, Nick responds that the past might already be out of Gatsby's reach (106). With all this in mind, let us now turn to the plot of the novel.

There is nothing particularly "great" about Jay Gatsby except perhaps his idealism. This is the bitter irony of the title and ultimately of the story too. He is a fraud and a charlatan, someone who deals in the nefarious world of illegal moneymaking. However, at the same time he is the low-class guy as well: the self-made man, who can never break through the glass ceiling of old money. From the moment he is introduced in the novel, readers somehow know that this inscrutable yet likeable rogue is doomed to fail, and that the real villains, embodied in the old money of Tom Buchanan and his wife Daisy, will avoid punishment. In this sense, Gatsby is someone with whom many readers may empathise. Much of that empathy is arguably afforded him in the way the book's narrator, Nick Carraway, presents him and the events surrounding his past. Nick does this mainly in the order he himself learns of the events. Nick gives us strong hints at the start of the novel before he launches into his flashback. The dramatic irony is for the reader a powerful, emotive tool. However, such is the length of the flashback that some readers may forget that it is one, and may disregard the information given at the beginning of the story.

As Bruccoli rightly suggests, Jay Gatsby is the hero, but Nick Carraway is the central figure (1992: xii). It has been suggested by Wayne Booth in *The Rhetoric of Fiction* that had the story been told by an omniscient narrator, it would have a completely different emotive tone and texture (1961: 345). This is true. Still, Nick is as much a spectator as he is an actor. I believe it is this distance in the telling that charges the story with that extra emotion to which involved and engaged readers respond.

After a brief reflection on the events of the last summer, the novel begins in earnest with Nick, a well-educated, relatively well-to-do young man, arriving from the Midwest to work in the New York bond business. He rents a small house next door to Gatsby's huge mansion on the peninsula of West Egg (presumably a fictitious place somewhere on Long Island), where the host gives many dazzling and lavish parties. Nick's cousin, Daisy Buchanan, is married to Tom but Tom is having an affair with Myrtle Wilson, the wife of the local garage owner George Wilson. The Buchanans are "old money" and live across the bay from Gatsby. Daisy also introduces Nick to her best friend Jordan Baker, and a lukewarm romance develops between the two of them. Jordan tells Nick that Gatsby had an affair with Daisy several years ago, but that she rejected his advances, primarily because of his common background and his lack of wealth. As Bruccoli puts it "she is for sale, but he doesn't have the right currency" (1992: xi). Gatsby, it seems, never stopped loving her and now he is back to reclaim his woman with his newfound wealth, the origins of which are the topic of much speculation. Gatsby has taken a house directly across the bay from Daisy so that he can stand on his lawn, stare across the water and stretch out his arms towards the green light at the end of her garden, which is a symbol that embodies all he desires. Gatsby craftily uses his friendship with Nick to become reintroduced to Daisy. Nick is fascinated by Gatsby but he is wary of him as well, especially when he learns about some of his dubious business acquaintances. Tom, who despises Gatsby, finds out about Daisy's earlier affair with him while they are all in New York at a hotel. In the huge argument that follows, Tom triumphs by making clear to everyone that the affair is over. They all return home, Daisy, for the last time in Gatsby's car. On the way home, Gatsby's car accidentally hits and kills Myrtle outside her husband's garage. Myrtle has run out into the road, thinking it might be her lover, Tom, coming to fetch her. The car drives on after the accident, but the hit and run is witnessed by the young Greek, Michealis, who runs a local coffee shop, and a driver passing in the opposite direction. As a result, Myrtle's husband, George, finds out. Gatsby tells Nick that Daisy was driving at the time and that is why they did not stop. Come what may, he will take all responsibility to protect Daisy and say that he was behind the wheel. Nick tries to persuade Gatsby to leave town, as he knows that he could be in danger, but Gatsby refuses.

Soon afterwards George Wilson, who was aware of his wife's adultery but not the identity of her lover, asks Tom Buchanan whose car killed his wife. He thinks that it may have belonged to her lover since she ran out into the street after it; Buchanan conveniently points the vengeful and distraught Wilson in Gatsby's direction, hoping to conveniently dispose his two problems in one go. Several hours later, Gatsby's body is discovered floating in his swimming pool. He had been shot dead. On the ground close by lay Wilson, who had turned his gun on himself. The Buchanans show a conveniently clean pair of heels and leave town for good. Gatsby is buried, but the hundreds of hangers-on and sycophants who frequented his parties at his expense are not present. Just one partygoer turns up at the funeral: an old drunk. He, Nick, the servants, the postman, and Gatsby's father, who is a poor farmer from Minnesota, make up the painfully low funeral turnout.

The novel ends with the piece I will be focusing on in this chapter and the next one. Nick walks through the deserted grounds of Gatsby's old mansion for one last time before he returns home to the Midwest for good. From the old deserted house he looks across the bay to the green light that held Gatsby spellbound, and ponders the meaning of his friend's life and death. In doing so, he holds up a mirror to his listeners, as indeed Fitzgerald does at another level for all his readers, of what being and nothingness mean for us all.

Here, then, are those closing lines, the ones I asked the thirty-six subjects in the survey to read. It is from the Penguin edition (2000: 171–72, ed. Tanner). I have retained the words "orgastic" and "farther" as they appear in the authorised text of most other editions. The readers actually read from the line starting "Gatsby's house was still empty when I left—the grass on his lawn had grown as long as mine" some two pages before the end. For practical purposes, however, the text below starts three paragraphs later and represents solely the closing lines.

> Most of the big shore places were closed now and there were hardly any lights except the shadowy, moving glow of a ferry boat across the Sound. And as the moon rose higher the inessential houses began to melt away until gradually I became aware of the old island here that flowered once for Dutch sailors' eyes—a fresh, green breast of the new world. Its vanished trees, the trees that had made way for Gatsby's house, had once pandered in whispers to the last and greatest of all human dreams; for a transitory enchanted moment man must have held his breath in the presence of this continent, compelled into an aesthetic contemplation he neither understood nor desired, face to face for the last time in history with something commensurate to his capacity for wonder.
>
> And as I sat brooding on the old, unknown world, I thought of Gatsby's wonder when he first picked out the light at the end of Daisy's dock. He had come a long way to this blue lawn, and his dream must have seemed so close that he could hardly fail to grasp it. He did not know that it was already behind him, somewhere back in that vast obscurity beyond the city, where the dark fields of the republic rolled on under the night.
>
> Gatsby believed in the green light, the orgastic future, that year by year recedes before us. It eluded us then, but that's no matter—tomorrow we will run faster, stretch out our arms farther . . . And one fine morning—
>
> So we beat on, boats against the current, borne back ceaselessly into the past.

We now turn to question 15 in the NRQ survey which, unlike all the previous questions, has ten separate, related parts pertaining to a number of issues, including style, themes and reader epiphany. I will also investigate further two ideas I started in the previous chapter that emoted readers might slow down and even read in specific chunks of text when they reach the end of a much-enjoyed novel. I will deal with each of the ten sections below separately. These sections, named A–J, have been divided into four parts. Part I (A) is of a general nature, designed to discover whether the subjects had read the whole novel as requested and not just the text fragment at the end. The next five sections (B–F) constitute Part II and relate to the style of the piece. These questions ask if any of five linguistic aspects I list have had an emotive effect on them. These are words, clauses, sentences, punctuation and rhythm. Part III is made up solely of question G which pertains to themes. Lastly, Part IV is composed of three questions (H–J), which pertain more to somatic aspects, and refer to felt affects on the body and mind while reading. They also sought to elicit responses pertaining to whether a reader was emoted or not during the reading experience. The responses of this section depended to a significant extent on question A, namely whether a subject had read the whole book and not just the last fragment. The last question in the survey (J) was included in case question A received a low affirmative response.

In the original questionnaire ample space was left for subjects to insert lengthy open responses should they so wish. They could also expand this space by hitting "enter". Underneath this final question in the NRQ I added a text as a guideline and also as a final plea to the subjects to consider reading the whole novel, as opposed to just the text fragment. That text read as follows:

> Here are the closing lines from the popular novel *The Great Gatsby*. Some of you may know this novel well, some slightly and some not at all. Ideally, the fragment should be read in the context of the entire novel. Please do not read it from the screen but instead print and read it in whichever location/position you feel most apt. I realise that I cannot make large scale demands on your time but if you would like to grasp the chance to read this novel right now for reasons of pure personal pleasure, then you are encouraged to do so. It is a short novel and can be easily read in a day. You certainly won't regret reading it—or indeed re-reading it.

It should be stated that although I gave them approximately three pages of text to read, my main analytic interest in the passage concerns the final two paragraphs, starting with the lines "And as I sat there . . . ". The reason I gave them more text to read was to offer a reasonable amount of co-text that would be helpful for those who had not re-read the novel but still knew enough about it from a previous reading. I believed that in addition this strategy might also offer some sense of co-text to those who had ignored my appeal to read the book. Let us turn to the first question that was put to the group of thirty-six readers.

## NRQ—15 a   Did You Only Read This Piece or Did You Decide to Read the Whole Novel so That You Could Enjoy These Closing Pages in a Fully Contextualised Manner?

Twenty subjects admitted to only reading the fragment. I had hoped that more students would choose to read this short and accessible novel. Even the sixteen who did read it did not all do so of their own accord. The nine students from the Roosevelt Academy Middelburg were obliged to read the book a part of the curriculum. This will have consequences for the questions on style and themes, but even more for the later somatic questions about reader epiphany. Despite this, the raw data may still yield some interesting insights for at least three reasons. First, one can perhaps expect a number of those who did not read the novel this time had read it sometime in their past or had seen one of the several films based on the book. Second, the fact that I had given them three long paragraphs preceding the closing ones did give them some co-textual context to work from. Third, as explained previously, I had already built in a question (J) at the end of the survey that would try to account for just this kind of none-reading situation.

Question B was the first that actually dealt with the notion of style head on. I should report at this stage that there appeared to be a problem with some of the labels I proposed. With the exception of six respondents, the subjects seemed unable to differentiate between a word, a clause and a sentence. This led to a somewhat jumbled mix of answers in the data. For example, when subjects were asked to give words, they gave clauses or even sentences, and vice versa. As a result, I have decided to be pragmatic and present the data to these three questions (B–D) in one section.

## NRQ—Q.15b/c/d   Did Any Particular Words / Clauses / Sentences in This Piece Emote You? (Please List Them and Try to Explain Why.)

Would the subjects select categories of words that came up in my earlier discussion on themes and style in Chapters 5 and 6? Let's fist look at some of the most frequently selected words and phrases and thereafter some clauses and sentences. The words (and phrases) that were listed most included "vast obscurity" (three times), "this blue lawn" (five times), "green light", (five times) and, "orgastic future" (eight times). Comments given by the readers pertaining to these included:

- "this seemed hopeless" (for "vast obscurity")
- "I like the sound of this" and "It gave me a sense of sadness and a sense of what Gatsby was feeling every time he was standing on that lawn"(for "blue lawn")
- "It represents hope and sadness"(for "the green light")
- "It gives me a huge kind of explosion" (for the "orgastic future")

Furthermore, three subjects highlighted the word "dream", one commenting "that is what he failed to grasp, his dream, and that was what he was after and that is really sad". Three others mentioned "one fine morning", one commenting "it sounds kind of clichéd, but it is recognisable". The terms "ceaselessly" and "recede" were also highlighted three times. A comment referring to the former was "it somehow conveys a sense of hopelessness and futility", whereas one referring to the latter was "it makes me think of sadness, emptiness—slowly losing something". The words "future" and "past" were also mentioned by two readers, one of whom added the comment "it made me think that life is a cycle".

A couple of respondents grouped a number of words together and made a joint comment about them. For instance, one said of the four words/phrases "vast obscurity", "dark fields", "dreams" and "tomorrow" that "these words described Gatsby's endless search for something he can never obtain. They make me feel pretty melancholic". Another respondent could make no distinction between lexis and syntax and just grouped words together with larger units of text and then commented on them as a whole. The text fragments he/she highlighted were "the green light", "orgastic future", "blue lawn", "old, unknown world", "hardly fail to grasp it", "that year by year recedes before us", "somewhere back in that vast obscurity beyond the city, where the dark fields of the republic rolled on under the night" and, finally, "so we beat on, boats against the current, borne back ceaselessly into the past". He/she then added: "these are poetically written words that you find in your dreams, words far away from you, ones that you only hear in books and in your mind". Can some of these emoting lexical concepts highlighted here be labelled as "distal"? If so, do they match or perhaps echo any of the categories I mentioned in my discussion on themes and style? While there are few one-to-one matches, one would be hard-pressed to give an absolute negative response.

Let us now look at some clauses and sentence that were highlighted by readers as having had an emotive effect on them. For ease of understanding I will present all the responses below in terms of sentences only. I shall focus on the six sentences in the analysed passage, and I set out below how often subjects highlighted a sentence as "emotive". These "sentences"—as I have temporarily called them—do not all conform to the formal syntactic norms of what a sentence should be. This is therefore used as a term of convenience here. Some comments have been listed immediately after they appear in the sentence in question. Are any of these "distal" in nature?

- 1. *And as I sat brooding on the old, unknown world, I thought of Gatsby's wonder when he first picked out the light at the end of Daisy's dock.*
  o (Highlighted as emotive by *three* respondents)
- 2. *He had come a long way to this blue lawn and his dream must have seemed so close that he could hardly fail to grasp it.*
  o (Highlighted as emotive by *fourteen* respondents)
- 3. *He did not know it was already behind him, somewhere back in that vast obscurity beyond the city, where the dark fields of the republic rolled on under the night.*
  o (Highlighted as emotive by *eleven* respondents)
- 4. *Gatsby believed in the green light the orgastic future, that year by year recedes before us.*
  o (Highlighted as emotive by *ten* respondents)

- 5. *It eluded us then, but that's no matter—tomorrow we will run faster, stretch out our arms further . . . And one fine morning—*
    - o (Highlighted as emotive by *twenty-two* respondents)
- 6. *So we beat on, boats against the current, borne back ceaselessly into the past*
    - o (Highlighted as emotive by *sixteen* respondents)

The final two sentences were seen as the most emotive with the penultimate one being the most affective of all. The opening sentence is the least emotive. Interestingly, if you were to plot these sentences on a graph you would get something not too dissimilar to the classical structure of a novel: rising action leading to a peak just before the end followed by a slight fall. It is as though the final paragraph acts out a classical plot structure at a micro level. Let us now look at some of the raw response data linked to these six sentences.

- Sentence 1

    - o Daisy's dock is a symbol for the yearning and the distance between the two

- Sentence 2

    - o I like this part, it makes me sad. Gatsby did much for his dream, and didn't reach it. It happens many times in real life too. We work hard for something and then it is gone
    - o I think it's a beautiful line although you never really grasp the meaning because it is so subjective

- Sentence 3

    - o This gives a sense of futility, the waste of a life, of something that was doomed from the start; the inevitability of failure
    - o Gatsby thinks he has something but he is wrong. I feel sad when I read this because I want him to be chasing something that is still reachable
    - o I like the imagery, "dark fields of the republic that roll like the sea under the blanket of night". It has a nice rhythm to it
    - o I think it means everything that lies beyond what is visible is unknown. This reminds me of my place on earth

- Sentence 4

    - o This is the whole point of the story, Gatsby trying to get his dream, and is convinced that he would o You really see this mystical green light on the other side of the shore, that nicely represents Gatsby's dream, and it will stay a dream now always.

- Sentence 5

  o This second part (running faster and stretching out arms) makes me feel better, there is a breeze of hope and chance of better times
  o This seems to say "never give up" we must keep going, the dream has not ended
  o I like this sentence very much. It makes me think, but also calms me down
  o This evokes a feeling of a new day, it will all get better. Sounds very American to me. The American dream
  o "And one fine morning" gives me a sense of hope and belief but then in the next sentence a sense of sadness. You get the feeling your belief will never be fulfilled, your goal will never be achieved
  o The last part "and one fine morning" sounds very dreamy to me, it makes me picture a sunrise with a calm see, sea gulls and the cold air of the morning

- Sentence 6

  o It really touched me that he talks about rolling into the past, instead of the future, it really shows the "mood" of the book
  o I think that the repetition of B in beat, boat, borne, back gives a kind of constancy and energy. I don't know how though
  o This emotes me because of the alliteration and the imagery; because of the melancholic and sad feeling it gives you. Even though you want to move on, you are still pulled back by the past. It's a beautiful thought, but also a sad one
  o This last section emoted me most. It is slowly written, you can dance a little bit on the rhythm of the words. It looks like a combination of thoughts and telling
  o This piece grabs me because it is written in a calm way. It is peaceful, it help me to dream away
  o The "boats against the current" part reminds us of the fact that will and persistence can bring us a long way. And also how things can seem so futile when you are in the middle of them but at the end can seem so meaningful
  o This line speaks more words by the image it gives the reader than the words that are in these lines. I think that the image of a boat against the current is very telling

Let us now look at some of the raw data pertaining to the question on the emotive effects of punctuation and rhythm in this text.

## NRQ—Q.15e    Did Any Particular Aspects of Punctuation in This Piece Emote You? (Please List Them and Try to Explain Why.)

Eighteen of the respondents highlighted that the ellipsis marks in the sentence "*It eluded us then, but that's no matter—tomorrow we will run faster, stretch out our arms farther . . . And one fine morning—*" had some emotive effect on them. This is close to the number who highlighted the same text when commenting on sentences in the previous section and suggests that the punctuation did stand out as it drew the affective attention of half of the thirty-six readers. Could this essentially textual matter, combined with what subjects cognitively brought to bear on the text, help create an embodied sense of "felt movement" while reading the next (and final) sentence? Interestingly, twelve of these eighteen affirmative responses came from the group of sixteen that had read the entire novel. Here is the raw data (eleven responses) on the emotive power of punctuation in this closing text.

1. It gives me a feeling that it will go on forever
2. I like the way it gives you the feeling that one day you will grasp your dreams but then in the next sentence shows that although you think it will happen it never will
3. It leaves me with an excited feeling, as though the sentence is just out of reach
4. I think that the dots are actually trying to jump
5. It triggers a feeling of something that can never really happen
6. The dots kind of give hope but then the dash after "morning" shows that there is no hope
7. The dash after "morning" represents the hopes and dreams and ambitions of mankind really, as well as the inevitability of failure or in the few cases when someone is successful, the futility of the success
8. The dots and bars give a kind of indescribable sense of distance
9. It is as though the writer is thinking this at the moment he writes it
10. The sentence ends so abruptly. It kind of intensifies the unpronounced meaning of it somehow
11. Yes, this punctuation scores with me. It didn't disturb me in any way. It made the reading easier

It will be recalled from Chapter 6 that I suggested ellipsis marks and aposiopesis—the sudden breaking off of a piece of discourse by failing to provide the final words of a clause or sentence—often go hand in hand. I cited there Demetrius, who wrote, "in certain cases conciseness, and especially aposiopesis, produce elevation, since some things seem to be more significant when not expressed but only hinted at". I also cited Sloane, who said that such a figure can simulate the impression of a person so overwhelmed by emotions that he or she is unable to continue speaking, something I termed "the rhetoric of silence". I suggested too that elliptical punctuation employed in this fashion in such literary closure can enact a kind of pathos or poignancy and is even capable of creating the conditions for powerful emotions in readers. The comments of some of the readers in the above data seem to support this in part.

Interesting responses include respondent one who claimed "it gives me a feeling that it will go on forever" and respondent two who wrote "it leaves me with an excited feeling, as though the sentence is just out of reach", and also respondent nine who said "the dots and bars give a kind of indescribable sense of distance". The most interesting response, however, might perhaps be respondent five who remarked "I think that the dots are actually trying to jump". What does this reader mean by this? Is it the punctuation doing the jumping or is it a felt sense of jumping taking place in the embodied mind of the emoted reader? I will address this later. Next we turn to rhythm.

## NRQ—Q.15f  Did the Rhythm of the Piece do Anything to You Emotionally?

Would the rhythm of the piece affect the readers, especially in the last two sentences? Moreover, could it act as a kind of "fluvial" priming device to help induce a kind of heightened emotive, even epiphanic, state in certain engaged readers? Seventeen subjects, almost half the readers, said that the rhythm of the final section emoted them. Plausibly, the fact that most readers had only read the text fragment, rather than the entire novel, kept the number below half of the readership. The following two comments from the data appear to support this idea.

- This fragment is too short for me to able to say anything about the rhythm. I should have read the whole novel, of course, but I don't have time for that
- No, not really. But that is because I did not read the whole book

Of the sixteen subjects who read the entire novel, nine belonged to the group of seventeen who said that the rhythm of the piece emoted them. There were fifteen qualitative responses.

1. Yes, especially the very last sentence. That one is very rhythmical. It gives a special feel to the sentence

2. The whole of the last section from "Tomorrow, . . . " and especially the last sentence "beat, boats, borne, back". They make them very "easy" and "sad"

3. I really liked the rhythm from "Gatsby believed in . . . " up until the end

4. I like the rhythm of the last sentence very much. It makes me think, then calms me down

5. The ending was beautiful. The rhythm made me think

6. Nice rolling sentences in all of the closing piece

7. I was struck by how the rhythm of certain words and sentences mimicked the waves of the sea, rolling in and out, symbolizing of running synchronically to Gatsby's hope and failure, his belief and disillusion in the text. That rhythm, reflected in the last sentence struck me

8. The commas helped the rhythm. Pulling me and making me nostalgic

9. The rhythm is beautiful. It flows. It goes up and down like a wave

10. I felt like it was very smooth, the rhythm and the use of clauses and punctuation

11. The rhythm was the best in the last section. It has got the rhythm of a nice little river. It spoke to me very much and I could find my rest in it. It made me peaceful

12. At the end the rhythm is faster as a result of the shorter sentences. This makes it more emotional, since it feels like you have to breathe faster

13. The rhythm becomes more staccato towards the end of the piece. This made me read a little more intense towards the end. I can recall the end better than the beginning of the fragment

14. I like the rhythm of the repetition. In the last sentence all those b's make the read easier and quicker, but it is also as if you are singing a song. A wonderful concluding line

15. The last part had very emotional rhythm

Can we find support for the questions posed above in these data? An interesting response is made by reader seven who noted that the rhythm of certain words and sentences appeared to have "mimicked the waves of the sea, rolling in and out". Another intriguing comment is made by respondent nine, who observed that the rhythm was beautiful, in part because it flows: "it goes up and down like a wave". Respondent eleven said that the rhythm was the best in the last section, in part, because "it had the rhythm of a nice little river". This person added that he/she "could find rest in it, it made him/her peaceful". As in the previous section on punctuation, a sense of real movement and felt movement were indicated as well in some of the responses. They included observations about "nice rolling sentences in the closing piece" (response 6), and that the commas helped the rhythm to pull him/her in and make him/her nostalgic' (response 8). There were also direct references to physiological, embodied phenomena. Respondent twelve, for example, noted that "at the end the rhythm is faster as a result of the shorter sentences. This makes it more emotional, since it feels like you have to breathe faster". These responses are interesting and give some credence to the idea that punctuation can act as a kind of fluvial priming device to help induce a kind of heightened emotive state in certain engaged readers.

Having looked at the more stylistic aspects, let us now go in search of evidence of certain themes in this passage and their possible effects on the readers.

## NRQ—Q.15g What Kind of Central Underlying Themes do You Think This Piece Deals With and What Emotive Effect, if Any, Did They Have on You?

Twenty-four of the thirty-six readers responded to this question.

1. Longings and desires
2. Dreams and goals not being reached
3. Lost chances and not being able to turn back time
4. Chasing your dreams and not succeeding
5. A lost chance, something that should have been taken when it was there
6. Not being able to live life to the full, but being left behind
7. Ambition and futility, loss, the passing of time—these themes made me feel sad, but also gave me a sense of peace, calmness and comfort
8. The past and its regrets, the future and its opportunities. Not being able to let go. Trying to bring something back from a long time ago—it makes me sad and empathetic for Gatsby. We can learn a lesson from this, so in a way Gatsby didn't die for nothing (even though he is fictional)
9. Death, future-past, loss
10. The past, dreams (individual and those of the whole human race)— these affected me because I think that they deal with what you can expect from your life in terms of the value of what you hope and dream you will be able to do or have in your life as opposed to the realities of life
11. Unfulfilled plans and life goes on no matter what
12. How temporary life is, death, self deception—it has a depressing affect on me
13. Timelessness; past, present and future are one. I love that idea that everything seems connected. One universal time. It makes you kind of think of the world and everything that is happening in it. Perhaps it makes you more aware of things or makes you look at things in a different way. It makes you feel tiny—there is also a sense of lost dreams.

When he breaks off after " . . . And one fine morning—" it gives the impression that he does not believe in that fine morning. It leaves you with a sad desolate feeling

14. Death, departure, saying farewell. This theme pleased me. The end piece focuses on a "we" that "beat on". This "we" could also involve myself. Also the fact that this world will keep turning one I am gone is touched on in this piece. It also shows themes in a larger whole, of which I, as a reader, am apart as well

15. Light and dark, past and future, the sea

16. Leaving things behind, a new beginning, excitement of the unknown, hope—I felt these kind of emotions too

17. Loss, disappearing friendships and love

18. Looking back, reflecting on death and guilt

19. Loss, friendship, death, the past—These themes made me feel melancholic

20. Life, dreams, hope. I had a kind of "it's sad, but it is for the best" sensation

21. Things go by and eventually finish, nothing is forever, past friend-ships—The main theme is something that is over. I feel sad for the narrator because something that was dear to him is over and can never return. I would like for him that the things he loved still existed

22. The loss of something. You feel the pain of the character. You can also feel the grief he has because the hope his friend had never became reality

23. It made me think about the sea, but I am not sure what it is about

24. The death of the American dream. Reliving the past

There are some interesting comments here. The idea of (metaphorical) distance is suggested in response 2 about dreams and goals not being reached. The notion of nostalgia was hinted at much more strongly in remarks about "longings and desires" (response 1); "loss, the passing of time" (response 7) and "looking back, reflecting on death and guilt" (response 18) and several others. There were no direct references to the idea of incommunicability. Other interesting responses included number 8, which highlights the importance of character empathy as a source of emotion in readers; response 13, which mentioned the notion of cir-cularity and connection as an emotive theme, and response 22, which emphasises that readers can "feel the pain" as characters and narrators do. Others included responses 15 and 23, which made mention of the sea, e.g. "it made me think about the sea, but I am not sure what it is about".

Let us now move on to the final section of sub-questions from ques-tion 15 in the NRQ and pose questions related to heightened emotions and reader epiphany.

## NRQ—Q.15h   Did This Piece do Anything to You Emotionally or Bodily?

Twenty-one readers responded affirmatively and this includes twelve of the sixteen who had read the whole novel. There were twelve comments in total from this group of twenty-one. There was also a comment from a reader who had not read the whole novel, namely, "no, but if I had read the novel, then I think I would have". This is purely hypothetical. The real question of interest here is would the subjects who had answered affirmatively refer to emotion or some physiological aspect of what was happening to them in the raw data? Below are six responses that point to diverse bodily reactions to the text-processing event.

1. At the end I couldn't swallow
2. I wanted to cry
3. I cried
4. At the end I felt the hairs on my arms rise
5. I felt like I could really grasp the emotion or something
6. I had an empty feeling, a bit of a belly-ache, a nagging feeling. I also wanted to cry but couldn't

Response number 1 refers again to the mouth playing a role in reading but this time it is swallowing that is affected by the emotive nature of the reading event rather than breathing. This semi-gustatory aspect is continued in response 6, which highlighted feelings in the stomach. Response 4 refers to goose bumps on the arms. In short, the body appears to be involved in this emotive literary reading process, at least for these subjects. The next set of responses pertains to more general emotions:

7. It depressed me
8. It did something emotional because of the teller and the rhythm, but I don't know what
9. I felt rejected and wanted to stop reading
10. I felt pain
11. It evoked emotions of nostalgia and disappointment
12. I felt the gloominess

I then posed a second question that went a little further by asking the subjects about experiencing reader epiphany. The twenty who did not read the entire novel can be excluded from this part of the experiment.

## NRQ—Q.15i Did This Passage Have Any "Reader Epiphany" Effect on You at All?

Of the sixteen who had read the entire novel six responded affirmatively. Of the twenty who has not read the entire novel, one subject responded affirmatively. The reader in question said that he/she experienced a reader epiphany because of the "beautifully written, beautiful imagery, rhythm and balance", adding "this combined with the sad-toned content made me become highly emoted". In short, seven of the thirty-six readers felt that they had undergone some kind of reader epiphany while reading this text at closure. Of course, we cannot take this at face value because we cannot be sure that the readers in question knew what a reader epiphany was. Below are some responses from subjects who had read the book and reported experiencing some kind of reader epiphany.

1. It made me feel somewhat at ease, yet emotional ... A soft smile
2. I read every word carefully and seemed to feel the importance of every word
3. The final part especially "Gatsby believed in the green light ... " and so on. It rounds it off so beautifully. My epiphany is probably there because the final part has such beautiful imagery rhythm and balance. Combine that with the sad-toned content and you've got me very emoted
4. Yes, a little bit. I felt like what Gatsby felt. It is really hard to describe. It's a feeling. It all had something of a dream
5. The literary value of the piece drew me to it and gave me a reader epiphany

Very few responses refer directly to felt physiological effects, the like of which we read about in the earlier Ginsberg example in the previous chapter. However, some qualitative aspects of the data are interesting. For example, the feeling of ease in response number 1, the rhythm and balance in response 3 and the notion of an epiphany drawing a person in as seen in response 5.

I will return to this topic in the next chapter. For the time-being, from a methodological perspective, it can be said that the conditions I created to explore reader epiphany were far from ideal, even though I allowed readers to read at home, in their own time and I encouraged them to read the whole novel. To illustrate just one aspect of the general problem here, one subject who answered "no" to this question also wrote: "I think I would have needed to have read the whole story for this to happen. Now it seems a bit sudden to just fall in to the middle of things". This comment seems to sum up one of my main methodological problems. To get more insight into this, I posed a final question. As I explained earlier, I added this question in case only a few of the subjects read the novel in full. The question is hypothetical and as such has little argumentative force. The raw data, however, may prove productive for later surveys and experiments.

# NRQ—Q.15j   If You Have Answered "no" to the Above Question, do You Think That if These Closing Lines Had Been Read in a More Normal/Natural Novel-reading Situation, i.e. in Your own Time and on Your Own Terms, These Closing Lines Might Have Had the Power to Trigger a Reader Epiphany in You or Indeed in Another Reader?

You may recall that this question pertains to just twenty of the readers. Fifteen responded affirmatively, two negatively and three said that they were unable to say, a valid answer given the hypothetical nature of the question. Let us look at the responses, twelve in total, in three different groups.

1. I think these sort of themes and styles could trigger some strong emotion in me had I read the book. Whether this would be a reader epiphany or not, I can't tell. I have only experienced this twice before in my life. Since these were both long books that I read for days on end perhaps the fact that I was going to finish a book I'd been reading intensely for a long time caused this reader epiphany

2. Because I only read the last bit of the novel, I couldn't get into the story. Had I read the whole story, then it probably would have been different. It takes me a while to really get into a story and these passages were just too short for that

3. If I had read the whole book, then I think I would have felt the reflection of the man who is described in these paragraphs

4. I think in the ideal situation, this has the power to cause an epiphany in anyone because it deals with issues that everyone is emotionally involved in or at least would have some kind of emotional reaction to

5. Yes, I guess I could have felt a reader epiphany if I had read the whole novel

Some other responses listed below hinted at the important role of both mood (numbers 6 and 7) and location (numbers 8 and 9) for reader epiphanies to take place.

6. I think that it is possible that I would have become emotively affected if I had read it under my own terms—as a choice of my own

7. In a less stressful situation (I've got a lot on my mind at the moment) and when I have read the whole book, then I could be touched by it. It is impressive and nostalgic enough for this to happen

8. I want to read it at my own speed, in my own moment, when I choose. I want to be able to choose when to read

9. I have read this book before many years ago and I remember the emotive effect it had on me. A reader epiphany is best experienced when

reading non-stop for a long while, where and when I want, right up to the finish. A short excerpt like this does not do the trick for me

There are some persuasive arguments here for the importance of the *kairos* of the reading situation for an affective reading to take place: the time, the place, the mood, the moment.

Other respondents suggested that the actual experiment may have prevented a reader epiphany from taking place

10. If I had been drawn into the story good and proper, and if I hadn't had to analyze it right after reading it, and if I hadn't felt the pressure of it being "a questionnaire" it might have. Then again, it might not. It depends on the rest of the novel, which I haven't read
11. Yes I do think a reader epiphany is possible under different circumstance. Now I was so aware of the fact that I had to read and was reading that I couldn't really "fall" into the story. Not having a context (just an ending) didn't really help either
12. Had I read the novel in its entirety I would have been able to see the strength of the passage. Besides, reading it in your own time changes things as well. You can take the time you want to read it and are not obstructed by the idea that you have to read it in order to answer questions that, I think, causes you to read in a different way as well. You are aware that you have to focus on certain aspects of the passage more than on the other and you are consciously aware of this

The spectre of the empirical tester, distorting that which he/she seeks to observe—not discussed in any real depth in the book—raises its head here. Is it really possible to elicit genuine emotive responses to real reading situations by using subjects in a survey or experiment? As respondent twelve points out, reading literature in your own time does influence the way it is processed, interpreted and received. There is much to be said on this topic—and much methodological progress still to be made in literary reception studies and especially in those experiments that seek to elicit emotive responses to aesthetic objects like works of literature.

Other responses in this section pertained to the role of specific book themes such as "reader epiphanies can be triggered in me, but this is not my kind of book". Another reader remarked "the context is very important for epiphany and the structure and composition of the story, where you can have that final climax of the content. I did enjoy this text and will read the book sometime to see if it does have that kind of effect on me".

This final remark concludes this chapter on how thirty-six readers read the closing lines of *The Great Gatsby*. Some important questions not considered here included whether the fact that almost all of these subjects are non-native speakers of English affected the responses. Perhaps the poetic quality of the text might have been lost on some. A problem I came up against was how to get subjects to read an entire short novel when asked to do so, because literary epiphanies are not going to be measured that accurately in future empirical studies using just closing text fragments. Perhaps copies of novellas should be purchased for every subject in the experiment. This, I believe, would produce far more relevant and far more accurate results than just paying students a small sum of money to take part in the experiment (even though I did not do this in my survey). The subjects would then be allowed to keep the books and also write in them while reading; an important aspect of emotive literary engagement not dealt with here. Respondents could be given a whole semester (approximately fifteen weeks) to read the novel at their leisure, when they feel like it, in a location and at a time of their own choosing. Thereafter, they could complete the questionnaire how, where and when they wanted. They could also refuse to take part and just keep the book. Although this approach will have many methodological control problems, I believe it would be offer another perspective.

Throughout this section, I have been concerned with the responses of thirty-six undergraduate students reading the closing lines of *The Great Gatsby* in a take-home, reader response survey. As stated earlier, the collected data are meant as an illustration, not as empirical evidence. We gained some insights as to how the style, themes and rhythm of the piece of text might affect certain readers and their reading process. In addition, some suggestive comments have been made as to how readers read, and how the combination of all the affective inputs I have previously discussed may lead to heightened emotion in a reader. In the next chapter I shall draw on some of these affective observations when making my own cognitive stylistic analysis of the same passage. The literary critic Ronald Berman has noted of *The Great Gatsby* that "the novel has a surface, with uncharted depths" (cited in Prigozy 1998: xxiii). It will be the purpose of my analysis to fathom those depths to explore, as it were, the affective cognition both at and under the linguistic surface structure. Moreover, in the next chapter I will leave the term "reader epiphany" behind and replace it with my notion of reader "disportation", a concept that is much more appropriate for a cognitive stylistic study of literary reading processes.

# 10 A Cognitive Stylistic Analysis of the *The Great Gatsby* at Closure

In this chapter I conduct my own cognitive stylistic analysis of the closing lines of *The Great Gatsby*. Afterwards, I discuss the outcome of my analysis and compare it to some of the reader response data from the previous two chapters to look for similarities and differences. My analysis is simply about how I as an individual, avid reader, believe I read this text. My focus will be on how cognitive linguistic phenomena like image schemata and space grammar can be employed as a method of analysing literary discourse. Because there is no existing methodological framework to follow, I will be constructing my own way of schematically representing how I read in embodied image-schematic terms. In this chapter, I will try to show how readers such as myself, might draw on style-based inferences when reading the closing lines of a much-enjoyed novel. These are inferences that are grounded in previous, embodied, experiences of reading at closure. This mode of reading applies core aspects of the theoretical model of affective reading that I described in Chapter 7 of this book. One of the claims from that model is that highly abstract "memories" of affective linguistic/stylistic structures exist pre-conceptually in the non-reading phase, which can become activated by numerous activities such as those discussed in Chapter 4 on mood when one is approaching the end of a much-enjoyed novel.

So, what are image schemata? Well the first important thing to know is that they have little to do with mental images. In fact, they are more concerned with the concept of felt motion and are thus more somatosensory than they are visual. It is therefore better, I believe, to think of them as soma-schemata, even if they are named differently. Image schemata are thus dynamic, skeletal narratives that are grounded in embodied patterns of meaningfully organised experience. The notion of narrative is key to image schemata as they are based on our concrete interaction with the world, which, by its very temporal nature, must be experienced in narrative form. A number of abstract structures are set out by Mark Johnson (1987), who first meaningfully described image schemata: these include CONTAINERS, BALANCE, COMPULSION, BLOCKAGE, ATTRACTION, PATHS, LINKS, SCALES, CYCLES, CENTER-PERIPHERY, etc. (206). Johnson describes image schemata as:

a recurring, dynamic pattern of our perceptual interactions and motor programs that gives coherence and structure to our experience. The VERTICALITY schema, for instance, emerges from our tendency to employ an UP-DOWN orientation in picking out meaningful structures of our experience. We grasp this structure of verticality repeatedly in thousands of perceptions and activities we experience every day, such as perceiving a tree, our felt sense of standing upright, the activity of climbing stairs, forming a mental image of a flagpole, measuring our children's heights, and experiencing the level of water rising in the bathtub. (1987: xvi)

Similar rudimentary story-structures can be seen in cognitive schemata such as SOURCE-PATH-GOAL, BALANCE, SYMMETRY, UP-DOWN, IN-OUTT etc. Through a process of metaphorisation, these gestalt structures, originating in our early bodily experiences, provide the foundation for our later, more abstract thought.

There is a crossover between the concept of image schemata and at least two other cognitive linguistic domains: cognitive grammar and figure and ground relationships.[1] Cognitive grammar, also known as space grammar, claims that human beings have experiential and cognitive processing capacities that can be specified to language tasks (see Langacker 1991). It therefore denies that language is a separate and autonomous faculty. Figure and ground relationships focus on that which is foregrounded against that which is back-grounded. Cognitive linguistics takes these concepts from Gestalt psychology and uses the terms "trajector" and "landmark" to represent "figure" and "ground". A third term used in the cognitive version of figure and ground analysis is "path", which represents the distance that a specific trajector travels in relation to a specific landmark. "Path" often concerns a preposition or a dynamic verb. For example, in the line from the nursery rhyme "the cow jumped over the moon" "over" is the path, "the cow" is the trajector and "the moon" is the landmark. One of the reasons why image schemas are linked to space grammar and figure and ground relations is because all three are concerned with our everyday recurring bodily interactions with the world, which in turn we use for structuring other less concrete aspects of our experience.

Space grammar makes many interesting claims and provides useful tools for cognitive stylistic analysis. However, I will only choose a limited selection of those tools for my analysis. A significant aspect of space grammar for my study relates to the processing of written language by readers. Langacker postulates two ways of reading, namely "summary scanning" and "sequential scanning", which reflect the fact that our minds allow for two kinds of observations: either we see something as one whole, with all the elements displayed at once (summary), or we watch something step by step, as an ongoing process (sequential). Interestingly, there are clear links here to some of the discourse psychological work we saw in the opening

chapters of this book, not least to Sanford and Garrod's ideas on immediacy and incrementality in discourse understanding and processing.
Langacker claims that the difference between these methods of discourse
processing constitutes the distinction between "atemporal" relations on
the one hand and "processes" on the other (1991: 22). Summary scanning, by and large, involves such traditional grammatical categories as
prepositions, adjectives, adverbs, the non-finite infinitives and participles,
whereas sequential scanning is coextensive with the finite or tensed form
of verbs (1991: 78). Langacker illustrates this with (a) *there is a bridge
across the water*, and (b) *a hiker waded across the water*, which both
employ the word "across". When scanning or reading example (a) *there
is a bridge across the water*, the bridge, which is the trajector, appears
to simultaneously occupy all the points on the bridge spanning the river,
which is the landmark, in a holistic fashion. This is summary scanning.
The preposition "across", in this first example, has an atemporal quality.
From a discourse processing perspective it seems that summary scanning
has a weaker force. However, this force can change once the whole discourse unit has been read: "once the entire scene has been scanned, all
facets of it are simultaneously available and cohere in a single gestalt"
(1991: 78). So at the end, in reflection, the force grammar can be strong
as well, even if it is somewhat delayed.

By contrast, when scanning or reading example (b) *a hiker waded across
the water*, where the hiker is the trajector and the river once again the landmark, readers appear to read in a serial fashion, that is, they move from
stage to stage, sequentially. There is a more distinct sense of movement
here, a more urgent sense of dynamism, as a new forward space is activated
and occupied, thus causing a previously occupied space to become deacti-
vated. So, unlike in summary scanning, the activated spaces do not remain
activated throughout. It is thus according to Langacker non-cumulative in
the sense that there is no "building" effect. This is sequential scanning,
prompted, in this example, by the active verb "waded (across)".[2] Langacker
helps to ease the understanding of his somewhat complicated division with
the following analogy of studying a photograph and watching a motion
picture. Here he shows how there is flexibility in his division and that summary scanning can at times be conceived as dynamic and sequential scanning as static:

> Summary scanning is suited by nature to the conception of static
> situations, while sequential scanning lends itself to the conception of
> changes and events. We nevertheless have the conceptual agility to con-
> strue an event by means of summary scanning. Thus we can watch the
> flight of a ball and then mentally reconstruct its trajectory, which we
> can even visualize as a line with a definite curvature. In terms of the
> photographic analogy, employing summary scanning for an event is
> like forming a still photograph through multiple exposures. (1991: 79)

From the perspective of literary discourse processing, I claim that sequential scanning can be said to have a stronger force while in progress, but quickly diminishes after the discourse unit has been processed. This is not a claim from cognitive linguistics but my own intuition as an avid reader.

Peter Stockwell, in his own extensive cognitive stylistic work, has elaborated on Langacker's ideas and has claimed that summary scanning mostly involves nominals, stative modifiers, participles and stative verbs (stand, sit, lie, to be, etc.) (2002a: 66). Conversely, dynamic linguistic elements, involving relational, active processes, are scanned and processed sequentially. For example, the important final lines of the passage that I will shortly analyse will primarily be made up of active verbs such as "run", "stretch", bear (borne), "beat", etc. This suggests sequential scanning. However, these are preceded by a number of primarily stative verbs such as "sit" (sat), "brood", "wonder", "believe", etc., which indicates summary scanning. Some categories, however, like some prepositions, show overlap. Stockwell makes an important point here, namely that "labelling" or compartmentalising categories of grammatical words is not the main focus of space grammar (2002a: 66). Instead, it is more concerned with trying to account for discourse processing and the cognitive processes that are tied to processing. This will be my aim too in my subsequent analysis in which I will adopt space grammar in conjunction with image schemata as my methodological tools.

An important aspect of image schemata, my main methodological tool, is that they are gestalt structures. Johnson defines a gestalt structure as "an organized unified whole within our experience and understanding that manifests a repeatable pattern or structure" (1987: 44). He goes on to identify some specific gestalts for force relationships (1987: 45–48). As I have explained, all of these have their basis in our everyday interaction with the world. Johnson highlights seven abstract, highly structured, image-schematic gestalts, whose forces and vectors can be either real or potential (1987: 48). These are:

- COMPULSION: where a force comes from nowhere, has a given magnitude and moves along a path in a particular direction
- BLOCKAGE: where a force encounters a barrier and as a result takes a number of possible directions (e.g. rebounding, going over, going through)
- COUNTERFORCE: where two forces of equal strength meet head on resulting in stasis
- DIVERSION: where a force is diverted as a result of two forces meeting head on
- REMOVAL OF RESTRAINT: where a potential barrier is removed (or was not really there in the first place), thus allowing a direct movement from a to b

- ENABLEMENT: where there is a total absence of barriers and a force vector feels like it can move anywhere at will
- ATTRACTION: where an object is pulled towards a certain, non-gravitational, power source

Image schemata find form in a variety of dynamic, locative expressions. These can be by use of both direct linguistic prompts and metaphors. They are also often dealt with individually in analytical situations. For instance, it is said that X is an example of the BALANCE schema or that Y is an example of the UP-DOWN schema or that Z is an example of the SOURCE-PATH-GOAL schema, etc. Viewed this way, i.e. individually, as most analytic scholars have done since the publication of *The Body in the Mind*, they are very persuasive. However, I hope to show in my analysis that the integrity of image schemata increases even further when they are viewed operating on a continuum; that is, when they appear to lose their boundaries and flow into each other. During my analysis and discussion I will seek to show how image-schemata can become fluvial and dynamic during highly affective moments of literary discourse processing at closure. Although I will focus mainly on the SOURCE-PATH-GOAL schema, I will extend this to include the BALANCE and the IN-OUT schemata too. Here, I will show how all three can become one continuous image schema in certain affective literary reading situations, and, as such, can be seen as one infused PATH schema.

The three image schemata mentioned above are crucial to our everyday experience. SOURCE-PATH-GOAL is important, not least because of the fundamental temporal narrative that underlies our human existence: birth, school, work, death. BALANCE is important because, as Johnson states, it is basic for our coherent experience of the world and is learned because we have bodies (1987: 74). He goes on to say that there are a number of important modifications of the BALANCE schemas. These include a TWIN-PAN (or "see-saw") balance schema and an EQUILIBRIUM balance schema. The latter can be seen as a continuous mapping of symmetrical force vectors that meet at a point on a curved surface. Indeed, as Johnson claims, this systemic equilibrium is crucial (1987: 99). He points out that balance is seen in a number of other areas including psychological ones. This is especially the case with regard to emotion, which relies to a large extent on the homeostatic model, i.e. emotional pressures build up, causing an imbalance. The release of pressure eventually leads once again to a state of balance: when one is emotively "drained" one needs to reenergise in order to restore homeostasis (1987: 88–89). IN-OUT is important because it is involved in much of our life, from leaving rooms or entering buildings, where our body is the trajector, to more central bodily phenomena like eating, defecating, copulating, giving birth and, perhaps most basic of all, breathing, where our bodies become the landmark. Human beings experience all of these interactions in a fully embodied manner.

In my literary investigation, I will seek to go further than current cognitive stylistic analysis has done to show how the dynamism and fluviality of image schemas can, under certain circumstances, help facilitate what I call "disportation". This idea of fluvial, dynamic image schemata might seem somewhat implausible, but as Johnson himself has stated: image schemata are "relatively fluid patterns that get altered in various contexts" (1987: 30). He claims, furthermore, that image schemata exist in a *continuous* fashion in our understanding (1987: 23, my emphasis). This fluviality is something that seems to have been largely forgotten by scholars since, although in his original work Johnson clearly highlighted the core kinaesthetic character of image schemata, claiming "they are not tied to any single perceptual modality, though our visual schemata seem to predominate" (1987: 25). One of the aims of my analysis will therefore be to re-emphasise the fluidity and extensiveness of image schemata.

Thus far there has been little concrete neurobiological evidence for image schemata. However, cognitive-neuroscientist Turner has suggested in *The Literary Mind* that the best neural evidence for image schemas is to be found in "orientation tuning columns" located primarily in the visual cortex, particularly in the V2 area of the brain (1996: 23). There appears then to be a direct link between such image-schematic structures and visual neural activities, in effect between felt motion and perception. This is in essence what Ulric Neisser posited in influential 1976 work *Cognition and Reality*. Turner's claim is backed up by Johnson's previously quoted remark that vision plays an important role in image schemata. However, to my mind, there must also be a direct link between image schemata and sensory-motor systems of the brain—and perhaps even a further link to proprioceptory mechano-receptors and to the F5 area of the pre-frontal cortex, which is where mirror neural activity is initiated, as we saw in the discussion in Chapter 2. This suggests further the existence of memory-based sources for image schemata. Indeed, one of the examples Johnson himself gives of an image schema in the opening quotation of this chapter is "forming a mental image of a flagpole" (1987: xvi). It must be conceded that this is hardly an image schematic act primarily mediated by real-time visual input. In Chapter 2 where I discussed the workings of mirror neurons, I started to suggest there that the memory of an event could bring it back into full sensory-motor "consciousness", and that given the puissant nature of LRI, reading prose fiction was an ideal environment for this to take place.

In more concrete terms, I make two claims here, which will be further explained in my analysis. The first is that at the close of a much-enjoyed literary reading experience, when a reader is in, or is moving toward, a heightened state of emotion, readers can process a literary text in discrete "chunks" of discourse. I propose this in spite of a lack of affirmative data from my thirty-six young co-readers. These units of discourse are not bound to traditional propositional sentence structures or to standard predicate-argument sentences. Rather, discourse, in such highly affective contexts, is more likely to be processed in image schematic ways, aided by space grammatical cognitive structures. In short, certain aspects of discourse processing, such as the affective literary reading environment at closure, are not always based on formal propositions, but can involve embodied image-schematic processing when context and occasion demand it.

The claim that literary texts are always processed by readers in well-structured propositional units has been convincingly challenged by several scholars, including Miall (1989), Oatley (1992) and Gibbs (1994). They all insist that there is another important factor in literary text processing that propositional accounts of reading almost always ignore, although it has an important role in the actual processing in specific contexts. This crucial factor is human emotion. These mainly psychological arguments that literary readers may be induced to read in non-propositional ways is supported in current literary-critical thinking. According to Manguel, for instance, "we read in gusts of sudden pleasure" (1996: 303). I believe that this has significant embodied consequences. In using the term "gusts", Manguel appears to reject propositional accounts of literary discourse processing and defines reading instead as though readers were taking huge gulps of air as they move through a novel. This, it may be recalled, is something that, rightly or wrongly, several of my reader-respondents reported had happened to them. I will return to this bodily notion of reading later in my analysis.

The processing of literary discourse is, of course, facilitated to a significant extent by the language used in the actual text. Rhetorical and stylistic linguistic features are major factors here. Lexis and syntax are often the most significant factors, but other, "less immediate" aspects of style, such as the use of punctuation, ellipsis and rhythm can be equally important in specific contexts. Such textual phenomena are crucial but not the only input in the literary meaning-making process, for the reading is mediated as well by memories of previous similarly affective, embodied reading experiences. One might argue that although this is largely a subconscious process, the more affective the impact of the previous reading experience—and the more it was grounded in previous bodily experience—the more accessible such experiences are to activation in the reader's subconscious during the act of reading. Likewise, the more readily they can be channelled into full consciousness. My second claim, as I stated previously, will be that when the affective inputs are optimal for an engaged reader, there is an increased chance of what I call "disportation" taking place at literary closure. This, of course, presumes that the image schemata are optimum (both textually and cognitively) in their potential for fluvial interaction and that the five affective inputs are available for deployment.

In what follows I will mainly concentrate on just one image-schematic structure, namely SOURCE-PATH-GOAL. This process will be primarily, although not exclusively, text-prompted, as it will involve reference to dynamic linguistic signs. However, as I will show in a subsequent analysis, once the text has ended, at least two other image schemata, or soma-schemata, can come into play, which is especially the case in potentially "disportive" situations. The two additional schemata that I will highlight here are BALANCE and IN-OUT. When these image-schematic structures are all activated—as they will be for emotionally-engaged readers, processing the final lines of the *The Great Gatsby*—they will, I believe, operate not monolithically, but in a fluvial, single continuum, just as Johnson originally suggested. It is this sense of infusion that, together with ongoing, affective mind-fed inputs, helps to facilitate reader disportation. As far as it is currently possible, I will show as well how this process can be accounted for in neural and physiological terms as I discussed earlier with regard to such phenomena as mirror neurons and proprioception.

Here I show how I, an avid and engaged reader, read the closing lines of *The Great Gatsby*. This cognitive stylistic analysis, like all stylistic analyses, is my own, personal reading. However, I hope that other readers might recognise and experience some of my responses. I believe, just like Iser, that "the subjective processing of a text is generally still accessible to third parties, i.e. available for intersubjective analysis" (1978: 49). It will be recalled that I am using my own methodological framework, which may make extra demands on you, the reader. Before I move on to the analysis I briefly set out the *kairos* or rhetorical situation of my reading experience. I am doing this so that I might come to understand the mind-fed inputs at work in my pre-reading stage. Of course, all of this is self-reflective and, due to the inaccuracy of human memory, necessarily imperfect.

- **Occasion:** I decided long ago that before conducting my cognitive stylistic analysis of the closing lines of *The Great Gatsby* I would reread the entire novel. I read the Scribner paperback version (2003 edition). I did not read the editorial introduction, preface or the publisher's Afterword at this sitting
- **History:** I selected this novel for analysis for a number of reasons; first, for its aforementioned acclaimed style and popularity; second, for its relative brevity, and third because I quite like the story, although I am by no means an admirer of Fitzgerald's other works. I have read the novel on four occasions before (in childhood, adolescence and twice in adulthood) not always out of choice, but as part of a curriculum. My last reading of the novel was approximately eight years ago.
- **Time:** I chose a Saturday in late September 2005 to reread the book. I cancelled all appointments for that day. My plan was to start after breakfast and end in the late afternoon. This is how it roughly turned out. I planned to start my cognitive stylistic analysis on Saturday evening, writing out my main ideas and responses, and then flesh them out on the Sunday. This is what happened
- **Location:** The entire reading event took place at home, alone, while I sat on the couch. I was comfortable and had all amenities (food and

drink) close at hand. As it turned out, my reading was just as highly emotive at the close as it had been eight years earlier

- **My resulting pre-reading affective cognition:** Before I started reading, my pre-reading cognition was, as I recall, emotionally charged in a positive, anticipatory sense. It was in this frame of mind that I read the closing lines of the novel late on that warm Saturday afternoon back in September 2005. Below, as a reminder, are those closing lines.

And as I sat brooding on the old, unknown world, I thought of Gatsby's wonder when he first picked out the green light at the end of Daisy's dock. He had come a long way to this blue lawn, and his dream must have seemed so close that he could hardly fail to grasp it. He did not know that it was already behind him, somewhere back in that vast obscurity beyond the city, where the dark fields of the republic rolled on under the night.

Gatsby believed in the green light, the orgastic future that year by year recedes before us. It eluded us then, but that's no matter—tomorrow we will run faster, stretch out our arms farther . . . And one fine morning—

So we beat on, boats against the current, borne back ceaselessly into the past.

Before embarking on my cognitive stylistic analysis I wish to draw some language and style based observations on the closing lines and especially on the last couple of sentences. My reason for this, as I have argued elsewhere (Burke 2005; 2007), is that cognitive stylistics does not replace literary stylistics, rather, it augments and enhances it. As such, stylistic analyses should seek to draw on diverse aspects and levels of emotion, cognition, language and rhetoric. I will start by looking in the text for the ten affective style aspects that I listed in Chapter 6. Thereafter I will make some more general stylistic observations at a number of linguistic levels.

There is little modality in this piece, and I find no examples of hypothetical future or subjunctives. However, ellipsis marks (dots and dashes) are present, accompanied by aposiopesis. Punctuation and ellipsis are capable of communicating important iconic aspects of meaning to readers, both here and in other literary texts. The modification of the flow of discourse is indicated in the closing lines first by a dash, then by three ellipsis points and thereafter by a dash once again.

It eluded us then, but that's no matter—tomorrow we will run faster, stretch out our arms farther . . . And one fine morning—

These dashes and dots can be said to act like boundaries that help moderate the units of discourse as I read. They also help to determine the all-important rhythm of the piece. The text is written in plain style. It appears to rise to a crescendo in the second half, approximately when the pronouns shift from the third person singular "he" to the third person plural "we/us/our", which are mentioned four times in the closing sentences. From a narrative perspective one might say that the speaking voice shifts from Nick in the first part to some implied narrator in the second. In this sense, the final sentence almost becomes an insert story, albeit one with deep philosophical undertones. This juncture or volta is supported too by the verb choices: the stationary-cognitive "brooding, knowing and believing" eventually give way to the physical dynamism of "recede, elude, run, stretch, beat and bear". Another of my ten distal affective style features, namely the gesture of stretching and grasping, also occur in this piece. There is the visual stretching in Nick's reflection on Gatsby "picking out" the green light across the bay, as well as the cognitive metaphorical grasping of an idea. This sense of dynamism at closure is observable in the varied prepositional phrases as well such as "against the current" and "into the past", which are preceded by "under the night". The noun phrases are patterned. Head nouns like "light" and "obscurity" are modified by adjectives such as "green" and "vast". If there is an underlying dominating semantic field here, it is one of vision or colour.

At the level of a more general literary stylistic analysis, I am immediately drawn in by the opening word "and". This, in formal terms coordinating conjunction, is used functionally as some kind of discourse marker, and in that sense it deviates from its normal usage. It further acts as a demarcation point, separating what has already been in the text from what is yet to come. This sets up a reflective tone, which is, of course, strengthened by the brooding nature of the narrating voice. For me, it acts as a starting point for the penultimate paragraph, which is brought to a close by use of the same technique in the next-to-last line, "And one fine morning—". This "bookending", as it were, is a kind of "discoursal antimetabole". It sets up the final lines as a discrete unit. This is, of course, facilitated too by the marked shift in pronouns and narrating voice, which I have noted previously.

I wish to look at the stylistic properties of the last line, focusing primarily on two of my ten affective style aspects: parallelism and rhythm. There is parallelism at a number of levels. At the phonological level we find the assonance of the long high front vowel /i:/ sound in "we/beat". From a metrical perspective, the last line can be divided into four discrete sections. The first, "so we beat on", has four beats equally distributed across the four monosyllabic words. The stress pattern is strong-weak-weak-strong (one could perhaps argue that the first beat is also weak). The metre is a trochee followed by an iamb. In effect, the beat pattern is inverted like a mirror image. The second section "boats against the current" is not as balanced. Here there are six stresses in essentially trochaic metre. The most likely pattern is strong-weak-strong-weak-strong-weak. This appears to be well balanced but the last two beats are pronounced much quicker than the first four and can even be pronounced as one beat instead of two because of the weakness of the final syllable. The third section, "borne back cease-lessly" has a strong-strong-strong-weak-weak irregular stress pattern and does not echo the first two in any obvious way. Its closest metrical pattern is trochee/dactyl combination. The fourth and final unit "into the past" is a very close copy of the first. It too has four beats; the stress pattern is strong-weak-weak-strong. The metre is a combination of trochaic and iambic. It now becomes clear that units 1 and 4 not only match closely at the metrical level, but are also mirror images of each other in this respect. An analogy can be drawn here with a style figure from classical rhetoric, namely epana-lepsis, which is the repetition of a word at the end of a clause that appeared at the beginning of that same clause. Corbett and Connors write that such a scheme is rare in prose, adding that "it is a heightened language" that "springs spontaneously from intense emotion" (1999: 392). Might this be one of the reasons why this metrical repetition works on me so powerfully at a subconscious level and why it has had such an intense emotive effect on me? As mentioned, metre and rhythm are important as well for prose. The metre and rhythm in these closing lines do not appear to posses any special or noticeable qualities. This changes, however, in the last line: this most foregrounded of positions. This is not in an overt sense, but more in a "felt" one: that is, it is not over-structured or too noticeable or too metric. This is precisely what Aristotle recommended in his *Art of Rhetoric*: "the form of the diction should be neither fully metrical nor completely without rhythm" (1991: 230, ed. Lawson-Tancred). He remarked too that "the end-ing must be obvious, not because of the writer or the full stop, but because of the rhythm" (1991: 231, ed. Lawson-Tancred).

The last piece of text, akin to last notes of music, is left ringing most strongly in our minds once the physical reading has finished. It is thus a strong candidate to enter and re-enter into affective meaning making in the post-reading stage. It is also a strong candidate to become stored in the deep backwash of a person's oceanic mind in the non-reading phase. Recall that according to Fitzgerald, "the purpose of a piece of fiction is to appeal to the lingering after effects in the reader's mind". The metre of a final line of prose, that subliminal aesthetic persuader, goes some way to contributing to those lingering after effects. It also channels subcon-scious thematic memory fragments from previous readings. These are lines of seemingly similar philosophical, rhythmic or rhetorical depth. In this particular instance, my mind is filled with echoes of "the great shroud of the sea rolling on as it rolled five thousand years ago" from *Moby Dick*; "events revolving in circles of time" from *The Moonstone*; and the single final word "tomorrow" from Arundhati Roy's *The God of Small Thing*. With this in mind, let us now move on to my cognitive stylistics analysis.

Although there are seven sentences, seven boundaries, seven syntactic and propositional units—and although I broadly chose these boundaries when discussing the group responses—I realise that I do not read this text systematically in whole sentences or clauses in an affective cognitive mode at literary closure. After careful monitoring of, and reflection on, my own reading manner, I have set out below, as accurately as I could, how I believe I have read this text. I have divided what I experience as the units of discourse into twelve main reading sections, the twelfth of which may also be seen as two inter-dependent discourse units. In the following schematic representation, each discourse unit has been assigned five pieces of information that are positioned in rows. They are preceded by the passage in question and are followed by a short discussion. These are:

- (1) The viewpoint (labelled as "*origo*/present")
- (2) The phases (X-1–2–3-Y)
- (3) The text displayed in the diverse phases (supported by arrows to show the direction)
- (4) A spatial deictic orientation overview, with terms such as "then", "here", "there", etc.
- (5) The SOURCE-PATH-GOAL orientation (referred to here henceforth simply as the PATH schema)

The image-schematically prompted units of text that reflect my reading experience are set out in bold below and are numbered 1–12. Most of the five pieces of information listed above are self-explanatory. However, the second of these, "the phases", needs some elucidation. "Phases" refers to the general starting point of the discourse utterance, indicated in the layout as "the *origo*/the present", so there is no one-to-one mapping with traditional tense forms here. This category is important because, as Johnson points out, orientation in the PATH-schema always presupposes a viewpoint from which the movement is observed (1987: 36). Phase 1 is the past, phase 2 the present and phase 3 the future. There are two other phases, labelled X and Y. The first of these refers to a distal or "yonder" past whereas the second pertains to a distal or "yonder" future. The phases line up, from left to right, as follows: phase X, phase 1, phase 2, phase 3, phase Y. Although I use the terms past, present and future, these do not correspond with grammatical tenses but rather to what might provisionally be called "felt cognitive categorisations" based on my own intuitive reading experience.

## 1.  And as I sat there brooding on the old, unknown world, I thought of Gatsby's wonder

From a cognitive stylistic perspective, I read this as a fairly single, coherent gestalt. In space grammar terms it is primarily scanned and processed in a summary fashion, and this is most likely partly facilitated by the two nominals in the sentence and the relatively stative verb forms, even though some of them carry a distinct sense of duration such as "brooding".

**2. ... when he first picked out the green light at the end of Daisy's dock (Table 10.1).**

This is a remembered visual event: the character is trying to see a long way ahead. It has a "from then to here to there" PATH structure/projection, passing from phases 1 to 2 to 3. The visual act of looking into the distance is, in image-schematic terms, similar to stretching out manually. In space grammar terms there are two sections of scanning: the first is "sequential" (channelled by the active verb "picked out") and the second is "summary" (channelled by two linguistic units, the preposition "at" and the nominal "the end"). In space grammar reading terms, this is a strong processing force, followed by a weaker sense of processing that becomes illuminated at the end, in hindsight. The space grammar force is therefore strong-weak-strong. In image-schematic terms, one can speak of a COMPULSION force structure, which involves a force that has direction moving along a path.

**3. He had come a long way to this blue lawn (Table 10.2)**

This is reflective and "inverted"'. It is facilitated by three different sign-fed elements: a verb form, a noun phrase and a prepositional structure. Gatsby's childhood may be regarded as the source and Gatsby's New York world (just prior to his death) the goal. This is a "from here to then to yonder past" structure immediately followed by a "from yonder past to then to here" projection. Interestingly, this PATH schema has a distinct wave-like, ebb and flow pattern. In space grammar terms there are two key processing elements here, one embedded in the other, namely, "had come (a long way)

*Table 10.1*  Image Schematic Reading of Section Two

|  | *Origo/Present* |  |  |  |
| --- | --- | --- | --- | --- |
| **Phase X** | **Phase 1** | **Phase 2** | **Phase 3** | **Phase Y** |
|  | *when he first picked out* ▶▶▶ |  |  |  |
|  |  | *the green light* ▶▶▶ |  |  |
|  |  |  | *at the end of Daisy's dock* ▶▶▶ |  |
|  | Then▶ | Here▶ | →There▶ |  |
|  | SOURCE▶ | PATH▶ | GOAL▶ |  |

*Table 10.2*   Image Schematic Reading of Section Three

| | | Origo/Present | | |
| --- | --- | --- | --- | --- |
| **Phase X** | **Phase 1** | **Phase 2** | **Phase 3** | **Phase Y** |
| | | *He* ◄◄◄ | | |
| | *had come* ◄◄◄ | *t* | | |
| *a long way* ◄◄◄ | | | | |
| | *to* ►►► | | | |
| | | *this blue lawn* ►►► | | |
| ◄Yonder | ◄Then | ◄Here | | |
| Yonder► | Then► | Here► | | |
| ◄SOURCE | ◄PATH | ◄GOAL | | |
| SOURCE► | PATH► | GOAL► | | |

to". The main one, which is scanned sequentially and has a strong pull, is the active verb, whereas the embedded unit "a long way" is nominal and is scanned in a summary fashion. It has a weaker pull. In sum, this phrase has a relatively strong space grammar force. In image schematic terms one can speak of an ATTRACTION force structure that involves a force (the blue lawn) that draws something to it along a path.

## 4.   and his dream must have seemed so close that he could hardly fail to grasp it (Table 10.3)

This is conceptual and hypothetical, an imaginary manual grasping, a stretching out. The goal is a fusion of "his dream", "the green light", "Daisy" and becoming "a socially and financially successful and respectable person". The goal therefore is also a fusion of earthly happiness, eternal love, life, etc. The goal is not attained here (hence the parenthesis and the "neg'" prefix). This element is negative, but this is unimportant, because the mentioning alone, even in a negative/non-happening context, is enough to activate the image schematic concept. This discourse unit has a "from here to (neg.)-there" structure/projection. Moreover, the two hypothetical terms "must have seemed" and "could", combined with the sense of negation in "hardly fail", might mean that it will be difficult to analyse. From a space grammar perspective this discourse unit should produce a mixed

*Table 10.3*    Image Schematic Reading of Section Four

| Phase X | Phase 1 | *Origo/Present* Phase 2 | Phase 3 | Phase Y |
|---|---|---|---|---|
| | | *and his dream must have seemed so close that he could hardly fail* ▶▶▶ | | |
| | | | *to grasp it* ▶▶▶ | |
| | | Here▶ | (neg-There)▶ | |
| | | SOURCE▶ PATH▶ | (neg-GOAL)▶ | |

weak-strong force. In image-schematic terms it is difficult to analyse as well. Of all the seven force structures that Johnson sets out, none map completely. Perhaps the closest is the REMOVAL OF RESTRAINT force structure, the difference in this case being that one cannot be entirely sure that the restraint has actually been removed.

## 5.   He did not know that it was already behind him (Table 10.4)

This is an "unknowing", essentially "inverted", structure: while Gatsby is facing forwards, unbeknown to him the narrator makes a kind of SOURCE-

*Table 10.4*    Image Schematic Reading of Section Five

| Phase X | Phase 1 | *Origo/Present* Phase 2 | Phase 3 | Phase Y |
|---|---|---|---|---|
| | | *He did not know* ◀◀◀ | | |
| | *it was already behind him* ◀◀◀ | | | |
| | ◀Then | ◀Here | | |
| | ◀SOURCE | ◀PATH ◀GOAL | ◀GOAL | |

PATH-GOAL projection behind him. This discourse unit has a "from here to then" PATH structure/projection. Even though the unit begins with the important "he did not know", the prominent space grammar item here is the preposition "behind", suggesting that this discourse unit is processed in a summary fashion that becomes illuminated and strong only in hindsight, once the whole unit has been processed. In image-schematic terms, the best force that fits here is DIVERSION, albeit in the sense of something rebounding off a surface and being behind one before one has time to notice. "He" is already deceased, unaware of the narrator's reflections.

## 6. somewhere back in the vast obscurity beyond the city, (Table 10.5)

The events that are taking place and the movements are again all behind the character, in what is plausibly his incommunicable past. It starts at a distal/yonder past and moves "forward", as it were, to the past in phase 1. "Yonder" can be seen here as a blend of the spatial and the temporal. This discourse unit has a "yonder-then" PATH structure/projection, although plausibly this could also have been inverted. There is also an implied sense of a goal from the present (phase 2), which is not unimportant. Prominent space grammar items here are the prepositions "beyond" and "in" as well as the adverb "back". I process this discourse unit in a summary, weak fashion that only becomes illuminated and strong in hindsight, once the whole unit has been read. Interestingly, "beyond" is usually associated in our Western embodied orientation with forward yonder space, not backward yonder space as I have positioned it here. In image-schematic terms, there is no direct force structure to represent this. One that comes closest is the REMOVAL OF RESTRAINT force in as much as there is an important structure, i.e. "the city" that may have potentially hampered movement beyond it.

*Table 10.5* Image Schematic Reading of Section Six

|  |  | Origo/Present |  |  |
| --- | --- | --- | --- | --- |
| Phase X | Phase 1 | Phase 2 | Phase 3 | Phase Y |
| *somewhere back in the vast obscurity* ◀◀◀ |  |  |  |  |
|  | *beyond the city* ◀◀◀ |  |  |  |
| ◀Yonder | ◀Then | ◀Here (implied) |  |  |
| ◀SOURCE | ◀PATH | ◀GOAL (implied) |  |  |

## 7.    Gatsby believed in the green light

I process this phrase as a single coherent gestalt. Just like the first text unit, it is therefore less interesting for this type of analysis. This is facilitated by the stative phrasal-prepositional verb "believed in". In space grammar terms it is primarily scanned and processed in a summary fashion. This is particularly fitting as the sentence becomes momentarily illuminated as one whole gestalt only at the very end of the processing— the word that triggers that illumination, most fittingly, and most iconically, is "light".

## 8.    the orgastic future that recedes before us (Table 10.6)

This discourse unit suggests a somewhat intangible path (and goal) that remains equidistant from the reader no matter how quickly one attempts to proceed towards it. The goal is thus never reached (hence the parentheses and the prefix "neg."). This PATH structure starts in the future (phase 3), as the future is the mysterious/orgastic subject of the text fragment. It then moves to a distal/yonder future, making the goal appear to move on a kind of ever-ebbing tide. This discourse unit has a "there to yonder" PATH structure / projection. In space grammar terms it is a classic example of sequential scanning, as items are illuminated one at a time, the previous item decaying as a new one is ignited. In image schematic terms, we have here a COMPULSION force with some aspects of the ATTRACTION force structure. If something "recedes before us" it can also mean that we remain equidistant from it, primarily through the efforts of our own "pursuit". This is the COMPULSION aspect. However, the object draws us as well, as it is referring back to the subject of this sentence, namely, the green light, which appeared in the previous discourse unit.

*Table 10.6*   Image Schematic Reading of Section Eight

|  |  | *Origo/Present* |  |  |
| --- | --- | --- | --- | --- |
| Phase X | Phase 1 | Phase 2 | Phase 3 | Phase Y |
|  |  |  | *the orgiastic future* ▶▶▶ |  |
|  |  |  |  | *that recedes before us* ▶▶▶ |
|  |  |  | There ▶ | Yonder ▶ |
|  |  |  | PATH ▶ | (Neg)-GOAL ▶ |

## 9.   It eluded us then, but that's no matter (Table 10.7)

The second clause, "but that's no matter", is a kind of impromptu aside that is less significant for my analysis. I will therefore deal with the first part only. This clause has a strong sense of "a failed future in the past". This is somewhat difficult to represent schematically without referring to some other cognitive linguistic method, such as mental spaces or possible worlds or text world theory. What can be said is that it has a "then to yonder" structure. Moreover, it scans sequentially in space grammar terms, owing to the verb form "eluded". In image-schematic parlance it does not fit any of the seven structures comfortably. The closest is perhaps COUNTERFORCE, where a great effort results in nothing because of some counterforce, which can be "actual" or, as in this case, merely "potential" (Johnson 1987: 48). In a way, it is also the antithesis of the ENABLE-MENT force, which gives one the feeling of being capable of achieving anything.

## 10.   to-morrow we'll run faster, stretch out our arms farther . . . (Table 10.8)

This is a projected (future) embodied aspect of mobility. The discourse unit has an "(implied here) from there to yonder" projection. The "here" part is implicit, as the text already begins with the word "tomorrow". The goal is not known and apparently unattainable, but very much desired. We can say that it is almost as though it is in two stages. In space grammar terms this exemplifies sequential scanning, although some aspects should be labelled "summary". Take the first text fragment, *"to-morrow we'll run faster"*. Strictly speaking, only "we will run" would be a prime candidate for sequential scanning. All the other words, the nominal "to-morrow" and the adverbial "faster" should belong to a more summary scanning mode. But somehow they seem to defy this because they both

*Table 10.7*   Image Schematic Reading of Section Nine

|  | Origo/Present |  |  |  |
| --- | --- | --- | --- | --- |
| Phase X | Phase 1 | Phase 2 | Phase 3 | Phase Y |
|  | It eluded us ◄◄◄ |  |  |  |
| Then ◄◄◄ |  |  |  |  |
| ◄Yonder | ◄Then |  |  |  |
| ◄SOURCE | ◄PATH ◄ GOAL |  |  |  |

*Table 10.8*   Image Schematic Reading of Section Ten

| | | Origo/Present | | |
|---|---|---|---|---|
| Phase X | Phase 1 | Phase 2 | Phase 3 | Phase Y |
| | | | *To-morrow we'll run faster,* ▶ ▶ ▶ | |
| | | | | *stretch out our arms farther* ▶ ▶ ▶ |
| | | Here (Implied) ▶ | There ▶ | Yonder ▶ |
| | | SOURCE/PATH (implied) | GOAL 1 ▶ | GOAL 2 ▶ |

harbour a sense of sequential, forward movement. The future categorisation of "tomorrow" is strengthened at a morphological/graphological level by the hyphen that is place between "to" and "morrow". The effect of this graphological deviation is to stretch even further, iconically mirroring the stretching-out of Gatsby. This may plausibly lead to the triggering of mirror neural activity in some engaged readers, especially if we recall how reading and mirror neurons use the same general neural (F5) area, which is analogous to Broca's region. The adverbial "faster" is also somehow sequential, even though its word class would be summary. The second text fragment *"stretch out our arms farther"* continues in a similar vein. "Stretch out" is clearly sequentially processed whereas "farther" should be processed in a summary way. The effect should be a strong force followed by a weak one. However, the adverb "farther" appears to stretch out beyond the discourse unit and, in doing so, pulls the word from summary into sequence. From an image-schematic perspective, this sentence blends a number of force schemas. They include COMPULSION and, most significantly, ENABLEMENT as there is a distinct sense of there being a potential force vector that would allow a person to do almost anything. There are no potential barriers—but one gets the sense that this is only for the time being.

## 11.  And one fine morning—

In space grammar terms this text is primarily scanned and processed in a summary fashion. It has a weak force and is therefore less interesting for this type of analysis. Its positioning here is telling though, as I will explain later.

## 12  So we beat on, boats against the current, borne back ceaselessly into the past (Table 10.9)

This unit of discourse starts by pushing forward, projecting a "from here to there" structure in two sections. However, the word "against" followed by "current" can give the reader a sense of being somatically driven back by natural forces (ones that appear to be greater than any human being, irrespective of material, intellectual or spiritual strength) before reaching the "goal". The projected structure is an inversion from SOURCE-PATH-(almost)GOAL to (almost)GOAL-PATH-(implied)SOURCE. In cognitive rhetorical terms it can be seen as a near example of a cognitive-iconic figure from classical rhetoric, namely, antimetabole, a repetition of words in successive clauses in reverse grammatical order. This last line can be said to be the embodiment of what reading-induced affective cognition is, as I will show in the next chapter. It is also this flowing and ebbing; the changing of direction can potentially help to send a highly-emoted reader into a state of heightened emotion at the close of this novel as we will see in the next chapter.

*Table 10.9*  Image Schematic Reading of Section Twelve

| Phase X | Phase 1 | Origo/Present Phase 2 | Phase 3 | Phase Y |
|---|---|---|---|---|
| | | *So we beat on,* ▶▶▶ | | |
| | | | *boats against, the current* ▶▶▶  ◀ | |
| | | *borne back ceaselessly* ◀◀◀ | | |
| | *into the past* ◀◀◀ | | | |
| (◀◀◀) | | | | |
| | | ▶Here | ▶(almost) There  ◀ | |
| ◀Yonder (implied) | ◀Then | ◀Here | | |
| | | ▶SOURCE/PATH | ▶(almost) GOAL  ◀ | |
| ◀SOURCE (implied) | ◀PATH | ◀GOAL | | |

Linguistically, "beat on" and "borne back" are two key terms that demand a sequential scanning procedure. They light up concepts individually and allow others to decay in a non-cumulative fashion. This provides a strong sense of a pushing force. However, towards the end this text segment reveals dynamic aspects of summary scanning. These include the prepositions "against" and "into". There are nominals too that also give a sense of sequential movement, among them the word "current". In addition, there are adverbials such as "ceaselessly" that have a similar effect. These should be classed as holistic units that are only highlighted at the end, in hindsight, but somehow they seem to have both a sequential and a summary scanning effect. As a result, the whole piece exerts a strong force. The fact that it ends with the prepositional phrase "into the past" allows readers to review all elements of the sentence ignited again in its fullest glory.

From an image schematic perspective, this closing text fragment is very special indeed. It starts with "so we beat on", which is a COMPULSION force scheme. A force comes from somewhere and drives us along a given path toward an unspecified goal, though within a given trajectory. This is followed by "boats against the current" which is a COUNTERFORCE scheme where two similar forces meet head on, resulting in inertia. It then continues with "borne back ceaselessly" and "into the past". Here, there is a blend of (i) the BLOCKAGE force schema, where an obstacle is struck by a vector and rebounds, (ii) the DIVERSION force schema, which adds to this effect of "being rebounded" by sending a vector off in a converse direction, and (iii) the ATTRACTION force schema, which, paradoxically attracts that same vector, drawing it inevitably into the past. It is the number of force vectors in this final text fragment, and more importantly the great variety of force schemas employed either individually or in concert, that helps create the effect of this felt, embodied "ebbing" and "flowing". This continuous mapping of force vectors also appears to correspond to what is according to Johnson the most perfect sense of the BALANCE schema, namely, EQUILIBRIUM. It is here, at this zenith of counterpoise, where the force vectors can easily spill over into a state of cognitive schematic IMBALANCE. It is this heightened moment of embodied force vector fusion, this image-schematic confluence, which is one of the key facilitators that I shall describe in the next chapter as disportation. Let us now discuss my cognitive stylistic reading of this text.

From this analysis it becomes clear that there are many divergent SOURCE-PATH-GOAL projections (or PATH schemas) in the closing lines of this novel, which are channelled mainly by diverse linguistic prompts. This channelling is not only initiated by prepositions through their characteristic locative nature, but also, as has been seen, by certain verb forms and even noun phrases. The units of discourse that I have focused on sometimes employ combinations of these grammatical categories. What links all of these linguistic, sign-fed elements is that they all have some embodied sense of dynamic movement. Some examples can be seen in Table 10.10.

As I have shown and argued, *The Great Gatsby* is a well-crafted novel. As a highly-wrought work of literature, it contains a mix of rhetorical and

*Table 10.10*   Embodied Movement in Diverse Linguistic Elements

| Text fragment | Discourse unit | Grammatical category |
|---|---|---|
| *at* the *end* of Daisy's dock | #2 | prepositional |
| He *had come* a *long way* | #3 | verbal and nominal |
| *behind* him | #5 | prepositional |
| *beyond* the city | #6 | prepositional |
| the . . . future . . . *recedes before* us | #8 | verbal and prepositional |
| *stretch out* our arms *farther* | #10 | verbal and adverbial |
| *on / against / borne back / ceaselessly / into* | #12 | prepositional, verbal and adverbial |

stylistic structures at the close. In this case, from a cognitive stylistic perspective, it pertains to a series of seemingly alternating SOURCE-PATH-GOAL conceptual PATH structures. To show more clearly what I mean, these are listed in Table 10.11. In this table I use the terms "flow" and "ebb" to represent forward and backward movement. Again, the five phases employed are: X = yonder (past), 1 = past, 2 = present, 3 = future and Y = yonder (future).

These projections vary in strength and direction. As I have arranged them here, there are actually fourteen, not twelve, units (numbers 3 and 12 have two each), eleven of which are active. Six of these involve movement pointing outward or forwards: I have labelled these "flow". For the sake of parity, the five travelling inwards or backwards have been called "ebb". At the beginning, (discourse units 2–3) several of these have what can be termed a strong force or pull, i.e. they take up more than two of the five cells in the table (across the phases). As a result, the PATH trajectory is also longer. In the beginning of this closing paragraph, the direction of the flow is mixed, involving both flow and ebb. They are structured in the following way: first there is a strong flow which is followed by a strong ebb. This in turn is followed by a strong flow once again (these last two are in the same discourse unit). There is also an IN-OUT PATH schema in these three units. Discourse units 4 and 5 consist of a flow followed by an ebb and also have an appropriate wave-like image-schematic pattern. This is strengthened because they both begin in the "present", mirroring each other, and both have the same mild force. Discourse unit 6 is ebb, but has an ambiguous sense of flow to it as well as was alluded to earlier. Unit 7 is at rest but unit 8 shows mild flow, while unit 9 exhibits mild ebb. Unit 10 continues this undulating pattern with mild flow. Interestingly, this produces a mirror image. Unit 6 starts in the past and travels to the yonder/distal past, as does unit 9. Conversely, unit 8 starts in the future and travels to the yonder/distal

*Table 10.11*  Alternating Image-Schematic Projections as Closure

| Discourse Units | X | 1 | 2 | 3 | Y | | Direction |
|---|---|---|---|---|---|---|---|
| 1. *less applicable* | - | - | - | - | - | - | - |
| 2. from thn to here to there | | ► | ► | ► | | Flow | OUT |
| 3. from here to then to yonder | ◄ | ◄ | ◄ | | | Ebb & | IN |
| & from yonder to then to here | | ► | ► | ► | | Flow | OUT |
| 4. from here to there | | | ► | ► | | Flow | OUT |
| 5. from here to then | | ◄ | ◄ | | | Ebb | IN |
| 6. from yonder to then | ◄ | ◄ | | | | Ebb | IN |
| 7. *less applicable* | - | - | - | - | - | - | - |
| 8. from there to yonder | | | | ► | ► | Flow | OUT |
| 9. from then to yonder | ◄ | ◄ | | | | Ebb | IN |
| 10. from there to yonder | | | | ► | ► | Flow | OUT |
| 11. *less applicable* | - | - | - | - | - | - | - |
| 12a. from here to there & | | | ► | ► | | Flow & | OUT |
| 12b. from here to then to (implied yonder) | (◄) | ◄ | ◄ | | | Ebb | IN |

future, as does unit 10. It may seem strange to have such a weak force in such an important place, as the text approaches closure. This, however, has its purpose. At the end of the passage the force becomes strong once again, as it was in the beginning of this text, taking up more cells in the table. This highlights the change towards a strong pull/flow as the novel reaches the end. Discourse unit 11 is "at rest". This might be the "silence before the storm", represented semantically most aptly with the words "And one fine morning—". In sections "a" and "b" of discourse unit 12, we find the strongest force of the entire closing paragraph. Being in the position they are, they also enjoy heavy foregrounding in stylistic terms. Unit 12 starts with a flow PATH schema. However, it runs out of legs, so to speak, loses its homeostasis and is pulled back along the same trajectory into what is the strongest ebb PATH schema in the piece: one that potentially has no end. As a result, there is a powerful back and forth feeling, even more so than in the rest of the piece. Here, it is somehow a more regular ebb and flow rhythm, plausibly giving an engaged highly-emoted reader the sense that he/she is being rocked back and forth by an infusion of affective inputs.

To illustrate more clearly what I have been discussing here the table below (Table 10.12) includes four pieces of information: (1) the direction (flow-ebb) of a discourse unit, (2) the start and finish point across the phases *and* the force exerted across the five phases (strong/mild), (3) the space grammar force (strong/weak/mixed), and (4) the image schematic gestalt.

*Table 10.12* An Overview of Forces and Image-Schematic Gestalts across the Phases

| Direction | Force across the Phases | Space Grammer Force | Image Schematic Gestalts |
|---|---|---|---|
| 1. at rest | ---- | ---- | ---- |
| 2. flow | past-present-future (*strong*) | Mixed | COMPULSION |
| 3a. ebb & | present-past-(yonder) past (strong) | Strong | ATTRACTION |
| 3b. flow | & yonder (past)-past-present (*strong*) | Strong | ATTRACTION |
| 4. flow | present-future (*mild*) | Mixed | REMOVAL OF RESTRAINTS |
| 5. ebb | Present-past (*mild*) | Weak | DIVERSION |
| 6. ebb | yonder (past)-past (*mild*) | Strong | REMOVAL OF RESTRAINTS |
| 7. at rest | ---- | ---- | ---- |
| 8. flow | future-yonder (future) (*mild*) | Strong | COMPULSION & ATTRACTION |
| 9. ebb | past-yonder (past) (*mild*) | Strong | COUNTERFORCE |
| 10. flow | Future-yonder future (*mild*) | Strong | COMPULSION & ENABLEMENT |
| 11. at rest | ---- | ---- | ---- |
| 12a. flow & | Present-future (*mild*) | Strong | COMPULSION, COUNTERFORCE, REMOVAL OF RESTRAINT & DIVERSION |
| 12b. ebb | & present-past-(implied yonder (past) (*strong*) | Strong | BLOCKAGE, ATTRACTION & ENABLEMENT |

There are at least two interesting things to be observed here. First, there is a comparable match throughout between the force across the phases and the space grammar force. This shows an element of consistency in my approach to define and describe the important force vectors in the text. However, there is a mismatch in discourse units 8–10 (and at the start of 12), where the space grammar suggests a strong force in contrast to the mild force across the phases. I said earlier that it seems a little strange that there should be a mild force here, as too much silence before a storm may be disadvantageous. Although there is a mild force in the one sense, across the phases, in another, space grammatical, sense, the force is perhaps already building up, at a subliminal level, for the powerful ending in the closing lines. This idea that a hidden force is building for a powerful closure seems more appropriate.

A second interesting point is that each discourse unit appears to employ just one, or sometimes two, image schematic gestalts. This appears to be the case throughout. With regard to the last unit, however, (12a and 12b) one could quite easily ascribe all seven of Johnson's force structures to it. This coming together of various force vectors at closure reinforces my comment on the EQUILIBRIUM balance structure. That all these force vectors are present at closure, evoking this complex balance structure, makes it easier for an engaged reader to experience a feeling of heightened balance followed immediately by imbalance, as the structure appears to tip over, spill out and run away: a process which is facilitated by the physical ending of the discourse. The accumulation of force vectors at closure succeed in transporting this engaged reader, at least, from experiencing one single image schema, namely, SOURCE-PATH-GOAL, to experiencing at least two others: BALANCE-IMBAL-ANCE and IN-OUT. Here, the three separate image schemas are experienced at an embodied level as one single FLUVIAL schema, which, to adopt a term from space grammar, is activated and experienced in a sequential fashion. I will say more about this in the next chapter.

This concludes my analysis which has largely focused on linguistic prompts in the text. However, it is important to remember that such acts of discourse processing are not purely based on texts, although the text at this stage plays the primary role. Rather, one should speak of a combination of inputs, both text and mind-based, which make such PATH schemas possible. The latter of these involves abstract affective cognitive structures that come into being both prior to the text interface and as a result of the text itself, in the form of intertextual and autobiographical memory-based inputs, the like of which I described in my model of affective reading in Chapter 7. These subconscious prompts are often gleaned from earlier affective reading experiences as I argued in Chapter 6. All of these meaning-making inputs go into the ongoing meaning-making fusion of affective cognition.

The last few waves of discourse in the *Gatsby* text are also iconic in the sense that a blend of their image-schematic form and linguistic form helps to imitate the meaning of the actual text. The effect is not unlike a baby being cradled in the arms of a mother; or a child being pushed gently on a swing by a primary caregiver. The combination of this strong forward force suddenly changing into a strong backward force at the very end of this text plausibly projects a number of iconic effects. One of these is related to breathing and includes effects of a last deep breath, followed by a short top-up breath and then a final long slow exhale followed by silence—it might be recalled at this juncture how one of the readers echoed this idea of being able to draw a single breath. Additionally, this could iconically represent the point of death itself. A second possibility is that this unit of discourse is akin to an imaginary wave breaking on an illusory shore. The first strong push forward is when the wave breaks with all its might and runs up the beach. The long pull backward starts as the wave comes to a halt, momentarily stops, tips back and drains in a long steady ebb out to sea.

I have suggested that aspects of the text's structure are like waves of discourse. Alberto Manguel's "gusts of sudden pleasure" echoes this general motion. Indeed, Fitzgerald himself wrote that the language he used in *Gatsby* followed "a pattern of incremental repetition" (Prigozy 1998: xxx). Here the text flows relentlessly to a climactic point, before the final sense of "release" and return. This climax is shown in my cognitive stylistic analysis, in which the pulls and pushes are much stronger in the last few discourse units. It can be claimed too that image schemata somehow appeal to readers in somatic and embodied ways when reading. Moreover, it is in part the very invitational nature of these SOURCE-PATH-GOAL image schematic structures that draws a reader into processing the discourse in such wave-like ways. This has certainly been the case in my engaged reading of the text. I would be surprised to learn I am unique in this.

I have suggested that a fusion of language and affective cognition can produce a number of diverse image schemas, which, when structured in alternating ways, as they are here, may help to induce a back-and-forth effect. I will expand on this in the following chapter. It is my belief that this rocking effect is experienced and felt as well in the motor cortex of a reader, even though the reader is not in motion, and also in the F5 area of the pre-frontal cortex, where the mirror system is housed. As we saw in Chapter 2, the idea that the "visual" mind can trigger mirror neural activity, just like visual perception can, is held by a number of neurobiologists, including McGlone, Howard and Roberts. Following Grafton et al., they researched the role of an observer's imagination in mirror neural activity. My claim therefore is that mirror neurons are not just triggered by visual perceptual input but by mental "perceptual" input as well, which, in this case, is channelled by literary words on the page, as well as by the residues of pre-reading affective cognition and mind-based intertextual echoes, which may, in part, be brought about by the language and the structure of the text. This process is also aided by fragmentary LRI from long-term memory. The question that remains is whether this phenomenon can lead to felt motion in a reader immediately after the text processing has ended. This will be the central topic of the next chapter.

In the foregoing text, I set out my cognitive stylistic reading of the closing lines of *The Great Gatsby*. I now wish to check its relevance to what the reader respondents reported. I am particularly interested in discovering whether there are any links between what I have described in my reading and their responses. The subjects in the experiment in Chapter 8 offered some evidence that when they slowed down at the close of a novel they read in essentially non-propositional ways. One respondent wrote, for example, that stylistic devices would make his/her reading speed slow down which will affect "the chunks of text I read in one go". Another respondent spoke of reading more slowly at closure but not stuttering ("stammer" was the actual word he/she used) in his/her reading patterns. He/she added that they get the feeling of "being sucked into the end of the story". This feeling of getting "sucked in" at closure can be traced back to one half of the back-and-forth nature of the image schematic structures. It is evident too in the cognitive embodied forces being produced. This sense of motion can be seen in the way the last few lines seem to manipulate the reader by pushing him/her outward and then drawing him/her inward at the close of the novel. This could very well be one of the cognitive stylistic triggers bringing about a sense of "being sucked in". A third respondent admitted to always holding his/her breath when reading the end of a novel, in order to see if the tension caused by not breathing was reflected in the language that is used. This discussion on when to breathe, or indeed whether or not to breathe, is something that also occurred in my image schematic analysis in the previous section while discussing certain iconic aspects. Moreover, it will not have gone unnoticed that the notion of "holding one's breath" while reading at closure is something that has come up, not just in reader responses in Chapter 8 but in diverse reader responses as well through my NRQ survey. Can all this merely be coincidence? It is difficult to say with any certainty, but I believe that the image schematic force structures at the close of a much-enjoyed novel can somehow regulate our breathing patterns. The pattern has a kind of reciprocal structure as reading is first affected by embodied experience and this then, in turn, affects our physiology. Fittingly perhaps, this process also has a skeletal wave-like structure. A fourth respondent spoke of "being pulled along into a novel at closure". That person identified "metaphor and deviant (disrupting) style" as the main means of achieving this. These four examples appear to lend some support to my views on my own reading patterns and the underlying forces set out in my analysis. However, it should not be forgotten that set against the other responses these ones represent a minority. Moreover, there were some interesting data in Chapter 9, which specifically addressed the reading of the closing lines of *The Great Gatsby*. These responses can be seen as potentially more relevant to my own analysis of the text. One respondent commented: "this last section emoted me most. It is slowly written. You can dance a little bit on the rhythm of the words". Interestingly, this response emphasises the emotive significance of the rhythm as I did too. A second respondent commented: "it seems like you get pulled further a bit more after every comma". This highlights the significance of punctuation and ellipsis for the rhythm of a reader being "pulled in". These force "flow" structures represented a significant point in my analysis of the discourse unit with ellipsis dots and dashes. A third comment was: "it feels like you have to breathe faster". Once again, this is a response that points to irregular breathing patterns at closure. It ties in with what I have said about the image schematic iconicity of breathing and the physiological effects it might have.[3] It seems not unlikely that breathing and reading patterns at literary closure have something in common. I conjecture that the innate physicality of in-out breathing patterns that informs our image-schematic sense of what in-out means in a whole host of everyday tasks, including discourse processing, becomes physically activated during such intense moments of reading. Why this happens is, as yet, unclear to me and only further theoretical work, preferably combined with later empirical testing, will shed more light on it. An alignment of breathing and reading patterns leads to acts of literary reading that are more intense, emotive and embodied.

These reader responses, although relevant and interesting, have thus far merely alluded to what I felt in my own reading, but upon closer inspection of the data we can also find responses that seem to be saying something quite similar to my remarks about the wave-like structure of some units of discourse that are processed in an affective mode at literary closure. One of these responses was: "It has got the rhythm of a little river . . . it made me peaceful". A second was: "the rhythm is beautiful. It flows. It goes up and down like a wave". And a third was: "I was struck by how the rhythm of certain words and sentences mimicked the waves of the sea, rolling in and out". Such comments appear to map onto the force and structural aspects of my own act of reading, suggesting that what I experienced as an avid reader might be felt by others too.

On a final note, it may be recalled that a small number of readers claimed that they had actually experienced some kind of "reader epiphany" at the end of reading this text. The responses were:

- I felt as if I had reached a higher level of understanding
- Quite excited. Climactic (in the reading sense) . . . Just like waking from a vivid dream or coming off a roller-coaster
- Very emotional. Disappointed and euphoric at the same time. But also calm and focused (in a Zen sort of way) taking it slow
- I felt a sort of release
- Thrilled. Heightened attention. Intense experiences and excited expectation

- Excited, euphoric . . . somehow I am still reading in my mind

I asked too whether specific memories were triggered at this moment of reader epiphany, for I expected that there might be some overlap with the themes of childhood, the childhood home, a primary caregiver, distance, death and incommunicability. This is what was reported:

- It was a bit of a blend. Some memories were concerned with a specific location (a train station), but also with my friends and a specific event was taking place. We were saying goodbye
- It reminded me of myself, when I was young
- The memories are blends of special persons and special events from my past
- Things you recognise, like relationships . . . Also descriptions of places I've been, locations that I remember. Sometimes my attention goes straight to that place instead of staying with the novel. That happens at the end of a novel but I am not sure that is the only place it happens

If we are to consider these responses seriously, we have to ask a number of questions: (i) Did image schemata have anything to do with such a heightened sense of emotion? (ii) If they did, how did it occur and what happened during this heightened state of literary-reading-induced emotion? And, (iii) Can specific stages be ascribed to this phenomenon? In the next and final chapter of this work, I will seek answers to these questions by investigating a phenomenon that I call disportation, upon which I will now expand.

# 11 Disportation

In this chapter I will illustrate my theoretical notion of disportation based on my cognitive stylistic reading of the ending of *The Great Gatsby* and the reader-response data discussed earlier. This will be supported by a reactivation of some cognitive and neural empirical data discussed in all the earlier chapters of this work. After introducing the term "disportation", I will first show how it can occur in a single SOURCE-PATH-GOAL structure during literary closure while reading the final few paragraphs. I will combine this with the affective theme of "stretching out". Next, I will show how it can occur at the very moment of closure, i.e. when reading the very last words. Both these examples aim to show that disportation can be facilitated when image-schematic structures become confluent. In the discussion that follows on the assumed cognitive and neural underpinnings of disportation I will suggest that this highly skeletal cognitive process in all probability occurs simultaneously with mirror-neural and proprioceptive activity. I will conclude by discussing the essentially post-textual, affective-cognitive phases of this phenomenon, followed by a concise philosophical discussion on what the effects of disportation may be and why such embodied phenomena occur during acts of literary discourse processing. In doing this I seek to highlight an embodied secular form of consolation that might compete with the increasing number of disembodied non-secular ones that abound at the start of our twenty-first century.

So what is disportation? Discussing literature and emotion, Herrnstein Smith writes that "varying degrees or states of tension seem to be involved in all our experiences, and that the most gratifying ones are those in which whatever tensions are created are also released" (1968: 3). She then shows how this is the case in poetic closure. Tension building toward a sense of release at poetic closure suggests that some kind of change takes place in a reader or some shift from one state to another. Disportation is the label I propose to define this embodied affective-cognitive event. The word has an etymological basis incorporating notions of movement and affect. I examine it in this chapter, as it occurs at the end of the physical reading cycle. However, such events can plausibly take place at almost any part of the text, and echoes of such events remain in implicit memory during the post-reading, pre-reading and non-reading stages that I have described (see Figure 7.1). Depending on the context, its primary triggers can also be cognitive rather than exclusively linguistic. When I use the term disportation I am referring to a heightened emotive state that occurs in affectively-engaged individuals while reading literature. It is characterised by a distinct feeling that a reader undergoes for a few seconds whereby a person feels that he/she is in motion even though this is not the case. This is a process that I recognise from my own engaged reading experiences and believe other avid readers may engage in such a process too. Disportation, an example of the human mind in an affective, oceanic processing mode, is what the previous three chapters have been working towards. It will be recalled that according to Nichols, cognitive studies should be able to illuminate the concept of literary epiphany. Disportation is my answer to this. In order to facilitate it, two things must occur: (i) the focus of investigation must be moved from specific epiphanic events that happen to characters in novels, to the felt motion and felt release experienced by real readers when they read literature, especially when they approach the end of a much-enjoyed novel, and, (ii) the focus must not just be on the text but rather on the ongoing confluent interplay between text and the affective cognition of the engaged reader. An important topic here is felt movement, as we have already seen in the image-schematic work of Johnson and others. Below I analyse and discuss two examples. The first takes place *during closure* and is primarily text-based, with some cognitive input. The second occurs *at the very moment of closure and beyond*, and has a more significant level of affective-cognitive input. After these two analyses I move on to reflect why disportation occurs at all and what its function might be in both physiological and philosophical terms.

Herrnstein Smith writes that "in lines which involve references to terminal motion (such as falling or sinking), there is a kinesthetic aspect to our responses, as if we were subliminally, but nevertheless physically, participating in the motion so described" (1968: 178). She adds that phrases like "stretched painfully" or "stood on tiptoe" can evoke what might be called a *kinesthetic image*, "not as a picture of the event from outside, as it were, but a sense of what it feels to be engaged in it" (1968: 178). Indeed, the novelist and critic Jeanette Winterson makes a similar claim when she suggests that books are kinetic (1995: 123). This sense of motion is important for Johnson too, when he claims that "image schemata have a certain kinesthetic character" (1987: 25). Herrnstein Smith also suggests that "references to terminal motion may strengthen the reader's experience of closure by inviting him to re-enact the physical event which itself terminates in repose or stability" (1968: 178). That invitation to re-enact, I believe, takes place at an affective-cognitive level. Herrnstein Smith adds that this "more or less subliminal kinesthetic identification is not, of course, confined to the experience of poetry or even of language or art. A spectator at a ballet performance or a football game may be physically exhausted at the end of it though he never left his seat" (1968: 178). Almost four decades after this was written, advances in the fields of discourse psychology, cognitive linguistics and neurobiology have made it possible to start fleshing out Herrnstein Smith's astute literary intuitions with regard to this particular kind of text processing, which includes poetic closure in novels. My notion of disportation can be seen as a part of that ongoing "fleshing out" process.

As Herrnstein-Smith suggests, felt motion can be triggered by direct textual reference to several different kinds of motion events, terminal or otherwise. These could include events like "losing one's grip", "reaching out and missing", "losing one's balance", etc., and might be extended to some of the emotive linguistic features I have discussed in my chapter on style. All of these references can be either literal or metaphorical. In some cases it can be triggered as well by the memory of such an event while reading, induced by associative intertextual mind-fed echoes or by other, normally unassociated, words triggering heightened emotion. The triggering might take place at a higher thematic level; perhaps activating some of the emotive themes I discussed in my earlier chapter. However, there is more to activation than "the world out there". Recall Kintsch's comment that neither direct linguistic referents nor associative ones need be present for a cognitive concept to be evoked. In such cases the implicit memories of previous episodes of LRI, a comfortable reading location and one's pre-reading mood may play a part. In the rest of this section, I will pull this confluent process apart in order to focus on the effects that textual input can have on triggering disportive feelings in readers.

The closing lines of *The Great Gatsby* contain a number of textual elements that might induce disportation in a reader. As suggested, approaching the end of a novel we have some distant felt sense of what we can expect, through the prior unconscious experience of rhythmic embodiment and mirror neural remembrance. Arguably, expectations are higher here than anywhere else in the entire cycle of reading. As Herrnstein Smith suggests, one reason why poetic styles are important in the study of closure is that formal and thematic elements that typically appear at closure can activate past experiences of similar discourses within a particular culture. In short, there is convention in poetic closure. So, for example, a repeated final line in a poem may seem familiar to a Western reader because of the nature of such repetitions found in nursery rhymes and ballads (1968: 30–31). It is also interesting to note that the poetic examples she gives here are almost always first learned in childhood.

The textual element I wish to focus on here fall under "acts of stretching out" and include manual, visual or even cognitive acts of stretching. Four are mentioned in Table 11.1. In the right-hand column I have tried to include both literal and figurative meanings. I believe that there are image-schematic PATH structures at the cognitive core of such events.

All four of these examples contribute to the image-schematic attraction of this passage. However, I shall only analyse one here. Because the final lines of the text have proved most fruitful thus far, both in the group

*Table 11.1*    Acts of Stretching Out

| | | |
|---|---|---|
| 1. | When he first picked out the light at the end of Daisy's dock | Visual |
| 2. | His dream must have seemed so close that he could hardly fail to grasp it | Cognitive and Manual |
| 3. | The orgastic future, that year by year recedes before us | Cognitive |
| 4. | To-morrow (we will run faster), stretch out our arms farther ... | Manual and Cognitive |

responses and in my own analysis, I will focus on the fourth example, which appears in the text just prior to the final, powerful IN-OUT/EBB-FLOW force structures in discourse unit twelve. From the semantic content of this unit of discourse and the context of the rest of the story one can guess that a person (or group of people) have previously tried and failed to achieve something. This can also be assumed from the word "tomorrow", and the comparative "faster" that suggests that a previous "fast" must have failed. The most important thing is that readers are given the strong impression that a previous attempt has been unsuccessful and, in light of this, the next one will too, despite the apparent optimism of the speaker, whose ponderings appear to be influenced by the spirit of Gatsby himself. Affective themes such as childhood locations and returning home may also get triggered here, albeit primarily implicitly.

My previous image-schematic analysis showed how this clause involved the following: (i) a projected (future) bodily mobility, (ii) a "from there to yonder (future)" projection, and (iii) "goal not known, unattainable, but very much desired". I suggested that the goal has not been attained because either the stretching out had led to no contact or incomplete contact, that is, the desired object was touched, but was beyond reach to be properly grasped. Both of these events lead to chain-event embodied notions of (i) "balance", (ii) "loss of balance", and (iii) a plausible "spilling over", but in different ways. In the first case, balance is lost, for instance, because an attempt at a swipe or grasp has been made without contact, which causes the person doing the grasping to lose his/her balance and fall to the ground. We know this may occur because of our world knowledge and our own bodily experiences of imbalance. This embodied knowledge is fundamental to how image schemata inform comprehension. It is accentuated by the fact that our brain and most of our sensory processing are located in our head, which is some distance from the ground.

In the second case, the imbalance is where the object "spills" out of our hand. It is thus a sudden loss of grip or an incomplete grip, resulting in the object falling to the floor. Interestingly, the linguistic SOURCE-PATH-GOAL event is accompanied by a similar physical one. The hand at rest, with the arm coiled inwards, can be viewed as the SOURCE stage, the movement towards extension by means of the fully outstretched arm can be seen as the PATH, and grasping is the GOAL. In cognitive-linguistic terms the hand can be seen as the trajector and the arm the landmark. In addition to the textual SOURCE-PATH-GOAL of "stretching out", the notions of grasping for one's goal and missing it, as occurs in the text, albeit implicitly, has a sense of a "loss of balance". This can evoke the BALANCE image-schema. Further, the sense of something being grasped at and missed evokes the IN-OUT image-schema. Both of these evocations take place automatically because we are human beings with embodied minds and we have built up a wealth of both conscious and subconscious knowledge about our personal past experiences. The BALANCE/IN-OUT image that I am trying to describe might be represented in more concrete terms by imagining a container first filling up with a fluid and then overflowing. It is at the point of overflowing where the BALANCE schema gives way to the IN-OUT schema.

Since metaphorical thought informs language it is not surprising that such representations have entered our lexicon. For example, in English, if a person catches and then immediately drops an object, one can say colloquially that it has "spilled" out of his/her hands. This idiom is often heard in the commentary of diverse sports journalists. These three image schemata, i.e. SOURCE-PATH-GOAL, BALANCE, and IN-OUT, should not be viewed as monolithic conceptual structures. Instead, they function in my notion of disportation in an infused fashion. In this sense, when they come together they can be seen as a single FLUVIAL schema.

This can occur in part because, in addition to the linguistic sign-fed input, there is a strong mind-fed presence that is brought to bear on working memory almost immediately. In top-down cases this may occur already in anticipation. I will say more about what is happening in both cognitive and neural terms during disportation in a moment. For now, I will just state that if all the five affective inputs that have been discussed in this work are in place when an engaged, emoted reader learns about Nick's thoughts on Gatsby's failure, then those readers are capable of experiencing a similar feeling of grasping and missing, albeit in a neurally-embodied way. This process is facilitated by mirror neural and proprioceptive simulation inputs. In this way certain readers may experience heightened emotion that may, in turn, lead to the felt sense of disportation. The affective cognitive processing of such "stretching out" events described here during emotive episodes of literary reading, whether they be manual, cognitive or visual, can lead to the firing of mirror neurons in the cortical premotor areas of the brain. This is irrespective of whether they are manual, cognitive or visual in nature. This process coincides with the embodied movement that is felt to take place in an individual during disportation. My following post-closure example will clarify what I mean.

This work started some eleven chapters ago with the quote by F. Scott Fitzgerald that "the purpose of a work of fiction is to appeal to the lingering after-effects in the reader's mind". I believe that Fitzgerald was talking about more than just conscious, post-reading reflection here. The question is then; if not reflections on reading, what was he speaking of? Some of the reader respondents in my NRQ survey suggested that their reading process did indeed appear to continue in some affective form after they had finished reading the text, even though there was nothing concrete on the page left to read. Others also appeared to suggest that this was accompanied by, or even facilitated by, a heightened emotive state. Perhaps the best example for this was the respondent who said at the end of the novel he/she was "excited, euphoric . . . somehow I am still reading in my mind". But how can a reader still be reading in his/her mind once the text has finished? And what does a sense of excitement and euphoria have to do with this? The answer to these questions may lie in the infused, continuum-like image schemata and more specifically in the notion of disportation. As I have suggested, this mode of processing occurs in the post-reading and the subsequent non-reading stage of literary discourses processing.

Below, I show an example that uses the same mechanism as described in the previous "stretching out" one. However, this time it will occur not *during closure* of the text (while a person is still reading) but *at the very point of closure* (as the physical reading ends). Although there is one predominant image schema in the text, namely, the SOURCE-PATH-GOAL one, when reader epiphany occurs two other schemata may be evoked that are not specifically textually represented. These are not solely linguistically prompted, even though they come into being because of the initial sign-fed text producing the SOURCE-PATH-GOAL schema. Instead, they are embodied structures that somehow get evoked because of the context of the literary discourse processing. The two inference-generated, embodied-cognitive structures that I mentioned previously are BALANCE-IMBALANCE and IN-OUT. Not only can they occur individually but, as suggested, they can also come into being as a kind of chain reaction. The PATH schema gets extended from the text base into the non-textual domain. In short, the PATH schema in this example begins with primarily textual prompts and ends with primarily cognitive ones. The three image schemata therefore blend to become one fluvial PATH schema. Below I will explain how this works in practice. Here again (in Table 11.2) are the closing lines and the relevant image-schematic SOURCE-PATH-GOAL "pull" from the previous chapter: "So we beat on, boats against the current, borne back ceaselessly into the past".

Here we see how the SOURCE-PATH-GOAL image schema is first turned one way and then another: the forward flowing "on" and "against" are immediately followed by the ebbing "back" and "into" ending with the word "past". The eye-tracking reading experiments of Just and Carpenter discussed in the opening chapters showed that readers appear to focus longer on content words than function words. Readers also appear to focus longer on words at the opening and closing of sentences. This being the

*Table 11.2* The Image-Schematic SOURCE-PATH-GOAL "Pull"

| Discourse Units | | | | | | | | Direction |
|---|---|---|---|---|---|---|---|---|
| | The Five Ohases | X | 1 | 2 | 3 | Y | | |
| 12a. from here to there & | | | | ► | ►<br>◄ | | Flow & | OUT |
| 12b. from then to yonder | | (◄) | ◄ | ◄ | | | Ebb | IN |

case, we might ask whether the word "past", being the final word of the final paragraph of the final chapter of *The Great Gatsby*, receives more of our reading attention—and, if so, whether this somehow helps facilitate the effects of disportation?

The many prepositions also have a significant function. This forth and back motion can affect the reading patterns, mood and emotions of an engaged reader and in doing so prepare the ground for possible disportation. This will have already been primed by affective elements of the style and rhetoric of the piece, the like of which I have discussed earlier. As can be seen, the SOURCE-PATH-GOAL structures are principally text-driven by prepositions, although subconscious mind-fed inputs from previous reading experiences may come into the equation, enriching and even (re)directing the effect. There need not be a one-to-one match, and indeed often there is none. The BALANCE schema is not primarily text-driven but is activated on the PATH continuum at the very moment when the written language on the page ends. The expected yet nonetheless abrupt shift from a blend of text and cognition to the purely mind-based inputs helps to facilitate a sense of loss of balance. This now in turn triggers the BALANCE schema. However, since its only linguistic prompt is the sudden lack of text, it does not form a new image schema but is, rather, a continuation of the SOURCE-PATH-GOAL schema. The two operate in this context on a continuum, with the one blending effortlessly and seamlessly into the other as one embodied cognitive procedure. This process is facilitated in implicit neuro-cognitive ways by a reader's rapidly increasing sense of affective cognition. The effect is also helped by the ongoing continuation of mind-based inputs as well as the residue of the underlying force effects highlighted earlier. Many of those mind-fed inputs will be guided by, and consist of, affective cognitions that have been stimulated and charged by all of the possible affective inputs I have mentioned, from LRI to reader mood and location and the themes and style of the work itself. It is at this moment that readers might feel like the poet Allen Ginsberg did or the scholar Alice Kaplan, whose epiphanic reading experiences were described in Chapter 8.

All of this can be seen as happening on the cusp of a further fusion of image schemata, namely from the BALANCE-IMBALANCE schema to the IN-OUT schema. Here, the IMBALANCE part of the schema is the starting point for the OUT part of the IN-OUT schema. The IN part thus overlaps with the BALANCE schema. For those readers who are affected at closure, this feeling of "overflowing" will be the first real moment of felt movement after the tingling sense of rapture which is the apex of balance. This is akin to a feeling of a vertiginous ecstasy. The OUT part of the IN-OUT schema is the very moment when a reader may feel that he or she is moving while still stationary. This is the very core of felt motion and thus of disportation. From a physiological perspective there is no real bodily movement at all. Perhaps the only thing moving will be the hairs standing on end on a reader's arms as goose bumps appear. Indeed, recall how some of the reader respondents remarked that they subconsciously appear to hold their breath and only exhale during the descent into the post-reading phase.

In space grammar terms, during such acts of disportation, it is as if even though the closing lines are processed sequentially, lighting up as they go, by the end point of disportation the whole lights up once again. This is what ordinarily happens in summary scanning. In image schematic terms, this process can also be viewed as an "arrival" at some goal. In abstract terms it is, as it were, an arrival at, and, by extension, an insertion into, a new "container". This facilitates the regaining of equilibrium in the BALANCE schema and is supported by the phenomenon of homeostasis. Let us now take a step back and try to account for what is actually happening during disportation in both cognitive and neural terms, by reintroducing some of the theories, studies and survey results discussed in earlier chapters.

In Chapter 7 I illustrated by means of charts and diagrams how cognitive and neural phenomena are thought to operate during regular emotive literary reading experiences. At the end of that chapter I put forward a number of propositions:

(i)   that style and themes are in the mind as well as on the page

(ii)   that in the pre-reading stage themes, style fragments and LRI are already drifting in and out of working memory before a reader's eyes have met the page (suggesting that intertextuality is active much earlier than we might think)

(iii)   that during engaged acts of literary reading it is impossible to separate sign-fed and mind-fed sources, due to their constant ebbing, flowing and coalescing and that they should henceforth be known as the *affective inputs* of literary discourse processing

(iv)   that literary reading is not just about the actual text interface. Instead, there are plausibly four confluvial parts that make up the *literary reading loop*

(v)   that *affective cognition* in literary reading is made up of *affective inputs*

(vi) that *oceanic cognition* is to some extent the interactive, ever-fluvial combination of explicit and implicit memory, together with cognitive emotion and affective cognition

(vii) that engaged acts of reading at literary closure involve an intensification of all affective inputs

I also suggested that to understand oceanic cognition, and the oceanic mind, we need to look not just at the emotive events encountered while reading literature, as was mainly the case in Chapter 7, but also at those intense emotive moments that come about while reading fiction, namely disportation.

During disportation, when endorphins flood the synapses, a reader is overwhelmed by intense emotion, and experiences a sense of rapid rising and forward movement followed by a gentle felt sense of slowing and descending. How can this be accounted for? Let us first look at structure. Just as there are three parts to the image-schematic model I have just discussed, there are also three stages to disportation: (i) the start and rapid rise, (ii) the pinnacle, and (iii) the decline, gentle reverberation and rest. The first stage is dependent on anticipation, which, as Frijda explained earlier, extends the period of time over which a given event exerts emotional influence and intensifies considerably the emotional experience itself. Reading-induced disportation is no different. At the moment of disportation, the continual priming of fragmentary personal memories, the like of which Hogan has described, explodes in a torrent of affective cognition "beyond the text" in the embodied mind of the engaged reader and out into the post-reading phase, eventually settling on a low-swell in the non-reading phase.

This general idea, that there can be phases in intense emotive responses to literature, was supported by Hogan's comments that literature-induced euphoric emotions involve "'thresholds'". He maps out three stages concerning orientation, expression and control. In stage one mood is dominant and volition on the part of the reader still present. In stage two, control is ebbing: tears may dominate here but there is still control over actional impulses. In stage three all control is lost. We see a parallel with disportation in the loss of volition. This leads to states of euphoria tinged with sadness. It is this third state of what, following Hume, I have named a state of "agreeable melancholy" that typifies disportation. Another model was observed in the literary description of epiphany by Langbaum who constructed four stage-like criteria: (a) psychological association (i.e. epiphany is secular not divine); (b) momentousness (i.e. the epiphany is fleeting but leaves a lasting effect); (c) suddenness (i.e. a shift takes place in sensory perception) and (d) fragmentation or "epiphanic leap" (i.e. the text never quite equals the epiphany). Aspects of most of these can be found in my account of disportation.

Perhaps the best structural fit for disportation is Berlyne's theory of aesthetic response, although it is only a two-stage model. We recall that Berlyne spoke of "tension" and "release" in his theory of aesthetic arousal, using the terms arousal "boost" and "jag". Tension involves activation, a readiness to respond emotionally or attentionally, whereas jag refers to a drop in heightened emotion. My claims seem to agree with Berlyne's empirically tested model—my second "pinnacle" category occurs between "boost" and "jag". It will be recalled that according to Frijda there is a drive to regain homeostasis since long exposure to high levels of arousal is unpleasant. The "jag" or "relaxation" thus becomes more pleasurable than even the object of arousal. This also seems to be the case in disportation, which ties in with Bachelard's remark that readers might feel a "poetic power rising within them" and after the original "reverberation" they are able to experience "resonances, sentimental repercussions, reminders of their past". This, in my opinion, is the very stuff of disportation in philosophical form. Further, alluding to the seemingly oceanic nature of the reading mind, Bachelard added that this state of poetic reverie must always "set the waves of the imagination radiating". As Frijda noted, being moved by aesthetic objects (as happens in my model when I speak of disportation) should not be seen in mere terms of "tension release", for it is not simply a physiological matter. Rather, it should be thought of as "surrendering to something greater than oneself" (1986: 358). Aesthetic emotion is then to my mind not only less cognitive, but it also involves what Frijda called a relevance to desire, to join and to possess. This includes proximity, coherence and additionally "losing oneself" (1986: 358). Could this "joining" be during disportation a desire to be reunited with a childhood past and primary caregivers from that past? In a later section I will explore this essentially philosophical question.

Felt disportation, a sense of "delay" (i.e. rising or "boost") followed by "catch-up" (i.e. descending or "jag") might be explained as well in neurobiological terms. In the earlier chapter of this work we learned that blood flow is crucial to memory and cognitive processing and that fMRI-scans measure activity *later,* rather when it actually occurs. This is because blood flow needs time to respond to a stimulus. In fact there is a 3–4 second delay in fMRI scanning. The whole process of blood being redirected to a part of the brain to process information and then moving away again once the action has taken place can take up to 25 seconds in total. So what neurolinguistic researchers see on the monitor during language experiments using fMRI scanning equipment is not language processing but rather its "shadow" or "echo". Might this, in part, account for what is felt during disportation, adding to what I have already claimed about implicit memory and affective cognition? Furthermore, the seeming immediacy in the "boost" stage of disportation can be accounted for by the operation of mirror neurons. Morrison observed that mirror neurons fire at an *early* visuomotor stage of processing, so that memory processing of this information occurs downstream from mirror perception. In short, the feeling of movement comes *before* the actual memory of the event. She added that mirror perception contributes at a relatively early stage to a cascade of responses that couple perception with action, and action disposition with memory. As we saw earlier, reading and the mirror system are linked because reading is an essentially non-vocal procedure that involves both Broca's area and motor areas. The fact that Broca's is analogous to the F5 mirror neural area facilitates the link from silent reading to felt movement and disportation. A third plausible neurobiological link pertains to the "jag" of disportation which leads to neural and cognitive relaxation. Interestingly, when a person is in a relaxed and awakened state possibly with closed eyes, as one may be at the end of disportation, he/she produces what is known as alpha waves in the brain.

Let us now step back and recap before looking at the psychological aspects of disportation. Literary readers are often egocentric, surreptitious beings, who have basic subconscious goals even before they come to the first page of a novel. One of their aims may be to strive to achieve disportation; the idealised preferred final outcome, as Tan put it, of several engaged and committed lovers of books. From a neural perspective, the overwhelming part of literary reading is principally a stimulus-thalamus-cortex-amygdala or high road event, as Hogan calls it. However, reading-induced disportation is almost certainly a low-road (thalamo-amygdala) phenomenon. This observation calls into question Hogan's claim that in literature, as opposed to the visual arts, we cannot have low road responses. So why is it that emotion can appear to dominate in literary reading so much so that disportation no longer seems to be a cognitive act of text processing, but more a somatic-emotive event? A number of facets need to be explored in order to answer this question. First, as we saw from my discussion in chapter 7, there is an ongoing "oceanic" interaction between what I termed affective cognition on the one hand and cognitive emotion on the other. This operates in tandem with implicit and explicit memory (see Figure 7.6). Second, we also saw that there are two processing routes: one that skips the higher cortical processing areas before moving on more or less directly to the subcortical emotive areas of the brain, and the other that does not (see Figures 7.4 and 7.5). Further, I showed that reading has four confluent phases: pre-reading, reading and post-reading as well as non-reading (see Figure 7.1).

When a reader is engulfed in a disportive state at literary closure, the body takes on a major processing role in that immediate post-reading phase. But how is this possible? The answer in part lies in affective cognition, which in some measure is made up by the five affective inputs. Affective cognition works so effectively in literary discourse processing because at the very moment of disportation the physical text processing stops, either because the novel has ended or because the reader has encountered a disportive moment in the reading process. Here, the cognitive emotion of text processing begins to coalesce, not just sporadically, but in earnest, with affective cognition. In effect, a neural and cognitive ebbing back and forth between these two processing centres is set in motion. This would mean that the body is represented in working memory, but this is not formally mapped out in existing accounts and models. We know from LeDoux's findings in *The Emotional Brain* that the body indicates changes back to other parts of the brain via the somatosensory cortex. This input then becomes part of the meaning-making appraisal maelstrom that is somehow played out in the working memory. Alan Baddeley's aforementioned model of working memory (Baddeley and Hitch 1974) has just three slave (or "buffer") systems that interact with the central executive, the supervisory system that controls the back and forth flow of information to and from those slave systems. As mentioned, these are the phonological loop, the visuo-spatial sketchpad and the episodic buffer. The last of these was only added relatively recently and is responsible for linking information across the existing domains by structuring it in a kind of chronological narrative to make visual or phonological information comprehensible. It also has strong links with long-term memory (see Baddeley 2000). This is plausibly where Kintsch's earlier mentioned "retrieval cues" are located. Below is a schematic representation of Baddeley's model of working memory.

However, if somatic inputs are as important as so many cognitive neuroscientists tell us (e.g. Damasio, LeDoux, Kintsch, Gibbs, etc.), then there must be an additional slave system that will help account for a whole host of felt phenomena, including disportation. For example, in *Comprehension*, Kintsch suggests that introspectively, it appears plausible that working memory contains a set of somatic markers in addition to cognitive

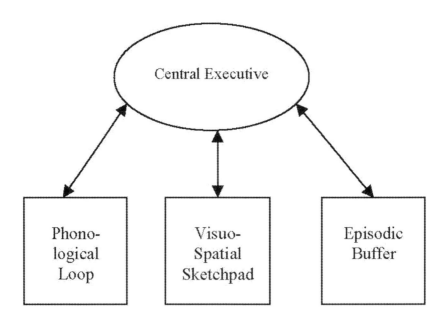

*Figure 11.1*    A schematic representation of Baddeley's model of working memory.

nodes (1998: 410). Let us then attempt to model this and call this new system "the somatic cushion". The addition of such a new buffer zone gives structure to Damasio's observations on "somatic markers" i.e. feelings we have about our own body. The way I imagine this working is during disportation, wavelets of information come together and intermingle in what Damasio described as "convergence zones".

Furthermore, it would also help to account for Kintsch's claims that we react to the world not only with our sense organs but with gut-level feelings too (1998: 412). Hence, the things that excite us, please us and scare us are most closely linked to the body. Indeed, if Kintsch is to be believed, our innermost memories are the ones most intimately linked to our body. The somatic cushion must therefore have links with the somatosensory cortex, the amygdala and the pre-frontal cortices. This may be so, since we have previously learned from LeDoux that the amygdala, together with the pre-frontal cortices, represent information and feelings about a person's body. These areas also control the state of the body. We know further through LeDoux's experiments that processed stimuli may activate the amygdala without activating explicit memories or otherwise being represented in consciousness, and that links between cues and responses are basic, and memories robust and open to strengthening as times wears on—unlike the hippocampal memory system (1998: 203). Indeed, from Gruber's earlier discussion on mirror neurons in Chapter 2 we are also aware of the crucial link that exists between working memory, Broca's area and other areas of the premotor cortex. These neurological findings match Schank's psychological ones, which show that the mind is at its core a collection of stereotypical experience-based stories. Recall is therefore about the brain deploying and replaying the nearest match. Indeed, Bartlett observed that when we recall an event it is never an exact copy of the information that was originally stored. Affective attitudes influence recall and the nature of the recalled event may tend, in particular, to produce stereotyped and conventional reproductions that adequately serve all normal needs, although they are very unfaithful to their originals (1995: 55). Further, we saw how at times the amygdala can have direct access to the central processing parts of the brain. The following diagram (Figure 11.2), an extended version of Baddeley's model, shows my added category of the somatic cushion in operation.

Recall from Chapter 6 how Kintsch described short term memory as "a dynamically changing stream" awash with "changing patterns of activation" (1998: 411). My model goes some way towards accounting for this, even if the basic arrows used in this rudimentary model in no way do justice to the reality of the constant ebbing and flowing of information across, between and beyond these areas. I believe that the strong somatic-emotive felt effects of disportation are so overwhelming, because they are capable of ebbing back and forth via the somatic cushion from short-term to long-term memory; and beyond them too, in and out of higher

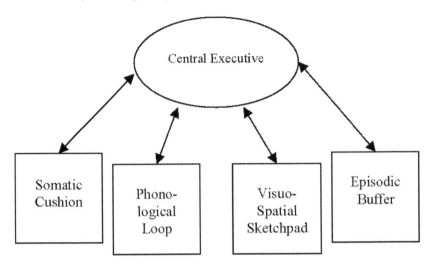

*Figure 11.2*    A schematic representation of Baddeley's model of working memory with the somatic cushion.

cortical and sub-cortical regions. This is not implausible; remember how Barsalou's idea of "event fragmentation" involves memory sources flowing into each other. This oceanic process brings with it the fragmentary memories of places and people. The role of the episodic buffer in this process is to provide narrative structure between the somatic cushion and the other slave systems, especially the visuo-spatial sketchpad. It may be remembered how Barsalou showed that from a PSS perspective short-term memory and long-term memory share neural systems with perception: the long-term system harbours the simulators while working memory implements specific simulations (1999: 604). The addition of the somatic cushion helps to explain and facilitate this process. Perceptual symbols fit into a disportive framework as they, (i) function unconsciously (1999: 583), (ii) reside at the neural level (1999: 583), (iii) are dynamic in nature, (1999: 584), (iv) produce componential images rather than holistic ones (1999: 584), (v) produce simulators "that are *always* partial and sketchy, *never* complete" (1999: 586; emphases as in original), (vi) are multimodal not just visual, including introspection (1999: 586), i.e. cognition and emotion and proprioception.

In Barsalou's terms, all this produces a simulation of the earlier event that differs from the original perception because of fewer bottom-up constraints. The neural centres and patterns responsible for these images, as he explained, are located in the early sensory cortices of varied modalities. Indeed, Barsalou suggested that memories of the same component then become organised around a common "frame": an integrated system of perceptual symbols that is used to construct specific simulations of a category (1999: 590). This leads to the implementation of a "simulator", which can produce limitless simulations of the component. This is what Barsalou calls "dispositional space": unconscious, implicit knowledge where images can be reconstructed and processed in recall. The link that the somatic cushion maintains between memory systems allows for this implicit content. Even though affective cognition and implicit memory have the upper hand during disportive reader states, emotive cognition and explicit memory also play a role through the involvement of short-term memory. The link between these two mnemonic systems was already theorised by LeDoux in his claim that there are many neural connections between the hippocampus and the amygdala as well as between lots of other cortical regions (1998: 203). He also stated that in order to have a fully embodied emotive experience the amygdala system must be activated (1998: 201).

With this knowledge, let us review a chart (Table 11.3) that I proposed in Chapter 7 to which I now add a column on the left that attempts to account for disportation.

Here, in the added category of "during highly emotive reading (especially at closure)" the textual aspects of styles and themes hover between the explicit and implicit, and in doing so tip the overall balance of the emotive reading experience into the domain of affective cognition. This is one explanation why it seems that during that most cognitive of events, discourse processing, emotion appears to take over from cognition during episodes of disportation. Cognition is, of course, involved at all stages, but affective cognition, charged with somatic inputs, from both short-term and long term areas, and implicit memory, takes over the text processing during such deeply subconscious, highly-emoted moments of reading. The role of the somatic cushion is of central importance in this process.

*Table 11.3*   Disportation and Affective Cognition during the Literary Reading Loop

|  | During highly emotive reading (especially at closure) | During reading | Pre-reading and post-reading | Non-reading |
|---|---|---|---|---|
| *Cognitive emotion* | Styles, themes | Styles, themes | XXXXXXXXX | XXXXXXXXX |
| *Affective cognition* | (strong) Styles, themes, LRI, mood, location | LRI, mood, location | *(strong) Styles, themes, LRI, mood, location* | (weak) Styles, themes, LRI, mood, location |

In sum, we can conclude that, from a neural perspective, many cross-cortical processes must be taking place during disportation. This is possible because of the deeply fluvial and cross-cortical nature of mind and brain processes. Call to mind, for example, that human brains and minds use both parallel and distributed processing strategies. Consider also that the brain processes do not work like computers, in distinct stages, for the brain is continually awash with processing activities, allowing sensory input to continually cascade back and forth in and out of working memory and the buffer zones that surround it. According to the neuroscientist Zull, many, if not most, pathways of signalling in the brain include a combination of neurons that send signals in one direction and neurons that send signals in the other one. Zull notes further that during emotive and cognitive episodes many parts of the human brain can be active at once, "in neuronal networks of incomprehensible complexity" (2002: 100). Specifically with regard to reading we previously learned how recent fMRI experiments have revealed that there is a vast network of cortical areas that are active in the different stages of reading. In fact, there appear to be about a dozen regions involved, spread across the entire brain.

Other aspects of disportive confluent cognition include neural simulations of movement that have their base in proprioception (for force), the vestibular function (for balance) and mirror neurons (for the integrated feeling of felt motion). Indeed, all of these may very well be triggered simultaneously. In addition to these pre-cortical and sensory-motor areas, the sub-cortical emotive areas of the brain must also be fully engaged at this stage, producing the smiles and the tears and the affective memories that were all too obvious in the previously cited examples, including Kaplan's tearful reading of the closing lines of *The Great Gatsby* and the comments of the NRQ respondents. Indeed, like Kaplan, one the NRQ reader-respondent recalled that he/she "always had to cry near the end" while his/her thoughts "wandered off, slowing down the reading process".

Readers therefore "stay in the story" during disportation, as one NRQ survey respondent put it so aptly and so accurately. This may be so, because a person feels as though he/she is being "sucked into the end of the story" as another respondent stated. As we have seen, textual elements play a role in this process too. Some evidence for this is given by the respondent who admitted that "metaphors and disrupting style at the end always pull me into the novel and affect how I read it". We observed actual indications of disportation in some of the earlier NRQ responses, for instance, when one person admitted to "feeling strange" at the moment of finishing a much-enjoyed novel and another one remarked tellingly that "it was like I was still living in the story". All of these real responses from real readers allude to different phases of disportation. The last one, in particular, alludes to a reading that takes place in the post-textual phase. Similarly, one person wrote that he/she was "quite excited, climactic—just like waking from a vivid dream or coming off a roller-coaster" and another admitted being "very emotional: disappointed and euphoric at the same time but also calm and focused". Two comments, however, that best highlighted disportation were very brief. These were "I felt a sort of release" and "somehow I am still reading in my mind." The former puts into words the very act of entering a disportive state, whereas the latter, as suggested earlier, provides anecdotal evidence for the mainly mind-fed and affective cognitive processing that takes place in the post-reading phase, as well as the non-reading and pre-reading phases, in what I have termed, the literary reading loop.

The felt nature of movement during disportation suggests as well that mirror-neural activity occurs simultaneously with conceptual image-schematic processing. This in turn implies that in addition to a known processing area for image-schematic structures in the visual cortex, set out by Turner and discussed earlier, there is as well a currently undiscovered neural activity in the pre-motor areas. This is where the processing of mirror neurons takes place and other motor areas employed in proprioception and this could also plausibly involve the visuo-spatial sketchpad, linked to the somatic cushion via the episodic buffer. Since the human brain uses many areas when processing visual data, as explained in Chapter 3, it can be assumed that the emotive sub-cortical regions of the brain must also be part of the neural processing network. There are no technological means available to support my theoretical claim just yet. However, improved neural scanning techniques of the future may go some way toward shedding more light on this, although the location of the reading event will always remain a stumbling block with regard to observing what really happens in the brains and bodies of real readers when they read literature in an engaged and emotive manner.

To conclude this cognitive-neurobiological section, I have tried to show how disportation may work at literary closure, how three image schemata can become one by flowing into each other along an affective cognitive continuum and how mind and language are involved in confluent ways. This all takes place in a matter of seconds, milliseconds even. I have shown too that this can cause a highly emoted reader to undergo a form of image-schematic "vertigo", which can be the starting point of reader disportation. I have termed this phenomenon of several image schemata becoming one in specific discourse processing environments the FLUVIAL schema. As I have shown, this whole process is supported in force terms by all the image gestalt force vectors coming together to set up the EQUILIBRIUM version of the BALANCE schema at the moment the discourse ends. I have also shown how this sense of the vertiginous has the capability to send an emoted literary reader spinning into a sensory maelstrom, which has the feeling of moving upward and outward in a FLUVIAL/PATH-like fashion. This exemplifies the affective-cognitive way in which the oceanic human mind can work, facilitated by the somatic cushion. This is the sense of euphoria and elevation that all those who have experienced reader disportation should be able to recognise.

In image gestalt terms, the forces of REMOVAL OF RESTRAINT and ENABLEMENT dominate here. In cognitive image schematic terms, in reaching a state of disportation a reader transgresses the image-schematic notion of a CONTAINER, namely a bounded space with an interior and exterior. Hence, disportation, as it is channelled here in this text, contains, in my opinion, a blend of three image schematic structures: (1) the transition from SOURCE to PATH (on the way to the GOAL); (2) BALANCE, followed by IMBALANCE; (3) a movement from INSIDE to OUTSIDE. In order to mentally visualise this in more concrete terms, imagine a container, as indeed our bodies are, at the very moment it overflows. At the moment when disportation starts, at least three image schemata become fluid and flow into each other. This supports Johnson's largely forgotten claim that image schemata are "dynamic", "continuous", "flexible" and most importantly of all, "relatively fluid" (1987: 30).

All of the above is, of course, in part facilitated by the main themes in *The Great Gatsby*. By the time a reader reaches the end of the book, the characters' "longing to return" and the "yearning for a state of true contentment" will have set in place an abstract PATH schema in the affective cognition of an engaged reader. Readers might also empathically project—in the embodied way, as Lakoff and Johnson described it—for both Gatsby and Nick. It is towards the end of the book that readers might conceptually feel the "blockage", as it were, in Gatsby's life-journey, as both Nick and we, as readers, come to realise that his dream was already behind him, in his irretrievable, incommunicable past. It is at this stage that we recall Gatsby's stretching-out through Nick's reminiscing/mental stretching. Readers are prompted to experience the disportive, emotive infusion of image schemata. Another important point is that since an empathetic sense of projection is involved, readers might map Gatsby's flawed life onto aspects of their own life. This ties in both with Scheff's earlier mentioned idea of experiencing emotions through art "at a safe aesthetic distance" and with Aristotle's cathartic insights into pity and fear. Let us now look at some potential philosophical implication of my disportation theory.

Why can disportation occur during highly emoted episodes of literary reading, in this case at closure? And does this phenomenon have any function in the wider sense? It seems plausible that disportation occurs principally because of our biological need to experience intense emotional states like moments of euphoria. This is a somewhat sweeping statement and will need some clarification. I have used the word "principally" here quite purposely. Frijda, for example, points out that emotional intensity is not a clear-cut concept (1986: 32): "the relationship between arousal and experienced emotional intensity is complex" (1986: 226). Probing this matter further, Rita Carter has suggested in her work *Mapping the Mind* that some moments of euphoria are only arrived at after considerable conscious processing (2000: 130–31). Although the end-product is largely physiological, the immense amount of explicit and implicit cognitive processing that is needed to reach that state must not be forgotten. In short, as Carter points out, "there must be an elaborate exchange of information taking place between the conscious cortical areas of the brain and the sub-cortical limbic system" (2000: 130–31). It would seem, therefore, that we are neurologically wired to undergo such states of euphoria from time to time, be they religion-induced, art-induced or otherwise. Even though reading, and especially literary reading, is a new medium in evolutionary terms, and even though reading is what Kosslyn and Koenig rightly call an example of "opportunistic processing" in its use of neurocognitive pathways meant for other activities such as object identification (1995: 168), literature is an abstract art par excellence and as such is well-suited for emotive-cognitive embodied events. As Mortimer Adler and Charles van Doren rightly argue, "one reason why fiction is a human necessity is that it satisfies many unconscious as well as conscious needs" (1967: 220). The reason why disportation can occur is because we have bodies and minds that facilitate it. The question here, however, is not *how* it occurs while reading literature, which I have already attempted to explain in the previous chapters of this work in neural and cognitive terms, but *why*?

Can one assume that readers in a disportive state may momentarily gain entry to the normally inaccessible parts of their subconscious and their long-term memory? When disportation occurs, a reader may sometimes appear to "travel back", perhaps to the remembered locations of the past, which may also include the felt, fragmentary presence of primary caregivers. This felt regression has the effect of appearing to distance the reader from his/her inevitable death. Returning to my above example in abstract cognitive terms, all this appears to happen when the OUT part of the IN-OUT schema is activated. This is the "ebbing away", as it were. So the question is, whether disportation can be viewed as some kind of "portal to the past"? Might such an *Erhebung* without motion"—to borrow a phrase from the poem "Burnt Norton" in *Four Quartets* by the poet and critic T.S. Eliot—be a form of secular revelation? Can literary disportation momentarily appear to ward off death and offer a reader a soft landing into the reality of his/her undeniable mortality? Might such LRI of past locations in which a reader is a child again; skipping, running, jumping or swinging, momentarily soften the inevitable drift that is to come? I will now look at some of these questions in more detail.

A first important matter is that there is no guarantee that disportation will occur in a reader; indeed some engaged readers may never experience it. Second, if it takes place, it must be accompanied by a series of physiological states that ordinarily should include an increase in heart-rate, body temperature and blood pressure, erratic breathing patterns, a reddening of the skin colour of the face and neck, etc. This will begin with the person becoming suddenly highly emoted by an essentially empathetic mechanism, but one which is based on a reader's socio-cognitive knowledge of both other texts and other worldly events, especially those that impinge on that person's life or of his/her loved ones.

So what is disportation and why does it occur? Below I will offer support for the following five statements:

- Disportation has some of the characteristics of spirituality but is not a form of spiritualism
- Disportation is a transformational phenomenon in the sense described earlier by Winnicott
- Disportation is an embodied phenomenon
- Disportation helps us to close the gap between culture and cognition
- Disportation helps us to both understand and deal with our own mortality

Are such literary effects, as set out in my disportation hypothesis, akin to a religious "state of mind"? The answer to this is both yes and no. Let me start by returning to a question I posed to a group of readers in Chapter 3 of this work: "Do you think that literary reading has anything to do with spirituality?" Of the fifteen subjects asked, nine answered affirmatively. Eight of the fifteen subjects added an additional comment all of which I have listed in Chapter 3. Some said it depended on the spiritual content of the book; a sign-fed prompt, while others said it depended on the existing spirituality of the reader, a mind-fed trigger. Others were more eclectic, saying "mental imagery and spirituality are both really personal", and "I sometimes get spiritual experiences when a book is very captivating".

For Langbaum, literary epiphany is "the Romantic substitute for religion" (1999: 59). Literature of a certain kind can indeed be an important aspect of modern spirituality for some individuals, as has previously been claimed. The nineteenth-century poet and critic Matthew Arnold argued in his 1888 critical essay "The Study of Poetry" that in the future people would turn to poetry and prose for sources of inspiration and comfort. The literary form would not only console and sustain us, but it would help us to understand better what life is about (who we are, where we came from, where are we heading, and why?). He also predicted that in time poetry would replace philosophy and religion. Although I agree with the first part of Arnold's claims, I cannot fully concur with the second; not simply because poetry is less ideological and political than religion, but also because there are too many other discrepancies between the two. Marcel Proust famously said in his essay titled "On Reading" that "reading is at the threshold of spiritual life; it can introduce us to it. It does not constitute it" (cited in Gilbar 1995: 39). My position is somewhere between Arnold's "consoling ", and "sustaining" claim and Proust's suggestion that reading can only take one to the borders of spirituality. Acts of disportation do comfort and maintain us, whether we are consciously aware that they are happening to us or not, but this is not spirituality in the true sense. Disportation is an ideal for life, not an insurance policy against death.

The idea that heightened emotive moments within a framework of affective literary reading might act as some kind of surrogate for a long-dead caregiver might seem outlandish, but as we saw earlier Winnicott argued in his work on transitional phenomena that our experience of human culture develops in the space that opens up between our infant selves and our mothers (or, in some cases, another primary caregiver). In the beginning, infant and mother are one, but then they slowly but surely begin to separate, and blankets, pacifiers and teddy bears begin to fill the space between them. These surrogate objects are, in effect, the transitional phenomena. The object represents the mother, or to be more exact, it represents the child's relationship with the mother. Although the object is not the mother, it has similar soothing and calming effects on the child. Later in life, the space gets filled with such things as language and culture, which become the new transitional phenomena, the new comforters. Mirroring Winnicott's ideas, cognitive psychologist Oatley has also quite recently argued that "without the space that grows in between the mother and infant there would be no culture" (2000: 104). It is my contention that disportation, as experienced during affective interfaces with literary texts, is an apt example of a language-based cultural transitional phenomena for adults, an experience through the medium of literature. I propose further that the feeling experienced will be stronger in an older reader and in the reader whose favourite primary caregiver is deceased. In a way, the older the reader, the narrower the transitional space, in the sense that it waxes into maturity, then wanes in old age. This may indicate that disportation may occur more frequently in such older readers. The transitional space in which disportation operates grows until our loved ones and primary caregivers start to die. At this point it peaks, and then turns and starts to shorten again. Accordingly, it seems plausible that if a person lives into old age, the disportive transitional space that a reader will have to travel will be only slightly longer than it was in pre-adolescence.

Winnicott's psychoanalytic claims on location are embodied in some of the philosophical ones of Bachelard, who suggested that we comfort ourselves by reliving memories of protection through the poetry of space. Is this perhaps one of the reasons why we desire to encounter childhood locations, namely in order to be able to re-participate in the original locative intimacy and warmth. In another work *The Poetics of Reverie* (1960/1971), he makes the claim that childhood lasts all through life. He suggests that it somehow returns quite frequently to affect long segments of our adult lives. He adds, most poignantly, that it is poets who will help us to find this living childhood within us (1971, from the Introduction to section six).

Perhaps the late eighteenth-century German novelist and philosopher Novalis was not too wide of the mark when he said that all philosophy is about homelessness and homesickness and only the novel can transcend this distance. Critiqued in the early twentieth-century by eminent Marxist literary critics such as Georg Lukács for its hopeless romanticism, I believe this idea warrants a reappraisal—for although nostalgia is thoroughly anti-modern, and therefore problematic, secular nostalgia, as it occurs in the confluence of culture and cognition, is centrally humanist and is thus worthy of our renewed attention.

In light of the above one might conclude that from a psychoanalytic perspective literary readers who seek to undergo disportation are akin perhaps to perennial infants, unable to tear themselves away from the site of the mother's breast, or, worse still, individuals who are locked into some kind of self-indulgent, pseudo-onanistic state. Although such psychoanalytic interpretations of disportation may prove fruitful, they are beyond the remit of this book. Nonetheless, they should be explored in future research. Perhaps, though, they appear to miss the main point of an embodied, affective cognitive mind. This is summed up succinctly by one of the reader respondents who said that he/she felt "climactic" but "climactic in the reading sense". Because disportation is channelled by an art form, it is an aesthetic emotion, and as cognitive psychologist Frijda states "aesthetic emotion is not mere pleasure, like that produced by sexual climax" (1986: 357). However, there is one enticing psychoanalytic claim brought up by May while discussing epiphany-like impressions in novels: "a suitable succession of such moments would be the ideal psychoanalysis, the means to perfect self-understanding" (1977: 66). This is an appealing point and one that echoes some of my own claims about disportation.

Disportation is also a fundamentally embodied experience, not an "out-of-body" occurrence. The idea of "stepping outside oneself" is something that has remained popular in Western philosophy since the time of the pre-Socratic Pythagoreans and their ponderings about the "transmigration of the soul". Twenty-first-century philosophical investigations of heightened affective states during literary reading should remember that human bodies and human brains do not merely cause cognitions and emotions, they house and facilitate them as well. Motion during disportation is at all times "felt"; it is a simulation, not a physical performance. It is a kind of cognitive shadow-play; an event that sends us "moving through the silence without motion" to cite a line from the Joy Division song "Shadowplay" written by Ian Curtis. Disportation is thus a rhythmic sense of embodied cognition that is at the centre of the oceanic human mind.

My disportation hypothesis also shows how aspects of culture and cognition are blended. Culture nourishes the brain with language, literature, art, science and religion, and the brain, in turn, both facilitates and reverberates those cultural phenomena back out into the apperceived world, until the stimulus-driven and concept-driven enter a confluence of emotive human appraisal. These cultural phenomena are also all, to a greater or lesser extent, human-designed cerebral safety nets, as L. S. Vygotsky once remarked in *Mind in Society*. They are strategies of survival, to counter the greatest danger of consciousness, namely that we know that one day we will die. Humans arguably need the comfort of culture and/or religion, since both may act as life-preservers. The disportation hypothesis puts forward the claim that one of the most buoyant of such life-preservers may be located in the literary reading adventure. To extend on this point: without culture there would be no human brain as we know it today. Culture allows our brains to grow so that we can imbibe and create more culture. Culture does not oppose the biological processes of the brain but is at its very heart, because it is to a large extent responsible for its enlarged cortical state. One might even say that culture is the source of the human brain, the source of human cognition and, as such, the source of human emotion. This is why when speaking of the "embodied" human mind we are speaking of a mind that is grounded in a blend of biology and society. In effect, the oceanic mind that I have been describing is neuro-culturally grounded.

So what might the purpose of disportation be? Can its effects somehow stave off the inevitability of our ensuing death—albeit in perceived and felt terms rather than in reality? Reading and death, as concepts, might seem far removed from each other: some, however, would disagree. The writer Stanley Elkin has claimed in his essay "Where I Read, What I Read" that the reason we read is to die—or, more specifically, to learn how to die (cited in Gilbar 1995: 114). Similarly, Harold Bloom suggests in *How to Read and Why* that "one of the uses of reading is to prepare ourselves for change, and the final change alas is universal" (2000: 21). Literary reading, it would therefore seem, may well be considered both the midwife and mortician of human emotion.

In sum, literary reading is, indeed, a cognitive activity, but it is a confluent cognitive emotive and affective cognitive phenomenon involving both explicit and implicit memory, all of which occurs within the embodied basin of the oceanic human mind. Oceanic cognition is therefore confluent cognition. Moreover, I view disportation in all engagements with art as an evolutionary survival strategy. During disportive moments, when feel-good chemicals flood the synapses of the brain, readers feel they have been successful in momentarily stopping time, even though this is not factually the case. Not only that, but in appearing to stop time they also facilitate a process whereby they can flow back to whence they believe they came. This felt embodied journey has the function of empowering the reader for the real journey that is inevitably to come. Engaged and committed literary readers can enjoy a momentary window in time, plausibly sending those individuals back to their indistinct locations of their remembered, or pseudo-remembered, childhood. The ability therefore of the embodied mind to travel back may be a survivalist strategy that has evolved to a higher function of the embodied mind. Moreover, this process keys into being conducive to well-being and happiness. In this way, the effects of literary reading are fundamentally *eudaemonistic* in the Aristotelian sense. Prior to literature and reading there were other, less-abstract, art forms that facilitated this, such as basic rhythms and image paintings on rocks.

Disportation does not ward off the inevitable descent into death, as nothing can, but it does offer readers the option of a parachute for a softer landing than otherwise might have been the case. When our time comes it may very well be our longing for the safety and comfort of a childhood location or childhood moment or childhood object that will fill our minds. And when that moment is upon us, we may reach out, but when we do, we are preordained to flail and miss; such is the human condition. And in doing so we will be borne back ceaselessly, into our incommunicable pasts: all the wiser for the experience; all the milder for the deliverance.

As the psychologist Esther Salaman noted earlier, "we are all exiles from our lives; we need to recapture it". I believe that one of the ways to accomplish this is to read literature in an engaged and committed manner. I propose that there is a familiar childhood space that drifts deep in the undertow of our embodied oceanic minds. This place has long disappeared from the real world and has dissolved in the shifting memories of our individual pasts. But there is a common cultural process requiring a confluence of the sociological world and the biological body that allows us to reclaim fragments of this lost time. In doing so it permits us to drift back momentarily on the backwash of our subconscious memory to a time of protection and comfort, even if, in reality, this was very different. Such is the deceptive quality of memory. Such acts of literary reading are facilitated by the affective-cognitive processes of the embodied, oceanic reading mind. Like Stevenson's shipwrecked character, described in Chapter 3, we come to realise as we grow older that we too are marooned. Thankfully, as there was for him, there is a cultural process whereby we can momentarily become furnished with a distal sense of those lost childhood locations and those cherished primary caregivers. So if you want to go in search of lost time, of some distal half-remembrance of things past, simply wait till your mood is optimal, take down a book, make yourself comfortable, open that book, and start to read.

With that final thought we find ourselves at the end of this reading journey. In Chapter 4 I quoted the writer Harold Brodkey, who thought that the act of reading literature as it really occurs is obscure. He was right. It has been the aim of this book to try to shed some light on that fascinating and elusive process, to explore what may be occurring in what Brodkey termed "the altered tempos of reading". In this work I set out to discover what happens in the minds and bodies of readers when they make the conscious decision to sit down and engage with literature. My aim was to make a small theoretical contribution with my humanities experience towards shedding some light on this. I chose to narrow this huge research question and focus on just three issues, which in hindsight, were still vast: (i) what role does emotion play in a cognitive event like literary text processing?, (ii) which kinds of bottom-up and top-down inputs are most prominently involved in literary reading, and how do they interact in meaning-making?, and (iii) what happens in the minds and bodies of readers when they experience intense or heightened emotions at literary closure? My main claim was that during the affective cognitive act of reading literature, comprehension often takes place within the theatre of what I called "oceanic cognition". My idea of oceanic cognition suggested that there is a dynamic, free-flow of bottom-up and top-down affective-cognitive inputs during literary reading, and that reading does not begin or end when eyes apprehend the words on the page, but long before that and indeed long after it. In light of the dynamic ebb and flow of affective mind processes during engaged acts of literary reading, I concluded that the human mind might best be considered not as mechanical or computational, but as oceanic. I believe that I have gone some way towards producing some support for this claim even if many questions have been left unanswered.

This work has not offered a complete theory of emotive poetics. My notions of the oceanic mind, the disportation hypothesis, affective cognition, the somatic cushion, the literary reading loop and my five affective inputs are still very much "in the making". They are hypotheses that need to be tested, and where necessary reconsidered, refined and restructured. For instance, I now see that an additional affective input to complement the location of the act of reading could be the time or timing of that reading event. In short, this study constitutes the very beginning of my own thinking on affective inputs in the oceanic, literary reading mind—not the end.

I have suggested that cognition works in an oceanic fashion in contexts of emotive literary reading. But the question is, is it just limited to literary reading situations? It is now broadly acknowledged that the world of literary reading and the real world are not wholly disconnected. Recent psychological studies have shown how literary narratives can have a real effect on people's lives (Gerrig and Rapp 2004) and substantially alter real-world beliefs (Green et al. 2004). Perhaps, then, oceanic cognition could be the modus operandi behind the processing of many ordinary mental events, like daydreaming, recollecting, planning and thinking. Perhaps too, the fragmentary childhood locations that I believe are evoked while reading literature may very well be visualised in all kinds of everyday thinking procedures. Might the flow of all thought be "like the waves in an ocean", as one of my reading respondents claimed? Although the hard proof is still missing, and may continue to be so for some time yet, the mounting neurobiological, psychological, linguistic and literary evidence seems to be pointing increasingly in that general direction.

In sum, I have tried to search for those "lingering after-effects in the reader's mind" to which a work of fiction appeals. Have I managed to do that? And further, have I been successful in proposing the beginnings of an oceanic theory to account for the affective cognitive processes that come into play when an engaged and committed reader sits down to read literature? Only time and tide will tell.

So we read on—books against the current—born back ceaselessly—into our pasts.

# Notes

## NOTES TO CHAPTER 1

1. The original work was published in 1983. It is from this most recent (1999) work that I cite here in this section.
2. Zull points out how a difference can be made in working memory saying that "spatial working memory more frequently engages the upper part of the frontal cortex and object working memory the middle and lower parts" (2002: 183).

## NOTES TO CHAPTER 2

1. At the source of this discovery are two seminal articles: Rizzolatti and Arbib (1998) "Language within Our Grasp" and Gallese and Goldman (1998) "Mirror Neurons and the Simulation Theory of Mind Reading".
2. Since the theory expounded on here is part of Richard Lazarus's ongoing work, I will refer only to him in subsequent references. The perspective cited below on emotion in the appraisal process is one that runs through much of his influential cognitive psychological work.
3. This became known too as the "Cannon-Bard Theory" in recognition of the similar work done by physiologist Philip Bard.

## NOTES TO CHAPTER 3

1. This research was presented at the 2005 conference for *Text and Discourse Studies* held at the Free University, Amsterdam (VU). The talk was entitled "Discourse Dimensions in Autobiographical Memories of Younger and Older Adults".
2. Of course, it should be said that all of Bachelard's ideas in *The Poetics of Space* are almost certainly contingent on having had a non-traumatic childhood.
3. Bachelard also said "the home of other days has become a great image of lost intimacy" (1958: 100).
4. This idea of a confluence of the locative childhood space and the maternal (i.e. primary caregiver) also appears in an earlier work entitled *La Terre et les Rêveries de Repos* (1946), where, when discussing the reading of a poem by Milosz, Bachelard makes mention of a reading-induced mental construct

"where the mother image and the house image are united" (also cited in *The Poetics of Space* 1958: 45).

5 The final question in the NRQ (question 15) pertains exclusively to the reading of this novel and especially to the reading of its closing paragraphs. Chapter 9 of this study will be devoted to looking closely at the results of this case study.

## NOTES TO CHAPTER 4

1. One of the most comprehensive versions of Jauss's ideas is to be found in "Toward an Aesthetic of Reception" (1982).
2. A breakdown of these students and the conditions under which this survey took place can be found in the previous chapter. Throughout this chapter, and all of the ones that will follow, for practical purposes, I no longer make the distinction between the responses of the VU subjects and the RA subjects.
3. See Manguel (1996: 141–47) for a more detailed overview of this development upon whose account my synopsis is based.
4. This account is cited in full in Gilbar 1995 (see 109–18).
5. Cited from a digital letter to customers (dated 20 November 2007) from Jeff Bezos, founder and CEO of Amazon.

## NOTES TO CHAPTER 5

1. This episode was broadcast on BBC 1, on 28 July 2001. Portmeirion was actually quite famous in the 1960s, because it was used as the setting for Patrick McGoohan's cult television series *The Prisoner*.
2. This according to a survey conducted by the British Council, which interviewed 40,000 people in 102 non-English speaking countries. ("Mum's the Word, Says the World", 26 November 2004,www.newsvote.bbc.co.uk).
3. By "above themes" I mean the ten that appear in the question previous to this one in the original layout of the NRQ, namely question 12.

## NOTES TO CHAPTER 6

1. It is customary in cognitive linguistics to write such metaphors in small capitals. I will employ this convention throughout the rest of this book.
2. For more on this see the entry on "Rhetoric and Music" in the *New Grove Dictionary of Music and Musicians* (Sadie and Tyrell 2003).
3. I am using the English language version of Benjamin's *Illuminations* (with an introduction by Hannah Arendt). The Flaubert piece discussed by Benjamin is thus based on the English translation that appears there.
4. The original text is:
    "C'est là ce que nous avons eu de meilleur!" dit Frédéric. "Oui, peut-être bien? C'est là ce que nous avons eu de meilleur!", dit Deslauriers.
5. Indeed, for similar examples see Rumelhart 1975 and Mandler and Johnson 1977. This is also acknowledged in narratology (see Propp 1968 and Prince 1973).

# NOTES TO CHAPTER 10

1. There is also some similarity here with Len Talmy's notion of "force dynamics" (1988). Generally speaking force dynamics operate at a higher abstract level than image schemata.

2 This has been simplified here. In Langacker's space grammar it is presented in a much more complex way. For example, a verb's temporal profile will also play an important role in how and when it is processed. (For more on this see Langacker 1991, 149–63, in his chapter titled "Abstract Motion".)

3. I have written elsewhere briefly on the idea that literary texts may channel breathing patterns (see Burke 2001).

# Bibliography

Abrams, M. H., ed. *A Glossary of Literary Terms*. 5th ed. Orlando, FL: Holt, Rinehart and Winston Inc., 1988.

Adler, Mortimer J., and Charles van Doren. *How to Read a Book*. 1940 ed. New York: Simon and Schuster, 1967.

Alcott, Louisa May. *Little Women*. New York: Signet Classics, 2004.

Aristotle. "On the Art of Poetry." In *Aristotle, Horace, Longinus: Classical Literary Criticism*, 29–76. Harmondsworth, Middlesex: Penguin, 1965.

———. *On the Art of Rhetoric*. Translated by Hugh Lawson-Tancred. London: Penguin, 1991.

———. *On the Soul*. Translated by Hugh Lawson-Tancred. London: Penguin, 1987.

Arnold, Matthew. "The Study of Poetry." In *Essays in Criticism*. London: J. M. Dent and Sons, 1964.

Augustine, St. *Confessions*. Translated by Henry Chadwick. Oxford Oxford World's Classics, 1998.

Bachelard, Gaston. *La Terre Et Les Rêveries De Repos*. Paris: José Corti, 1946.

———. *The Poetics of Reverie*. 1960 ed. Boston, MA: Beacon Press, 1971.

———. *The Poetics of Space*. 1958 ed. Boston, MA: Beacon Press, 1964.

Baddeley, Alan. D., and G. Hitch. "Cognitive Psychology and Human Memory." *Trends in Neuroscience* 11.4 (1988): 176–81.

———. "The Episodic Buffer: A New Component in Working Memory?" *Trends in Cognitive Science* 4 (2000): 417–23.

———. "Working Memory." In *The Psychology of Learning and Motivation: Advances in Research and Theory*, edited by G. H.Bower, 47–89. New York: Academic Press, 1974.

Bal, Mieke. *Narratology*. 2nd ed. Toronto: Toronto University Express, 1997.

Barsalou, Lawrence W. "The Content and Organization of Autobiographical Memories." In *Remembering Reconsidered: Ecological and Traditional Approaches to the Study of Memory*, edited by Ulric Neisser and Eugene Winograd, 193–243. Cambridge: Cambridge University Press, 1988a.

———. "The Instability of Graded Structure: Implications for the Nature of Concepts." In *Concepts and Conceptual Development: Factors in Ecological and Intellectual Categories*, edited by Ulric Neisser 101–40. Cambridge: Cambridge University Press, 1987.

———. "Intra-Concept Similarity and Its Implications for the Nature of Concepts." In *Similarity and Analogical Reasoning*, edited by S. Vosniadou and A. Ortony. Cambridge: Cambridge University Press, 1988b.

———. "Perceptual Symbols Systems." *Behavioral and Brain Sciences* 22 (1999): 577–660.

Barthes, Roland. *Camera Lucida: Reflections on Photography.* Translated by Richard Howard. 1981 ed. London: Vintage Books, 1993.

Bartlett, Sir Frederic C. *Remembering: A Study in Experimental and Social Psychology.* 1932 ed. Cambridge: Cambridge University Press, 1995.

Beja, Morris. *Epiphany in the Modern Novel.* Seattle ,WA: University of Washington Press, 1971.

Benjamin, Walter. "The Storyteller." In *Illuminations,* edited by Hannah Arendt, 83–109. New York: Schocken Books, 1968.

Bergman, Ingmar. "Introduction." In *Four Screenplays.* London: Secker and Warburg, 1960.

Berlyne, Daniel E. *Aesthetics and Psychobiology.* New York: Appleton-Century-Crofts, 1971.

———. *Conflict, Arousal and Curiosity.* New York: McGraw Hill, 1960.

———. *Studies in the New Experimental Aesthetics: Steps Towards an Objective Psychology of Aesthetic Appreciation.* London: Taylor & Francis, 1974.

Best, John B. *Cognitive Psychology.* St. Paul, MN: West Publishing Company, 1986.

Biber, Douglas, and Edward. Finnegan. "Adverbial Stance Types in English." *Discourse Processes* 11 (1988): 1–34.

———. "Styles of Stance in English: Lexical and Grammatical Marking of Evidentiality and Affect." *Text* 9 (1989): 93–124.

Black J. B., and Seifert C. M. "The Psychological Study of Story Understanding." In *Researching Responses to Literature and the Teaching of Literature,* edited by C. R. Cooper, 190–211. Norwood, NJ: Ablex, 1985.

Blair, Hugh. *Lectures on Rhetoric.* Edited by Grenville Kleisner. 1783 ed. Whitefish, MT: Kessinger Publishing, 2004. Reprint, 1911.

Bloom, Harold. *How to Read and Why.* London: Fourth Estate, 2000.

Booth, Wayne. *The Rhetoric of Fiction.* 2nd ed. Chicago: University of Chicago Press, 1961.

Boulton, Marjorie. *The Anatomy of Prose.* 1954 ed. London: Routledge and Keegan Paul, 1980.

Bower, Gordon H. and Joseph Forgas. "Affective Influence on the Content of Cognition." In *Handbook of Affect and Social Cognition,* edited by Joseph Forgas, 95–120. Mahwah, NJ: Lawrence Erlbaum Associates, 2001.

Brecht, Berthold. *Brecht on Theatre: The development of an aesthetic.* Trans. John Willet. New York: Hill and Wang, 1977.

Brewer, W. F. "Schemas Versus Mental Models in Human Memory." In *Modeling Cognition,* edited by P. Morris, 187–97. Chichester: Wiley, 1987a.

———. "What Is Autobiographical Memory?" In *Autobiographical Memory,* edited by D. C. Rubin, 25–49. Cambridge: Cambridge University Press, 1987b.

Brodkey, Harold. "Reading, the Most Dangerous Game." In *Reading in Bed: Personal Essays on the Glories of Reading,* edited by Steven Gilbar, 101–8. Jaffrey, NH: Godine, 1995.

Broyard, Anatole. "Rereading and Other Excesses." *New York Times,* 3 March 1985.

Bruccoli, Matthew. "Introduction." In *The Great Gatsby,* edited by F.Scott Fitzgerald, vii–xvi. New York: Scribner, 1992.

Burke, Michael. "Cognitive Stylistics." In *Encyclopaedia of Language and Linguistics,* edited by Keith E. Brown., 218–21. Amsterdam: Elsevier, 2006.

———. "Cognitive Stylistics in the Classroom: A Pedagogical Account." *Style* 39.1 (2004): 491–510.

———. "How Cognition Can Augment Stylistic Analysis." *The European Journal of English Studies* 9.2 (2005): 185–96.

————. "Iconicity and Literary Emotion." *European Journal of English Studies* 5.1 (2001): 31–46.

————. "Progress Is a Comfortable Disease: Cognition in a Stylistic Analysis of E. E. Cummings." In *Contemporary Stylistics*, edited by Marina Lambrou and Peter Stockwell, 144–55. London: Continuum, 2007.

————. "Rhetoric and Persuasion." In *The Cambridge Encyclopedia of the Language Sciences*, edited by Patrick Colm Hogan. Cambridge: Cambridge University Press, 2010.

Buzsáki, György. *Rhythms of the Brain*. Oxford: Oxford University Press, 2006.

Caffi, Claudia, and Richard V. O. Janney. "Towards a Pragmatics of Emotive Communication." *Journal of Pragmatics* 22 (1994): 325–73.

Cannon, Walter. B. "The James-Lange Theory of Emotion: A Critical Examination and an Alternative Theory." *American Journal of Psychology* 39 (1927): 106–24.

Carter, Rita. *Mapping the Mind*. London: Phoenix, 2000.

Cataldi, S. *Emotion, Depth and Flesh*. Albany: State University of New York Press, 1996.

Cather, Willa. *My Ántonia*. 1918 ed. New York: Bantam Books, 1994.

Chafe, Wallace. "Integration and Involvement in Speaking, Writing and Oral Literature." In *Spoken and Written Language: Exploring Orality and Literacy*, edited by Deborah Tannen, 35–53. Norwood, NJ: Ablex, 1980.

Chase, W. G., and K. A. Ericsson. "Still and Working Memory." In *The Psychology of Learning and Motivation*, edited by G. H. Bower, 1–58. New York: Academic Press, 1982.

Cicero. *De Oratore*. Translated by E. W. Sutton and H. Rackham. Vols. I and II. Cambridge, MA: Harvard University Press, 1942.

Clark, Urszula, and Sonia Zyngier. "Towards a Pedagogical Stylistics." *Language and Literature* 12.4 (2003): 339–51.

Clore, Gerald, L., and Karen Gasper. "Feeling Is Believing: Some Affective Influences on Belief." In *Emotions and Beliefs: How Feelings Influence Thoughts*, edited by Nico H. Frijda, Antony S. R. Manstead and Sacha Bem, 10–44. Cambridge: Cambridge University Press, 2000.

Coleridge, Samuel Taylor. *The Collected Works of Samuel Taylor Coleridge, Volume 14: Table Talk 1*. Princeton, NJ: Princeton University Press, 1990.

————. *The Complete Poems*. London: Penguin, 1997.

Collins, Wilkie. *The Moonstone*. 1868. Wordsworth Classics ed., 1993.

Conley, Thomas C. *Rhetoric in the European Tradition*. Chicago: University of Chicago Press, 1990.

Conrad, Joseph. *Lord Jim*. 1900 ed. Oxford: Oxford University Press, 1983.

Conway, Martin A. "Conceptual Representation of Emotions: The Role of Autobiographical Memories." In *Lines of Thinking: Reflections on the Psychology of Thought. Vol. 2 Skills, Emotion, Creative Processes, Individual Differences and Teaching Thinking*, edited by K. J. Gilhooly et al. Chichester: Wiley, 1990.

Conway, Martin. A., and Debra. A. Bekerian. "Situational Knowledge and Emotions." *Cognition and Emotion* 1 (1987): 145–91.

Cook, Guy. *Discourse and Literature: The Interplay of Form and Mind*. Oxford: Oxford University Press, 1994.

————. *Language, Play and Learning*. Oxford: Oxford University Press, 2000.

Corbett, Edward P. J., and Robert J. Connors. *Classical Rhetoric for the Modern Student*. 4th ed. Oxford: Oxford University Press, 1999.

Crystal, David. *The Cambridge Encyclopaedia of the English Language*. Cambridge: Cambridge University Press, 1995.

Csábi, Szilvia, and Judit Zerkowitz, ed. *Textual Secrets: The Message of the Medium.* Budapest: Akadémiai Nyomda Martonvásár, 2002.

Cupchik, Gerald C., and Janos László. "The Landscape of Time in Literary Reception: Character Experience and Narrative Action." *Cognition and Emotion* 8.4 (1994): 297–312.

Cureton, Richard. "The Auditory Imagination and the Music of Poetry." In *Twentieth-Century Poetry: From Text to Context*, edited by Peter Verdonk, 68–86. London: Routledge, 1993.

Curtis, Ian. "Shadowplay." In *Unknown Pleasures*: Factory, 1979.

Damasio, Antonio R. *Descartes' Error: Emotion, Reason and the Human Brain.* New York: Avon Books Inc., 1994.

———. *The Feeling of What Happens: Body and Emotion in the Making of Consciousness.* Orlando: Harcourt Inc., 1999.

Danesi, Marcel. "The Neurological Coordinates of Metaphor." *Communication and Cognition* 22.1 (1989): 73–86.

Dehaene, Stanislas. «Natural Born Readers.» *New Scientist*, 5 July 2003, 30–33.

Demetrius. *On Style.* Translated by Doreen C. Innes and W. Rhys Roberts. rev. ed. Cambridge, MA: Harvard University Press, 1996.

de Montaigne, Michel. *The Essays of Montaigne.* Translated by E. J. Trechmann. Vol. 1. Oxford: Oxford University Press, 1970.

de Vega, I. M., and J. M. Díaz. "The Representation of Changing Emotions in Reading Comprehension." *Cognition and Emotion* 10.3 (1996): 303–21.

Dronkers, Nina F., Steven Pinker and Antonio Damasio. "Language and the Asphasias." In *Principles of Neural Science*, edited by James H. Schwartz and Thomas M. Jessel and Erik R. Kandel, 1169–87. New York: McGraw-Hill, 2000.

Eliot, T. S . *Four Quartets.* 1944 ed. London: Faber and Faber, 2000.

———. *Selected Essays.* London: Faber and Faber, 1976.

Elkin, Stanley. "Where I Read, What I Read." In *Reading in Bed: Personal Essays on the Glories of Reading*, edited by Steven Gilbar, 109–18. Jaffrey, NH: Godine, 1995.

Emmott, Catherine. "The Experience of Reading: Cognition, Style, Affect and Social Space." In *Thematics: Interdisciplinary Studies*, edited by Szilvia Csábi and Judit Zerkowitz. Budapest: Akadémiai Nyomda Martonvásár, 2002.

———. *Narrative Comprehension.* Oxford: Oxford University Press, 1997.

———. "Reading for Pleasure: A Cognitive Poetic Analysis of 'Twists in the Tale' and Other Plot Reversals in Narrative Texts." In *Cognitive Poetics in Practice*, edited by Joanna Gavins and Gerard Steen, 145–59. London: Routledge, 2003.

———. "Responding to Style: Cohesion, Foregrounding and Thematic Interpretation." In *Thematics: Interdisciplinary Studies*, edited by Max Louwerse and Willie van Peer, 91–117. Amsterdam: John Benjamins, 2002.

Empson, William. *Seven Types of Ambiguity.* 1930 ed. New York: New Directions, 1966.

Engler, Balz. "The Poem and Occasion." In *Twentieth-Century Poetry: From Text to Context*, edited by Peter Verdonk, 159–70. London: Routledge, 1993.

Epicurus. *The Essential Epicurus: Letters, Principal Doctrines, Vatican Sayings and Fragments.* Translated by Eugene O'Connor. New York: Prometheus Books, 1993.

Ericsson, K. A., and Walter Kintsch. "Long-Term Working Memory." *Psychological Review* 102 (1995): 211–45.

Eysenck, M. W., and M. T. Keane. *Cognitive Psychology: A Student's Handbook.* Hove/Mahwah, NJ: Lawrence Erlbaum Associates, 1990.

Farrah, Martha. J. "Is Visual Imagery Really Visual? Overlooked Evidence from Neuropsychology." *Psychological Review* 95 (1988): 307–17.

———. "Psychological Evidence for a Shared Representational Medium for Mental Images and Percepts." *Journal of Experimental Psychology* 114 (1985): 91–103.

Fiedler, Klaus, and Herbert Bless. "The Formation of Beliefs at the Interface of Affective and Cognitive Processes." In *Emotions and Beliefs: How Feelings Influence Thoughts*, edited by Nico H. Frijda, Antony S. R. Manstead and Sacha Bem, 144–70. Cambridge: Cambridge University Press, 2000.

Finke, Ronald A. *Principles of Mental Imagery*. Cambridge, MA: MIT Press, 1989.

Fish, Stanley E. *Is There a Text in the Class?* Cambridge, MA: Harvard University Press, 1980.

———. "What Is Stylistics and Why Are They Saying Such Terrible Things About It?" In *The Stylistics Reader: From Roman Jakobson to the Present*, edited by Jean-Jacques Weber, 94–116. London: Arnold, 1996.

Fitzgerald, F. Scott. *The Great Gatsby*. 1925 ed. New York: Scribner, 1992.

———. *This Side of Paradise*. Cambridge: Cambridge University Press, 1995.

Flaubert, Gustav. *Sentimental Education: The Story of a Young Man*. Translated by Robert Baldick. 1869 ed. New York: Viking Press, 1991.

Flesch, Rudolf. *How to Test Readability*. London: Harper, 1951.

Foertsch, Julie, and Morton A. Gernsbacher. "In Search of Complete Comprehension: Getting 'Minimalists' to Do Work." *Discourse Processes* 18 (1994): 271–96.

Fogassi, Leonardo, and Vittorio Gallese. "The Neural Correlates of Action Understanding in Non-Human Primates." In *Mirror Neurons and the Evolution of Brain and Language*, edited by Maxim I. Stamenov and Vittorio Gallese, 13–35. Amsterdam: John Benjamins, 2002.

Forgas, Joseph, P. "Feeling Is Believing? The Role of Processing Strategies in Mediating Affective Influences on Beliefs." In *Emotions and Beliefs: How Feelings Influence Thoughts*, edited by Nico H. Frijda, Antony S. R. Manstead and Sacha Bem, 108–43. Cambridge: Cambridge University Press, 2000.

———. "Mood and Judgment: The Affective Infusion Model (Aim)." *Psychological Bulletin* 117.1 (1995): 39–66.

Frazier, Lyn, and Keith Rayner. "Resolution of Syntactic Category Ambiguities: Eye Movements in Parsing Lexically Ambiguous Sentences." *Journal of Memory and Language* 26 (1987): 505–26.

———. "Taking on Semantic Commitments: Processing Multiple Meanings vs. Multiple Senses." *Journal of Memory and Language* 29 (1990): 181–201.

Frijda, Nico H. *The Emotions*. Cambridge: Cambridge University Press, 1986.

Frijda, Nico H., Anthony S. R. Manstead and Sacha Bem, ed. *Emotions and Beliefs: How Feelings Influence Thoughts*. Cambridge: Cambridge University Press, 2000.

Frijda, Nico H., and Mesquita, Batja. "Beliefs through Emotions." In *Emotions and Beliefs: How Feelings Influence Thoughts*, edited by Antony S. R. Manstead, Sacha Bem and Nico H. Frijda, 45–77. Cambridge: Cambridge University Press, 2000.

Galen. *On the Natural Faculties*. Translated by Arthur J. Brock. Cambridge, MA: Harvard University Press, 1916.

Gallese, Vittorio, and A. Goldman. "Mirror Neurons and the Simulation Theory of Mind Reading." *Trends in Cognitive Science* 2.12 (1998): 493–501.

Gardner, Esther P., Martin, John H. and Thomas M. Jessell. "The Bodily Senses." In *Principles of Neural Science*, edited by Eric R. Kandel, James H. Schwartz and Thomas M. Jessell, 430–50. New York: McGraw-Hill, 2000.

Georgakopoulou, Alexandra, and Dionysis Goutsos. *Discourse Analysis*. Edinburgh: Edinburgh University Press, 1997.

George, Orwell. *1984*. 1949 ed. London: Penguin, 1970.

Gerrig, Richard J. *Experiencing Narrative Worlds: On the Psychological Activities of Reading*. New Haven, CT: Yale University Press, 1993.

Gerrig, Richard J., and David N. Rapp. "Psychological Processes Underlying Literary Impact." *Poetics Today* 25.2 (2004): 265–81.

Gibbs, Raymond W. Jr. *Embodiment and Cognitive Science*. Cambridge: Cambridge University Press, 2006.

———. "Feeling Moved by Metaphor." In *Textual Secrets: The Message of the Medium*, edited by Szilvia Csábi and Judit Zerkowitz, 12–27. Budapest: Akadémiai Nyomda Martonvásár, 2002.

———. *Intentions in the Experience of Meaning*. Cambridge: Cambridge University Press, 1999a.

Gibbs, Raymond W. Jr., *Poetics of Mind: Figurative Thought, Language and Understanding*. Cambridge: Cambridge University Press, 1994.

———. "Taking Metaphor out of Our Heads and Putting It into the Cultural World." In *Metaphor in Cognitive Linguistics*, edited by Raymond W. Gibbs Jr. and Gerard Steen, 145–66. Amsterdam: John Benjamins, 1999b.

Gibbs, Raymond W. Jr., and Gerard Steen, ed. *Metaphor in Cognitive Linguistics*. Amsterdam: John Benjamins, 1999.

Gilbar, Steven, ed. *Reading in Bed: Personal Essays on the Glory of Reading*. Jaffrey, NH: Godine, 1995.

Ginsberg, Allen. "The Art of Poetry Viii: Interview with Allen Ginsberg." *Paris Review* 37 (1966): 13–55.

Graesser, Arthur C. *Prose Comprehension Beyond the Word*. Berlin: Springer, 1981.

Graesser, Arthur C., and R. J. Kreuz. "A Theory of Inference Generation During Text Comprehension." *Discourse Processes* 16 (1993): 145–60.

Graesser, Arthur C., M. Singer and T. Trabasso. "Constructing Inferences During Narrative Text Comprehension." *Psychological Review* 101 (1994): 371–95.

Grafton, S. T. et al. "Localization of Grasp Representation in Humans by Positron Emission Tomography: 2. Observation Compared with Imagination." *Experimental Brain Research* 112 (1996): 103–11.

Green, Melanie C., Jennifer Garst and Timothy C. Brock. "The Power of Fiction: Determinents and Boundaries." In *The Psychology of Entertainment Media: Blurring the Lines between Entertainment and Persuasion*, edited by Schrum L. J., 161–76. Mahwah, NJ: Lawrence Erlbaum Associates, 2004.

Greenfield, Susan. *Brain Story*. London: BBC Worldwide Ltd., 2000.

Gruber, Oliver. "The Co-Evolution of Language and Working Memory Capacity in the Human Brain." In *Mirror Neurons and the Evolution of Brain and Language*, edited by Maxim I. Stamenov and Vittorio Gallese, 77–87. Amsterdam: John Benjamins, 2002.

Halliday, Michael. A. K. *An Introduction to Functional Grammar*. 1985. 2nd ed. London: Arnold, 1994.

Henry, Anne C. "Ellipsis Marks in a Historical Perspective." In *The Motivated Sign: Iconicity in Language and Literature 2*, edited by Olga Fischer and Max Nänny, 135–55. Amsterdam: John Benjamins, 2001.

Herodotus. *The Histories*. Translated by Aubrey de Sélincourt. 2nd ed. Penguin Classic Edition, 1954.

Herrnstein Smith, Barbara. *Poetic Closure: A Study of How Poems End*. Chicago: University of Chicago Press, 1968.

Hogan, Patrick Colm. *Cognitive Science, Literature and the Arts*. New York/London: Routledge, 2003a.

————. *The Mind and Its Stories: Narrative Universal and Human Emotion.* Cambridge: Cambridge University Press, 2003b.

————. "Towards a Cognitive Science of Poetics." *College Literature* 23.1 (1996): 164–78.

Hoorn, Johan. "Metaphor and the Brain: Behavioural and Psychophysiological Research into Literary Metaphor Processing." Diss: Vrije Universiteit Amsterdam, 1997.

Horace. "Ars Poetica." In *Aristotle, Horace, Longinus: Classical Literary Criticism*, 77–96. Harmondsworth, Middlesex: Penguin, 1965.

Hume, David. "Of the Delicacy of Taste and Passion." In *On the Standard of Taste and Other Essays*, edited by John W. Lenz, 25–28. New York: Liberal Arts Library, 1965.

Isen, Alice M. "Toward Understanding the Role of Affect in Cognition." In *Handbook of Social Cognition*, edited by T. Wyer and T. Srull, 179–236. Hillsdale, NJ: Lawrence Erlbaum Associates, 1984.

Iser, Wolfgang. *The Act of Reading.* Baltimore: Johns Hopkins University Press, 1978.

————. *The Implied Reader: Patterns of Communication in Prose Fiction from Bunyan to Beckett.* Baltimore: Johns Hopkins University Press, 1974.

Ishiguro, Kazuo. *The Remains of the Day.* London: Vintage, 1993.

Jakobson, Roman. "Closing Statement: Linguistics and Poetics." In *Style in Language*, edited by Thomas A. Sebeok, 350–77. Cambridge, MA: MIT Press, 1960.

James, William. *Essays in Psychology.* Cambridge, MA: Harvard University Press, 1983.

————. *The Principles of Psychology.* New York: Holt, 1890.

————. "What Is an Emotion?" *Mind* 9 (1884): 188–205.

Jauss, Hans, R. *Toward an Aesthetic of Reception.* Translated by Timothy Bahti. Minneapolis: University of Minnesota Press, 1982.

Johnson, Mark. *The Body in the Mind: The Bodily Basis of Meaning, Imagination and Reason.* Chicago: The University of Chicago Press, 1987.

Joyce, James. *A Portrait of the Artist as a Young Man.* 1914–15 ed. London: Penguin, 1992.

Just, Marcel A., and Patricia A. Carpenter. "A Theory of Reading: From Eye Fixations to Comprehension." *Psychological Review* 87 (1980): 329–53.

Kafka, Franz. *The Trial.* Translated by David Wyllie. Teddington Middlesex: Echo Library, 2006.

Kandel, Erik, R. "The Brain and Behaviour." In *Principles of Neural Science*, edited by Eric R. Kandel, James H. Schwartz and Thomas M. Jessell, 5–18. New York: McGraw-Hill, 2000.

Kandel, Eric R., Irving Kupfermann and Susan Iverson. "Learning and Memory." In *Principles of Neural Science*, edited by Eric R. Kandel, James H. Schwartz and Thomas M. Jessell, 1225–46. New York: McGraw-Hill, 2000.

Kandel, Eric R., James H. Schwartz and Thomas M. Jessell, ed. *Principles of Neural Science.* 4th ed. New York: McGraw-Hill, 2000.

Kandel, Eric R., and Robert H. Wurtz. "Constructing the Visual Image." In *Principles of Neural Science*, edited by Eric R. Kandel, James H. Schwartz and Thomas M. Jessell, 492–506. New York: McGraw-Hill, 2000.

Kaplan, Alice. *French Lessons: A Memoir.* Chicago: University of Chicago Press, 1993.

Keats, John. *The Letters of John Keats (1814–1821).* Edited by Hyder Edward Rollins. Cambridge, MA: Harvard University Press, 1958.

Kintsch, Walter. *Comprehension: A Paradigm for Cognition.* Cambridge: Cambridge University Press, 1998.

Kosslyn, Stephen. *Image and Brain. The Resolution of the Imagery Debate*. Cambridge, MA: MIT Press, 1994.

———. *Image and Mind*. Cambridge, MA: Harvard University Press, 1990.

———. "Information Representation in Visual Images." *Cognitive Psychology* 7 (1975): 341–70.

———. "Measuring the Visual Angle of the Mind's Eye." *Cognitive Psychology* 10 (1978): 356–89.

Kosslyn, Stephen M., and Olivier Koenig. *The Wet Mind: The New Cognitive Neuroscience*. 1992 ed. New York: The Free Press, 1995.

Kövecses, Zoltán. *Emotion Concepts*. New York: Spriner Verlag, 1990.

———. *Metaphor and Emotion*. Cambridge: Cambridge University Press, 2000.

Krakauer, John, and Claude Ghez. "Voluntary Movement." In *Principles of Neural Science*, edited by Eric R. Kandel, James H. Schwartz and Thomas M. Jessell, 756–81. New York: McGraw-Hill, 2000.

Kristeva, Julia. "Stabat Mater." In *The Kristeva Reader*, edited by Toril Moi, 160–86. Oxford: Blackwell, 1987.

Lakoff, George, and Mark Johnson. *Metaphors We Live By*. Chicago: Chicago University Press, 1980.

Lakoff, George, and Mark Turner. *More Than Cool Reason: A Field Guide to Poeticmetaphor*. Chicago: University of Chicago Press, 1989.

Lakoff, George. *Philosophy in the Flesh: The Embodied Mind and Its Challenge to Western Thought*. New York: Basic Books, 1999.

Langacker, Ronald. *Concept, Image and Symbol*. Berlin: Mouton de Gruyter, 1991.

———. *Foundations of Cognitive Grammar. Vol I: Theoretical Prerequisites*. Stanford, CA: Stanford University Press, 1987.

———. *Foundations of Cognitive Grammar. Vol II: Descriptive Application*. Stanford, CA: Stanford University Press, 1991.

Langbaum, Robert. "The Epiphanic Mode in Wordsworth and Modern Literature." In *Moments of Moment: Aspects of the Literary Epiphany*, 37–60. Amsterdam: Rodopi, 1999.

Lazarus, Richard. S. *Emotion and Adaptation*. Oxford: Oxford University Press, 1991.

———. "On the Primacy of Cognition." *American Psychologist* 39 (1984): 124–29.

Lazarus, Richard S., and Bernice N. Lazarus. *Passion and Reason: Making Sense of Our Emotions*. Oxford: Oxford University Press, 1994.

LeDoux, Joseph E. "Emotion: Clues from the Brain." *Annual Review of Psychology* 46 (1995): 209–35.

———. *The Emotional Brain*. New York: Phoenix, 1998.

———. "The Neurobiology of Emotion." In *Mind and Brain Dialogues in Cognitive Neuroscience*, edited by Joseph E. LeDoux and W. Hirst, 301–54. Cambridge: Cambridge University Press, 1986.

Leech, Geoffrey N., and Michael H. Short. *Style in Fiction: A Linguistic Introduction to English Fictional Prose*. London: Longman, 1981.

Libet, Benjamin. "Timing of Cerebral Processes Relative to Concomitant Conscious Experience in Man." In *Advances in Psychological Sciences*, edited by I. Meszaros, G. Adam and E. I. Banyai. Elmsford, NY: Pergamon Press, 1981.

Lindberg, David C. *Studies in the History of Mediaeval Optics*. London: Variorum Reprints, 1983.

Locke, John. *An Essay Concerning Human Understanding*. 1690 ed. Oxford: Oxford University Press, 1979.

Lohafer, Susan. *Reading for Storyness: Preclosure Theory, Empirical Poetics and Culture in the Short Story*. Baltimore: Johns Hopkins University Press, 2003.

Losey, Jay. "'Demonic' Epiphanies: The Denial of Death in Larkin and Heaney." In *Moments of Moment: Aspects of the Literary Epiphany*, edited by Wim Tigges, 375–400. Amsterdam: Rodopi, 1999.

Lucretius. *On the Nature of the Universe*. [De Natura Rerum] Translated by R. E. Latham. rev. John Godwin. Harmondsworth, Middlesex: Penguin, 1994.

Lukács, Georg. *The Theory of the Novel: A Historico-Philosophical Essay on the Forms of Great Epic Literature*. Translated by Anna Bostock. Cambridge, MA: M.I.T. Press, 1971.

Mandler, Jean M., and N. S. Johnson. "Remembrance of Things Parsed: Story Structure and Recall." *Cognitive Psychology* 9 (1977): 111–51.

Manguel, Alberto. *A History of Reading*. London: Penguin, 1996.

May, Keith, M. *Out of the Maelstrom: Psychology and the Novel in the Twentieth Century*. New York: St. Martin's Press, 1977.

McCrum, Robert. "E-Read All About It." *The Observer*, 15 January 2006, 17.

McCullers, Carson. *The Member of the Wedding*. Harmondsworth, England: Penguin, 1946.

McCune, Loraine. "Mirror Neurons' Registration of Biological Motion: A Resource for Evolution of Communication and Cognitive/Linguistic Meaning." In *Mirror Neurons and the Evolution of Brain and Language*, edited by Maxim I. Stamenov and Vittorio Gallese, 315–22. Amsterdam: John Benjamins, 2002.

McGlone, Francis, Matthew Howard and Neil Roberts. "Brain Activation to Passive Observation of Grasping Actions." In *Mirror Neurons and the Evolution of Brain and Language*, edited by Maxim I. Stamenov and Vittorio Gallese, 125–34. Amsterdam: John Benjamins, 2002.

McKoon, Gail, and Roger Ratcliff. "Inferences During Reading." *Psychological Review* 99 (1992): 440–66.

———. "The Minimalist Hypothesis: Directions for Research." In *Discourse Comprehension: Essays in Honour of Walter Kintsch*, edited by S. Mannes, C. A. Weaver and C. R. Fletcher, 97–116. Hillsdale, NJ: Lawrence Erlbaum Associates, 1995.

Melville, Herman. *Moby Dick*. Ware, Hertfordshire: Wordsworth Classics, 1992.

Miall, David. S. "Affect and Narrative: A Model of Response to Stories." *Poetics* 17 (1988): 259–72.

———. "Anticipation and Feeling in Literary Response: A Neuropsychological Perspective." *Poetics* 23 (1995): 275–98.

Miall, David. S. "Beyond the Schema Given: Affective Comprehension of Literary Narratives." *Cognition and Emotion* 3.1 (1989): 55–78.

Miall, David. S, and Don Kuiken. "Feeling and the Three Phases of Literary Response." In *Empirical Approaches to Literature. Proceedings of the Fourth Conference of the International Society for Empirical Study of Literature, Igel, Budapest 1994*, edited by Gebhard Rusch, 282–90, 1995.

———. "Foregrounding, Defamliarization, and Affect: Response to Literary Stories." *Poetics* 22 (1994): 389–407.

Morgan, Jerry. L., and Manfred B. Sellner. "Discourse and Linguistic Theory." In *Theoretical Issues in Reading Comprehension*, edited by Rand J. Spiro, Bertram. C. Bruce and William F. Brewer. 165–200. Hillsdale, NJ: Lawrence Erlbaum Associates, 1980.

Morrison, India. "Mirror Neurons and Cultural Transmission." In *Mirror Neurons and the Evolution of Brain and Language.*, edited by Maxim I. Stamenov and Vittorio Gallese, 333–40. Amsterdam: John Benjamins, 2002.

Murphy, S. T., and Robert B. Zajonc. "Affect, Cognition and Awareness: Affective Priming with Optimal and Sub-Optimal Stimulus Exposures." *Journal of Personality and Social Psychology* 64 (1993): 723–39.

Nadel, L., and W. J. Jacobs. "The Role of the Hippocampus in Ptsd, Panic and Phobia." In *Hippocampus: Functions and Clinical Relevance*, edited by N. Kato. Amsterdam: Elsevier Science, 1996.

Neisser, Ulric. *Cognition and Reality*. San Francisco: W. H. Freeman, 1976.

Neubauer, John. *The Emancipation of Music from Language: Departure from Mimesis in Eighteenth-Century Aesthetics*. New Haven, CT: Yale University Press, 1986.

Newman, J, E. Cusick and A. La Tourette, eds. *The Writer's Workbook*. London: Arnold, 2000.

Nichols, Ashton. "Cognitive and Pragmatic Linguistic Moments: Literary Epiphany in Thomas Pynchon and Seamus Heaney." In *Moments of Moment: Aspects of the Literary Epiphany*, edited by Wim Tigges, 467–80. Amsterdam: Rodopi, 1999.

Novakovich, Josip. *Fiction Writer's Workshop*. Cincinnati, OH: Story Press, 1995.

Novalis. *Heinrich Von Offerdingen*. Translated by Palmer Hilty. Long Grove, IL: Waveland Press, 1990.

Nussbaum, Martha C. *The Fragility of Goodness: Luck and Ethics in Greek Tragedy and Philosophy*. Cambridge: Cambridge University Press, 1986.

Oatley, Keith. *Best Laid Schemes: The Psychology of Emotions*. Cambridge: Cambridge University Press, 1992.

———. "The Sentiments and Beliefs of Distributed Cognition." In *Emotions and Beliefs: How Feelings Influence Thoughts*, edited by Nico H. Frijda, Antony S. R. Manstead and Sacha Bem, 78–107. Cambridge: Cambridge University Press, 2000.

Oatley, Keith, and P. N. Johnson-Laird. "Towards a Cognitive Theory of Emotions." *Cognition and Emotion* 1 (1987): 29–50.

Oatley, Keith, and Jennifer M. Jenkins. *Understanding Emotions*. Oxford: Blackwell, 1996.

O'Connor, Eugene. *The Essential Epicurus*. Translated by Eugene O'Connor. New York: Prometheus Books, 1993.

Opdahl, Keith. *Emotion as Meaning: The Literary Case for How We Imagine*. Lewisburg, PA: Bucknell University Press, 2002.

Otten, M., and J. J. A. van Berkum. "Discourse-Based Anticipation During Language Processing: Prediction or Priming?" *Discourse Processes* 45.6 (2008): 464–96.

Paley, Grace. "A Conversation with My Father." In *Enormous Changes at the Last Minute*, 161–67. New York: Farrar, Straus and Giroux, 1981.

Pearson, P. David. *Handbook of Reading Research*. Mahwah, NJ: Lawrence Erlbaum Associates, 2000.

Penfield, Wilder, and P. Perot. "The Brain's Record of Visual and Auditory Experience: A Final Summary and Discussion." *Brain* 86 (1963): 595–696.

Plato. *Phaedo*. Translated by David Gallop. Oxford: Clarendon Press, 1975.

———. *Philebus*. Translated by R. Hackforth. Cambridge: Cambridge University Press, 1972.

Polanyi, L. *Telling the American Story: A Structural and Cultural Analysis of Conversational Storytelling*. Norwood, NJ: Ablex, 1985.

Prigozy, Ruth. "Introduction." In *The Great Gatsby*, edited by F. Scott Fitzgerald, vii–xxxv. Oxford: Oxford World's Classics, 1998.

Prince, G. *A Grammar of Stories*. The Hague: Mouton, 1973.

Propp, Vladimir. *Morphology of the Folktale*. 1928 ed. Austin: University of Texas Press, 1968.

Proust, Marcel. "On Reading." In *Reading in Bed: Personal Essays on the Glories of Reading*, edited by Steven Gilbar, 39–44. Jaffrey, NH: Godine, 1995.

————. *Remembrance of Things Past*. Translated by C. K. Scott Moncrieff. London: Chatto and Windus, 1976.

Pulvermüller, Friedmann. *The Neuroscience of Language: On Brain Circuits of Words and Serial Order*. Cambridge: Cambridge University Press, 2002.

Quintilian. *Institutio Oratoria*. Translated by H. E. Butler. Vol. Books I–XXII (in six volumes). Cambridge, MA: Harvard University Press, 1921–22.

Quirk, Randolph S. et al. *A Comprehensive Grammar of the English Language*. London: Longman.

Ramachandran, Vilayanur S. *A Brief Tour of Human Consciousness: From Imposter Poodles to Purple Numbers*. London: Pi Press, 2005.

Ramachandran, Vilayanur S. and Diane Rogers-Ramachandran. "The Neurology of Aesthetics: How Visual Processing Systems Shape Our Feelings About What We See." *Scientific American Mind* October/November (2006): 16–18.

Rapp, David N., Richard J. Gerrig and D. A. Prentice. "Readers' Trait-Based Models of Characters in Narrative Comprehension." *Journal of Memory and Language* 45.4 (2001): 737–50.

Reisner, B. J., J. B. Black and R. P. Abelson. "Knowledge Structures in the Organization and Retrieval of Autobiographical Memories." *Cognitive Psychology* 17 (1985): 89–137.

Rizzolatti, G., and M. Arbib. "Language within Our Grasp." *Trends in Neuroscience* 21 (1998): 188–94.

Rizzolatti, Giacomo., Laila Craighero and Luciano Fadiga. "The Mirror System in Humans." In *Mirror Neurons and the Evolution of Brain and Language*, edited by Maxim I. Stamenov and Vittorio Gallese, 37–59. Amsterdam: John Benjamins, 2002.

Roach, Peter. *English Phonetics and Phonology*. Cambridge: Cambridge University Press, 1983.

Robinson, Andrew. *The Story of Writing: Alphabets, Hieroglyphs and Pictograms*. London: Thames and Hudson, 1995.

Roy, Arundhati. *The God of Small Things*. London: Flamingo, 1997.

Rumelhart, David E. "Notes on a Schema for Stories." In *Representation and Understanding: Studies in Cognitive Science*, edited by D. G. Bobrow and A. M. Collins, 211–36. New York: Academic Press, 1975.

Rumelhart, David E. "Schemata: The Building Blocks of Cognition." In *Theoretical Issues in Reading Comprehension: Perspectives from Cognitive Psychology, Linguistics, Artificial Intelligence and Education*, edited by et al R. J. Spiro, 22–58. Hillsdale, NJ: Lawrence Erlbaum Associates, 1980.

Rumelhart, David E. et al. "Schemata and Sequential Thought Processes in Pdp Models." In *Parallel Distributed Processing: Explorations in the Microstructure of Cognition*, edited by J. L. McCleland et al, 7–57. Cambridge, MA: MIT Press, 1986.

Sacks, Oliver. *The Man Who Mistook His Wife for a Hat*. London: Picador, 1985.

Sadie, Stanley and Tyrell, John, ed. *Rhetoric and Music*. 2nd ed, The New Grove Dictionary of Music and Musicians. Oxford: Oxford University Press, 2003.

Salaman, Esther. *A Collection of Moments*. London: Longman, 1970.

Sanford, Anthony J., and Simons C. Garrod. "Incrementality in Discourse Understanding." In *The Construction of Mental Representation During Reading*, 3–27. Hillsdale, NJ: Lawrence Erlbaum Associates, 1999.

————. "Selective Processing in Text Understanding." In *Handbook of Psycholinguistics*, edited by M. Gernsbacher, 699–719. New York: Academic Press, 1994.

————. *Understanding Written Language: Explorations in Comprehension Beyond the Sentence*. Chichester: John Wiley and Sons, 1981.

Saper, Clifford B., Susan Iverson and Richard Franckowiak. "Integration of Sensory and Motor Function: The Association Areas of the Cerebral Cortex and the Cognitive Capabilities of the Brain." In *Principles of Neural Science*, edited by Erik R. Kandel, James H. Schwartz and Thomas M. Jessel, 349–80. New York: McGraw-Hill, 2000.

Scarry, Elaine. *Dreaming by the Book*. Princeton, NJ: Princeton University Press, 1999.

Schacter, Daniel L. *Searching for Memory: The Brain, the Mind and the Past*. New York: Basic Books, 1996.

Schachter, Stanley, and Jerome Singer. "Cognitive, Social and Physiological Determinants of Emotional State." *Psychological Review* 69 (1962): 379–99.

Schank, Roger C. *Dynamic Memory Revisited*. Cambridge: Cambridge University Press, 1999.

————. *Dynamic Memory: A Theory of Reminding and Learning in Computers and People*. Cambridge: Cambridge University Press, 1983.

Schank, Roger. C., and R. Abelson. *Scripts, Plans, Goals and Understanding*. Hillside, NJ: Lawrence Erlbaum Associates, 1977.

Scheff, Thomas J. *Catharsis in Healing Ritual and Drama*. Berkeley: University of California Press, 1979.

Schwartz, James, H. . "Neurotransmitters." In *Principles of Neural Science*, edited by Erik R. Kandel, James H. Schwartz and and Thomas M. Jessel, 280–97. New York: McGraw-Hill, 2000.

Schwartz, Lynne Sharon. "True Confessions of a Reader." In *Reading in Bed: Personal Essays on the Glories of Reading*, edited by Steven Gilbar, 127–34. Jaffrey, NH: Godine, 1995.

Seilman, Uffe and Steen F. Larsen. "Personal Resonance to Literature: A Study of Remindings While Reading." *Poetics* 18 (1989): 165–77.

Semino, Elena. *Language and World Creation in Poems and Other Texts*. London and New York: Longman, 1997.

Shamay-Tsoory S. G., R. Tomer and J. Aharon-Peretz. "The Neuroanatomical Basis of Understanding Sarcasm and Its Relationship to Social Cognition." *Neuropsychology* 19 (2005): 288–300.

Short, Mick *Exploring the Language of Poems, Plays and Prose*. London/New York: Longman, 1996.

Simon, Herbert A. *Reason in Human Affairs*. Stanford: Stanford University Press, 1983.

Singer, M, Arthur C. Graesser and T. Trabasso. "Minimal or Global Inference During Reading." *Journal of Memory and Language* 33 (1994): 421–41.

Sloane, Thomas O. *Encyclopedia of Rhetoric*. Oxford: Oxford University Press, 2001.

Smith, Mark, A. *Alhacen's Theory of Visual Perception: The First Three Books of Alhacen's "De Aspectibus'*. Philadelphia: American Philosophical Society, 2001.

————. "Alhazen's Debt to Ptolemy's Optics." In *Nature, Experiment and the Sciences*, edited by T. H. Levere and W. R. Shea, 146–64. Dordrecht, 1990.

Solso, Robert L. *Cognitive Psychology*. 4th ed. Needham Heights, MA: Allyn and Bacon, 1995.

Spivey, M., M. Grosjean and G. Knoblich. "Continuous Attraction toward Phonological Competitors." *Proceedings of the National Academy of Sciences* 102.29 (2005): 10393–98.

Stamenov, Maxim, I., and Vittorio Gallese. *Mirror Neurons and the Evolution of Brain and Language*. Amsterdam: John Benjamins, 2002.

Sterne, Lawrence. *Tristram Shandy Ii*. London: Everyman Library, 1956.

Stevenson, Robert Louis and Lloyd Osbourne. "Books Which Have Influenced Me." In *Reading in Bed: Personal Essays on the Glories of Reading*, edited by Steven Gilbar, 35–38. Jaffrey, NH: Godine, 1995.

———. *The Ebb Tide*. 1894 ed. Teddington Middlesex: Echo Library, 2007.

Stockwell, Peter. "Cognitive Grammar." In *Cognitive Poetics: An Introduction*, 59–74. London: Routledge, 2002a.

———. *Cognitive Poetics: An Introduction*. London: Routledge, 2002b.

———. "Miltonic Texture and the Feeling of Reading." In *Readings in Cognition and Literature*, edited by Elena Semino and Jonathan Culpeper. Amsterdam: John Benjamins, 2002c.

Stoljar, Margaret Mahony. *Novalis: Philosophical Writings*. New York: State University of New York Press, 1997.

Talmy, Leonard. "Force Dynamics in Language and Cognition." *Cognitive Science* 12 (1988): 49–100.

Tan, Ed S. H. *Emotion and the Narrative Film: Film as an Emotion Machine*. Hillsdale, NJ: Lawrence Erlbaum Associates, 1996.

Tan, Ed S. H., and Nico H. Frijda. "Sentiment in Film Viewing." In *Passionate Views: Film, Cognition and Emotion*, edited by Carl P. Plantinga and Greg M. Smith. Baltimore: Johns Hopkins Press, 1999.

Tannen, Deborah. "Introduction." In *Linguistics Incontext: Connecting Observation and Understanding*, edited by Deborah Tannen. Norwood, NJ: Ablex, 1988.

———. *Talking Voices: Repetition, Dialogue and Imagery in Conversational Discourse*. Cambridge: Cambridge University Press, 1989.

Tanner, Tony. "Introduction." In *The Great Gatsby*, edited by F. Scott Fitzgerald, vii–lv. London: Penguin, 2000.

Trabasso, T., T. Secco and Paul van den Broek. "Causal Cohesion and Story Coherence." In *Learning and Comprehension of Text*, edited by H. Mandl, N. L. Stein and T. Trabasso, 83–111. Hillsdale, NJ: Lawrence Erlbaum Associates, 1984.

Turnbull, Andrew, ed. *The Letters of F. Scott Fitzgerald*. London: Bodely Head, 1964.

Turner, Mark. *Death Is the Mother of Beauty*. Chicago: Chicago University Press, 1987.

———. *The Literary Mind: The Origins of Thought and Language*. Oxford: Oxford University Press, 1996.

———. *Reading Minds: The Study of English in the Age of Cognitive Science*. Princeton, NJ: Princeton University Press, 1991.

Unwin, Timothy. *The Cambridge Companion to Flaubert*. Cambridge: Cambridge University Press, 2004.

van Berkum, J. J. A. et al. "Anticipating Upcoming Words in Discourse: Evidence from Erps and Reading Times." *Journal of Experimental Psychology* 31 (2005): 443–67.

van den Broek, Paul et al. "The Landscape Model of Reading: Inferences and the Online Construction of a Memory Representation." In *The Construction of Mental Representations During Reading*, edited by Herre van Oostendorp and Susan. R. Goldman, 71–98. Mahwah, NJ: Lawrence Erlbaum Associates, 1999.

———. "A 'Landscape' View of Reading: Fluctuating Patterns of Activation and the Construction of a Stable Memory Representation." In *Models of Understanding Text* edited by Bruce K. Britton and Arthur C. Graesser, 165–87. Mahwah, NJ: Lawrence Erlbaum Associates, 1996.

van Dijk, Teun A. "Context Models in Discourse Processing." In *The Construction of Mental Representation During Reading*, edited by Herre van Oostendorp and Susan R. Goldman, 123–48. Hillsdale, NJ: Lawrence Erlbaum Associates, 1999.

van Dijk, Teun. A., and Walter Kintsch. *Strategies of Discourse Comprehension.* New York: Academic Press, 1983.

van Oostendorp Herre, and Susan R. Goldman, eds. *The Construction of Mental Representations During Reading.* Mahwah, NJ: Lawrence Erlbaum Associates, 1999.

van Peer, Willie. "Emotional Functions of Reading Literature." In *Literature and the New Interdisciplinarity*, edited by Roger D. Sell and Peter Verdonk, 209–20. Amsterdam: Rodopi, 1994.

———. "Towards a Poetics of Emotion." In *Emotion and the Arts*, edited by Mette Hjort and Sue Laver, 215–24. Oxford: Oxford University Press, 1997.

Verdonk, Peter. "Style." In *Encyclopaedia of Language and Linguistics*, edited by Keith E. Brown, 196–210. Oxford: Elsevier, 2006.

———. *Stylistics.* Oxford: Oxford University Press, 2002.

Virgil. *The Aeneid*, Trans. David West. London: Penguin, 1990.

Vogeley, Kai, and Albert Newen. "Mirror Neurons and the Self Construct." In *Mirror Neurons and the Evolution of Brain and Language*, edited by Maxim I. Stamenov and Vittorio Gallese, 135–50. Amsterdam: John Benjamins, 2002.

Vygotsky, L. S. *Mind in Society: The Development of Higher Psychological Processes.* Cambridge, MA: Harvard University Press, 1978.

Wales, Katie. *A Dictionary of Stylistics.* 1989. 2nd ed. London: Longman, 2001.

Walker, Alice. *Meridian.* London: The Woman's Press, 1976.

Werth, Paul. *Text Worlds.* London: Longman, 1999.

Wierzbicka, Anna. *Emotions across Languages and Cultures.* Cambridge: Cambridge University Press, 1999.

Wimsatt William K. Jr., and Monroe K. Beardsley. *The Verbal Icon: Studies in the Meaning of Poetry.* New York: The Noonday Press, 1962.

Winnicott, D. W. *Playing and Reality.* London: Routledge, 1971.

———. "Transitional Objects and Transitional Phenomena." In *Collected Papers: Through Paediatrics to Psychoanalysis.* London: Tavistock Publications, 1958.

Winterson, Jeanette. *Art Objects: Essays in Ecstasy and Effrontery.* New York: Vintage, 1995.

Wolf, Phillipp. "The Lightening Flash: Visionary Epiphanies, Suddenness and History in the Later Work of W. B. Yeats." In *Moments of Moment: Aspects of the Literary Epiphany*, edited by Wim Tigges, 177–93. Amsterdam: Rodopi, 1999.

Wolfe, Thomas. *Look Homeward, Angel.* London: Heinemann, 1973.

Wolfson, N. *The Conversational Historical Present in American English Narrative.* Dordrecht: Fortis, 1982.

Wordsworth, William. *The Poetical Works of William Wordsworth.* Oxford: Oxford University Press, 1946.

———. *The Prelude.* Cambridge: Cambridge University Press, 1991.

Wright, M. R., ed. *Empedocles: The Extant Fragments.* New Haven, CT: Yale University Press, 1981.

Wurtz, Robert H., and Erik R. Kandel. "Perception of Motion, Depth and Form." In *Principles of Neural Science*, edited by James H. Schwartz and Thomas M. Jessel and Erik R. Kandel, 548–71. New York: McGraw-Hill, 2000.

Zajonc, Robert B. "Feeling and Thinking: Preferences Need No Inferences." *American Psychologist* 35 (1980): 151–75.

———. "On the Primacy of Affect." *American Psychologist* 39 (1984): 117–23. .

Zeki, Semir. *Inner Vision: An Exploration of Art and the Brain.* Oxford: Oxford UP, 2000.

———. *A Vision of the Brain.* Oxford: Oxford University Press, 1993.

Zull, James E. *The Art of Changing the Brain: Enriching the Practice of Teaching by Exploring the Biology of Learning.* Sterling, VA: Stylus, 2002.

Zwaan, Rolf. *Aspects of Literary Comprehension.* Amsterdam: John Benjamins, 1993.

# Index